Frances Moore Lappé has been involved in research and writing on the world food issue since 1969. Her best-selling book, *Diet for a Small Planet*, has been translated into several languages and she has also published numerous articles in academic and popular journals.

Joseph Collins has made a special study of multinational corporations and the policies of first-world governments in third world areas. He has collaborated with Richard Barnet and Ronald Muller in research for the book *Global Reach: The Power of the Multinational Corporation*.

Frances Moore Lappé and Joseph Collins

FOOD FIRST

First published in Great Britain by
Souvenir Press Ltd 1980

Published in Abacus 1982 by
Sphere Books Ltd
30–32 Gray's Inn Road, London WC1X 8JL

Reproduced, printed and bound in Great Britain by
Hazell Watson & Viney Ltd, Aylesbury, Bucks

Contents

Acknowledgements

During the years devoted to this book, one of our greatest satisfactions has been the discovery of a diverse network of people throughout the world, working hard on these difficult problems and willing to share their information and insights. We thank all of them. The very existence of this growing network is significant: it suggests that for more and more people the paradox of hunger in a world of plenty is catalyzing both deeper probing and a greater commitment to action.

We especially wish to thank three people whose contribution was so varied that it is impossible to detail but so invaluable that the book would have been impossible without them – Deborah Hepworth, Sue Kanor, and Judy Warneck.

The book benefited greatly from the research assistance of Henry Frundt, Robert Olorenshaw, David Kinley, Erica Byrd, Connie Phillips, Clark Fisher, Sandra Callier, Peter Mann, and Tonia Heinrichs.

We are grateful to Kathe Flinker, Ann Nicols-Jones, Irene Rusnak, and Sonia Senkiwsky, who helped organize a library of thousands of documents from around the world on which this book draws. We are also grateful for the secretarial assistance of Jo Ann Isaacs, Ellen McAvoy, Jan Martin, Ina Moore, and Diane Spatz.

We also appreciate the help of Ruth Bua, John Callahan, Irene Fleming, Irene Gifford, Joan and Doreen Pietropaulo and Paul and Jeanette Lappé, who lovingly cared for Frances's children, Anthony and Anna, while this book was in progress.

We want to acknowledge those whose work we found especially useful and whose advice we valued highly – Keith Abercrombie, Peter Adamson, Cynthia Hewitt de Alcántara, Silvio Almeida, George Anthan, Gonzalo Arroyo, Jun Atienza, George Baker, Solon Barraclough, David Baytleman, Fred Beck, Joe Belden, Alan Berg, Thierry Brun, Roger Burbach, The Centre for Rural Affairs, Jacques Chonchol, Harry Cleaver, Robert Cohen, Barry Commoner, Kim Conroy, Kenneth Dahlberg, Susan DeMarco, Erik Eckholm, Richard Edwards, Richard Elsner, Ron Erickson, M. Taghi Farvar, Ernest Feder, Pat Flynn, Gil Friend, Isao Fujimoto, Johan Galtung, Susan George, Richard Gilmore, Ole

Gjerstad, Harris Gleckman, Jerry Goldstein, Marcel Ganzin, Keith Griffin, Ross Hall, Merle Hansen, Jim Hightower, Anne-Marie Holenstein, Angus Hone, Michael Jacobson, Erich Jacoby, Brennon Jones, Jacques Kozub, Al Krebs, Ken Laidlaw, Robert Ledogar, Al Levinson, Cassio Luiselli, Arthur MacEwan, James McQuigg, Larry Minear, David Morris, Ingrid Palmer, Cheryl Payer, Andrew Pearse, Marco Quiñones, Christopher Robbins, Clodomir Santos de Morais, Susan Sechler, David Stohlberg, Colin Tudge, Liszt Aragon Vieira, Peter de Vries, Jean-Marc von de Weid, H. Garrison Wilkes, and Ben Wisner.

We want to express here our gratitude to all those who read all or part of the rough drafts, offering helpful comment – Ann Barnet, Richard Barnet, Erna Bennett, Richard Berliner, Roger Blobaum, Stephen Bossi, Michael Carder, Arthur Domike, Marion Gallis, Michael Gertler, Grace Goodell, Michael Henry, Marc Lappé, William Luttrell, Maureen MacKintosh, Harry Magdoff, Ali Manwar, Leah Margulies, John Moore, Fatemah Moyhadam, Vahid Nowshirvani, Ted Owens, Pascal de Pury, Marcus Raskin, Idrian Resnick, Mark Ritchie, Plinio Sampaio, Paul Sweezy in addition to many of those previously mentioned.

There are many whose general support and encouragement has been valuable to one or both of us – Eqbal Ahmad, Angus Archer, Sherry Barnes, Victoria Bawtree, Clifflyn Bromling, Diana Calafati, Dick Clark, William Sloane Coffin, Bettina Connor, Rusty Davenport, John Dillon, Frank Dobyns, Norman Faramelli, Edmundo Flores, Ramon Garcia, Nathan Gray, Ted Greiner, Joan Gussow, Steve Hayes, Jack Healey, B. Henderson, Nick Herman, Fred Just, Rich Killmer, Arthur Lincoln, Michael Locker, Ellen McAvoy, Brian MacCall, Julie Marshall, Eleanor McCallie, Mike McCoy, Dan McCurry, Michael Moffitt, Bill Moyer, Charles Paolillo, Elliott Postol, Jim Ridgeway, Doug Ross, Emma Rothschild, Jacobo Schatan, Nevin Scrimshaw, Jay Steptoe, Milo Thornberry, Erica Thorne, Mark Vermillion, Stanley Weiss, Edie Wilson, and Debbie Wright.

We want to take this opportunity to thank our friends at World Hunger Year – Bill Ayres, Jeri Barr, Rory Bedell, Harry Chapin, Lyn Dobrin, Diane Feyler, and Wray MacKay.

We are grateful to Harry Chapin, Samuel Rubin (through the Transnational Institute), and Stanley Weiss for their much-needed financial assistance for parts of this project.

We want to thank Joan Raines, our literary agent, and Ronald

Busch and George Walsh at Ballantine Books for their unwavering faith in this project and Robert Cowley at Houghton Mifflin for his supportive editorial contributions with the assistance of Dale Conway and Mandira Sen.

Finally, our thanks to Frances's brother, John Moore, Jr., for hitting upon *Food First* as just the right name for our book.

Acknowledgments for the Revised Edition

Our first thanks must go to our associates here at the Institute— to David Kinley who contributed valuable research assistance, and to Adele Beccar-Varela, Toby Stewart, Rodney Freeland, Robert Gabriner, Terry McClain and Bruce Johnson. Their contributions have been manifold and are deeply appreciated. In addition, we wish to thank Wendy Tanowitz and Patty Neel for their assistance. The revised edition, just as was the first edition, is truly the product of a dedicated team.

In addition, the revised edition especially benefits from the work of Charles Avila, Lasse and Lisa Berg, James Boyce, Steve Commins, Richard Franke, Jo Froman, Robert Gersony, Kathleen Gough, Guy Gran, Betsy Hartmann, Tony Jackson, Grace and William Liu, Mitch Meisner, Jim Newcomer, Bill Shurtleff, Yash Tandon, and Henry Weinstein.

The revised edition could not have gone forward without the financial support of funders who, like we, see the critical nature of the issues we discuss in this book. For the support of this and all the projects of the Institute, we are grateful to the: Samuel Rubin Foundation, Stern Fund, United Presbyterian Church USA, Church of the Brethren, Jesuit Council for Theological Reflection, Tides Foundation, Episcopal Church USA, and First United Church of Oak Park, Illinois.

It is doubtful if we could have prepared this special Souvenir Press edition of *Food First* without the resourceful collaboration of Dexter Tiranti of the *New Internationalist*. Dexter worked with us closely (spiritually, if not geographically) on the extensive special editing and on the British-oriented insertions. He authored the 'What We Can Do' essay and the appendices. John Clark in turn worked with Dexter in researching a number of the British-oriented materials and especially those on European food aid. Rosalynde de Lanerolle at Souvenir encouraged us in this unique Anglo-American collaboration. Our compliments and gratitude to all three.

Introduction to the Revised updated Edition

This Souvenir edition of *Food First* is being published over three years after we finished the manuscript for the American hardcover edition. During the intervening time at the Institute for Food and Development Policy we have continued to study, investigate, travel abroad, write and speak – often with people throughout the world, many of whom have vast experience in the problems we write about in *Food First*.

As we expected and hoped, our book has stirred controversy. In debating the issues, we feel our grasp of the problems has become ever firmer. We have also come to see why some of our ideas have been misunderstood or misconstrued by some.

'Food First' has been reduced at times to mean that the pat solution to hunger is simply to replace luxury export crops with local food crops. Export agriculture is said to be *the* enemy. In this edition, we counter this misrepresentation in several ways. In Chapter 1, we now prelude the book by pointing to the ways in which inequality in control over productive resources is the primary constraint – both on food production and on equitable distribution. Thus, until the question of who controls the production process is confronted, no shift from one crop to another, even to a nutritious food, will solve the problem of hunger.

Moreover, we have pulled out and developed some critical material subsumed in other chapters in order to create a new part, titled 'Inefficiency of Inequality' (Part V). Here we explore in some depth the constraints on production built into anti-democratic structures that we mention in Chapter 1. In this new Part V we also have added an entirely new Chapter where we address the impact of land reform on agricultural output.

A closely related misreading of our book relates to trade. Is *Food First* advocating autarky and isolationism? In a word, no. We explicitly summarize our position in Chapter 19 on export agriculture. Moreover, in Chapter 30 we contrast trade from a self-reliant base with the vulnerability resulting when survival desperately depends on trade.

In this edition, the positive guidelines for food self-reliance called Food First Fundamentals, are more fully developed. Again in Chapter 30, we devote more space to reflecting on the rich historical experience that indicates the elements necessary to create food security for all.

Furthermore, a principal benefit of returning to the book after two years is that our own field investigations and communications with others working here and in the Third World have provided us with a clearer understanding and more concrete cases with which to analyse the role of development aid and such powerful institutions as the World Bank. Besides adding such clarifications and fresh material, this new edition afforded the opportunity to update information where pertinent.

We hope that this revised edition also will elicit comment, criticism, and controversy. Only then will this book be of service to all of us – honing our critical awareness and igniting our passion to confront the arduous task of constructing forms of social organization capable of ending hunger and deprivation.

Frances Moore Lappé
Joseph Collins
Institute for Food and Development
Policy

Why This Book?

Writing a positive book about world hunger sounds to most people like trying to make a joke about death – there just isn't the material! This attitude comes home to us every time we are introduced to someone and attempt to describe what we are doing. A typical response is a sigh of sympathy overlaid with a look of bewilderment: 'Why would any normal person choose to think all day and every day about starving people?' Sometimes we sense latent feelings of guilt because we inevitably appear as individuals who are 'making a sacrifice.'

We, too, feel uncomfortable. How can we explain in a few sentences that we are not dwelling only on the tragedy of hunger and deprivation? Instead, we are learning for the first time where our own self-interest lies. Rather than being a depressing subject to be avoided, the world food problem has become for us the most useful tool in making sense out of our complex world. That is why we decided to write a book.

To discover the positive message hidden in the apparent 'hopelessness' of the world food problem we must first face the forces now pushing us into positions of guilt, fear, and ultimate despair. Everywhere newspaper headlines carry a clear message:

POPULATION BOMB AND FOOD SHORTAGE: WORLD LOSING FIGHT FOR VITAL BALANCE

New York Times, August 14, 1974

WORLD FOOD CRISIS: BASIC WAYS OF LIFE FACE UPHEAVAL FROM CHRONIC SHORTAGES

New York Times, November 5, 1974

We are all in a life-and-death contest, we are told, between growing numbers of people and limited amounts of food. We are in a race and some must inevitably lose. The implicit message is that not everyone will have enough to eat. And how will we come out? According to C. W. Cook, retired chairman of General Foods, if we have 'to compete with . . . an increasingly crowded and hungry world, providing adequate nutrition to millions of lower-income Americans could become an impossible dream.'

Since there are *already* so many hungry people in the world, many think it obvious that even now we do not have sufficient food to go around. 'Malthus has already been proved correct,' declares the president of the Rockefeller Foundation, Dr John Knowles. Another officer of the Rockefeller Foundation has likened the growth of the world's population to our most dreaded disease, cancer. It is not, however, mere numbers but *whose* numbers are increasing. President Nixon told us that 'the frightening fact is that the poor are multiplying twice as fast as the rich.'

Some writers threaten complete 'catastrophe.' They refer not just to starvation but to the spectre of the submersion of our 'civilized values' and the emergence of 'thousands of desperadoes for every one now terrorizing the rich today.' Thus not only our diet appears to be at stake, but the very fabric of our civilization is threatened by the hungry seeking our food.

To this dual threat our new, and potentially valuable, environmental awareness adds its own version of the apocalypse. Lester Brown warns that 'new signs of agricultural stress on the earth's ecosystem appear almost daily as the exponentially rising food demand, fuelled by population growth and rising incomes, presses the ecosystem's finite capacities. . . . There is no way to calculate the trade-off between increases in population and improvements in the quality of life – a choice we must now make as we press against the finite limits of our ecosystem.' Such warnings lead people to believe that increases in food production will necessarily damage the environment and threaten our future food supply. We are made to fear that there is no way out of scarcity without making our children pay the price.

There is also an equally deceptive and ultimately negative message pulling us in the opposite direction. Well-intended attempts to stir public action have shifted the world food crisis out of the political-economic arena onto the ground of individual morality. Our consumption is tirelessly contrasted with deprivation elsewhere; the message being that *our* consumption causes *their* suffering. We are told, for example, that the amount of fertilizer used on US lawns, golf courses, and cemeteries equals all of what India uses to grow food. We inevitably experience some shame, feeling our wastefulness must reflect a moral failing. With no understanding of how hunger is actually created, we are defenceless against a diffuse but powerful sense of guilt – guilt for just being amongst the lucky affluent few. The hungry are made into a powerful threat and, at the same time, a burdensome responsibility. We are torn.

To resolve our conflict, one appealing answer has emerged: 'Lifeboat ethics' – the simple notion, popularized by scientist Garrett Hardin, that the earth now constitutes a lifeboat in which there is not enough food to go around. Isn't it then only logical that food should go to those most likely to survive, that you do not risk the safety of all by bringing new passengers on board? 'What happens if you share space in a lifeboat?' asks Dr Hardin. 'The boat is swamped, and everyone drowns. Complete justice, complete catastrophe.'

The remedy offered to ease the pain of our conflict is simple: *Stop feeling*. We are told that the Judaeo-Christian ethic is out-moded in this new era of scarcity; that compassion is a luxury we can no longer afford; that Judaeo-Christian do-gooderism is the true root of the world's present predicament. We are told we must learn a *new ethic*, the ethic of detached reason; we must learn to let people die for the ultimate survival of the human race.

Such voices do offer one resolution of our conflicting feelings. In the words of writer Peter Collier, they offer us 'novocaine for the uneasy soul.' But must we take the novocaine? Do we have to deaden our sensibilities in order to find some surcease for our anxieties? Or can we transform what appears to be the most impossible problem of our generation – the world food crisis – into the most useful and constructive tool for understanding the complex forces that limit our own lives? Can we, moreover, on the strength of that new insight, gain a sense of personal power over those forces – forces that increasingly diminish our own freedom of choice and our own well-being?

Why Food First? We met each other on the first national Food Day in the spring of 1975 at Ann Arbor, Michigan. Frances had been invited as the author of *Diet for a Small Planet* and Joe, because of his work on *Global Reach*, a book on multinational corporations, and his coauthorship of *World Hunger: Causes and Remedies*, a work countering establishment wisdom at the time of the 1974 World Food Conference. Following our talks, the students asked us the same urgent questions we each had been asked many times before, and we tried to answer them. Yes, we did have some answers. But we were not satisfied. Finally, we concluded that together we would throw all our energy into a search for answers to all the toughest questions that we ourselves had ever asked or that we had ever been asked by others about the causes of hunger.

Most fundamentally *Food First* means that whether or not people are hungry appears to us as the primary test of a just and effective social and economic system. The security of any people has historically rested on meeting its own basic food needs. Thus every country should mobilize its own food resources to meet its own needs first. Only then can trade serve to expand choices rather than to deprive people of the benefits from the resources rightfully theirs.

As we studied, read, travelled and interviewed, we found that the themes of scarcity, guilt, and fear are all based on myths. We learnt that:

No country in the world is a hopeless basketcase
Food redistribution is not the solution to hunger.
The hungry are not our enemies.

Our task is clear. We, the citizens of the affluent world, need to build a movement – a movement that lays bare the truth that it is a single system, supported by governments, corporations and landed elites, that is undermining food security both in our countries and in the Third World. The forces in Africa, Asia and Latin America cutting people out of the production process and therefore out of consumption turn out to be the same forces that have converted the food system into one of the most tightly controlled sectors of our own economies. Ever fewer land operators and food companies control a larger and larger portion of our food. We get increased and needless processing, exposure to dangerous chemicals, less nutrition, and consistently higher prices, resulting even in hunger for some and malnourishment for many. In fighting the forces tightening their hold over our food economies, we are directly fighting some of the very forces that promote hunger in other countries.

Many have been misled to believe that if justice were made a priority, production would be sacrificed. The opposite is true. It is the land monopolizers, both traditional landed elites and corporate agribusiness, who have proved themselves to be the most inefficient, unreliable and destructive users of food-producing resources. Democratizing the control over food-producing resources is the only road to long-term agricultural productivity for others and for us.

The greatest reward of our work has been the discovery of realistic and liberating answers to *the* most urgent question: What can we do? To find an answer, we had to grasp that hungry people can free themselves from hunger once they have overthrown the obstacles in their way. Indeed, wherever people now are not feeding themselves, you can be sure that powerful obstacles have been placed in their way.

The first step in putting Food First is demystifying the problem of hunger. Perhaps this is where our work can help most. We did not start out as experts. We began just as you might. We became interested. Hunger loomed as the greatest problem of our lifetime. As we learned more and more, read what the 'experts' read, travelled through our own country and abroad, we found that the solution to world hunger is no mystery. It is not locked inside the germ plasm of a seed waiting for a brilliant young agricultural scientist to discover it. It is not spelled out in econometric studies of development planners. The real block to the solution to world hunger is the sense of powerlessness we are made to feel: *that the enormity of the problem is outside our control and that it should be entrusted to others.* In truth, however, the solution to hunger is firmly in all of our hands.

PART I THE SCARCITY SCARE

1 : Too Many People, Too Little Land?

To diagnose hunger as caused by scarcity of food and land is to blame nature for people-made problems. There are at least 500 million undernourished and starving people in the world. This hunger exists in the face of abundance; therein lies the outrage.

One way to demonstrate that land and food scarcity is not the true cause of hunger is to show that there is no scarcity of either. The second is to explain what really does cause hunger. In·this book, we will seek to do both.

Measured globally, there is enough food for everyone now. The world is producing each day two pounds of grain – more than 3,000 calories and ample protein – for every man, woman and child on earth.[1] This 3,000-calorie estimate, more than that consumed by the Western European, does not include the many other nutritious foods people eat – beans, nuts, fruits, vegetables, root crops, and grass-fed meat. Thus, on a global scale, the idea that there is not enough food to go around simply does not hold up.

But global figures mean little, except to dispel the widespread notion that we have reached the earth's limits. What counts is whether adequate food-producing resources exist in countries where so many people go hungry. The resources *do* exist, we have found, but they are invariably underused or misused, creating hunger for many and surfeit for a few.

How can we measure this untapped potential? One way is to note the gaps between current production and possible production. According to a US Presidential Commission in the late 1960s and, more recently, studies by scientists at Iowa State University, only about 44 per cent of the world's cultivable land is now being cropped.[2] In both Africa and South America less than 20 per cent of the potentially arable land is cultivated.[3] Grain yields in the underdeveloped countries could more than double before reaching the average yields of the industrial countries. And there is no physical reason why production per acre in most underdeveloped countries could not *exceed* that of the industrial countries. In many underdeveloped countries, land presently harvested only once yearly could provide two or even more harvests.

Barriers to unleashing this productive capacity are, in most cases, not physical; rather, they are social: Wherever there is unjust, undemocratic control over productive resources, their development is thwarted.

In most countries where people are hungry, large landholders control most of the land. A study of 83 countries showed that slightly more than 3 per cent of all landholders, those with 114 acres or more, control a staggering 79 per cent of all farmland.[4] But these large landholders are the *least* productive. Studies in seemingly diverse countries reveal that large landholders consistently harvest lower yields per acre than the smallest farmers, as we detail later (pp. 141ff.). Furthermore, many who hold large amounts of land for prestige or as an investment, not as a source of food, leave considerable acreage unplanted. A 1960 study of Colombia, for instance, found that the largest landholders, in control of 70 per cent of the land, planted only 6 per cent of their land.[5] Land monopolized by a few is inevitably underused. Moreover, the wealth produced is invariably not reinvested for rural development but drained off for conspicuous consumption and for investment in industries catering to the fancies of urban and foreign well-to-do.

In addition, low productivity results from economic and social injustice that obstructs agricultural improvements by small, poor farmers. The larger, more influential landholders monopolize access to extension services, markets, and perhaps most critical, nonusurious credit (money-lenders commonly charge the poor 50-200 per cent interest). And with no individual or shared ownership in the land, how can tenants, sharecroppers and landless labourers either be motivated or have the wherewithal to conserve and improve the land for better crops? They realize any improvement will overwhelmingly go to advance the landowners, not themselves.

Finally, co-operation is the most essential ingredient of development. We discuss this point, with examples from Bangladesh (pp. 25ff.). To build and maintain irrigation and drainage systems, for instance, it is essential that everyone in a village work *together* in order to be effective. The same is true for controlling pests. But co-operation is unlikely where there is such grossly unequal ownership of the land and other productive resources. Largeholders do not want their poor neighbours to progress; then the poor might become less exploitable by them.

In measuring the untapped potential of the earth to nourish

those who now are hungry, we should assess not only the under-used potential, as we have just done, but also the *mis*use of resources. Food-producing resources are misused when they are diverted, as they increasingly are, away from meeting basic food needs and toward the satisfaction of those already fed. Even though the majority of a country's population may be in grave need of food, if they have too little money to make that need felt in the marketplace, agricultural resources will be made to serve those who can pay – the local upper classes and high-paying markets abroad. Luxury crops expand, therefore, while basic food crops are neglected.

In Central America and the Caribbean, where in some countries as many as 80 per cent of the children are undernourished, approximately half of the agricultural land, invariably the best land, is made to produce crops and cattle for a domestic elite and for export instead of basic food for the people.[6] In 1973, 36 out of 40 of the world's poorest countries – those classified by the UN as being most seriously affected ('MSA's') by inflated world food prices – exported agricultural commodities to the United States.[7]

The pattern of diverting food-producing resources to the already well-fed continues even in the face of famine. Agricultural exports from the Sahelian countries to Europe actually increased during the late sixties and early seventies, in the face of worsening drought and widespread hunger. During the drought in Mali the area planted with the two most important export crops, peanuts and cotton, was expanded by almost 50 per cent and over 100 per cent respectively between 1965 and 1972.[8]

Many crops long considered basic staples have recently come to be used as luxury or export crops. Corn, sorghum, vegetables, cassava, and rice turn out to be increasingly grown for export and for fattening livestock for export or for the local elite.

In Mexico, more basic grains are consumed by livestock than by the country's peasants.[9] In Brazil, the most widely planted crop is corn, accounting for about one-fourth of Brazil's total crop area. But in 1977, well over one-third of this traditional crop went to fatten livestock, either in Brazil or Europe.[10] Brazil and Paraguay have been rapidly expanding soyabean acreage (largely through foreign investment); yet almost all of this protein-rich food is for export to fatten livestock.

Or consider cassava. In many countries, cassava has become

the belly-filler of last resort for the poor. But now, this poor folks' food is being 'discovered' by European firms as a low-priced feed for European cattle. In Thailand, urban elites are buying up large tracts of farm land to plant cassava. Continuous planting so rapidly depletes the soil that ever greater acreage is needed to get the same production. Cassava now takes up well over 2 million acres and has overnight become Thailand's leading export!!

When the earth's tremendous productive capacity is underused and when its bounty is increasingly siphoned off to feed the already well-fed, scarcity can hardly be considered the cause of hunger. While hunger is real, scarcity is an illusion. Throughout *Food First* we find that the illusion of scarcity is a product of extreme inequalities in control over food-producing resources that thwart their development and distort their utilization.

But isn't it true that the most densely populated countries are also the hungriest countries? Surveys around the world show no such pattern. Some nations very dense in people per acre also have adequately nourished populations. France has just about the same number of people for each cultivated acre as India.[12] China, where starvation has been eradicated in only twenty-five years, has twice as many people for each cropped acre as India.[13] On the other hand, countries with relatively few people per cultivated acre nevertheless are often ones where most of the people are malnourished. In Africa, south of the Sahara, one of the worst famine areas in the world, there are almost two and one-half *cultivated* acres per inhabitant, more than in the United States or the Soviet Union and six to eight times more than in China. And this estimate for Africa may represent as little as 12 per cent of the region's potentially cultivable land.[14]

Moreover, the population in many parts of Africa is probably less dense than it was in the sixteenth century before the slave trade. Indeed some economists have argued that certain African countries are *under*populated in terms of the labour force needed for agricultural development.

Latin America, like Africa, is a region of overall low population density. With 16 per cent of the world's cultivable land it has only 6 per cent of the world's population, yet proportionately more hungry people than in India, Pakistan, and Bangladesh. Here again there is no apparent relationship between the amount of agricultural land available per person and the extent of hunger.

In a country like Bolivia, severe undernourishment is a daily reality for most of the population; yet Bolivia has well over one-half acre of cultivated land per person, significantly more than France (and a potential of over ten cultivable acres per person). Mexico, where most of the rural population is poorly fed, has more cultivated land per person than Cuba, where now, virtually no one is underfed.

Certainly there are countries in Latin America with both relatively high population density and widespread hunger – countries like Haiti and the Dominican Republic. But they are the exceptions. Haiti and the Dominican Republic nonetheless, have just slightly less cultivated land per person, and a much longer growing season, than Italy.[15] This calculation does not even include the considerable additional area in Haiti and the Dominican Republic many observers agree is good agricultural land. This land is officially classified as 'permanent pasture' simply because the owners choose to graze livestock on it.

As long as food is something bought and sold in a society with great income differences, the degree of hunger tells us nothing about the density of the population.

Is Bangladesh the Exception?

Bangladesh for many is the archetype of a country whose population has simply overwhelmed its food-producing resources. 80 million people live in a country the size of England and Wales. So, even when our studies of countries around the world revealed in case after case that sheer physical limits are not the cause of hunger, we thought that Bangladesh might be an exception. It isn't.

Even now, with resources grossly underused, Bangladesh grows enough in grain alone to provide everyone in the country with at least 2,300 calories a day.[16] Yet, according to World Bank figures,[17] over half of the families in Bangladesh daily consume less than 1,500 calories per person, the minimum survival level. Two thirds of the population suffer from protein and vitamin deficiencies.

If enough is produced, then why don't the hungry in Bangladesh eat? Ironically, the hungry grow much of the country's rice. At harvest time, when prices are at their lowest, many are forced to sell so much of what they produce that they will not have enough to cover their own needs until the next harvest. They are forced to do so in order to pay back what they owe – with considerable interest – to the moneylender-merchants, from whom they needed to borrow food at much higher prices before the harvest. Many of those trapped in this vicious circle are tenant farmers who must pay for all the agricultural inputs and still give over half of their harvest to the landlord. Not surprisingly, many landlords have become moneylender-merchants. The moneylender-merchants' hoarding of grain is a prime cause of the very 'scarcity' on which they speculate.

Landless labourers, dependent on meagre wages, are particularly vulnerable. Precisely when floods and droughts deprive them of work altogether, speculative food prices due to the work of hoarders shoot up 200 to 500 per cent. Once we became aware of these realities, we were not surprised to learn that, while many starved after the 1974 floods, hoarders stacked up an estimated 4 million tons of rice because 'the vast majority . . . were too poor to buy it.'[18]

Not only is there no legitimate scarcity now, but Bangladesh has what it takes to grow much more food. Travelling about the country we were struck by its stunning fertility. For Bangladesh is blessed not only with a luxuriant tropical climate (abundant sun and water) but also with deep, rich alluvial soils annually deposited by three great rivers and their countless tributaries.

Sizing up Bangladesh's food potential, a 1976 report for the US Congress concluded, 'The country is rich enough in fertile land, water, manpower and natural gas for fertilizer, not only to be self-sufficient in food, but a food exporter, even with its rapidly increasing population size.'[19]

So what is the problem? Inequalities in control over the country's productive resources thwart its food potential.

One of Bangladesh's chief assets, for instance, is rainfall – 100 to 300 inches of it annually – but virtually all during the 3-4 month monsoon season. The trick then is to control water, otherwise you first have flooding and then drought. But what incentives are there for sharecroppers and labourers who work 90 per cent of the land, to build and maintain draining and irrigation canals and embankments when such investments would primarily benefit the landowners? And the smallholders fear that any improvement in the land might heighten the desire of the larger holder to take it over.

The sharecropper saves any extra effort for what little piece of land he might own himself. Hired labourers concern themselves with their wages, not the landlord's yields. And since the landlord pays for their labour, he uses it sparingly. Moreover, the landlord is increasingly likely to be absentee, perhaps a military officer or petty government official, living and investing in urban real estate or even abroad. In Bangladesh we were repeatedly told that it is not uncommon for a landlord to sabotage irrigation and other improvements simply because he does not wish his tenants to prosper and become less dependent.

Not surprisingly, only about 5 per cent of the country's cultivated land is irrigated. Simple irrigation, making the 'dry season' no longer dry, would amount to doubling the country's food base. And in much of Bangladesh an extra crop each year could result from reinstituting pre-colonial practices for collecting the monsoon rains.

Co-operation in digging and maintaining ponds was common before 1793 when the British instituted the individual ownership of land. Today in villages throughout Bangladesh we sadly noted many silted up ponds and canals hardly capable of holding much water. And they are no longer *village* ponds but private ponds.

Village-wide co-operative work is impossible when less than 10 per cent of the rural households own 51 per cent of the cultivated land and when almost half the families are, for all practical purposes, deprived of land.[20] The poor feel forced to compete against each other for sheer survival. Poor small farmers face the largeholders who scheme daily to further impoverish, in order to foreclose on, them. During the 1974 famine, rich landholders stood in line all night at land registry offices in order to buy land that hungry, mortgaged small farmers were selling as a last resort.

Consider also Bangladesh's inland fishing resources, which according to one FAO (Food and Agriculture Organization) report are 'possibly the richest in the world.'[21] At present, most of the fishing waters are controlled by absentee owners who are satisfied to sell a small quantity of fish at high prices to a few well-off consumers. With profits already so inflated, why should they invest in improving fishing methods? The fishermen, as mere hired hands, see no point in improving their fishing skills or the fish resources: they know they themselves would not benefit. The fishermen are, according to a confidential United Nations report,[22] severely exploited by the absentee owners, for the urban consumers pay about 500 to 600 per cent more than what the fishermen receive – prices moreover that keep fish out of the reach of millions.

So in Bangladesh, as in many countries we are made to perceive as hopelessly poor, it is the extreme inequality in the control over productive resources that makes co-operative work difficult and thwarts production. For this reason, a 1975 FAO report on Bangladesh concludes, 'A policy of really drastic land redistribution might promote both production *and* equity.'[23]

Co-operative farming structures could overcome the danger that redistribution would break up the land into units too fragmented to make efficient use of irrigation and drainage networks. Likewise, co-operative fishing could provide employment to hundreds of thousands of landless families. The fish would be an excellent protein source for millions of farming people who under the new order would be productive enough to buy it. Greater production would result because for the first time the *entire* rural population would sense that working together they could master the forces of nature and that they themselves would be the beneficiaries, not landlords and moneylenders. And an active, decision-making rural population would be the best foundation for democracy.

The obstacles in the way of these constructive developments are not the natural limits of the country. The key obstacle to development for the people of Bangladesh is the present power of a few that prevents the majority from realizing their common interests and the strength of their unified effort. Bangladesh is by no means a hopeless famine case.

2 : Are People a Liability or a Resource?

This question reflects several widely held beliefs that we have found to be myths.

Myth one: Agriculture in underdeveloped countries is held back because there are just too many people in the countryside to be productively put to work.

If too many workers per acre really stood in the way of production, wouldn't countries that have a *more* productive agriculture have *fewer* workers per acre than their less successful neighbours? Yet, what do we find? Japan and Taiwan, both thought of as agriculturally successful, have more than twice as many agricultural workers per acre than the Philippines and India. The value of production per acre in Japan is seven times that of the Philippines and ten times that of India.[1] The overall trend, in fact, seems to show a *positive* relationship between the number of workers on a unit of land and the level of agricultural output. This may be hard for us to accept because we are taught to measure productivity in terms of how *few* people it takes to grow food. Such a measure makes no sense at all in underdeveloped countries with vast, untapped human labour resources.

Countries we think of as heavily overpopulated – countries that we assume could not use even one more farmer – are not necessarily overcrowded agriculturally. When China attempted to increase production utilizing its human labour potential, it found that it could gainfully triple or even quadruple the labour input per acre. According to the World Bank, if countries like India could attain Japan's level of labour intensity – two workers per hectare (2.5 acres) – their agriculture could absorb all the labour force expected by 1985.[2] The significant difference, of course, is that countries like Japan and China have developed labour-intensive farming that *productively* employs the additional labour; India and the Philippines have not. Clearly, a large rural population is far from the handicap it is often perceived to be.

Myth Two: Since agriculture cannot absorb any more people, the overflow from rural areas must go to the cities where new jobs in industry must be created for them.

It was exactly this analysis of the problem that prompted both the neglect of agriculture and the promotion of industrialization by development planners during the 1950s and 1960s. The result was a lot of capital investment but remarkably few new industrial jobs.

The percentage of the total workforce in underdeveloped countries from 8.5 per cent to 7.6 per cent of the total labour force between 1900 and 1950.[3] This pattern holds even in countries like Brazil touted as 'miracles' of industrial development. In India between 1950 and 1964, the government increased the capital invested in large-scale manufacturing fifteen-fold. Yet during the same period, the number of workers employed by such manufacturing only slightly more than doubled.[4] Foreign corporations with their labour-saving technologies from countries with high labour costs, have aggravated the chronic 'jobs crisis'. Two hundred and fifty-seven multinational corporations studied in Latin America employ less than one half the number of people per unit of sales as do local companies.[5]

A corporation invariably claims its investment 'created' so many hundred jobs. Many economists have come to recognize, however, that a new modern factory employing a couple of hundred persons might well put thousands of local craftsmen out of business. Moreover, local savings borrowed by a foreign corporation to create a factory could have been used in entirely different ways that would have created many more jobs.

Efforts to solve the unemployment problem by creating jobs in centralized, urban areas are misplaced in any case. In underdeveloped countries agriculture and small-scale decentralized workshops serving the needs of local agriculture have the greater potential to absorb workers. China has been able to reduce the percentage of its workforce in full-time agricultural jobs to about 54 per cent in contrast to the 70 to 85 per cent in most underdeveloped countries. This was accomplished by developing small factories and workshops throughout the countryside to make farm implements and basic consumer goods. China's large *rural,* but nonagricultural, population also represents a sizeable reserve labour force for agriculture – on hand to deal with peak season farm labour bottlenecks that in many countries are the common excuse for mechanization that both squanders scarce financial resources and takes away jobs when there are no others.

Myth Three: Population growth is a tremendous burden to Third World economies since it means having to generate more jobs when 15 to 30 per cent of the population is already without work and many of the so-called employed are really underemployed. The result is increasing numbers of half-starved, marginal people living outside the economy.

Researching this book helped us to understand that 'marginal' people are not born. They are not caused by the *inevitable* overflow of a limited land base or by the fixed capacity of an economy to absorb workers. In sixteenth-century England and nineteenth-century Scotland a shift in land use led directly to the appearance of 'too many people.' The landed gentry had decided that sheep would be more profitable than farming. Sheep, however, need a lot of land and only a few shepherds. Land, therefore, was 'enclosed' and thousands of farming peasants were shut out. Many contemporary commentators saw in the growing number of landless vagabonds sure evidence of 'too many people' – a view that helped to motivate overseas colonizations. The overpopulation existed, of course, only in relation to a sheep-based agricultural economy. The total population of England in the sixteenth century was less than in any one of several present-day English cities.[6]

Colonial powers similarly created such marginal people by reducing highly diversified agricultural systems to single crops – monocultures on which the most profit could be made in foreign markets. Converting whole countries into production sites for one or two crops meant that planting and harvests were no longer staggered throughout the year. Employment opportunities were therefore limited to the cycle of the one or two main export crops. Thus, in the predominantly sugar-plantation economy of Cuba during the 1950s a half million sugar workers were employed only a few months a year – during the sugar harvest.[7]

Indeed, people are being made to appear marginal today by the further transformation of agriculture taking place in most underdeveloped countries. Agriculture, once the livelihood of millions of self-provisioning farmers, is becoming the profit base of influential commercial entrepreneurs – traditional landed elites, city-based agricultural speculators, and foreign corporations. These new agricultural entrepreneurs use profits both to enlarge their landholdings at the expense of the small farmer and the landless and to mechanize production at the expense of the labourer's job. Some examples:

- Pakistan: A Pakistan Planning Commission official states that full mechanization on farms of twenty-five acres or more could displace 600,000 to 700,000 workers in fifteen years.[8]
- Latin America: Each tractor displaces about three workers in Chile and about four in Colombia and Guatemala. A conservative estimate is that two and a half million labourers have been already displaced by tractor mechanization in Latin America.[9]
- India: In the Punjab it was expected that by 1980 the demand for hired labour in field crop production would all but disappear.[10]

Displacing tenants and labourers with machines means a larger marketable harvest and more profit for the commercial cultivator – in addition to freedom from the 'management problem' of a sizeable underpaid labour force. Replacing people with machines in countries with immense untapped labour resources is not, of course, of social value. The value accrues only to the individual operator who can use machines to maximize the profit made on each labourer. As this process proceeds, however, all the outsider sees is more unemployment and therefore concludes that there are just too many people.

The economic success of a nation does not depend so much on rich natural resources as on how effectively its people can be motivated and their labour utilized. People appear as a liability *only* in a certain type of economic system: one in which economic success is not measured by the well-being of all the people; one in which production is increasingly monopolized by a few; and one in which technology is used to exclude people from the production process so as to maximize the profit the landlord makes on each worker. People are not born marginal.

3 : Birth Control and Wealth Control

Surely it doesn't help the Third World people to have large families? The more children they have, the deeper their poverty and hunger? These questions suggest that people in underdeveloped countries desire large families out of ignorance of their own interests. But we have found their reasons for increasing family size reflect their powerlessness and poverty not their ignorance.

Most Third World families are rural. Survival for them often depends on having children to bring in extra food or money for the family and to provide minimal old age security for the parents. At the age of 45, people in underdeveloped countries may be wasted and old. And with nutrition, sanitation and health services poor or nonexistent, parents know all too well that their children often die. Giving birth to 'extras' is the only way to increase the likelihood that enough will survive.

Those of us in urban industrial societies might disbelieve that any child can earn more than he or she consumes. But demographers have calculated that a rural child at the age of 10 or even 8 can bring a net food or income benefit to the family.[1] Children, for example, herd animals, fetch water, firewood and dung, transplant rice, glean fields, and cut stubble. We also have seen all of this in our field investigations.

Most of us might see such children – and certainly the mothers who bear the burden of so many pregnancies and childrearings – as exploited. But as long as the social order keeps isolated family units as the only basis of productive work and security, there is little hope for change. This is plainly the case, given that the usurpation of resources by the powerful few leaves the majority of families little or no land and only miserable-paying jobs.

For each such family, the number of children determines the number of workers it can field to support itself. If the family has little or no land, its income might depend on the number of children that can be hired out as labourers in the fields of others. If the family survives by sharecropping a rich family's land, then the more children it has, the more land it can try to contract to work. And a poor family with some land of its own sees children as an asset too. As one Indian farmer explained to a population researcher: 'Just look around. No one, without sons or brothers to help him, farms his land. He rents it out to others with large families. Without sons, there is no living off the land. The more sons you have, the less labour you need to hire, and the more saving you can have.' Another peasant in northern India summed it up this way: 'A rich man invests in his machines. We must invest in our children.'[2]

Parents may also need many children simply because they have no alternative old-age security. Milkha Singh, a farmer in Manupur, a village in the Indian Punjab, put it this way: 'You think I am poor because I have too many children.' He laughed, 'If I didn't have my sons . . . God knows what would happen to me and their mother when we are too old to work and earn.'[3]

In such societies a family cannot be sure of meeting its need for a family labour force and for old-age security through having just one or two sons. According to a computer simulation, an Indian couple would have to bear an average of 6.3 children to be confident (at a 95 per cent level of probability) of the survival of one son.[4]

Powerlessness of Women

Even given the deprivation of the majority of rural families, the question of family size is also not an uncomplicated 'the more, the better'. For many mothers, so often undernourished, the burden of yet another pregnancy and child outweighs any prospective gain from an additional labourer in the family. But many women are powerless to make reproductive decisions. Having no personal autonomy, it is impossible for them to even ask their husband if he would allow the use of contraceptives. In a survey for the United Nations Fund for Population Activities, social worker Perdita Huston, interviewing rural women in Tunisia, the Sudan, Kenya, Sri Lanka, Mexico, and Egypt, found that it is not women who need to be convinced to have fewer children. In each of the six very different cultures she repeatedly heard variations of, 'I am tired. Look at me. I am nothing but a beast working in the fields and bearing all the children. I don't want any more but my husband says I must have as many as come'.[5]

Lowering birth rates is not a matter of overcoming ignorance. The poor often know their own best interests. Birth rates cannot come down until the poor overcome their powerlessness, including women's special powerlessness vis-à-vis men.

The Population Bomb

Because of the way the 'population bomb' has been thrown into the public's consciousness, most people are convinced that the poor are multiplying faster than ever. In reality, at least eleven underdeveloped countries are undergoing an even more precipitous decline in their birth rates than did any of the now industrialized countries, during their 'demographic transition' of the nineteenth and early twentieth centuries.[6] This trend, added to the slowing rate of population growth in certain industrial countries, mean that the annual increment in world population has dropped in the last few years. In 1970 the growth in world population, that is, the excess of births over deaths, was 70 million. By 1977 the increase was probably closer to 68.7 million. When one considers that the *number* of people of reproductive age is still getting larger each year, any such drop in annual increment indicates a significant lowering of birth rates. The rate of world population growth appears to have reached an all-time high around 1970 and has since begun to subside.

The lowering of the population growth rate in certain countries is apparently *not* related to the growth rate of the Gross National Product (GNP) or even to the *level* of per capita income but to a trend toward *equal distribution* of income and services such as health care.[7] Where birth rates are declining – such as in Sri Lanka, Singapore, Hong Kong, Taiwan, Egypt, Argentina, Uruguay, Costa Rica, and Cuba, we find that governments have, or once had, some national policies favouring the low-income groups; whereas in Brazil, Venezuela, the Philippines, and Mexico the well-being of low-income groups is diminishing and birth rates are not declining significantly. The causal factors do not appear to be direct birth control programmes but a shift in resources toward the poorest groups.

Well-being is not measured in income alone. Other factors besides income distribution per se seem to correlate with declining birth rates. Two Asian examples of declining birth rates – the state of Kerala in India, and China – illustrate this. In Kerala, statistics show that the population is poorer than in many other Indian states, but there are critical social and political differences that may well contribute to Kerala's declining birth rate. Alan Berg, a

World Bank nutritionist, has noted that of all the states of India, Kerala has the highest literacy rate (it is the only state where the majority of women are educated); the highest per capita consumption of nutritionally important foods; the lowest infant mortality rate; and a death rate lower than that of the United Kingdom or West Germany.[8]

The average Indian birth rate has fallen from 41 to 37.2 per 1,000 over the last twenty years. By contrast, Kerala's birth rate has dropped from 37 to 27 per 1,000 during only a ten-year period.

China has the most comprehensive approach to providing what seem to be social and economic prerequisites to population limitation. After retirement, workers receive 50 to 75 per cent of their earnings while most other benefits, notably health care, continue. In the countryside, the commune maintains a welfare fund to provide for those unable to work. In both city and countryside the collective working group ensures that no family's income falls below a certain minimal level.[9] Women are encouraged to join the workforce; liberal maternity leave and convenient nurseries are provided.

In addition, you will recall from the previous comments of Indian farmers, families competing against other families must have their own labour supply for survival. But when labour and production is shared beyond the family through group ownership and work, as it is in China, then the need to raise one's own family work force disappears.

China demonstrates the capacity of people to change their rate of reproduction with impressive rapidity once basic security needs have been met. China's birth rate has declined at perhaps unprecedented speed – down from 32 per 1,000 in 1970 to between 20 and 25 per 1,000 five years later.[10] Since the Chinese people constitute one fifth of humanity, their efforts to lower their birth rate have significantly lowered world figures.

To those of us in the industrial West, the people in the countries experiencing real declines in their birth rates may still seem 'poor' – some with per capita incomes not much over $200 per year – but in most of these countries the lives of the poor are changing in critical ways. Viable income and old age security, needs that had previously been met only by bearing many children, are beginning to be met by social and political reform: by more secure land tenure, by more reliable food supply, by better health care, and by old age security.

Birth Control Programmes

What is necessary, then, is the reconstruction of the social order, providing all the people with basic material security, to make birth control a *rational* option. Then birth control programmes are essential to make having fewer children a *feasible* option as well.

But birth control programmes that simply aim to shower rural areas with contraceptives will never work. Moreover, they run the risk of actually harming the poor. Without regular oversight by trained health care personnel, women can suffer both physical and psychological damage. Reports from Bangladesh stress that symptoms caused by irregular supply of oral contraceptives and bleeding from IUD's have caused severe personal suffering. In Moslem culture a woman too weak to do her household tasks can simply be rejected in favour of another wife.

Moreover, without improved health care to reduce child mortality rates, families run the risk of severe loss. Sterilization programmes are becoming a major part of birth control programmes in the underdeveloped countries. But if child mortality rates are still high, parents who become sterilized run the risk of great economic loss if their children die and they are unable to replace them.

Thus birth control programmes can only be effective and serve the interests of the poor when they

—are integrated into a total health care system that is reducing child mortality rates;

—include the education of both men and women;

—are village-based, training people from the village in which they will serve;

—can become self-supporting and therefore permanent, through, for example, a health insurance programme;

—are part of an education programme in which people are becoming conscious of the economic groups that limit their lives. Without this the poor are unable to build effective organization to protect their own interests, so necessary when the village elite tries to sabotage their efforts.

China's extensive and successful birth control programmes illustrate that rapid population growth does not 'automatically take care of itself' once the social prerequisites are met. China's programmes also illustrate many of the above features that would need to be integrated into truly effective and beneficial programmes.

In China population planning activities are not limited to separate 'birth control programmes.'[11] Rather, population planning activities – discussion of the rationale behind limiting births and the means to achieve it – permeate the many different organizations, from trade unions to residential committees, to which almost everyone belongs. As part of the public health system, including neighbourhood health centres and mobile family planning units, birth control information and devices reach virtually every community. The health centres almost never close and are operated not by aloof, outsider professionals but by local residents who maintain ongoing contact with families. China is self-sufficient in all contraceptive devices. They are free and readily available.

China is thus successfully lowering birth rates by building on people's positive sense of responsibility to the common good. This is possible since economic changes have made it truly in the interest of the people to choose smaller families. In other countries, such as India where one-quarter of the family planning budget goes for material incentives, birth control programmes both take advantage of people's poverty and reinforce individualistic desires.

An important lesson in the Chinese success story is this: where the majority of people are participating in development, making decisions about how resources are to meet the needs of all – in short, where there is a more fair and equal control of the country's wealth – all people are more likely to respond to birth control programmes because they can see for themselves the limits of their resources.

Clearly we support the goal of slowing growth rates and stabilizing our global population. And we do not underestimate the need for positive action in providing family planning programmes once the social prerequisites are being met. However, we stand firmly against family planning programmes that *purport to alleviate the problem of hunger*. They carry the message that the poor are themselves to blame for their own hunger, masking the true economic and political roots of their suffering.

Because some might misinterpret our words, suggesting that we discount the problem of rapid population growth, we must be absolutely clear. Population density and rapid growth can of course be grave problems. These problems are, as we have seen, symptoms of the powerlessness of so many to choose fewer children. Population factors also can exacerbate the difficult tasks of social and economic restructuring necessary to eliminate hunger. The error, however, is to transform the problem of population – a *symptom* – into the *cause* of hunger. And this is no semantic squabble. Getting at the solution to a problem hinges entirely on how well one can pinpoint its cause. The root cause of hunger has to do with the relationships of people to each other and to the control over basic resources. As long as people think the fundamental causes are elsewhere, this root cause will go neglected and people will in fact become more hungry.

Continuing to grow at current rates will certainly undercut the future well-being of all of us. That is self-evident. But this self-evident truth adds, for us, even *greater urgency* to identify clearly the root causes of rapid population growth.

4 : Population Pressure on the Environment

The deterioration of our global ecosystem and its agricultural resources coincides with an increase in the population of human beings and livestock. Yet is there a *necessary* causal link? We have had to conclude there is not.

Much of the current destruction of the ecosystem in under-developed countries began with colonialism. The plantations established by the British, Spanish and other colonial powers put a double burden on the land. First, they expropriated the best land for continuous cultivation of crops for export. Second, they usually pushed the local farmers onto marginal, often hilly, land not at all suitable for intensive farming. Land that otherwise might have served for grazing, forestry, or recreation soon became ravaged by erosion.

This double burden – cash cropping for export and squeezing the majority of farmers onto erosion-prone lands – is being reinforced today. Take a Central American country like El Salvador. The country is mostly steep hills and mountains. The most fertile and productive lands are the middle volcanic slopes, some scattered interior river basins, and the coastal plain. Beginning with the Spanish conquest, these prime lands have been owned by large estates devoted to exports: cotton, sugar, and coffee crops and cattle ranches. Less than one in a hundred farms in El Salvador has more than 250 acres; but those few that do, together take up *half* of the total farming area of the country, including all of the prime land.[1]

The land left over, now mainly barren hills, is all that some 350,000 *campesinos* have on which to scratch out a subsistence living for their families. Much of the land they are forced to cultivate is so steep, it has to be planted with a stick. The erosion can be so devastating – one study concluded 77 per cent of the nation's land is suffering from accelerated erosion[2] – that the *campesinos* must abandon a slope after a single year's meagre yield. Where they will go in the future is not at all clear. Already the rapid soil depletion has set off a heavy migration of Salvadorians into neighbouring Honduras. This land search by desperate Salvadorians helped precipitate a war between the two countries in 1969. And we were told that this was the first war in history caused by the population explosion.

It is tempting to look at an area such as the Caribbean, where semitropical forests have been destroyed and soil badly eroded, and simply diagnose the problem as too many people. Currently, local farms feed only one third of the Caribbean population and 70 per cent of the children are malnourished.[3]

But before accepting 'too many people' as the cause, consider some figures on Caribbean land use. Over half of all the arable land is made to produce crops and cattle for export. In individual countries the usurpation of the best land for export crops is even more dramatic. In Guadaloupe over 66 per cent of the arable land produces sugar cane, cocoa, and bananas. In Martinique over 70 per cent is planted with sugar cane, cocoa, bananas, and coffee. In Barbados, 77 per cent of the arable land grows sugar cane alone.[4]

'Haiti,' comments environmental writer Erik Eckholm, 'is among the few countries that already rival or perhaps surpass El Salvador in nationwide environmental destruction.'[5] Not coincidentally, only a few people own the country's farmland. The best valley lands belong to a handful of elites and their foreign partners, who produce endless vistas of sugar cane, coffee trees, and cattle – all for export. We were particularly struck to see the miserable shacks of the landless along the edge of fertile irrigated fields growing feed for thousands of pigs that wind up as sausages for Chicago's Servbest Foods. Meanwhile the majority of Haitians are left to ravage the once-green mountain slopes in near futile efforts to grow food. In desperation thousands flee to the United States, where they compete with the poorest paid Americans for minimum wage jobs.

In Africa it is colonialism's cash crops and their continuing legacy, not the pressure of its population, that are destroying soil resources. Vast tracts of geologically old sediments perfectly suitable for permanent crops such as grazing grasses or trees have instead been torn up for planting cotton and peanuts. The soil becomes rapidly poor in humus and loses its cohesiveness. The wind, quite strong in the dry season, then easily erodes the soils. Soil deterioration leads to declining crop yields[6] and consequently to an expansion of cultivated land, often onto marginal soils.

In dramatic contrast to cash-cropping monoculture, the traditional self-provisioning agriculture that it replaces is often quite sound ecologically. It is a long-evolved adaptation to tropical soil and climate. It reflects a sophisticated understanding of the complex rhythms of the local ecosystem. The mixing of crops, sometimes of more than twenty different species, means harvests are staggered and provides maximum security against wholesale losses due to unseasonable weather, pests, or disease. Moreover, mixed cropping provides the soil with year-round protection from the sun and rain.

The problem of soil erosion *is* serious. But soil erosion occurs largely because fertile land is monopolized by a few, forcing the majority of farmers to overuse vulnerable soils. Moreover, soil impoverishment results, not from an effort to meet the basic food needs of expanding populations, but increasingly from the pressure to grow continuously nonfood and luxury export crops over large areas to the neglect of traditional techniques that once protected the soil.

Overgrazing: A Case Study in Land Misuse

Overgrazing is another sure way to ruin marginal lands. But to get at the cause one must ask, Who is overgrazing and why? And does it follow that marginal lands can never be suitable for livestock? Finally, since overgrazing means too many cattle on the land, must we conclude this reflects too many people?

Some outsiders see Africa's nomadic pastoralists as the culprits. We have come to learn, however, that nomadic pastoralists have traditionally made efficient use of vast stretches of semiarid land that otherwise would remain unproductive. While their migrations might look random to the outsider, they are, in reality, patterned to take advantage of variations in rainfall and vegetation. The nomads may herd their livestock over hundreds of miles from rainy season pastures to oases of perennial grasses in dry seasons. Pastoral nomadism, then, is a rational response to an environment characterized by the scarcity of water, seasonal drought, and widely scattered seasonal fodder resources. The nomads' tactics make use of resources that others would not even consider as resources.[7]

Another adaptation technique of traditional pastoralists is keeping a herd that consists of different types of livestock: camels, sheep, goats, donkeys, as well as cattle. A mixed herd can exploit a variety of ecological niches. Cattle and sheep graze on grasslands; and goats browse on shrubs and low parts of trees. Valuable protein for human consumption is thus produced by plants that humans cannot eat. Different species also have different reproductive cycles; staggered breeding seasons ensure some type of milk throughout the year. The hardiness of goats and camels make them good animals to fall back on in times of drought when cattle die off. A varied herd also acts as a walking storehouse for food, either directly or in exchange for grain, during annual dry spells and periodic droughts.

Pastoralists traditionally produced enough meat and dairy products to exchange with farmers for grain. In addition, the pastoralists' herds annually manured the fallow fields of the farmers. The animals thus gained good grazing land and the fertility of the farmers' soil improved. This symbiotic relationship allowed for remarkably dense populations to comfortably inhabit seemingly inhospitable lands.[8]

If raising livestock has been and can be such an excellent way to make marginal lands productive, what has gone wrong? What is behind the many reports of overgrazing in regions like the African Sahel, that vast stretch of semiarid land along the southern border of the Sahara?

To answer such questions we have to go back to the beginning of this century. The French colonial administration created arbitrary 'national' borders (today enforced by the newly independent governments) without regard to the need of the nomads to migrate. Endless restrictions have made it increasingly difficult for the nomads to shift their herds in response to the short- and long-term cycles of nature.

The French also slapped a head tax on each nomad. The tax had to be paid in French francs even though most nomads lived within a barter economy. The nomads needed, therefore, to raise more livestock, so that some could be sold for cash. Over the years, their need for money has been compounded by the growing lure of imported consumer goods.

Higher market prices also prompted pastoralists to build up their herds beyond the carrying capacity of the lands.

The expansion of lands for peanut and cotton production sharply decreased the amount of pasture available to herders. Farmers also began to keep small herds near their houses. These herds, kept in such a confined space, resulted in localized overgrazing.[9] Moreover, the urban and export demand for beef induced the pastoralists to upset the natural balance of a diversified herd in favour of cattle. Modern inoculations against disease also facilitated the build-up of herds beyond the carrying capacity of the grazing lands. Medicine that was meant to save these herds ultimately contributed to the death by starvation of tens of thousands of animals.

Aid agencies, including the United States Agency for International Development (AID), drilled deep water wells in the late 1950s and early 1960s. They ignored the reality that the only grazing pattern that would not overtax semiarid land is one relying on free migration over a wide area and that a year-round watering hole is an inadequate substitute, as experience would show. When the rains began to fail, the nomads started to move their cattle en masse to these wells. A well, however, acts as a false signal in the traditional culture's communication system. A well *appears* to be a good substitute for rain. Unlike rain, however, it does not make pasture grow. A seemingly continuous supply of water, usually the most fickle and limiting factor in their economy, convinced the nomads to keep on increasing the size of their herds.

Before long on average in the Sahel 6,000 head of cattle were milling about wells surrounded by grazing lands that at best could feed 600. After the cattle ate out the areas around the wells and trampled down the soil, the caked earth could no longer even absorb the scarce rains. One eyewitness reported that each well 'quickly became the centre of its own little desert forty or fifty miles square.'[10]

From 1955 to 1960, the number of cattle, goats, and sheep in Mali alone increased by 800,000. After 1960, when more boreholes were drilled, the total number of livestock shot up from five million to sixteen million, or more than three animals for every Malien. In the recent drought a large number of animals, crowded on the rapidly exhausted grazing lands around the wells, died, not of thirst, but of hunger.[11]

You probably have read that the plight of the pastoralists proves that these countries are overpopulated and have exhausted their resources. Does more cattle mean there are too many people? We think the answer is by now obvious: not necessarily. But there is no need to romanticize nomads. Undoubtedly they must come into a new ecological balance within the context of the rest of society. This will require some changes, such as regulation of herd composition and size. But it will also require even more fundamental changes in the larger society, for instance, the integration of agriculture and pastoralism, in part through equitable and *stable* values for the exchange of livestock and grain.

Outsiders, especially urban-based government elites who have pronounced pastoralism an anachronism and an ecological disaster (perhaps principally because they cannot control the nomads), invariably advocate ranching as the 'modern way.' Commercial ranching with fenced-in grazing and grain feeding that squanders precious grain – geared largely to exporting beef – stands in dramatic contrast to the ecological sanity of traditional pastoralism that utilizes a full range of resources otherwise not available for human consumption. Ranching looms as a grave threat to Africa's semiarid lands and their traditional inhabitants.[12]

Moreover, commercial ranching overlooks the vast potential of game animals in Africa. Game, unlike cattle, are not affected by the tsetse fly that inhabits large areas of central and southern Africa. As strange as it may sound, some scientists suggest the tsetse fly may be a blessing in disguise.[13] If the flies were eradicated cattle ranching would probably lead to the extinction of game animals which, properly 'cropped,' represent an enormous meat potential for Africans. The noted ecologist Dr Raymond F. Dasmann argues that game cropping 'has the capacity in Africa, in many areas, of producing more meat per acre than can be obtained from the traditional domestic animals on the same land.'

There is certainly a critical choice ahead for Africa. Commercial ranching would mean expensive, imported inputs with serious environmental risks, the extinction of many species of animals, and increased vulnerability to widely fluctuating foreign beef markets. The other alternative, the restoration of a balanced pastoral system and well-planned game 'cropping', could realize Africa's enormous natural protein potential through the optimum utilization of vegetation.

The choice would seem obvious. But are the lure of foreign exchange, foreign loans for cattle projects, the foreign demand for beef, and the beef mystique of African urban elites all too irresistible to oppose before it's too late?

The Amazon

Like the wildlife areas of Africa, the Amazon River basin has long been seen as one of the world's few remaining great natural preserves. Recently the public has become vaguely aware that it too is being threatened. The Amazon basin *is* being 'ravaged,' but is the cause overpopulation?

Since the mid-1960s Brazil's largest government project is the 'colonization' of this extraordinary region. The plans call for sweeping clean tens of millions of acres of tropical forest. Already legions of Caterpillar Tractors' gargantuan 35-ton D-9s, mounted with angle ploughs weighing 2,500 pounds each, are bulldozing the forest at 2,700 yards an hour, uprooting everything in sight. In some areas the job calls for two D-9s with a heavy chain between them rolling a huge hollow steel ball eight feet in diameter and weighing 6,000 pounds. As the tractors move forward, the chain jerks out the trees, destroying the extensive matted root system and exposing the thin tropical soil. Fires visible for miles devour the debris.[14] Such massive deforestation is, according to the President of the Brazilian Academy of Science, Warwick Kerr, 'taking place at a faster pace than Brazil and perhaps the world has ever known before. The Amazon forest will disappear in 35 years if it continues to be destroyed at the present rate.'[15]

Is it really Brazil's expanding population behind those unrelenting D-9 'jungle crushers'? No, the truth is that Brazil with 2.3 acres of already cropped land per person (slightly better than the ratio in the United States) hardly needs to invade its tropical forests in order to feed its people. The Amazon forest is earmarked for destruction for two entirely different reasons.

Settlement or 'colonization' schemes historically have been safety valves – primarily a way to sidestep the urgent need for land redistribution. In Brazil, a mere one per cent of the farms take up over 43 per cent of the country's total farmland, and the best land at that. In brutal contrast, 50 per cent of the farms are left with less than 3 per cent of the land. In addition, at least 7 million rural families own no land at all – in a country where, even without taking the Amazon region into consideration, there are potentially ten cultivable acres for every family. Four out of five rural families, even if they do find work on a large estate, earn less that $33 a month. Yet a family of three needs at least $65 a month to buy food alone. It all translates into a massive waste of human life. Almost 200 of every 1,000 babies born in rural north-east Brazil die in their first year of life.[16]

To avoid provoking Brazil's most powerful families by dividing up the large, generally export-orientated estates, the military government announced an absurd solution: move the rural poor to the Amazon basin, a tropical region totally unsuited for intensive and continuous farming.[17] Thus the pressure on the Amazon forest comes *not* from Brazil's population growth but from a government's effort to diffuse pressures for a just redistribution of land.

Ten years after much self-serving fanfare, the government has resettled a mere 10,000 small farmers. Even then, despite enormous bureaucratic expenditures, many of these farms have been soon abandoned, in part since their tropical soils cannot support intensive cultivation. Far from being concerned, the government has added insult to injury. Only a few years after trumpeting that prosperity for the rural poor was just a thousand or so miles down a not yet completed road, the government opted for a different type of pioneer. Kingdom-sized concessions, none smaller than 125,000 acres, were the new order of the day – mainly for export-oriented ranching and pulpwood production.

The 'pioneers' are some of Brazil's richest families, already among the country's largest landholders, a number of Brazilian corporations, and, for good measure, a few television stars. Also quick to find out what Brazil can do for them are many of the world's largest multinational corporations. These corporations include Anderson Clayton, Goodyear, Volkswagen, Nestlé, Liquigas, Borden, Mitsubishi and Universe Tank Ship (a low profile giant chartered in Liberia for tax reasons but in fact belonging to the aged American multibillionaire, D. K. Ludwig). The 'homesteads' of these pioneers run as large as 3.7 million acres, half the size of Holland.[18]

Never has a government given so much to so few for so little. A seemingly endless list of 'fiscal encouragements' is offered. One such incentive allows a corporation to invest in the Amazon half the taxes it owes on its earnings in Brazil.

Additional special incentives are offered to beef export operations. The goal is to make Brazil a major supplier of beef to Europe and the United States. Belem, at the mouth of the Amazon, is virtually as close to Miami as it is to the most populous cities of Brazil and five days closer by ship to Europe than are the Argentine slaughterhouses.

In 1975 a United States reconnaissance satellite's heat sensor detected a sudden and intense warming of the earth in the Amazon basin usually associated with an imminent volcanic eruption. A special alert mission was dispatched. And what did they find? A

German multinational corporation burning down one million acres of tropical forest for a cattle ranch. Unlike the slash and burn of a few acres here and there by Cayapó tribes, the corporation's burning a million acres means the death of most local wildlife.

Several corporations like Ludwig's, Georgia-Pacific, and Bruyznell are actively stripping the forest (which contains over a sixth of the world's remaining timberland) of its valuable lumber resources. They are in reality mining the forests. The plan is to sweep clean the unwanted trees with more D-9 Caterpillars backed up by power saws and voracious fires. The next stage calls for planting a 'homogeneous forest' of hundreds of thousands of gmelina trees uprooted from West Africa (who knows what environmental havoc this will cause?). The companies are betting the top soil will hold long enough for these fast-growing trees to be ready to be made into paper pulp for export. All this with government incentives and multimillions in profits, of course.

If you are wondering whether at least all this devastation will provide employment, the answer is that it won't. As with most mega-money corporations, the money invested goes mainly for machines, not to people. On his 3.7 million acres, Ludwig's cattle, pulp, and export-orientated rice operations expect to employ 1,200 permanent workers and a relative handful of seasonal hired hands.[19]

Some justify the whole Amazon scheme as necessitated by Brazil's or the world's population problem. In reality the scheme is a public relations fraud by the Brazilian government at the expense of the landless, a devastation of the country's natural resources to provide a fleeting profit for the rich. It is also, in the opinion of many noted environmental scientists, an ecological disaster in the making not only for Brazil but for the entire world. Many ecologists warn that such grand-scale tampering with the soil structure, drainage, and water evaporation rates might well set off chain reactions that could alter climates on a worldwide basis.

Conclusion

It is not, then, growing population that threatens to destroy the environment, either here or abroad, but a system that promotes the utilization of food-producing resources according to narrow profit-seeking criteria. Taking advantage of this system are land monopolizers growing non-food and luxury crops and colonial patterns of taxation and cash-cropping that force the rural majority to abuse marginal land.

Of course there are areas where population density exacerbates environmental deterioration. But, just as we said in our discussion of the cause of hunger, what is most critical is to distinguish exacerbating factors from the root cause. Where environmental destruction is most severe, halving the population would not solve the problem. Basic changes in the control of wealth remain the only path to an ecologically sane use of the land.

While taking credit for our tenacity and our considerable experience gained in manufacturing in 42 plants in 12 countries, Massey-Ferguson's success in Brazil certainly could not have been achieved without the enlightened policies of the Government since 1964 toward stability and development.

'Massey-Ferguson in Brazil,' statement by
Albert A. Thornbrough, President 1975

You can buy the land out there now for the same price as a couple of bottles of beer per acre. When you've got half a million acres and twenty thousand head of cattle, you can leave the lousy place and go live in Paris, Hawaii, Switzerland, or anywhere you choose.

An American rancher who owns land in the
Mato Grosso, as quoted in Robin Hanbury-Tenison,
A Question of Survival for the Indians of Brazil,
London, 1973

Mr. Ludwig doesn't want to waste time with research. He just wants to begin. Naturally we make mistakes, but we also get things done a lot faster.

An American manager of Ludwig's
Brazilian operation, quoted
in Time, November 15, 1976.

5 : The Price Scare

Approaching the 1970s, who would have thought that 'food crisis' was around the corner? 1969 was called the year of the 'Great Wheat Glut.' An article in *Nation's Business*, in September 1969, entitled 'Too Much of a Good Thing' pictured a farmer standing on a tractor in the middle of a 'field of plenty' waving the white flag of surrender. The article's conclusion: 'There are too many farmers, working too many farms, with too vast a capacity to produce.'

What we know as the 'food crisis of rising prices,' starting in 1972-1973, was largely the direct and intentional result of United States 'Food Power' policies that hit upon scarcity as a way to increase both the volume and price of agricultural exports. As we will show in Part VII, Food Power was a strategy to create demand and raise prices so as to increase the foreign exchange earnings of the United States. The stage had already been set by acreage cutbacks in the late sixties and early seventies to deal with the mounting surplus of grain. The acreage allotment figure for 1970 was only 75 per cent of that of 1967; less land was cultivated in 1970 than in 1948-1952.[1] In both 1969 and 1970 the amount of grain that could have been grown, but was not, on land held out of production amounted to over seventy million metric tons[2] – about double all the grain imported annually in the early seventies by the underdeveloped countries.

Against this backdrop, United States officials started to manoeuvre. By devaluing the dollar (thus making our grain cheaper abroad), by rescinding a law requiring that half of our grain going to the Soviet Union and Eastern Europe be carried by American ships, and by offering the Soviet Union financing for its grain purchases, the United States set the food bait. Other countries began to bite. The notorious Soviet grain deal was the first catch. Nineteen million tons of grain went not to feed the hungry, but to feed Soviet livestock.

Nature co-operated, too, with a late monsoon in India, drought conditions in West Africa, China, Australia, and Argentina and a precipitous drop in the anchovy fish catch (used for feeding livestock). But United States strategists could not depend on the weather to create scarcity. Although they must have been aware of these adverse weather conditions in many parts of the world, President Nixon and Secretary of Agriculture Earl Butz took another five million acres of wheat land *out* of production in September 1972. This act marked the largest holdout of cropland in several years – equal in size to all the farmland in the United Kingdom. Then in early 1973, when export sales had started to cool down, the United States devalued the dollar for a second time – suddenly making American grain 15 per cent cheaper for the Japanese. The Japanese jumped at the bait. A new cycle of scarcity was generated by the decisions of a few government policy makers.

The result was that world grain stocks that had stood at ninety five days worth of grain in 1961 were now down below thirty days. This planned and rapid depletion of grain reserves, more than any other single factor, contributed to the unprecedented increase and volatility in food prices. Scarcity, however, was *not* the problem; the world produced more grain per capita in the so-called scarcity year 1972-1973 – about 632 pounds – than it had in the year 1960, not considered a crisis year.

Yo-Yo Prices

The market system has built-in commodity cycles in which 'years of glut' follow 'years of want.' The result: Yo-yo prices.

Chemical fertilizer is one example. New plants were constructed in the 1960s. Profits dipped as supply outdistanced buyers because most of the world's farmers are too poor to afford chemical fertilizer. The companies then cut back production in hopes of increasing profits. As the world price of fertilizer climbed, the return on investment by the fertilizer industry jumped from 1.1 per cent in 1971 to 39.6 per cent in 1974.[3] Then, in less than a year, prices had soared so high that purchases again slowed down. In June, 1975, *Business Week* was covering the 'fertilizer glut.'

These alternating periods of glut and shortage occur because we have a food production system in which investment decisions are basically made only on assessments of *current* profitability. If prices are good now, farmers and livestock producers will plant or breed to take advantage of the prices. But since all other producers are following exactly the same cue, when the time comes to reap the harvest or slaughter the animal (in the case of cattle this may be thirty-two months from the initial decision to breed), there may well be a surplus, causing prices to drop. With prices down, farmers will be reluctant to plant or breed heavily; thus, there will be a future shortage, causing high prices. So the cycle begins anew.

When all farmers are planting at the same time in response to high prices, the result can be, not simply a drop in prices at harvest time but the waste of a tremendous amount of food. Farmers will decide it is less costly to let their crop rot in the ground than to harvest it at a loss. According to the US Department of Agriculture, the amount of fruit not harvested or discarded 'for economic reasons' amounted to over one *billion* pounds during the period from 1959 to 1973.[4]

We are told that price cycles represent the healthy balancing mechanism at the heart of a market system. The catch is that in a food processing and marketing system tightly controlled by a few corporations, consumer prices climb up in response to basic commodity cycles but often never come back down to where they were when the cycle began. Commodity price cycles then become a handy smoke screen for profit margin increases.

Chronic Surplus

We are asked to believe that the age of scarcity is upon us. Yet, as long as food is bought and sold like any other commodity and as long as a large portion of people are too poor to buy the food they need, the major problem of agricultural economists will continue to be the threat of surplus, not scarcity.

The theory that we are now entering the age of inevitable scarcity because our numbers have surpassed some supposed threshold cannot be substantiated. In a world where food stocks are deliberately depleted so that United States grain exports might earn the greatest foreign exchange and where the major headache of hundreds of Common Market officials is how to *reduce* mountains of so-called surplus, the notion of scarcity is worse than a distortion. It shifts the blame for scarcity onto nameless masses of people and onto the 'natural limits' of the earth.

6 : The Food Vs. Poison Trade-off

We have all read and seen on television frightening accounts of the dangers of manufacturing and using pesticides to increase food production. But won't we have to live with these dangers, since applying pesticides is one of the big reasons why we can produce so much food?

Perhaps Western food surpluses might allow for a slight cutback in pesticides such as the ban on DDT. But what can you say about the underdeveloped countries where every bushel counts for survival? Won't they need to use massive amounts of pesticides? Shouldn't food for starving people take precedence over all else?

Do Pesticides Help the Hungry to Produce Food?

We put this question to the chief of the Plant Protection Service of the FAO. He estimates that annually 800 million pounds of pesticides are used in underdeveloped countries. The 'vast majority,' however, are for export crops, principally cotton and to a lesser extent 'fruits and vegetables grown under plantation conditions for export.'[1]

An underdeveloped country, moreover, easily gets locked into producing more and more export crops, in part to earn foreign exchange to pay for more and more imported inputs such as pesticides. Pesticides lead to an agricultural environment requiring more pesticides. The diminishing financial returns per acre that result often step up the pressure to devote even more land to export crops. The entire process bypasses the need of local people for food.

Nor should we overlook the monetary cost to the individual farmer. Pesticides, in economic terms, are often just one more factor taking farming out of the hands of small, self-provisioning farmers.

Pesticide usage in underdeveloped countries is concentrated in little export-oriented enclaves that are functionally mere extensions of the agricultural systems of the industrial countries. In these enclaves pesticides are commonly applied so intensively that environmental scientists have the 'opportunity' to study the effects of extreme chemical farming.

One such opportunity came with the introduction of pesticides into the cotton fields of the Cañete Valley of Peru after World War II. By 1956, pests so overran the fields that cultivation had to be suspended. Dr Boza Barducci, the director of the region's agricultural experiment station, notes, 'In 1956 we concluded that it was nearly impossible, in practice, to obtain successful control of cotton pests by chemical methods, including the most efficient pesticides presently known.' He further comments, 'Such drastic losses as in the Cañete Valley disprove the worldwide belief in the theoretical efficiency of chemical products, an illusion created by the chemical industry.'[2]

Insecticides introduced into Egyptian cotton fields in the mid-1950s were hailed as 'a major triumph over nature.' By 1961 yields began dropping by 35 per cent a year. A similar pattern in northeastern Mexico brought a near halt to cotton production. In Malaysia and elsewhere, cocoa, palm oil, rubber, and other export crops have been devastated by pest attacks unleashed, ironically, by the introduction of pesticides.[3]

In Nicaragua cotton acreage was increased tenfold between 1950 and 1964. By the late 1950s the large growers, acting on the advice of United States Agency for International Development (AID) technicians, scheduled insecticide applications an average of eight times per season as well as liberal fertilizer treatments. Yields increased. But by 1966 the growers found it necessary to apply insecticides thirty times per season. Even then cotton yields began to drop: from 821 pounds per acre in 1965 to 621 pounds in 1968. Along the fertile Pacific coastal plain of Central America large cotton estates by the late 1960s had to schedule so many (45 to 50 a season) aerial sprays of a 'cocktail' of pesticides (including DDT) that cotton production ceased to be profitable. By 1968 Nicaragua had the dubious distinction of holding the world's record for the number of applications of insecticides on a single crop.[4]

In spite of (or because of?) heavy pesticide doses, food crops such as corn and beans, not themselves sprayed but merely located near the cotton fields, were for the first time heavily damaged by insects. Very little food could be harvested.

In regions where pesticides have been intensively used, mosquitoes have developed resistance. Malaria, once thought to have been 'eradicated' by DDT, has broken out again in Central

America and South Asia. In the Danli area of Honduras (population 32,000), only three years after the start of large-scale cotton production and pesticide sprayings, over one fourth of the population contracted malaria.[5] Similar outbreaks near cotton plantations using insecticides have been occurring throughout Central America.

What is happening? Why has everything seemingly gone wrong?

In country after country there is a regular progression of events. For the first few years insects are controlled at reasonable cost and yields are higher than ever before. The growers, seeing the bugs literally drop from plants, feel the pesticides give them power over forces that have always been beyond their control. Gradually, however, the pest species develop resistant strains through a survival of the fittest selection.

For it is not true that the only good bug is a dead bug. Some bugs are parasites or flesh-eating predators that live off the insect species doing the plant damage. Some eat only very specific parts of the crop plant. Studies show that the vast majority of insect species never cause sufficient damage to justify the cost of insecticide treatment. Their numbers are restricted below economic injury levels by the action of parasites and predators. But when an insecticide kills some of these parasites and predators, many ordinarily insignificant insects are able to multiply faster.

Because plant-eating pests generally are present in larger numbers than their predators, they statistically are more likely than their predators to contain a few individuals with inheritable resistance to the insecticide. As the few resistant pests gradually multiply, every application of the insecticide will kill more predators and fewer pests, compounding the damage to the crops. With this understanding we should not be surprised that twenty-four of the twenty-five most serious pests in California agriculture – those responsible for a million or more dollars in losses in 1970 – are either insecticide aggravated or actually insecticide-induced pests.[6]

Only twenty-five years ago the spider mite was a minor pest. Repeated use of pesticides supposedly aimed at other pests has decimated the natural enemies and competitors of the mite. Today the mite is the pest most seriously threatening agriculture worldwide.

Already by 1971 fifteen major pest species had developed resistance to the insecticides applied. The time taken to overcome susceptibility to an insecticide has ranged from four to fourteen years. The irony of nature is that the more effective an insecticide is in killing susceptible individuals of a pest population, the faster resistant individuals will evolve. Such is the case of several pest species (including the rice water weevil, the cabbage looper, the soyabean looper, the banded cucumber beetle, the two-spotted spider mite, and the banded-wing whitefly) for which no new insecticide has been developed to buy a few more years' grace. Ecologist Dr M. Taghi Farvar notes the alarming possibility that the present pest control strategy in Central America may be leading to resistant populations of pests on a hemispheric scale.[7]

Exporting Hazard

Half of the pesticides now exported from the United States go to the Third World. And pressure to expand the market for pesticides in the underdeveloped countries will undoubtedly step up if the introduction of alternative pest control strategies (which we will discuss later) actually begins to undercut the domestic pesticide market.

The question implies that these pesticide exports might well be a boon to the hungry who need food. But as we already pointed out, most pesticides used in the Third World are not applied to basic food crops. Just as important, it is often the hungry – the landless labourers working on export estates – who are put at risk precisely because of heavy exposure to pesticides, many of which have been deemed too hazardous to be used in the United Kingdom and the USA. According to the Environmental Protection Agency data, nineteen US-produced pesticides now being exported have either never been cleared by US authorities or have been restricted or banned in the United States.[8]

Even after the insecticide Phosvel had been linked to fatal human and water buffalo poisoning in Egypt, the Velsicol Chemical Corporation in Texas continued to manufacture it for export. Phosvel was designed to attack the central nervous system of insects. Apparently it can do the same thing to humans. Raymond David, a former supervisor at a Velsicol Corporation plant, reported that workers in the Phosvel section were dubbed 'the Phosvel zombies' because of their obvious nervous disorders. 'The company knew people were getting sick,' claimed David. But the management tried to dismiss the problem. 'They told me all those guys smoked marijuana. They said the guys were acid freaks,' recalled David. In 1975 David quit, feeling that he could no longer take responsibility for the hazards his subordinates faced. Former employees of Velsicol have brought a suit against the company for damage to their health, including muscle paralysis, nervous system disorders, blurred vision, and speech and memory blocks.[9] As a result, Phosvel production has been stopped. But sales in the Third World continue. Some vegetables imported from Mexico were recently found to be contaminated.

With low levels of literacy, meagre extension services, and heavy company propaganda about the chemicals' benefits, farmers in the Third World cannot be expected to appreciate the hazards of an apparently innocuous white powder. A research team in Pakistan in 1974 reported that 'one customer, lacking a suitable container, unwrapped his turban, poured a granular pesticide therein, and replaced it on his head for transport.'[10]

Most critically, people in underdeveloped countries, just like many farmworkers here who handle pesticides, have no voice in the conditions of their exposure. On Del Monte-controlled banana plantations in the Philippines, we saw workers exposed to pesticides in three ways. Twice each month, airplanes blanket everything below with deadly chemicals. Neither water sources nor people are protected. Secondly, workers carry tanks of pesticides on their backs into the fields and spray the plants directly. Third, in the packing house, women workers spray every bunch of bananas before loading them into boxes for export. None of the women are provided with protective clothing or masks. One showed us a large lesion on her leg caused, she said, when a fellow employee accidentally sprayed her.

In Central America, 'thousands of highland Indians who annually emigrate to the estates on the Pacific Coast to pick the cotton crop are poisoned by insecticides,' reports Dr Farvar. 'Hundreds of documented cases of death are recorded per year.'[11] In 1967-1968 in Nicaragua there were over 500 reported cases of human poisoning by insecticides with eighty deaths.[12] The United States Embassy in Mexico in 1974 reported 689 poisonings and seven deaths of agricultural workers due to insecticides manufactured by Shell and du Pont.[13] The National Academy of Sciences Special Commission on Pesticides found that severe occupational injuries 'might be seriously underestimated.'[14]

In Asia pesticides are destroying an important protein source of the rural population – fish. In the flooded rice paddies peasants have traditionally cultivated fish as a cash crop as well as an excellent low-cost source of protein to fall back on in times of declining rice prices. But today the widespread use of pesticides is sharply reducing fish production on rice farms in the Philippines, Malaysia, and Indonesia. In Indonesia in 1969-1970, German and Japanese multinational corporations began spraying over two million acres of paddy with the same chemical that allegedly only a few years before had killed millions of fish in the Rhine. Water buffalo, an important source of labour and food to the peasant population of Indonesia, reportedly have died.[15]

The Human Toll in the United States

United States pesticide safety regulations are much more lenient than those of most other industrial countries, largely due to lobbying by the powerful chemical corporations.[16] According to a comprehensive study of international standards, if the United States applied Japan's standards governing toxicity levels, we would have to 'do away with about half the organophosphate pesticides (the common substitute for DDT).'[17]

In 1974 the Environmental Protection Agency estimated that 'as many as 14,000 Americans may be non-fatally poisoned by pesticides in a given year, 6,000 seriously enough to require hospitalization.'[18] Other investigators estimate that 200 die annually.[19] In 1977, 14 of 27 men handling the soil fumigant, DBCP, were found to be sterile or to have low sperm counts. In addition to causing sterility, this pesticide, widely used on crops like carrots, peanuts, and tomatoes, has been shown to cause stomach and mammary cancer in rats. Health officials in Arkansas reported workers developing such cancer after two years' exposure.[20]

Although most of these ill effects are suffered by farmers and farmworkers, all of us are exposed through what we eat. Neither can we escape the poisons injected into the environment abroad. Our planet's ecosystem does not allow for the convenient quarantining of the underdeveloped countries. Despite the ban in most industrial countries, more DDT (over 150,000 metric tons) is annually deposited in the environment now than ten years ago.[21] One reason is that chemical corporation lobbyists have succeeded in persuading the US Congress to exempt exports from every ban or restriction on the domestic use of DDT and other pesticides. And, DDT, like all pesticides, just does not stay where it is put. Once applied to crops, it works its way into lakes, streams, rivers and oceans. Over one fourth of all DDT ever produced has wound up in our oceans. Fish are now almost universally contaminated.[22]

DDT applied to cotton in Nicaragua showed up in beef carcasses imported through Miami.

Pesticides easily enter into the food chain and wind up in human tissue. About 50 per cent of the food samples tested in a 1973 study contained detectable insecticide residues. Each young American adult already carries at least 0.003 ounce (0.085 gram) of pesticides permanently in his or her body fat.[23] Although this level of pesticide residue now presents no measurable health hazard, little is known about the effects of long-term pesticide dosages and residues.

The Poison Business

Despite the self-defeating cycle set off by heavy doses of pesticides and the documented, life-endangering hazards, pesticide sales are still increasing. The simple reason is that a pesticide corporation receives low marks from Stock Exchange analysts unless they maximize profits and expand at a steady clip sales that by 1975 were well over $2.5 billion a year.

Basic environmental security, not to mention truly effective pest control, clearly points to the need to develop pesticides that are as *target-specific* as possible and to study fully the effects of each new pesticide on nontarget insects, other wildlife, and people; but a chemical corporation's interests propel us in exactly the opposite direction. In order to maximize profit margins and expand sales, a chemical company seeks to minimize research and marketing costs and to come up with pesticides that kill the broadest spectrum of pests.

Pesticide sales are further expanded by promoting '100 per cent' pest elimination. Aiming for 100 per cent eradication, however, is extremely expensive, unnecessary, often fails, is likely to be dangerous and can result in costly 'overkills'.

Also, to maximize profits, the companies promote *scheduled* spraying, instead of spraying in response to a need. Scheduled spraying means greater and more predictable sales. It is easier for a chemical company manager to judge how much pesticide to produce and distribute to different outlets if he can simply multiply the number of acres his customers own by a given quantity per acre. That way he does not have to take into account predictions about how bad a particular pest really is going to be in a given year.

Poison for Beauty

What we gain from pesticides turns out in many cases not to be higher yields or better eating quality. We pay a heavy price in pesticides for skin-deep beauty. Our notion of what an orange or apple should look like is largely the creation of tens of millions of dollars spent on full-colour ads depicting 'perfect' fruit. In several Latin American countries the sharply increased use of dangerous and costly fungicides has nothing to do with efforts to grow more food for local people but with making sure that fruits and vegetables grown for export can meet the inflated beauty standards of the West.

Why do growers continue to release such deadly poisons into the environment and risk their own long-term welfare? One reason is that advertising by giant grower associations such as Sunkist, Inc., have conditioned the buying public to expect their fresh fruit to be blemish-free. Growers get premium prices only for such fruit. For example, in 1965, California growers received an average of $2.61 a box for navel oranges that passed the beauty standards. Navel oranges that were equally good inside yet destined for processing into juice due to small skin blemishes brought only 12c. a box. Tomato processors demand a visually perfect fruit, even when the tomatoes are destined to be smashed for paste, sauce, or puree. About two-thirds of the insecticide used on tomatoes grown for processing is to control the tomato fruit worm – an 'essentially cosmetic pest.'[24]

No plant-eating insects presently found in fruits and vegetables are harmful to people. Yet the United States Food and Drug Administration (FDA) has regularly lowered, over the last 40 years, the amount of insect residue that it will permit – in some cases, three to fivefold. In part to meet such standards, insecticide use on vegetables and fruits has jumped 100-300 per cent.[25]

Thus, an investigative team headed by Cornell's David Pimentel concluded that due to the heightened emphasis on cosmetic appearance by food processors, wholesalers, retailers and also the FDA's tightened insect residue standards, 10 to 20 per cent of insecticides used on fruits and vegetables serve only to improve the appearance. They in no way serve our health. In fact, this team points out the multi-layered price we are paying for blemish-free food : greater insecticide residues in our produce, more factory and farmworker pesticide poisoning, environmental pollution, increased energy consumption, and higher food costs.

Pesticides Versus Pest Management

In the last five years the potential for pest control sanity has taken form in what is now called 'integrated pest management'. 'Integrated' suggests that chemical control alone is not the answer. Chemicals are judiciously integrated into a total strategy that includes the manipulation of the natural environment to control pests: rotating crops to deprive a pest of its host plant; developing resistant varieties through genetic breeding; skilfully manipulating the predators and parasites that attack pests; and disrupting the reproductive behaviour of the pests themselves. 'Management' suggests that the goal is not necessarily the total obliteration of the pest but simply keeping the pest population below harmful levels.

'Integrated pest management,' in perhaps less sophisticated form, is the way pests were always dealt with before the pesticide blitz of the last 40 years. In the 1880's, for example, the cottony cushion scale, brought by accident to the US 20 years earlier, threatened the California citrus groves. The answer? Import the scale's predator too, the vedalia beetle. Only one and a half years later this hungry beetle had brought the entire scale threat under control. (And everything was fine until the 1950s, when the vedalia beetle succumbed to the growing applications of DDT.)[26]

For decades crop rotation proved effective in managing pests. The corn rootworm, for example, will not eat the soyabean plant, so that when soybeans alternate with corn, the rootworm has nothing to survive on.[27] But some weedkillers now commonly used on corn in the United States preclude this type of crop rotation. They remain in the soil and kill non-corn plants. Farmers who rely on pesticides thus must plant corn crop after corn crop, a practice that in itself tends to increase insects, disease and weed problems. (Given such a vicious cycle, it is not surprising that corn accounts for almost half the weedkillers in U.S. agriculture.) By now the corn rootworm has developed almost total resistance to major pesticides.[28]

In some areas crop rotation is mandated by the state authorities to control pests. To control the yellowing virus on sugar beets, a number of beet-free periods are enforced in California's several beet growing districts.

Mixed cropping patterns have been found to reduce the pest problem as compared to monoculture. Small cotton plots in Costa

Rica, scattered among those growing other crops, have less severe pest problems than cotton fields in Guatemala, where cotton grows in solid blocks covering as much as 50,000 acres.[29]

In underdeveloped countries with abundant rural labour, hoeing and corn knifing to control weeds require no machinery and create opportunities for productive employment. Mulching, simply covering the soil around the plants, can reduce weeds without using herbicides. A study in Nigeria showed that mulching reduced the competition from weeds to such an extent that corn yields doubled.[30]

The good news is that effective pest management methods minimize what underdeveloped countries and small farmers have least of – money for imported pesticides. Moreover, they create a demand for what is most available – labour power – and thereby involve more people in the production process.

Pest management can also include the selective use of pesticides. While agribusiness corporations are trying to promote 'blind,' scheduled spraying in underdeveloped countries such as India,[31] some farmers in the United States have realized that on top of environmental and health damage they were being just plain swindled. In Graham County, Arizona, cotton growers, working with scientists from the University of Arizona, proved they could save a lot of money by eliminating blind sprayings. Instead, they sent trained scouts out into the fields to measure pest levels. Pesticide expenditures dropped tenfold and so did pest damage. Even adding on fees paid to the 'pest scouts,' the total pest control costs were less than a fifth of what they had been with the scheduled approach. The chemical companies brought enormous pressure on the highest level of the university's administration to force the withdrawal of the scientists from the programme.[32]

Similar experiments on forty-two cotton and thirty-nine citrus farms in California reduced pesticide expenditures by more than 60 per cent.[33] A conservative estimate is that United States farmers could reduce insecticide use 35 to 50 per cent with no effect on crop production, simply by treating only when necessary rather than by schedule.[34]

Integrated pest management has achieved some marked successes in the United States in recent years. In the state of Washington, such integrated pest management programmes have reduced by 50 per cent the pesticide use on apples – the crop using the largest amount of pesticides per acre in the United States.

In China integrated pest management is carried out through the large-scale participation of the rural communities. Pests are controlled before they become a serious problem. With the guidance of experienced agronomists, young members of the production brigades organize themselves into a pest early-warning system. In Shao-tung county in Honan Province 10,000 youths patrol the fields and report any sign of pathogenic change. These youth teams are appropriately called the 'barefoot doctors of agriculture'. Their efforts have reduced the damage caused by wheat rust and the riceborer to less than 1 per cent and have brought under control the recurrent locust invasions. Such a people-intensive technique has greatly reduced the need for pesticides.[35]

The Knowledge Monopoly

Partly because of integrated pest strategies and the banning of certain dangerous chemicals, the use of insecticides in the United States has dropped somewhat in the last four years. But the use of chemical weedkillers – accounting for two-thirds of total pesticide sales – is climbing. Nonchemical weed control strategies are harder to come by. But even where integrated pest management has proven itself effective and less risky, farmers hesitate to switch from chemicals. Why is this? A recent study in California revealed that 'in 70 per cent of the cases, insect problem solving decisions originate with chemical company fieldmen.' And even so-called impartial sources – state and federal experiment stations – are dominated by research primarily on how to kill insects with chemicals. Even now, relatively little research is being done, for example, to pinpoint the economic injury level for a pest – a prerequisite for being able to apply pesticides only to manage pests below that level rather than having to go for the total obliteration of the pest.[36]

University of California professor of entomology Robert van den Bosch's hard-hitting *The Pesticide Conspiracy* documents the pressures put on scientists to suppress research unfavourable to pesticide-pushing corporations.[37]

Thus farmers (and many government officials throughout the Third World) continue to fall into the chemical trap in part because they lack information and advice about alternatives. In the US the Department of Agriculture and land grant colleges (many of whose trustees are connected to agrichemical corporations) have not taken the lead in exploring integrated pest management alternatives.

On the international level, the FAO is supposed to offer a pool of independent experts discovering and disseminating plant protection information, including the proper uses of chemical pesticides and alternatives. But more often than not FAO technicians work in direct collaboration with agribusiness corporations whose profits are directly threatened by any nonchemical alternatives. More and more FAO technicians see themselves as 'brokers' linking up an underdeveloped country and a multinational agribusiness firm.

Some pesticide firms already work so closely with governments that the two must be indistinguishable to most farmers. In Tanzania, Hoechst has become the adviser to the government on insecticides and spraying equipment. Hoechst even uses government agricultural extension officers to supervise the spraying for which they get a salary over and above the one they receive from the government. Hoechst has the power to fire a government extension officer who does not supervise 'properly.'[38]

We hope you now see through the false threat that poisoning our environment will be necessary if the hungry are to eat. Clearly pesticides are not being used by or for the hungry and, as will be abundantly clear from this book, lack of pesticides is not what is keeping them hungry. The real threat is that pesticide technology is in the hands of a few corporations that will profit only if they can continue to make farmers and 'concerned' people everywhere believe that our very survival depends on the increased use of their products.

The threat is even more ominous since some supposedly impartial bodies that could form a counter force to the power of multinational agribusiness have become, instead, their agents. Organizations such as the FAO, far from developing and disseminating suitable alternatives or even the knowledge of the appropriate use of pesticides, are becoming partners in promotion for the chemical corporations.

If possible sterility is the main problem (in handling pesticide DCBP), couldn't workers who were old enough that they no longer wanted to have children accept such positions voluntarily? Or . . . some might volunteer for such work posts as an alternative to . . . a vasectomy or tubal ligation, or as a means of getting around religious bans on birth control . . . We do believe in safety in the workplace but there can be good as well as bad sides to a situation.

Robert K. Phillips
Executive Secretary
US National Peach Council

PART II   BLAMING NATURE

7 : Famines and History

Throughout the history of mankind, it is often argued, there have been periodic famines. And these are associated with weather disasters which we surely can't control. But famines are not God ordained, they are man arranged. As one French historian remarked: 'The great French famines and food shortages of the Middle Ages occurred during periods when food stuffs were not lacking; they were indeed produced in great quantity and exported. The social system and structure were largely responsible for these deficiencies'.[1]

Most people believe famines in India have been constant phenomena related to a poor climate. But the frequency of famine in India has not been constant. Famine intensified under colonialism, especially during the second half of the nineteenth century, even though food production kept pace with population growth. After the opening of the Suez Canal in 1870, India became a major exporter of wheat to Britain, other Western countries, and Egypt. As Sir George Watt wrote in 1908, '. . . the better classes of the community were exporting the surplus stocks that formerly were stored against times of scarcity and famine.'[2]

Let us take a closer look at one of the most 'famous' famines of this century, that of Bengal, India, in the 1940s. By 1944, an official government report conservatively estimated that one and a half million lives had been lost by famine.

What caused such loss of life?

The immediate food crisis was precipitated by the exigencies of war. In 1943, Churchill ordered the Indians and the thousands of British military in India to 'live off their own stocks' when Japanese conquest of Burma had cut off a main outside source of rice for Bengal and all of India. A drought in 1942 translated into a poor winter rice harvest. But despite all this, the colonial government allowed rice to flow out of Bengal (185,000 tons was exported in the first seven months of 1942).[3] The food went where the money was and great profits were registered along the way. Similarly in a severe famine of 1876-1877 India exported record quantities of food grains. In 1943, The Royal Famine Commission – the twelfth such commission during the two centuries of British rule – commented:

> We have referred to the atmosphere of fear and greed which, in the absence of controls, was one of the causes of the rapid rise in the price level. Enormous profits were made out of this calamity, and in the circumstances, profits for some meant death for others. A large part of the community lived in plenty while others starved, and there was much indifference in the face of suffering. Corruption was widespread throughout the province. . . .[4]

The failure was one of the social and economic system, not merely of the rains.

The underlying causes of the Bengal famine are rooted in the long-term stagnation of Indian agricultural production under British rule. What few investments in agriculture the British did make were for nonfood crops. From the mid 1890s to the time of the Bengal famine, production of nonfood commercial crops (such as cotton and rape seed) increased by 85 per cent, while food production declined by 7 per cent. During the same period in eastern India, including Bengal, food (rice) production declined even more markedly, by 38 per cent per capita between 1901 and 1941.[5] The result was that by the early 1940s nonfood production equalled almost one third of total production.[6]

How should we react, then, the next time we see the Bengal famine referred to by writers such as Lester Brown as 'the last great famine due to the vicissitudes of weather'?[7]

The Land of Famine

As children we were all admonished not to leave any food on our plates because people were starving in China. Even if the connection wasn't clear, there was good reason for our parents to associate China and famine. According to Walter Mallory's 1928 book, *China: Land of Famine*,[8] China experienced famine in some province nearly every year and had done so for over a thousand years. A 1929 Red Cross report estimated that 3 million deaths a year could be attributed to starvation. The same report commented on the affluence of the elite.[9]

Official dynastic histories going back over 2,000 years record a total of 1,621 floods and 1,392 droughts – confirming Mallory's estimate of more than one disaster a year![10] Certainly, the 'vicissitudes of weather' in China have not changed. The North Plain, potentially the most productive area of the country, has undergone a drought, a flood, or both every year, for the past several years.

The weather has not changed but the *effect* of the weather on both the land and the people of China has changed and changed dramatically. In 1972-1973 when eighteen nations, containing one third of the world's people, were being hit by droughts, when western India was facing famine and herds of cattle were dying in the Sahel in Africa, China was also facing its third year of drought, the worst in three decades. But, China had no famine. In fact the provinces *most affected* reaped three years of record harvests.[11]

The difference is that in China food now comes first. The focus has not been simply on production and distribution but on the creation of an agricultural system that is less vulnerable to weather change. Traditionally, areas devasted by drought are just as likely to be vulnerable to floods next season, as in the case in Bangladesh. But a system of water control can make one season's flood into a blessing for the next.

The harnessing of the Hai River in Hopei province near Peking was one major effort at water control. In just eight years several hundred thousand men and women improved 1,700 miles of the riverbed, digging 200 new tributaries and 12,000 channels and building 50,000 bridges and tunnels, in addition to over 800 other major and medium construction works. In all, thirty-five large and medium-sized reservoirs in the mountains were built to store over 106 billion cubic metres of water.[12]

Complementing the water control projects were mobilizations to tap underground water resources. Under the slogan, 'We'll exchange sweat for water and water for grain,' the people of Hopei, Honan, and Shantung provinces organized themselves to sink hundreds of wells, sometimes working with picks and shovels or with labour-saving rigs they devised themselves. These three provinces now benefit from some 700,000 pump wells. During one year of the drought in Peking's Hopei province alone, this work expanded the irrigated land by over 850,000 acres.[13]

Just as important, all these projects were carried out with low capital expenditures. Instead of the usual huge sums spent on machinery, it was possible to mobilize the work power of millions of peasants because they knew *they* would be the beneficiaries – never again to experience famine. China, without a single World

Bank or Western aid project, has become the country with one third of the world's irrigated cropland.[14] Wind destruction and erosion have been controlled by widespread tree planting programmes. In the area around Peking alone, eleven million trees are being planted each year.[15]

So what has made the difference in China? The answer is clearly that the Chinese are developing a system that *assumes* the weather is going to be less than ideal. The people have built, largely by hand, an agricultural system that mitigates the negative impact of bad weather on production. But there is another factor – an economic system that mitigates the impact of weather on any given individual. In China even if there were a decline in total grain output, it would be shared more or less equally by all. No one feasts while others starve. In India, by contrast, the impact of drought falls almost entirely on the area affected and largely on the poorest. As the price rises in response to the drop in supply, it is the landless labourers, the unemployed, and the urban poor who suffer disproportionately.

We human beings have been on this planet long enough to know that adverse weather changes are to be *expected*. The evolution of human civilization can largely be defined as the process of working out many ingenious ways of protecting ourselves against the vagaries of nature. Therefore, when we hear of a widespread famine the first question we should ask is not 'What terrible natural event caused it?' but 'Why wasn't that society able to cope with the bad fortune? Why is it that one country can suffer natural disasters and have no deaths and another have a million deaths?'

China quite literally cannot feed more people . . . the greatest tragedy that China could suffer, at the present time would be a reduction in her death rate . . . millions are going to die. There can be no way out. These men and women, boys and girls, must starve as tragic sacrifices, on the twin altars of uncontrolled reproduction and uncontrolled abuse of the land and resources.

William Vogt, *Road to survival*, 1948

8 : Drought in the Sahel

Many falsely assume that the Sahelian drought beginning in 1969 was *the* Sahelian drought. But climatologists consider drought to be an 'integral part' of the climate of the region.[1] Most of the older inhabitants of the Sahel believe that the drought years of 1910-1913 were more severe than the recent, much more publicized ones and the figures bear them out.[2] Rainfall, lake, and river levels were not as low in 1969-1973 as they were during the earlier drought. By studying the retardation in the growth of tree-rings scientists have detected that there have been severe droughts several times over the past three centuries and numerous dry spells from time to time. The most recent study we know of concluded 'there is no indication of any long continued upward or downward trend in rainfall nor is there any obvious cycle.' Thus the expansion of the desert cannot be attributed to any long-term climatic change.[3]

In any case, desertification is not a one-way process. Deserts *can* be reclaimed – and without great financial expense – if great reserves of labour power are invested. For example, Algeria is today the site of a massive and successful reforestation programme. The goal over the next twenty years is to plant six million trees in a 1,000 mile belt across the northern fringe of the Sahara.[4] Between 1965 and 1970, 160 acres were reclaimed at the Saharan village of Bou Saadu in Algeria, through planting acacia and eucalyptus trees. These gave protection from sandstorms and increased surface humidity. According to one report, 'Soon grasses and shrubs sprang up and later [farmers cultivated] citrus fruits, olives, figs and pomegranates, grain, tomatoes, potatoes, peas, beans and onions.'

Over the centuries the small farmers of the Sahel had developed a profound understanding of their environment. They knew the necessity of letting land lie fallow for up to twenty years and they cultivated a wide variety of crops, each adapted to a different microenvironment and yet together offering nutritional complementarity. Nomads and cultivators often developed a mutually beneficial relationship. The cultivators offered the nomads lands for pasture in the dry season and grain in exchange for milk, manure for the fields, and donkeys for ploughing.

Sahelian Mali was once known as the breadbasket of Africa. It could always be counted upon to trade grain in times of neighbours' needs. The Sahelian precolonial custom was to construct small farming and village granaries for storing millet for flour and in some cases for even more years of consumption, knowing full well that small-harvest years should be expected. One United Nations study, arguing against the idea that the Sahel is overpopulated, noted that, if the traditional storage practices were followed, the 'carrying capacity' of the land in people and animals would be that of the average years and not that of the poorest years.[5]

What happened to a system that was adapted over centuries to deal with periodic drought? First, even before the French conquest in the late nineteenth and early twentieth centuries, these civilizations had already been severely undermined by two centuries of forced depopulation as millions of the youngest and strongest were taken as slaves to the New World. Then came the French and years of bloody fighting. Having established a permanent presence, the French looked for ways to make their new subjects pay for the administrative costs of occupation. As Thurston Clarke poignantly writes of Niger at this period, 'The Nigerien people were self-sufficient; the colonial administration was not.'[6] The French solution to this problem of their own making was to force the peasants to cultivate crops for export, particularly peanuts and cotton. Cotton was needed for France's textile mills since Britain controlled most other sources. Peanuts were to provide a cheap substitute for walnut oil then commonly used in France.

Where previously complementary crops such as millet and legumes were rotated, crop after crop of peanuts or cotton were cultivated until the soils were exhausted. To maintain cotton exports for the French, given the resulting decline in cotton yields, farmers were forced to expand the acreage in cotton in part by reducing planting of millet and sorghum. Before the French pushed cash crops, Nigerien farmers planted several different strains of sorghum, each requiring a different amount of rainfall. Thus some strains were likely to survive even when rains were poor. But when farmers had to sacrifice so much food acreage to peanuts and cotton, they shifted to only one strain of sorghum – the one yielding the greatest quantity. This strain however, required the most moisture. Thus farmers had increased their risk that all their sorghum would fail.

The techniques of colonialism and their devastating impact on the land and its people are hardly realities only of the past. While the Sahelian countries achieved formal independence in 1960, the successor governments have often outdone the French in forcing export crop production. Taxes that farmers can pay only by producing crops for export have been increased. In Mali in 1929 the French levied a tax that required each adult over fifteen to grow between five and ten kilos of cotton to pay for it. By 1960, the last year of French rule, the tax had risen to the equivalent of forty kilos. By 1970, during the drought, the successor government forced each adult peasant to grow at least forty-eight kilos of cotton just to pay taxes.[7]

Higher taxes, as well as falling export prices, force the peasants to increase the production of export crops. But since colonial times, up to and including the recent drought years, these increases are mainly achieved by destructive methods of cultivation. Even deeper ploughing for planting cotton has eroded vast areas. With even less humus to retain water, it appears as though there is less rain. Larger and larger tracts are cultivated (more accurately, 'mined') against the norms of traditional wisdom on soil maintenance. Expanding export crop production means that lands once allowed to lie fallow for a number of years and manured by the pastoralists' herds, are forced into virtually uninterrupted cultivation.[8]

The circle is vicious. Continual cultivation rapidly depletes the soil, necessitating still further expansion of export cropping at the expense of food crops and pasture land. Chemical fertilizers that once raised yields of some export crops, making the expansion of cultivation less pressing, are now so costly that the peasants in the end are obliged to bring still more land under cash cropping. Moreover, as the farmers grow less grain, they have had little or none to exchange for milk with the pastoralists.

With less grain being produced, speculators force up prices. The pastoralists then must raise ever more cattle just to obtain the same amount of grain. In southern Niger before World War II, one cow was worth 30 sacks of millet. Just before the drought of the 1970s, it was worth only one. The result, as you can imagine, is hunger for farmers and pastoralists alike, starvation for thousands of animals – and an 'encroaching desert.'

It is embarrassing for those who blame drought and an encroaching desert for famine in the Sahel to explain the vast amounts of agricultural goods sent out of the region, even during the worst years of drought. Ships in the Dakar port bringing in 'relief' food departed with stores of peanuts, cotton, vegetables, and meat. Of the hundreds of millions of dollars worth of agricultural goods the Sahel exported during the drought, over 60 per cent went to consumers in Europe and North America and the rest to the elites in other African countries.[9] Marketing control – and profits – are still by and large in the hands of foreign, primarily French, corporations.

During the drought many exports from the Sahelian countries increased, some attaining record levels. Cattle exports during 1971, the first year of full drought, totalled over 200 million pounds, up 41 per cent compared to 1968. The annual export of chilled or frozen beef tripled compared with a typical year before the drought. In addition, 56 million pounds of fish and 32 million pounds of vegetables were exported from the famine-stricken Sahel in 1971 alone.[10] During the drought years 1970-74, the total value of agricultural exports from the Sahelian countries – a startling $1.5 *billion* dollars – was three times that of all cereals imported into the region.[11]

Mali was one of the countries most affected by the drought and principal recipient of emergency shipments of food.[12] During the five years before the drought, there had been a significant decline in the total area dedicated to food grain production. During this same period, the acreage devoted to cotton more than doubled. Raw cotton exports during the drought years reached record levels (approximately 50 million pounds or 10 pounds for every man, woman and child) – three to four times the levels of the years preceding the drought. The fact that cotton yields during the drought averaged considerably higher than during the years before the drought suggests that cotton was being planted on the best soils: those least vulnerable to the drought.

In 1934 peanuts occupied 182,000 acres in Niger. By 1954 the area had doubled and by 1961 it had increased five times. On the 'eve of the famine' in 1968, the area planted in peanuts covered a record 1,080,000 acres, six times the peanut area of 1934. Government campaigns, taxation and 'gifts' from peanut companies that had to be repaid at harvest, as well as extensive research on new varieties of peanuts were some key forces behind this extraordinary expansion. The expansion was at the expense of fallow zones of 'green belts', critical especially during drought years. The cutback on fallow land only compounded the soil depletion caused by the planting of peanuts year after year on the same soil. Peanut cultivation in the 1960s began to spread north, usurping lands traditionally used by pastoralists. This encroachment made the pastoralists and their animals more vulnerable to drought.

In the five years immediately before and during the drought Chad carried out a major programme (with fertilizer subsidized by the European Common Market countries) to increase cotton production. Two thirds of a million acres of the best of Chad's scarce resources are devoted not to food but to cotton. This increase in cotton production throughout the Sahel prompted one French nutritionist to observe, 'If people were starving it was not for want of cotton'.[13]

More important than the sheer number of acres in the Sahel producing for export are the governments that have pressured farmers and skewed every conceivable programme to favour export production (irrigation, fertilizers, credit, new land development, research to develop drought-resistant varieties, extension services and marketing facilities). And all this they do with the support of foreign aid agencies. A current major UN proposal to 'aid the hungry' in the Sahel is a quarter billion dollar Trans-Sahelian highway, a construction boondoggle, useful only to get production out to the principal ports. With such support for exports, it comes as no surprise that even *before the drought* food production was seriously deteriorating while export crops were booming.[14]

Why is it that the Sahelian governments push export crops?

To earn foreign exchange. That is the answer everyone gives. But much of this is used to enable government bureaucrats and other better-off urban workers to live an imported life-style – refrigerators, air conditioners, refined sugar, alcoholic beverages, tobacco, and so on. In 1974, about 30 per cent of the foreign exchange earned by Senegal went for just such items.[15] The peanut exports annually account for one third of the national budget of Senegal – but 47.2 per cent of the budget goes on the salaries of the government bureaucrats.[16] Between 1961 and the worst drought year, 1971, Niger, a country with marked malnutrition and a life expectancy of only thirty-eight years, quadrupled its cotton production and tripled that of peanuts. Together these two exports in 1971 earned about $18 million. But $20 million in foreign exchange was then used up importing clothing, over nine times the amount earned by exporting raw cotton. Over $1 million went for private cars and over $4 million for gasoline and tyres. In only three years, 1967-1970, the number of private cars increased by over 50 per cent, most of them driven by the miniscule elite in the capital. Over $1 million was spent to import alcoholic beverages and tobacco products.[17] On a visit to the capital city, Niamey, we found that the local elites were shopping in a well-stocked supermarket right out of Paris – complete with frozen ice cream cones from a shop on the Champs-Elysées.

Even when part of the export earnings is used to import food, it generally does not reach the poor, whose labour produces the cotton, peanuts and livestock, but is consumed by the better-off classes in the urban areas. More than half of the foreign exchange Senegal earned exporting peanuts in 1974 was spent to import wheat for French-owned mills that turn out flour to make French bread for urban dwellers.[18]

Even more shocking than the pushing of export crops in the face of declining food production is the fact that *every Sahelian country, with the possible exception of mineral-rich Mauritania, actually produced enough grain to feed its total population, even during the worst drought year.*[19]

Most farmers who grow cash crops find themselves without enough money or food reserves to meet their families' needs from one marketing season to the next. In order to survive what they call the 'hungry' season – the months of particularly arduous work right before harvest – they are forced to take out loans in cash or millet at usurious interest rates from the local merchants. Local merchants have the grain because they buy it from farmers during harvest time when abundant supply makes for low prices and when farmers must sell to pay their debts and taxes. When we visited the Tensobentenga region of Upper Volta, we found that even during the normal rainfall year of 1976 the price of grain virtually doubled between the time of harvest and seven months later. The merchants can sell the hoarded grain during the hungry season at two or three times the price originally paid, and even export it to higher income markets in neighbouring countries. An American AID officer in Ouagadougou, Upper Volta, shocked us with his 'conservative estimate' that two thirds of the grain that merchants obtain from peasants in payment of debts gets exported to the Ivory Coast and Ghana. In such societies where speculation in food is 'normal,' adequate production can still result in scarcity for many – even for the producers.

For farmers made vulnerable by the vicious cycle of indebtedness, drought *does* precipitate famine. Victimized by profiteers, farmers cannot afford to improve the quality of their land and are often forced to exhaust the soil and even to forfeit their land altogether. But clearly, hunger and the seeming expansion of the desert are the products not of drought but of a parasitic class of usurers and grain-hoarding speculators.

Far from being a forsaken waste land, there are those who see the Sahel as a potential granary. They point to the region's exceptionally large underground lake basin and three major river systems, including the Niger, the world's twelfth largest river. With this potential for irrigation and the region's gift of a tropical sun, they estimate the Sahel could produce at least six times more grain than at present, as well as startling quantities of meat, vegetables, and fruit for the lucrative European and Middle Eastern markets.

A special correspondent for *The Economist* (Oct. 6, 1973), wrote glowingly that big profits could be made with boats 'fitted as floating feedlots' bringing young feeder cattle from places like the Sahel to Western Europe, North America and Japan. He estimated that such 'golden calves' are worth 20 to 40 times more in the industrial countries than in the Sahel. On a recent visit to Upper Volta we found a German agribusiness firm experimenting with the use of a gas balloon to 'lift' vegetables and fruits from outlying villages to the Ouagadougou airport so that they could be airfreighted to Frankfurt.

Anyone who knows the Sahel knows that there is no doubt that much more could be produced. But if the government elites and multinational corporations control that production, it is unlikely the majority of the people will benefit.

An analysis of famine that puts the blame on an 'encroaching desert' will never come to grips with the inequalities in power at the root of the problem. Solutions proposed will inevitably be limited to the technical and administrative aspects – irrigation programmes, modern mechanization, new seed varieties, foreign investment, grain reserve banks, and so on. Such an analysis allows no reflection upon the political and economic arrangements that, far more than changes in rainfall or even climate, are at the root of low productivity and human deprivation.

We have seen that drought cannot be considered the cause of famine. Drought is a natural phenomenon. Famine is a human phenomenon. Any link that does exist is precisely through the economic and political order of a society that can either minimize the human consequences of drought or exacerbate them.

The recurrent drought of the past few years has made clear that the desert is encroaching on a large scale and that food production capacity in western Africa is seriously threatened. . . . What is now needed is a comprehensive international programme that, rather than ease the effects of the drought, will help roll back the desert.

Henry Kissinger, 1976

Above all, the Sahelian situation calls for the immediate launching of a major effort to slow and stabilize population growth in the region. Such a long-term co-operative international programme will have to be comparable in scope to the programme that launched the Green Revolution in the late sixties.

Lester R. Brown, *By Bread Alone*, 1975

Space-age farms, modern cattle ranches and lush market gardens in the middle of the Sahara. . . . This is no mirage. It is what experts from six of the world's most backward nations have conjured up for the future. Their idea is to roll back the desert and turn their drought-ravaged countries into a fertile green belt of productive crop land and pasture.

The plan calls for giant dams to harness the Senegal and Niger rivers and provide power; advanced irrigation systems to water the dust bowls; and forest walls to check the southern march of the Sahara.

It could eventually turn the rural subsistence economies of the west African nations of Chad, Mali, Mauritania, Niger, Senegal and Upper Volta into a vegetable garden for Europe and a vast beef belt.

To the Point International,
'The Sahel: Today's disaster area . . .
tomorrow's glorious garden?'
(October 5, 1974)

PART III COLONIAL INHERITANCE

9 : Why Nations Can't Feed Themselves

To answer the question 'why hunger?' it is counterproductive to simply *describe* the conditions in an underdeveloped country today. For these conditions, whether they be the degree of malnutrition, the levels of agricultural production, or even the country's ecological endowment, are not static facts – they are not 'givens.' They are rather the *results* of an ongoing historical process. As we dug ever deeper into that historical process for the preparation of this book, we began to discover the existence of scarcity-creating mechanisms that we had only vaguely intuited before.

We have received great satisfaction from probing into the past since we recognized it is the only way to approach a solution to hunger today. We have come to see that it is the *force* creating the condition, not the condition itself, that must be the target of change. Otherwise we might change the condition today, only to find tomorrow that it has been recreated – with a vengeance.

Asking the question 'Why can't people feed themselves?' carries a sense of bewilderment that there are so many people in the world not able to feed themselves adequately. What astonished us, however, is that there are not *more* people in the world who are hungry – considering the weight of the centuries of effort by the few to undermine the capacity of the majority to feed themselves. No, we are not crying 'conspiracy!' If these forces were entirely conspiratorial, they would be easier to detect and many more people would by now have risen up to resist. We are talking about something more subtle and insidious; a heritage of a colonial order in which people with the advantage of considerable power sought their own self-interest, often arrogantly believing they were acting in the interest of the people whose lives they were destroying.

The Colonial Mind

The colonizer viewed agriculture in the subjugated lands as primitive and backward. Yet such a view contrasts sharply with documents from the colonial period now coming to light. For example, A. J. Voelker, a British agricultural scientist assigned to India during the 1890s, wrote

Nowhere would one find better instances of keeping land scrupulously clean from weeds, of ingenuity in device of water-raising appliances, of knowledge of soils and their capabilities, as well as of the exact time to sow and reap, as one would find in Indian agriculture. It is wonderful, too, how much is known of rotation, the system of 'mixed crops' and of fallowing. . . . I, at least, have never seen a more perfect picture of cultivation.'[1]

None the less, viewing the agriculture of the vanquished as primitive and backward reinforced the colonizer's rationale for destroying it. To the colonizers of Africa, Asia, and Latin America, agriculture became merely a means to extract wealth – much as gold from a mine – on behalf of the colonizing power. Agriculture was no longer seen as a source of food for the local population, nor even as their livelihood. Indeed the British economist John Stuart Mill reasoned that colonies should not be thought of as civilizations or countries at all but as 'agricultural establishments' whose sole purpose was to supply the 'larger community to which they belong'. The colonized society's agriculture was only a subdivision of the agricultural system of the metropolitan country. As Mill acknowledged, 'Our West India Colonies, for example, cannot be regarded as countries. . . . The West Indies are the place where England *finds it convenient* to carry on the production of sugar, coffee and a few other tropical commodities'.[2]

Prior to European intervention, Africans practised a diversified agriculture that included the introduction of new food plants of Asian or American origin. But colonial rule simplified this diversified production to single cash crops – often to the exclusion of staple foods – and in the process sowed the seeds of famine.[3] Central Ghana, once famous for its yams and other foodstuffs, was forced to concentrate solely on cocoa. Most of the Gold Coast thus became dependent on cocoa. Liberia was turned into a virtual plantation subsidiary of Firestone Tyre and Rubber. Food production in Dahomey and south-east Nigeria was all but abandoned in favour of palm oil; Tanganyika (now Tanzania) was forced to focus on sisal and Uganda on cotton.

The same happened in Indochina. About the time of the American Civil War the French decided that the Mekong Delta in Vietnam would be ideal for producing rice for export. Through a production system based on enriching the large landowners, Vietnam became the world's third largest exporter of rice by the 1930s; yet many landless Vietnamese went hungry.[4]

Colonialism's public works programmes only reinforced export crop production. British irrigation works built in nineteenth-century India did help increase production, but the expansion was for spring export crops at the expense of millets and legumes grown in the autumn as the basic local food crops.

Because people living on the land do not easily go against their natural and adaptive drive to grow food for themselves, colonial powers had to force the production of cash crops. The first strategy was to use physical or economic force to get the local population to grow cash crops instead of food on their own plots and then turn them over to the colonizer generally for export. The second strategy was the direct takeover of the land by large-scale plantations growing crops for export.

Forced Peasant Production

As Walter Rodney recounts in *How Europe Underdeveloped Africa*, cash crops were often grown literally under threat of guns and whips.[5] One visitor to the Sahel commented in 1928: 'Cotton is an artificial crop and one the value of which is not entirely clear to the natives . . .' He wryly noted the 'enforced enthusiasm with which the natives . . . have thrown themselves into . . . planting cotton.'[6] The forced cultivation of cotton was a major grievance leading to the Maji Maji wars in Tanganyika and behind the nationalist revolt in Angola as late as 1960.[7]

Although naked force was used, taxation was the preferred colonial technique to force Africans to grow cash crops. The colonial administrations simply levied taxes on cattle, land, houses, and even the people themselves. Since the tax had to be paid in the coin of the realm, the peasants had either to grow crops to sell or to work on the plantations or in the mines of the Europeans.[8] Taxation was both an effective tool to 'stimulate' cash cropping and a source of revenue that the colonial bureaucracy needed to enforce the system. To expand their production of export crops to pay the mounting taxes, peasant producers were forced to neglect the farming of food crops.

Marketing boards emerged in Africa in the 1930s as another technique for getting the profit from cash crop production by native producers into the hands of the colonial government and international firms. Purchases by the marketing boards were well below the world market price. Peanuts bought by the boards from peasant cultivators in West Africa were sold in Britain for more than *seven times* what the peasants received.[9]

The marketing board concept was born with the 'cocoa hold-up' in the Gold Coast in 1937. Small cocoa farmers refused to sell to the large cocoa concerns like United Africa Company (a subsidiary of the Anglo-Dutch firm, Unilever) and Cadbury until they got a higher price. When the British governments stepped in and agreed to buy the cocoa directly in place of the big business concerns, the smallholders must have thought they had scored at least a minor victory. The following year the British formally set up the West African Cocoa Control Board. Theoretically, its purpose was to pay the peasants a reasonable price for their crops. In practice, however, the board, as sole purchaser, was able to hold down the prices paid the peasants for their crops when the world prices were rising. Rodney sums up the real 'victory':

> None of the benefits went to Africans, but rather to the British government itself and to the private companies . . . Big companies like the United Africa Company and John Holt were given . . . quotas to fulfil on behalf of the boards. As agents of the government, they were no longer exposed to direct attack, and their profits were secure.[10]

These marketing boards, set up for most export crops, were actually controlled by the companies. The chairman of the Cocoa Board was none other than John Cadbury of Cadbury Brothers, which was part of a buying pool exploiting West African cocoa farmers.

The marketing boards funnelled part of the profits from the exploitation of peasant producers indirectly into the royal treasury. While the Cocoa Board sold to the British Food Ministry at low prices, the ministry upped the price for British manufacturers, thus netting a profit as high as 11 million pounds in some years.[11]

These marketing boards of Africa only institutionalized what is the essence of colonialism – the extraction of wealth. While profits continued to accrue to foreign interests and local elites, prices received by those actually growing the commodities remained low.

Plantations

A second approach was direct takeover of the land either by the colonizing government or by private foreign interests. Previously self-provisioning farmers were forced to cultivate the plantation fields through either enslavement or economic coercion.

After the conquest of the Kandyan Kingdom (in present day Sri Lanka) in 1815, the British designated all the vast central part of the island as crown land. When it was determined that coffee, a profitable export crop, could be grown there, the Kandyan lands were sold off to British investors and planters at a mere five shillings per acre, the government even defraying the cost of surveying and road building.[12]

Java is also a prime example of a colonial government seizing territory and then putting it into private foreign hands. In 1870, the Dutch declared all uncultivated land – called waste land – property of the state for lease to Dutch plantation enterprises. In addition, the Agrarian Land Law of 1870 authorized foreign companies to lease village-owned land. The peasants, in chronic need of cash for taxes and tempted by foreign consumer goods, were only too willing to lease their land to the foreign companies for very modest sums and under terms dictated by the firms. Where land was still held communally, the village headman was tempted by high cash commissions offered by plantation companies. He would lease the village land even more cheaply than would the individual peasant or, as was frequently the case, sell out the entire village to the company.[13]

The introduction of the plantation meant the divorce of agriculture from nourishment, as the notion of food value was lost to the overriding claim of 'market value' in international trade. Crops such as sugar, tobacco, and coffee were selected, not on the basis of how well they feed people, but for their high price value relative to their weight and bulk so that profit margins could be maintained even after the costs of shipping to Europe.

Suppressing Peasant Farming

The stagnation and impoverishment of the peasant food-producing sector was not the unintended consequence of an over-emphasis on export production. Plantations – just like modern 'agro-industrial complexes' – needed an abundant and readily available supply of low-wage agricultural workers. Colonial administrations thus devised a variety of tactics, all to undercut self-provisioning agriculture and thus make rural populations dependent on plantation wages. Government services and even the most minimal infrastructure (access to water, roads, seeds, credit, pest and disease control information, and so on) were systematically denied. Plantations usurped most of the good land, either making much of the rural population landless or pushing them onto marginal soils.

In some cases a colonial administration would go even further to guarantee itself a labour supply. In at least twelve countries in the eastern and southern parts of Africa the exploitation of mineral wealth (gold, diamonds, and copper) and the establishment of cash-crop plantations demanded a continuous supply of low-cost labour. To assure this labour supply, colonial administrations simply expropriated the land of the African communities by violence and drove the people into small reserves.[14] With neither adequate land for their traditional slash-and-burn methods nor access to the means – tools, water, and fertilizer – to make continuous farming of such limited areas viable, the indigenous population could scarcely meet subsistence needs, much less produce surplus to sell in order to cover the colonial taxes. Hundreds of thousands of Africans were forced to become the cheap labour source so 'needed' by the colonial enterprises. Only by labouring on plantations and in the mines could they hope to pay the colonial taxes.

The tax scheme to produce reserves of cheap plantation and mining labour was particularly effective when the Great Depression hit and the bottom dropped out of cash crop economies. In 1929 the cotton market collapsed, leaving peasant cotton producers, such as those in Upper Volta, unable to pay their colonial taxes. More and more young people, in some years as many as 80,000, were thus forced to migrate to the Gold Coast to compete with each other for low-wage jobs on cocoa plantations.[15]

The many techniques of colonialism to undercut self-provisioning agriculture in order to ensure a cheap labour supply are no better illustrated than by the story of how, in the mid-nineteenth century, sugar plantation owners in British Guiana coped with the double blow of the emancipation of slaves and the crash in the world sugar market.

Would the ex-slaves be allowed to take over the plantation land and grow the food they needed? The planters, many ruined by the sugar slump, were determined they would not. The planter-dominated government devised several schemes for thwarting food self-sufficiency. The price of crown land was kept artificially high, and the purchase of land in parcels smaller than 100 acres was outlawed – two measures guaranteeing that newly organized ex-slave co-operatives could not hope to gain access to much land. The government also prohibited cultivation on as much as 400,000 acres – on the grounds of 'uncertain property titles.' Moreover, although many planters held part of their land out of sugar production due to the depressed world price, they would not allow any alternative production on them. They feared that once the ex-slaves started growing food it would be difficult to return them to sugar production when world market prices began to recover. In addition, the government taxed peasant production, then turned around and used the funds to subsidize the immigration of labourers from India and Malaysia to replace the freed slaves, thereby making sugar production again profitable for the planters. Finally, the government neglected the infrastructure for subsistence agriculture and denied credit for small farmers.

The most insidious tactic to 'lure' the peasant away from food production – and the one with profound historical consequences – was a policy of keeping the price of imported food low through the removal of tariffs and subsidies. The policy was double-edged: first, peasants were told they need not grow food because they could always buy it cheaply with their plantation wages; second, cheap food imports destroyed the market for domestic food and thereby impoverished local food producers.

Both the Governor of British Guiana and the Secretary for the Colonies Earl Grey favoured low duties on imports in order to erode local food production and thereby release labour for the plantations. In 1851 the governor rushed through a reduction of the duty on cereals in order to 'divert' labour to the sugar estates. As Adamson comments in his *Sugar Without Slaves,* 'Without realizing it, he [the governor] had put his finger on the most mordant feature of monoculture: . . . its convulsive need to destroy any other sector of the economy which might compete for "its" labour.'[16]

Many colonial governments succeeded in establishing dependence on imported foodstuffs. In 1647 an observer in the West Indies wrote to Governor Winthrop of Massachusetts: 'Men are so intent upon planting sugar that they had rather buy foode at very deare rates than produce it by labour, so infinite is the profitt of sugar workes. . . .'[17] By 1770, the West Indies were importing most of the continental colonies' exports of dried fish, grain, beans, and vegetables. A dependence on imported food made the West Indian colonies vulnerable to any disruption in supply. This dependence on imported food stuffs spelled disaster when the thirteen continental colonies gained independence and food exports from the continent to the West Indies were interrupted. With no diversified food system to fall back on, 15,000 plantation workers died of famine between 1780 and 1787 in Jamaica alone.[18] The dependence of the West Indies on imported food persists to this day.

Suppressing Peasant Competition

We have talked about the techniques by which indigenous populations were forced to cultivate cash crops. In some countries with large plantations, however, colonial governments found it necessary to *prevent* peasants from independently growing cash crops not out of concern for their welfare, but so that they would not compete with colonial interests growing the same crop. For peasant farmers, given a modicum of opportunity, proved themselves capable of outproducing the large plantations not only in terms of output per unit of land but, more important, in terms of capital cost per unit produced.

In the Dutch East Indies (Indonesia and Dutch New Guinea) colonial policy in the middle of the nineteenth century forbade the sugar refineries to buy sugar cane from indigenous growers and imposed a discriminatory tax on rubber produced by native smallholders.[19] A recent unpublished United Nations study of agricultural development in Africa concluded that large-scale agricultural operations owned and controlled by foreign commercial interests (such as the rubber plantations of Liberia, the sisal estates of Tanganyika and the coffee estates of Angola) only survived the competition of peasant producers because 'the authorities actively supported them by suppressing indigenous rural development.'[20]

The suppression of indigenous agricultural development served the interests of the colonizing powers in two ways. Not only did it prevent direct competition from more efficient native producers of the same crops, but it also guaranteed a labour force to work on the foreign-owned estates. Planters and foreign investors were not unaware that peasants who could survive economically by their own production would be under less pressure to sell their labour cheaply to the large estates.

The answer to the question why can't nations feed themselves must begin with an understanding of how colonialism actively prevented people from doing just that. Colonialism

- forced peasants to replace food crops with cash crops that were then expropriated at very low rates;
- took over the best agricultural land for export crop plantations and then forced the most able-bodied workers to leave the village fields to work as slaves or for very low wages on plantations;
- encouraged a dependence on imported food;
- blocked native peasant cash crop production from competing with cash crops produced by settlers or foreign firms.

These are concrete examples of the development of under-development that we should have perceived as such even as we read our history schoolbooks. But we didn't. Somehow our schoolbooks always seemed to make the flow of history appear to have its own logic – as if it could not have been any other way.

10 : The Legacy of Colonialism

The effects of colonialism could not be wiped clean simply by a proclamation of independence. The colonial enforcement of export agriculture handicapped future development by orienting indigenous production and trade patterns to serve narrow export interests. Internal trade that might have served as the means for autonomous development was disrupted or even destroyed in the wake of all-encompassing colonial cash crop systems geared to the needs of foreign interests. Thriving industries serving indigenous markets were destroyed. The onslaught of low-priced textiles from the mills of Lancashire ruined skilled village spinners and weavers in India and Africa.

Whole countries became synonymous with only one city – the capital – or, if it was inland, the capital and its port. Internal communications and trade never developed. Latin American Eduardo Galeano writes poignantly:

> Brazil has no permanent land connections with three of its neighbors; Colombia, Peru and Venezuela. . . . Each Latin American country still identifies itself with its own port – a negation of its roots and real identity – to such an extent that almost all intraregional trade goes by sea: Inland transport is virtually nonexistent.[1]

An ignored but perhaps the most pervasive effects of colonial plantation culture is this: A narrowing of the experience of agriculture to plantation work, especially with tree crops, has over generations robbed entire populations of basic peasant farming skills. Moreover, it is more difficult today for people to return to growing the food they need because farming has come to be associated in their minds with misery and degradation.

The transfer of people of one race and culture to work plantations in a foreign land was a basic strategy of colonialism in all parts of the world. People of different racial and cultural backgrounds were thrown together in conditions of extreme hardship. Racial differences and antagonisms among labourers were ways for colonizers to control the labour force.[2] It is not surprising that this forced mixing of races and cultures has left a legacy of social tensions that make co-operation and economic unity almost impossible. By the forced migration of people, the pitting of race against race for the crumbs from the colonial table, colonialism undermined development based on mutual co-operation.

Colonialism also undercut the moral substratum of traditional societies. Traditional societies appear to many as totally autocratic with the chief, the warlord, or the village headman having unlimited power. But while the peasants were obliged to serve their rulers in most traditional societies, the privileged elite were also under obligation to protect and provide for the welfare of the peasant majority. Because of this principle of reciprocity, such societies did have a degree of trust and compassion in human relationships. Hard times were shared to some degree.[3] In Vietnam before the French, for example, the rulers allowed communal land to be used to ensure that each family had at least a minimal food supply.

But colonialism destroyed the basis for this traditional moral system. First, the traditional rulers lost much of their authority in the eyes of the peasants when they proved unable to defend their territory against the colonial invader. With the introduction of a commercialized production system, traditional obligations were replaced by money-based ties. The belief that ruler and ruled were responsible for each other was replaced by the notion that a growing GNP would provide for all. Most important, while colonialism undermined the traditional respect for the elite class, it invested that class with greater real power. In eighteenth-century Bengal, India, for example, the British made the traditional elites – previously responsible only for fiscal and administrative duties – into landed proprietors, now responsible for collecting revenue from the tenant-cultivators for the crown. These *zamindars*, as they were called, used their power to acquire vast holdings of land for themselves.[4]

Before the British ruled India, debt was commonplace but the moneylender was not powerful. Part of the reason was that land was not owned privately. Without private ownership it was impossible to lose land through indebtedness. But once the British had established private ownership to facilitate tax collection, the position of the smallholders, as most were, became precarious. Rain or drought, good harvest or bad – the taxes had to be paid in cash. With private ownership, land became the collateral for loans with which to pay one's taxes in bad times. If hard times continued, cultivators lost their land as the colonial legal system put its weight behind foreclosures.

When colonial policy tried to stem this transfer of land to non-agriculturalist moneylenders, many moneylenders simply became landlords themselves. Also larger landholders took on the role of moneylending. They were hardly sorry to see their debtors fail since foreclosure meant they could add to their property. Here we find some of the origins of present-day India's mushrooming landless labourer class.[5]

In Java, before the Dutch, the peasants had substantial economic strength. But the Dutch introduced a system similar to the British one of indirect rule through an existing elite. Peasants unable to pay their taxes to the Dutch could only turn to the local Chinese moneylenders. When the peasants could not repay a loan, they in effect became tenants on their own land, forced to grow crops chosen by the creditors for a below-market price determined by the creditors.[6]

So colonialism, in its need to extract wealth from the colony, introduced a money economy and put its power behind the already well-placed. It promoted the increasing concentration of landholding by the few and the increasing landlessness of the many. It is this legacy that forms such a great obstacle to true agricultural development today.

But colonialism did more than simply reinforce the emergence of one class over another. Colonialism exacerbated regional inequalities. And, as colonial policy focused on the rapid development of the most potentially profitable regions, the less obviously well endowed were left behind. A few urban areas became the seats of colonial power. These imbalances still plague development efforts.

We have seen how colonialism stifled and distorted traditional agriculture to extract wealth in the form of luxury cash crops; how colonialism enslaved or forced the migration of the agriculturally productive population in search of wage labour to pay colonial taxes; how colonialism laid the foundation for racial and social strife as disparate cultures were thrown together in competition for survival; and how colonialism exacerbated inequalities in the countryside, ending land-tenure security, a security that is now recognized as the first prerequisite of agricultural progress.

Our knowledge of the past is fundamental to our understanding of the present. The history of the colonial period should be familiar to any of us, its outcome predictable by any of us: declining food production and greater food imports, increasing impoverishment, growing vulnerability to the constant fluctuations in the international market, and internally uneven growth.

But it has not been so familiar. In the 1960s as college students we read the latest textbooks on 'international development' that described these economies as 'dualistic' – meaning that one sector, the commercial export sector – had potential for dynamic growth as part of an expanding international economy while the other sector, the traditional sector, was hopelessly mired in the past. According to this analysis, the task of development was to give the subsistence sector a big shove into the modern world, into the international market economy.

But dualism describes a condition while ignoring a process. If, however, we describe underdevelopment as a *process* and understand its colonial roots, we know that the traditional and the modern sectors do not stand side by side by mere chance. This history of underdevelopment shows that the economic decline of the backward sector was the direct product of the formation of the other, commercial sector, tied into the international economy. Once colonialism has raked over a country, there is no such thing as a 'traditional' culture left for economic planners to push into the present.

PART IV MODERNIZING HUNGER

11 : The Narrow Focus on Greater Food Production

If people are hungry, everyone assumes there must not be enough food. Indeed, for at least thirty years the central question has been: how can more food be produced? We learn of supposed answers almost daily in what we call the 'news release' approach to hunger, one new breakthrough after another – protein from petroleum, harvests of kelp, extracts from alfalfa – all to expand the food supply. And the biggest 'breakthrough' to many, has been the 'Green Revolution'.

Yet in country after country where a narrow production focus has resulted in more food than ever before there are also more hungry people than ever before. We can draw two alternative conclusions:

Either the production focus was correct but soaring numbers of people simply overran even the dramatic production gains;

or, the diagnosis was incorrect. Scarcity is not the cause of hunger. A production increase, no matter how great, can never in itself solve the problem.

The simple facts of world food production make clear that the overpopulation-scarcity diagnosis is incorrect. Present world grain production alone could provide every person on earth with more than 3,000 calories a day. Even more to the point, between 1952 and 1972, 86 per cent of the total population living in underdeveloped countries lived where food production kept pace with or exceeded the rate of population growth.[1]

Indeed the narrow focus on increasing production has actually *compounded* the problem of hunger. Most useful to us in understanding just why and how a narrow focus on production undercuts the welfare of the poor majority has been to examine the Mexican origins of the Green Revolution, the most highly publicized attempt to increase production.

Agrarian Reform in Mexico

In 1910, 2 per cent of the Mexican population owned 97 per cent of the land while in most states 95 per cent of the rural population had no land at all. During the bloody revolutionary war between 1910 and 1917, well over one million peasants died fighting for land. Theoretically the revolutionaries were victorious. But for seventeen years the country's peasant majority saw less than revolutionary changes. Then, in 1934, Lázaro Cárdenas, a rural-born general in the revolutionary army, was elected president. His administration immediately enacted the country's most sweeping agrarian reform law. For the first time much of the country's better land was appropriated for distribution to the landless, some to be farmed individually and some co-operatively. By 1940, near the end of Cárdenas's term, 42 per cent of the entire agricultural population benefited from the distribution of over 78 million acres.[2] Together these small farmers owned 47 per cent of all farmland and produced an impressive 52 per cent of the value of the nation's farm output.[3]

One reason for such productivity was that a newly created national bank channelled credit and technical assistance specifically to the now numerous land reform beneficiaries. The provision of peasant-oriented services – literacy programmes, health services, farm-relevant schooling, and modest rural communications – injected new life into the countryside. Often the results were immediate. In the Laguna area, to cite but one example, the real income of land reform beneficiaries quadrupled between 1935 and 1938.[4]

The Cárdenas administration also invested in scientific research. The purpose, however, was not to 'modernize' agriculture in imitation of United States agriculture but to improve on traditional farming methods. Researchers began to develop improved varieties of wheat and especially corn, the main staple of the rural population, always concentrating on what could be utilized by small farmers who had little money and less than ideal farm conditions.

Social and economic progress was being achieved not through dependence on foreign expertise or costly imported agricultural inputs but rather with the abundant, underutilized resources of local peasants. While production increases were seen as important, the goal was to achieve them through helping every peasant to be productive, for only then would the rural majority benefit from the production increases. Freed from the fear of landlords, bosses, and moneylenders, peasants were motivated to produce, knowing that at last they would benefit from their own labour. Power was perceptibly shifting to agrarian reform organizations controlled by those who worked the fields.

Not surprisingly, by the end of his administration in 1940, Cárdenas had made powerful enemies. First were those who had seen their haciendas expropriated. Next were the urban-based monied groups, alarmed by the Cárdenas model of co-operative ownership of land and public ownership of certain industries. Instead of investing in rural services and collective enterprises, they wanted the state to pay for electric power, highways, dams, airports, telecommunications, and urban services that would serve privately owned, commercial agriculture and urban industrialization – from which they would profit.

Not the least of the enemies of Cárdenas was the United States foreign policy establishment. Land redistribution with co-operative ownership, as well as Cárdenas's nationalization of the Rockefeller Standard Oil subsidiary and foreign-owned railroads, caused 'concern' in Washington and on Wall Street. United States corporate investment dropped by about 40 per cent between the mid-thirties and the early 1940s.[5]

By 1942, these enemies of Cárdenas's rural reconstruction succeeded in seizing the balance of power within the administration of Cárdenas's successor Avila Camacho. The significance of this shift for the future of Mexican agriculture was immediately clear. President Avila Camacho's first agricultural plan stated that agriculture was now to serve as the basis for the 'founding of industrial greatness.'[6] Agricultural progress was no longer to be measured first and foremost in terms of the well-being of the rural majority but in how well it served growth elsewhere in the economy.

The United States only reinforced this fundamental shift. United States policy makers identified American interests with the stability of the Avila Camacho administration, with Mexico's ability to produce manufactured goods to support the war effort, and with private control over resources. Getting more food out of the rural areas and into the cities was seen as critical. More food in the urban areas meant lower food prices, an essential ingredient for quieting urban unrest and keeping industrial wages low. Low wages would ensure industrial profits high enough to attract investors, both local and foreign.

It was in this historical context that the Green Revolution was born. The Avila Camacho administration welcomed the Rockefeller Foundation to Mexico, and in 1943 the Foundation joined with the new administration to initiate an agricultural research programme. The result on one level was in the much-heralded technical package later to be publicized as the Green Revolution. On another level, it served to reverse the entire thrust of the Cárdenas rural reconstruction.

The field director of the Rockefeller Foundation in Mexico became head of a new office *within* the Mexican Ministry of Agriculture. His job was to oversee a technical revolution in Mexican agriculture. Policy choices systematically discarded research alternatives oriented toward the nonirrigated, subsistence sector of Mexican agriculture. Instead, all effort went to the development of a capital-intensive technology applicable only to the relatively best-endowed areas or those that could be created by massive irrigation projects. The focus was on how to make seeds, not people, more productive. Agricultural modernization came to substitute for rural development.

Rapid urban-centred industrialization, so profitable for a few, simply could not coexist with the type of rural development promoted by the Cárdenas administration. First, true rural development based on making each rural family productive and better-off would have meant that the rural majority itself would have eaten much of the increment in food production. This increment was exactly what the ascendant urban interests counted on taking *out* of the countryside to feed an industrial work force. Second, genuine improvement in rural life would have sharply diminished the steady exodus to the towns and cities. But it was just this ongoing influx of rural refugees that was so 'needed' to perpetuate low industrial wages.

Only one type of agricultural policy would serve the ends of the urban and industrial interests – one that wilfully neglected the problems of the land reform communities created by Cárdenas while lavishing public funds on increasing the production of a few large commercial growers, marketing outside the rural areas.

The Mexican government subsidized imports of agricultural machinery. In addition, between 1941 and 1952, 18 per cent of Mexico's federal budget and 92 per cent of its agricultural budget was spent on large irrigation projects to create vast new stretches of rich farmland in the North. This valuable land was then sold at low prices, not primarily to the landless poor, but to politically powerful families of businessmen and bureaucrats. Although by law no one in Mexico can own more than 250 irrigated acres, today the average farm in the Mexican Green Revolution area of Hermosillo has grown to 2,000 irrigated acres[7] with some holdings running much larger.[8] Not surprisingly, about 3 per cent of all farms accounted for 80 per cent of the production increase during the 1950s.

Here we have the model of agricultural development that has been actively exported to virtually all the underdeveloped countries within the sphere of influence of the United States.

Ignoring the Small Farmer

Ignoring overwhelming evidence from around the world* that small, carefully farmed plots are more productive per acre than large estates and use fewer costly inputs, governments, international lending-agencies and foreign assistance programmes have invariably passed over small farmers (not to mention the landless). The French agronomist René Dumont describes a Ford Foundation mission of thirteen North American agronomists to India in 1959. The mission argued that it was practically impossible to make simultaneous headway in all of India's 550,000 villages. So they advised subsidization of technical inputs in those areas that were well-irrigated – thereby leaving over half of the nation's farms totally out of the national agricultural development programme. It appeared easier to help a small number of large farmers increase wheat production by 50 per cent within just a few years than to mobilize the productive potential of 50 to 60 million farm families. Thus in the mid-sixties, India's New Agricultural Strategy to promote the improved seed varieties ended up concentrating on merely one tenth of the cultivable land and to a great extent on only one crop, wheat.[9]

Everywhere the large farmer has been directly favoured. A study of Gapan, Nueva Ecija, in the Philippines, in 1966, showed that the first seeds produced by the Rockefeller-funded International Rice Research Institute were distributed only to landholders owning 25 acres of rice paddy or more.[10] No seeds were sold directly to sharecroppers or tenants.

Once selected as the focus of government help, the large farmers have taken full advantage of their head start. Frequently the wealthiest landowning families have reaped additional profits by monopolizing distribution of fertilizers, pesticides, and machinery

*See Chapter 14

needed to make the new seeds respond. Associations of large commercial farmers like those in Mexico have been able to make considerable extra earnings by exporting the Green Revolution, selling thousands of tons of the new seeds annually to Asia and Africa.

Focusing narrowly on production totals transforms rural development into a technical problem – one of getting the 'right,' usually foreign-made, inputs to the 'progressive,' invariably well-placed farmers. We refer to this production focus as *narrow* precisely because it ignores the social reality of hunger – that the hungry are those with control over little or no food-producing resources. Until control over productive resources is democratized such 'agricultural modernization' will remain but a mirage of rural development – a mirage that undermines the interests of the majority of the rural population in order to serve those of a few – large landholders, money-lenders, industrialists, bureaucrats, and foreign investors.

The influx of public funds for the purpose of increasing production has turned farming into a place for profiteering and speculative investment. But to take part, one has needed some combination of land, money, access to credit, and political influence. That alone has eliminated most of the world's rural majority.

The Politics of the High-Yielding Seeds

The term 'high-yielding varieties' of seeds – HYV's as they are called in the Green Revolution literature – is, in fact, a misnomer. The new seeds are in no way neutral.

As part of a fifteen-nation study of the impact of the new seeds conducted by the United Nations Research Institute for Social Development, Dr Ingrid Palmer concludes that the term 'high yielding varieties' is a misnomer because it implies that the new seeds are high-yielding *in and of themselves*.[11] The distinguishing feature of the seeds, however, is that they are highly *responsive* to certain key inputs such as irrigation and fertilizer. Following Palmer's lead we have chosen to use the term 'high-responsive varieties' (HRV's) as much more revealing of the true character of the seeds. The Green Revolution is obviously more complicated than just sticking new varieties of seeds into the ground. Unless the poor farmers can afford to ensure the ideal conditions that will make these new seeds respond (in which case they wouldn't be poor!), their new seeds are just not going to grow as well as the ones planted by better-off farmers. The new seeds prefer the 'better neighbourhood'.

Just as significant for the majority of the world's farmers is that the new seeds show a greater yield variation than the seeds they displaced.[12] The HRV's are more sensitive to drought and flood than their traditional predecessors. They are particularly prone to water stress – the inability to assimilate nutrients when not enough water is getting to the plant roots, especially at certain stages in their growth cycles. Under these conditions it is often no more profitable to apply fertilizers to the new seeds than to the previous ones.[13] In 1968-1969 in Pakistan, for example, yields of Mexican dwarf wheat declined by about 20 per cent because of a two-thirds reduction in average rainfall and higher than normal temperatures. The locally adapted varieties, however, were not adversely affected by the weather changes. Instead their yields increased 11 per cent.[14] The new sorghums now being planted in Upper Volta in Africa are also less drought-resistant than their local cousins.[15]

The HRV's are more sensitive to both too much and too little water: they need, not mere irrigation, but sophisticated water management. The significance of this becomes clear in India's Punjab. Higher yields from the new seeds depend on a tubewell for a controlled water supply. But a tubewell is well beyond the means of the small farmer.

Taking advantage of the HRV's has required farmers to double or even triple their indebtedness. Since small farmers are already in debt for preharvest consumption and for other family needs – often at very high rates of interest – most will not be able to take on this heavy new burden.

HRV's are often less resistant to disease and pests. Vulnerability results from transplanting a variety that 'evolved' over a short period in one climate (with a little help from agronomists) to an entirely different climate, thus supplanting varieties that had evolved over centuries in response to natural threats in that environment. A small farmer, whose family's very survival depends on each and every harvest, cannot afford to risk crop failure. For the large farmer that risk is minimized. The difference is not just that the large farmer can better withstand a crop failure.

In addition, the new seeds have been restricted to well rainfed and irrigated regions. It is not coincidental that these favoured regions are inhabited by the more affluent farmers. Almost all of the HRV increases in wheat cultivation in India have taken place in the states of Punjab and Haryana, largely because the soil is alluvial and a canal system assures a year-round water supply.[16]

Nyle C. Brady, Director of the International Rice Research Institute, where many of the new strains have been developed, estimates that the 'new rice varieties may be suitable for only 25 per cent of the world's acreage, largely those areas with water for irrigation.'[17] Because the new varieties are less resistant to flooding, there are many parts of Thailand, Bangladesh, and South Vietnam in which they cannot be used.[18] None of the new seeds are successful in areas of constant high temperatures and rainfall, limited sun, and thin, badly leached soils.

Knowing the biological requirements of the seeds, we should not be surprised that as late as 1972-1973 the HRV's covered a very small percentage – only about 15 per cent of the total world area excluding the socialist countries.[19] Furthermore, they are highly concentrated: 81 per cent of the HRV wheat grows in a small area in India and in Pakistan; and four countries (India, the Philippines, Indonesia, and Bangladesh) account for 83 per cent of the HRV rice.[20]

The seeds, due to their need for ideal conditions, are restricted to certain favoured areas. They therefore have reinforced income disparities between geographic regions, just as they have exacerbated the inequalities between social classes.

Two other factors contribute to making the new seeds less than neutral. First, hybrids of corn and sorghum do not remain genetically sure year after year. To maintain high yields new hybrid seeds must be purchased each year. This requirement alone gives the edge to the wealthier farmer and to the farmer more closely linked to seed distributors and other credit sources. The many farmers with only enough land to grow the food their families need will never have the cash to purchase hybrid seeds.

Second, the new seeds, because they require special knowledge to be used effectively, are inherently biased in favour of those who have access to government agricultural extension agents and instruction literature. In many countries the large landowners monopolize the services of the extension agencies. A study in Uttar Pradesh, India, showed that, since 70 per cent of the family heads were completely illiterate, 'access to literature is thus primarily the prerogative of the better educated, wealthier landowners.' Non-written material was no more successful in overcoming the problem: the village headman regarded the radio as his private property and invited only his friends to listen.[21]

The bias can be quite subtle. As Andrew Peairse, a longtime student of the Green Revolution, so aptly describes it, 'The new technology puts a relative handicap on those whose assets include traditional knowledge of the local idiosyncrasies of soil and climate and whose energies are absorbed by the labours of husbandry . . . It gives the advantage to those skilled in manipulating influence.[22]

Still the idea that a seed, the product of impartial scientific research, must be neutral, is deeply rooted in most of us. Most assume it will just be a matter of time before the new seeds spread out to the poor and bring the standard of living up for all farmers. But the dependence of HRV's on *optimal* conditions makes that impossible in most areas today. Both the rich and the poor farmer certainly can plant the seed, but who can feed the plants the optimal diet of nutrients and water and protect them from disease and pests? Can the family who depends for their food on what they grow afford to gamble with the less dependable seeds?

The only way that such seeds can be neutral is if the society prepares the way – giving equal access to the necessary inputs to all farmers. If this means redistribution of control over all food-producing resources, including land redistribution, it can work. In Cuba, for example, between 75 and 90 per cent of the rice acreage is planted with the high-response seeds.[23] In Taiwan, also a country of fairly equal land distribution, the use of improved seeds is over 90 per cent. But where 'equalizing access' has merely meant credit programmes it has rarely worked.

In China, production of the new seeds does not take place in central experimental stations but is handled by ordinary families themselves.[24] Most communes have their own laboratories for locally developing new varieties. Spreading the new technology is therefore not a problem. As early as 1961 the Chinese were breeding seeds for less favourable climes. Chinese farmers have successfully developed seeds that are both higher yielding and *more* able to withstand bad weather and other dangers, such as barley strains adapted to high altitudes and cold-resistant strains of wheat.[25]

Once manipulated by people, nature loses its neutrality. Elite research institutes will produce new seeds that work – at least in the short-term – for a privileged class of commercial farmers.

Genetic research that involves ordinary farmers themselves will produce seeds that are useful to them. A new seed, then, is like any other technological development; its contribution to social progress depends entirely on who develops it and who controls it.

12 : The Results of the Green Revolution

For many outsiders looking at hunger in underdeveloped countries, the fact that greater production can bring cheaper grain appears as part of the solution. The mistake is in forgetting two points: First, many of the poor are also producers whose livelihood in part depends on selling their grain. Second, for those unable to take part in the new technology, yields have often *not* increased. With overall greater availability, however, and the failure of government policies to maintain prices, the poor farmers with the unimproved yields are in a worse plight than ever.

In Greece the agricultural credit corporations pressure farmers to sow foreign-bred HRV wheats. In the lowland areas occupied by large farms the result has been higher yields, thus increasing total Greek output. But in the mountains the HRV seeds yielded less than the varieties that had been grown for generations by the mountain people. As the national (and world) yields increased, wheat prices fell. The large commercial farms in the plains could withstand the price drop because their volume of production was large and increasing. But for the poorer farm on the mountain slopes the fall in income resulting from lower yields was often the final blow leading to the desertion of many mountain villages, as well as the loss to the world of wheat varieties unconsciously selected, over centuries, to thrive in more difficult conditions.[1]

Rents Go Up

Landlords in many countries have found they can transfer part of the burden of increased production costs onto the tenants or sharecroppers, in effect forcing the tenants to pay for the new technology. For instance, with the introduction of the new technology, the cash rents tenants must pay have gone up by about one-third to one-half. Crop share rents are changing from the traditional 50-50 division between the landlord and the tenant to 70-30 in favour of the landlord,[2] effectively cutting the tenant out of the production gains. In one area of India where the sharecropper used to get half the harvest, he now gets only one-third; another third goes to the landlord and the remaining third goes to pay off the debt for the tubewell the landlord purchased (it will, of course, go to the landlord once the tubewell is paid for).[3]

Traditional landlords once had very clearcut, reciprocal obligations to tenants or sharecroppers. The landlord would have never considered passing on his obligations to the tenants. But now that more and more landlords are absentee city dwellers, traditional face-to-face dealings are being replaced by impersonal, money-based relationships. Landlords increasingly demand cash payment of rent instead of payment in kind. In the northern states of Malaysia cash payments are required at the *beginning* of the season. The tenant has to come up with rent at just the time he is least likely to have it. He therefore has to borrow at high rates of interest – thus reducing his total income. Moreover, if the crops fail, the tenant still has to come up with the rent.

By the same token, many landlords now prefer to pay in money wages rather than in farm produce. In times of inflating food prices, however, it would be much better for the tenant-farmer to have part of the harvest than money. We learned of one district in India where landlords now pay only money wages, preferring to hoard and sell the rice later for enormous profit. In 1974, India's *Economic and Political Weekly* reported that in Thanjavur, Tamil Nadu, 'hordes of the police were stationed in the paddy fields to quell disturbances arising out of the landlords' refusal to pay even a part of the wages in kind.'[4]

Land Values Soar

In countries where food-resources are still allowed to be held for private gain, the inpouring of government funds in the form of irrigation works and subsidies for fertilizers and machinery have combined with the higher potential yields of the new seeds to turn farming into the world's hottest growth industry. Agriculture is increasingly seen as a lucrative opportunity by a new class of 'farmers' with the money or influence to get in on the action – moneylenders, military officers, bureaucrats, city-based speculators, and foreign corporations. In those areas targeted by the 'production strategy' land values have gone up three-, four-, or even fivefold as these so-called farmers compete for the land that they believe, often rightly, will make them a fortune.[5]

Here is development economist Wolf Ladejinsky's well-known

account of how nonfarmers in India buy up land for speculation.

The buyers are a motley group: some connected with land through family ties, some altogether new to agriculture. A few have unemployed rupees acquired through undeclared earnings, and most of them look upon farming as a tax-haven, which it is, and as a source of earning tax-free supplementary income. The medical doctor from Jullundur who turned part-time farmer is sitting pretty. The 15 acres purchased four years ago have tripled in value. To listen to him, he is in farming 'for the good of the country.' . . . His only vexation is whether or not he will succeed in buying another 10 acres he has his eyes on – and what a disappointed man he will be if they escape him! As we watched him supervise the threshing, he was anything but a 'gentleman farmer'.[6]

Nonfarmers are taking over agriculture not only because governments have made investments attractive, but because increasingly only the wealthier urban dwellers can obtain credit or afford to buy the higher-priced land and the necessary inputs. As the price of land rises, purchase by the smallholder or tenant, if unlikely before, becomes completely out of the question. In countries where security of tenure is legally guaranteed after the tenant has continuously cultivated a given plot for a certain number of years, some landlords manoeuvre to ensure that their tenants are never given legal title to the land, now that land is more valuable. In Tanjore, India, landlords shift sharecroppers from one plot to another each year to successfully dodge such tenure regulations.[7]

Moreover, as the market value of land increases, taxes increase. In Colombia wealthy potential buyers of small plots persuade tax authorities to revalue the land in order to put pressure on the small farmers. Peasants who cannot afford to plant the new varieties of coffee find that they cannot pay the higher tax bill and are forced to sell to larger landholders who usually can evade the tax by paying a bribe.[8]

Fewer People Control More Land

Fewer and fewer people control more and more of farm production. A pattern of increasing monopolization of agricultural land moves ahead in India, Bangladesh, Mexico, the Philippines, Colombia – in virtually all countries where officially subsidized 'modernization' now means that high returns stem from the sheer amount of land one can control, not from how well one farms.

In the area of Tamesis, Colombia, the better-off coffee growers able to adopt the new seed varieties increased the average size of their holding by 76 per cent between 1963 and 1970.[9] Similarly, in the government-subsidized irrigated zones of Morocco land concentration is increasing. In just five years, from 1965 to 1970 the average size of modern, Moroccan-owned farms in one irrigated area increased 30 per cent.[10]

Another sign of increasing concentration of land ownership is that the smallest farmers are selling their land. To some, the decline of the small farmer appears unfortunate, but, alas, inevitable. But the tightening of control over agricultural production is not inevitable. It results from the actions and even the planning of people. In the early 1950s, large farmers in the Mexican state of Sonora saw that land values were about to go up because of massive government irrigation plans for the area. They began to contrive to take over cheaply the land owned by thousands of smallholders. They turned to their friends within the National Agricultural Credit Bank – the government agency on which smallholders in the area depended for survival. The bank began to delay crop credit for smallholders. In some cases they received credit so late that their wheat, to take but one example, had to be planted out of season and thus failed during several years. The smallholders' expenses soared. They had several disastrous years. Then came the final blow: The government foreclosed on all properties with outstanding debts to federal agencies. The large farmers had succeeded. The majority of the smallholders in one devastated settlement ended up selling their land for about one ninth of the market price to two of the largest and most politically influential landowners in the state.[11]

The Creation of the Landless

In certain areas landlords are moving to push their tenants off the land. The landlords see several advantages. For instance, they are freed from tenants who might conceivably claim land under a land-to-the-tiller reform movement. Moreover, the large landowner finds it more profitable to mechanize production or take advantage of part-time labourers who have no claim on the land or on the harvest. A study for the World Bank on the size of farms in the

Indian Punjab during the 1960s concluded that farms that had been mechanized grew by an average of 240 per cent over a three-year period, primarily because the landlords decided to cultivate land they had previously rented out.[12] The landlord's gain – higher cash income – was society's loss, as a substantial number of tenants could no longer rent the land they needed to support themselves. In India, in 1969, there were 40,000 eviction suits against sharecroppers in Bihar alone and 80,000 in Karnatika (Mysore).[13]

As the control of land tightens and more tenants are evicted, the number of landless labourers mounts. In all nonsocialist underdeveloped countries 30 to 60 per cent of rural adult males are now landless. In Mexico between 1950 and 1960 the number of landless labourers increased much faster than the general population, from 2.3 to 3.3 million.[14] Between 1964 and 1970 the number of landless families in Colombia more than doubled.[15] During the fifteen years beginning in 1951, the number of landless labourers in Bangladesh had increased by two and a quarter times.[16] In India, between 1961 and 1971, the number of agricultural labourers increased by over 20 million (by 75 per cent). In the same period the number of cultivators decreased by 15 million (by 16 per cent). None of these startling figures includes the millions of landless refugees who, finding no farm work, join an often hopeless search for work in the urban areas.

So the number of landless mounts while the number of rural jobs shrinks. Traditionally in many countries even the poorest landless peasant had access to part of the harvest. In India, Bangladesh, Pakistan, and Indonesia the large landowner once felt obligated to permit all who wished to participate in the harvest to retain one sixth of what they harvested. Even the most impoverished were assured of work for a few bags of grain. Now, with the increased likelihood of profitable sales, the new agricultural entrepreneurs are rejecting the traditional obligations of the landowner to the poor. It is now common for landowners to sell the standing crop to an outside contractor before harvest. The outsider, with no local obligations, can seek the cheapest labour, even bringing in workers from neighbouring areas.

In Java, landless labourers were once permitted to squat on dry land in the off season to grow cassava and vegetables. With the new rice seeds, landlords are now interested in irrigating the land for year-round production for commercial markets. Squatters are no longer welcome.

Women Undercut

In the severing of rural people from control over food-producing resources we have just described, women are often doubly hurt: work demands on women increase while their effective control over family resources erodes.[17] The family now has less or no land; the men are more and more often forced to seek wage labour away from the home. Women who have traditionally laboured to grow a variety of crops near the home as the mainstay of the family's diet now must take sole responsibility, often with less land and fewer cash resources.

With the spread of commercialized agriculture, moreover, government extension services, credit and membership in marketing cooperatives are now overwhelmingly geared to the men, not the women. And income is largely under the control of the men also. With women in less control of the family's resources, the new cash income often goes for what one rural sociologist has called 'bachelor-type goods' – radios, wristwatches or bicycles. And even if the cash income gained from selling the commercial crop is used for the family's food, it is unlikely to be the nutritional equivalent of the home-grown diet.

The Green Revolution Imperative

Historically, the Green Revolution represented a choice to breed seed varieties that produce high yields under optimum conditions. It was a choice *not* to start by developing seeds better able to withstand drought or pests. It was a choice *not* to concentrate first on improving traditional methods of increasing yields, such as mixed cropping. It was a choice *not* to develop technology that was productive, labour-intensive, and independent of foreign input supply. It was a choice *not* to concentrate on reinforcing the balanced, traditional diets of grain plus legumes.

Moreover, in light of all these 'paths not taken,' we must ask ourselves: In our eagerness to embrace the new, in our rush to extend the scope of human knowledge and control, do we forget to work on *applying* the collected wisdom already handed down to us? Has our fascination with science prevented us from tackling the incomparably more difficult problems of social organization and the agricultural practices of real farmers? For the majority who are hungry, 'miracle' seeds are meaningless without control over land, water, tools, storage and marketing.

A series of major studies now being completed for the International Labour Organization (ILO) documents that in the seven South Asian countries comprising 70 per cent of the rural population of the nonsocialist underdeveloped world, the rural poor have become worse off than they were ten or twenty years ago. The summary study notes that ironically *'the increase in poverty has been associated not with a fall but with a rise in cereal production per head, the main component of the diet of the poor.'* Here are typical examples:

- The Philippines: Despite the fact that agricultural production increased by 3 to 4 per cent per year during the last fifteen to twenty years, about one fifth of the rural households experienced a dramatic and *absolute* decline in living standards, which accelerated during the early seventies. By 1974 daily real wages in agriculture fell to almost one third of what they were in 1965.[18]
- Bangladesh: Between 1963 and 1975, the proportion of rural households classified as absolutely poor increased by more than a third and that of those classified as extremely poor increased five times. Yet about 15 per cent of the rural households in Bangladesh had significantly higher real incomes in 1975.[19]
- Sri Lanka: Despite a rise in per capita income between 1963 and 1973, actual rice consumption *fell* for all except the highest income class. All workers experienced a fall in real wages, except for those in industry and commerce whose real wages remained static.[20]

Where All the Food Has Gone

In many countries huge capital investments made in the modernization approach to production did boost the yields of many better-off farmers. But what has happened to much of the increased production?

- Some of it goes to urban middle- and upper-income groups.

In countries like the Philippines and Mexico increased production has benefited emerging industrialists and their foreign partners who want to have cheap food for workers in urban industries in order to keep wage demands low. Total production increases have also helped government elites who fear urban unrest – such as the food riots in Mexican cities during the 1940s – if not enough food could be extracted from the rural areas.

· Some of it gets reduced into luxury products the poor cannot afford.

The governments of the United States and Pakistan collaborated with the New Jersey-based Corn Products Corporation to improve yields of Pakistani corn – traditionally a staple food grown by the rural poor. Hybrid seeds and other inputs did increase yields. The corn, however, is now a cash crop grown by relatively few large farmers for manufacturing a corn-based sweetener used in such things as soft drinks.

· Some of it gets fed to livestock to create meat that the majority of the local population cannot afford.

In 1971, an FAO report advised Third World countries on the problem of how to dispose of 'surplus' grain resulting from the success of the Green Revolution production campaigns. The FAO suggested using a greater proportion of wheat for animal feed or shifting to cultivation of coarse grains more suitable for livestock than wheat and rice. Could they be serious? FAO was advising countries with the most serious undernutrition problems in the world to deal with the so-called surplus problem by stepped up livestock feeding!

In 1973 two thirds of Colombia's Green Revolution rice was being fed to livestock or going into the production of beer. Increased yields of corn provided the raw material for starting up a chicken feed industry. Did this mean Colombia's undernourished would be eating chicken? For over a quarter of the country's families, buying just two pounds of chicken or a dozen eggs would require an entire week's earnings or more. Much of the increased egg production goes into processed foods such as snacks and mayonnaise sold by multinational food companies to elite urban groups.[21]

· Some of the increased production gets exported.

Where the majority of people are kept too poor to constitute a domestic market and agriculture is made to rely on imported inputs like fertilizers and machines, the colonial pattern of production for export is reinforced in the search for a paying market and the foreign exchange needed to pay for imported inputs. India exports such excellent staples as potatoes to countries like Sweden and the Soviet Union yet the amount of potatoes available to the Indian people has been reduced by 12 per cent between 1972 and 1974.[22] Central America exports between one third and one half of its beef to the United States alone.

· Some of the increased production simply gets dumped.

Fruits and vegetables produced in Central America for export to the United States frequently either are shut out from an over-supplied market or fail to meet United States 'quality' standards – size, colour, smoothness. Since the local population, mostly landless, is too poor to buy anything, fully 65 per cent of the fruits and vegetables produced, according to one study, 'must be literally dumped or, where possible, fed to livestock' (which in turn are exported).[23]

Neglect of redistribution of control over productive resources and concentration instead on the production advances of commercial growers have determined where the production goes. Since any increase in production is not met by a similarly enlarged buying public, no matter how much food is produced it will end up going to an urban elite, to an export market, or to make livestock products that can only be purchased by the well-off.

A Fundamental Law of Development

Many view the Green Revolution as a technical innovation and feel that, as such, it should not be expected to solve social problems. But what we have found is that there can be no separation between technical innovation and social change. A fundamental law of development is that inserting any profitable technology into a society shot through with power inequalities (money, landownership, privilege, access to credit) sets off the disastrous retrogression of the less powerful majority. The better-off and powerful in a society further enrich themselves at the expense of the national treasury and the rural poor. As those initially better-off gain even greater control over the production process, the majority of people are made marginal, in fact, totally irrelevant, to the process of agricultural production. In such societies the reserves of landless and jobless function only to keep wages down for those who do find jobs. Excluded from contributing to the agricultural economy, the poor majority are no longer its beneficiaries, for being excluded from production means being excluded from consumption. A thirty-six-cents-a-day labourer in Bihar, India, knows this truth well: 'If you don't own any land, you never get enough to eat,' he says, 'even if the land is producing well.'[24]

The Green Revolution has *not* bought us time. 'Modernization' overlaid on oppressive social structures entrenches the ownership classes who are now even better positioned and less willing to part with their new-found wealth. Thus, *to focus only on raising production, without first confronting the issue of who controls and who participates in the production process, actually compounds the problem.* It leaves the majority of people worse off than before. In a very real sense the idea that we are progressing is our greatest handicap. We cannot move forward – we cannot take the first step toward helping improve the welfare of the vast majority of the world's people – until we can see clearly that we are now moving backward.

In most of the developing nations, rural people have traditionally had little faith in the national governments. Governments' policies were usually regarded with suspicion and perhaps with good reason. . . . The rural people are beginning to regard this government with more trust and confidence, to feel to some degree at least, that it is their government. In this way, the Green Revolution can also be said to be contributing constructively towards political stability.

George Harrar, President of the Rockefeller
Foundation in his *Review and
Annual Report*, 1970

13: Undermining the World's Food Security

There is no true food security, no matter how much is produced, if the food-producing resources are controlled by a small minority and used only to profit them. In such a system the greater profit will always be found in catering to those who can pay the most – not the hungry.

Here is what we mean: If farm businessmen in Colombia find they can make more money growing livestock feed for processors like Ralston Purina than a staple like beans, they will grow feed. When a Mexican commercial grower in Sinaloa discovers he can make almost twenty times more raising tomatoes of export quality than raising wheat, he is likely to switch to tomatoes. If large operators in Central and South America find they can make more money growing flowers for export rather than corn for local people, they will plant flowers.

On a research trip to northwest Mexico, we came upon several distilleries newly built to produce brandy from grapes to be grown on thousands of irrigated acres, land on which local people could grow nutritious food. The next day the head of cereal research at a nearby government-sponsored research centre explained to us that a farmer in the area makes a profit of almost $500 per acre growing grapes – four times more than with wheat.

In a country like Mexico, where early childhood death due to malnutrition has gone up 10 per cent over the last ten years, acreage devoted to basic food crops – corn, wheat, beans and rice – actually declined 25 per cent over the same period. Not surprisingly, between 1973-76, Mexico had to import 15 per cent of its corn, 25 per cent of its wheat, and 45 per cent of its soybeans.

Mexico is a prime example of a country that has gone far down the path of entrusting its agricultural resources to large commercial growers. The result? The government has had to practically bribe the 'modernized' growers to keep them producing basic staples for the national market; the Mexican government had to hike price guarantees by 112 per cent between 1970 and 1975 and even then the proportion of land growing basic foods has declined. Because of the tight control of the commercial farming sector over production, the large commercial growers have been able to use threats of production cutbacks to get higher government-supported prices. At times they have carried out the threats – switching to feedgrains or export crops – until the support offered by the government for growing a basic food was raised high enough. The food security of a country in which large commercial growers virtually control food production is forever in jeopardy for yet another reason: The large growers can withhold food from the market in periods of rising prices in expectation of higher profits later. Entrusting a country's food supply to a pampered elite turns out to be a dangerous and costly choice indeed.

How Vulnerable is an Agricultural System to Natural Hazards?

Can we measure food security in production totals if the agricultural base that produced the gains is itself threatened?

Consider these apparently isolated events:

- Indonesia, 1974-1975: At least 500,000 acres of riceland planted with the new variety was devastated by a viral disease spread by plagues of brown leaf hoppers.[1] (Indonesia has since inaugurated a programme aimed at replacing HRV rice with its own locally improved varieties.)
- Philippines, 1970-1972: Tungro rice virus reached epidemic levels in the Green Revolution rice fields.[2]
- Zambia, 1970s: Disaster in the form of a newly identified mould called *fusarium* has struck new hybrid corn stairs grown by the commercial farmers while the traditional corn crops of the villagers appear free from attack.[3]

What do these examples of crop loss from disease and pests reveal?

Green Revolution fields are often more vulnerable to attack than fields planted in traditional ways with locally evolved seeds. Why? Part of the reason is simply that the denser stands in Green Revolution fields provide a more abundant diet for pests. Multiple cropping allowed by the faster-maturing new seeds also provides pests with a more even year-round food supply. Moreover, the new seeds were bred with the highest priority on the greatest yield possible, not on resistance to disease or pests.

The danger of crop loss is compounded because, while the new seeds present novel opportunities for disease and pests, effective traditional practices for dealing with these problems are becoming casualties of the Green Revolution. Historically, wet-rice farming involved flooding the fields for several weeks each year, thus drowning many pests. Unfortunately, the rigorous timing of the new seeds often does not accommodate this practice. Alternating the cultivation of a food crop with a soil-building crop (called green manuring) is a proven traditional way to control pests by eliminating their hosts for a season. This practice was widespread even in the United States until recently. But with increasing use of chemical fertilizers, green manuring has become passé. Puddling is yet another practice on the way out. (In case you are wondering, puddling means using water buffaloes to plod through the fields in order to aerate the soil, increase water retention, trample the weeds, and eliminate insects.)[4]

Finally, the genetic uniformity of the new seeds planted over large areas means that they are more vulnerable to epidemics. A few years ago, the United States had a glimpse of what this could mean. In 1970, the great southern corn leaf blight wiped out 50 per cent or more of the crop in many of the Gulf Coast states (15 to 20 per cent of the total domestic corn crop.) A more tragic example is the Irish potato blight in which over 1 million people died during the 1840s. Scientists now believe that the underlying problem was the lack of genetic diversity of the potato crop.

Today all the Green Revolution dwarf wheats* (now 20 per cent of all wheat grown) trace themselves to a *single* parent plant. The same is true of dwarf-rice varieties. Should the genes that those parents have for dwarfness ever be linked to one conferring susceptibility to a plant disease such as glume botch, root rot, or Karnal smut (real names!), the Green Revolution could turn black overnight.

Because of their denser stands, multiple cropping, and genetic uniformity, the new seeds can be more vulnerable to attack. Current plant research is therefore placing greater emphasis on breeding for resistance. But the issue is much more complex than simply finding a seed that is resistant to today's diseases. Nature is not static. Pests and diseases are constantly adapting.

Scientists such as Dr H. Garrison Wilkes, a specialist in corn genetics at the University of Massachusetts, believe that it is only a matter of time before a mutation of an existing disease will take place, permitting it to attack a new seed strain. Wilkes states that

*'Dwarf' refers to characteristic shortness of the plants that prevents their tipping over even when more abundant yields makes their tops heavier.

'In their wilderness state, both plants and diseases which attack them are forever adapting to each other through the evolutionary process. The diseases mutate new forms of attack, the plants new forms of resistance.' But, he warns, 'Under modern agriculture plants no longer mutate but are grown from new seeds each year for continuous high yields. *The mutation of diseases, however, cannot be stopped.*'[5]

This inevitability would not be so serious if we could always rush back to the lab to produce a new strain – keeping one step ahead of nature and losing at most one crop. But it takes time to develop a resistant strain. Could the world wait as many as ten to twenty generations of seeds, that is, four to five years, for a resistant hybrid?[6] Clearly the answer is no.

Moreover, this scenario presumes that the material will continue to exist from which plant breeders can always come up with a new resistant strain. But will it? We have talked here in Part V about the social and economic transformation of agriculture. But what of the transformation of world agriculture in terms of the plants themselves? What happens when commercialized, standardized agriculture penetrates almost every corner of the globe?

The human race historically cultivated over 3,000 species of plants for food, about half of them in sufficient quantity to enter into commerce. Today, in stark contrast, only fifteen species, including rice, corn, wheat, sorghum, barley, sugar cane, sugar beets, potato, sweet potato, cassava, the common bean, soybean, peanut, coconut, and banana actually feed the entire world, providing 85-90 per cent of all human energy. Of these, only *three* plants, wheat, rice, and corn now supply 66 per cent of the world's seed crop.[7]

Especially since there are now so *few* plants on which we all depend, the maintenance of genetic diversity within these species is absolutely critical. Genetic diversity, as we have already seen, is necessary to prevent the wholesale wiping out of a crop in which all the plants are vulnerable to the same pathogen, and it is also crucial as the storehouse of material from which to breed new resistant strains. The heritage of genetic diversity has not been evenly spread over the earth. In the 1920s, the Russian plant geneticist N. I. Vavilov discovered eight major and three minor centres of extreme plant gene diversity, all located in underdeveloped countries (along the Tropic of Cancer and the Tropic of Capricorn), in mountainous regions isolated by steep terrain or other natural barriers. These centres represent only one fortieth of the world's land area but have been the source of almost all our food plants. From these reservoirs have come many of the most valuable strains and genes used by plant geneticists in the last fifty years.[8]

Until now scientists have returned to these areas of diversity for new germ plasm with which to breed resistance. But this diversity has never been adequately protected. Collections of genetic material were often lost when scientists discarded them after hitting upon the genes that would serve their immediate purpose. Suddenly in the 1970s the problem worsened dramatically. As plant geneticist Wilkes puts it: 'We are discovering Mexican farmers are planting hybrid corn seed from a Midwestern seed firm, that Tibetan farmers are planting barley from a Scandinavian plant breeding station, and that Turkish farmers are planting wheat from the Mexican Wheat Programme.' He concludes, 'Each of these classic areas of genetic diversity is rapidly becoming an area of seed uniformity.'[9]

Once foreign strains are introduced, the native varieties can become extinct in a single year if their seeds are consumed and not kept. Dr Wilkes states, 'Quite literally, the genetic heritage of a millennium in a particular valley can disappear in a single bowl of porridge.'[10]

Some argue that our security against genetic 'wipe outs' will lie in establishing seed banks that would be treasuries of genetic diversity. Unfortunately, seed banks, too, are vulnerable. A major Peruvian collection of corn germ plasm, one of South America's largest, was irretrievably lost when the compressors for the refrigerators in which it was stored failed! And, the corn research centre in Mexico that produced the original Green Revolution seeds inadvertently lost some of its irreplaceable corn germ plasm collected during the 1940s.[11] Bangladesh still has some 1,200 different traditional varieties of rice and Indonesia has 600. How effectively can that genetic diversity be protected once it is removed from the field for cold storage in a seed bank? One alternative to seed banks proposed by many scientists is carefully selected natural preserves throughout the world that could maintain living collections in the field.

As long as such research is primarily the domain of a few corporations one wonders what protective measures will be taken. Already Pioneer Hy-Bred International, Inc. and DeKalb Ag Research supply 55 per cent of the hybrid corn market. These two, plus six others, dominate virtually all hybrid development and marketing.[12] Can such firms be expected to help maintain living treasuries of genetic diversity in which all countries might participate? Or will they guard their genetic research against competitors and promote only the currently most saleable variety?

How Self-Contained Is the Agricultural System?

This is the third measure of true food security. To measure how self-contained an agricultural system is one must first know who controls the farm inputs necessary to make the land productive. Take, for example, the new hybrid corn seeds. Since these seeds do not reproduce themselves perfectly, farmers who save seeds from one crop for the next planting find their yields and quality greatly diminished. The farmer – once he is hooked into the hybrid seed system – is dependent, therefore, on a new supply of seeds season after season. These seeds now come primarily from private companies able to produce them through controlled pollination. The US Department of Agriculture has just developed seeds called 'apomictic' hybrids that the farmers would be able to use year after year without new purchases from seed companies.[13] It is unlikely, we are told, that this development will be pursued by the big seed companies since their whole sales system would be threatened.

Reliance on imported chemical fertilizers also runs counter to the maintenance of a secure, self-contained agricultural system. Nevertheless, corporations and institutions based in the industrial countries are exporting the myth that chemical fertilizers are the best way to achieve production gains. This road to increased yields is a model most of us take for granted. From 1942 to 1967 chemical fertilizer use in the United States expanded tenfold – not because it was the only path to production gains but for other reasons. For one thing, chemical fertilizers became dirt-cheap. The cost of nitrogen fertilizer dropped to one half and in some cases one quarter of what it was immediately after World War II. The greater demand for nitrogen fertilizer can also be linked to the rapid promotion of meat consumption. (It takes about sixteen times more nitrogen to produce grain-fed meat than it does to produce plant protein.)

Even more significantly, chemical fertilizer use is accelerating in order to compensate for soil nutrient depletion due to the nitrogen lost by bad cultivation practices and resultant erosion. One estimate places the loss of soil nitrogen in rich soils in midwest America at 40 per cent in the last century.[14] It is estimated that fifteen to twenty years of returning organic matter – manure, crop residues, sewage sludge, and so on – would be necessary to restore the organic content and the nitrogen of American soils. Such soil depletion reveals much about American agriculture. Careful husbandry necessary to maintain fragile soils or enrich poor soils never evolved there because until now it simply did not seem necessary.

The critical importance of careful land husbandry came home to us recently. A Soil Conservation Service official in Iowa explained how, depending on the way the land is cared for, top soil might last only thirty-six years or for an indefinite period. If the soil is ploughed up and downhill in the fall and corn is planted year after year with no crop residue left, the entire six to eight remaining inches of Iowa's top soil will be lost from land with even a very slight slope. If, by contrast, no-till farming and contour terracing are practised and crop residue is left on all year, the eight inches of top soil could last indefinitely since new top soil would always be in formation. Yet, as of today, only one third of Iowa's agricultural land is protected by the kind of conservation practices needed to protect the top soil.[15]

Is this American record – neglect of soil maintenance and reliance on chemical fertilizers – a useful model for underdeveloped countries today?

Underdeveloped countries now import 55 per cent of their nitrogen fertilizer,[16] making them highly vulnerable to skyrocketing fertilizer prices. World fertilizer prices jumped threefold between 1970 and 1974. Crop production fell in many underdeveloped countries simply because they had become hooked on chemical fertilizers and yet could no longer afford to import them. But even if it *were* possible to rely on imported chemical fertilizer to increase food production, is this the place for underdeveloped countries to start?

Chemical fertilizers can increase yields but they cannot maintain or enhance the soil's organic matter. Organic matter, however, is the ultimate key to fertility; it maintains the porous soil structure, providing superior waterholding capacity (critical during droughts) and allowing oxygen to penetrate for use by soil organisms that break down manure, crop residues, and other organic matter. Relying primarily on chemical fertilizers can be self-defeating in the long-term. The more one relies on chemical fertilizers instead of manure, compost, crop rotation, and green manure, the more the organic matter declines, the less able plants are to absorb inorganic nitrogen in chemical fertilizers.

Chemical fertilizer must, therefore, never be thought of as a *substitute* for organic sources. First, all sources of organic matter should be mobilized and returned to the soil. Then, for countries like China and Algeria with petroleum available to produce chemical fertilizer, developing and using that potential can make sense. (Furthermore, even though China is making a big push to utilize its petroleum for fertilizer, 70 per cent of its fertilizer is still from organic sources, enough to guarantee sufficient food production.)

Even if there are no local resources for chemical fertilizer production (and this is the case for most underdeveloped countries), yield gains can be achieved by mobilizing the now wasted potential of organic matter. Conservatively estimated, waste material from animals, plants, and humans in underdeveloped countries could supply *six to eight times* more nutrients than these countries obtained during 1970-1971 from the use of chemical fertilizers. In 1973, the economic value of such organic wastes in underdeveloped countries was estimated at over $16 billion. Using labour-intensive methods, urban waste in India could be processed into fertilizers at one-third the cost of imported chemical fertilizers.[17] Yet virtually none of this potential has been tapped.

Most measures of food security fixate on global statistics of agricultural production. But food security simply cannot exist in a market system where food is a business. Commercial growers cannot be relied upon to keep growing food for hungry people when they can make more money growing luxury crops for the minority who can always pay more. Moreover, we have seen that much of the increased production has been at the price of increased vulnerability, *and unnecessarily so*. Increased production approached as a mere technical problem has completely re-shaped agriculture itself, reducing a very complex, self-contained system into a highly simplified and dependent one. The Green Revolution approach converts a recycling, self-contained system into a linear production formula: pick the 'best' seeds, plant uniformly over the largest area possible, and dose with chemical fertilizer. The reduction of agriculture to this simple formula leaves crops open to attack and soils highly vulnerable to deterioration.

Such reductionist agriculture turns chemical fertilizers and pesticides into necessities to cover for its built-in vulnerabilities. True food security is further undermined as production is made increasingly dependent on external sources of supply over which there is no local control. We are all exposed repeatedly to catchy corporate ads that attempt to scare us into believing that the corporate-marketed inputs are the only safeguards against hunger. Yet the increasing capital costs of this way of producing food exclude ever larger numbers of rural people abroad as well as in the United States from a livelihood and push the price of food beyond the means of those who most need it.

This system of agriculture has been in operation no more than twenty-five years in the industrial countries, yet it is being exported as the sure, indeed, the only, answer for the entire world. That is an incredibly risk proposition, however you look at it.

We have learned that real food security simply cannot be measured in production figures. Production figures may well go up while the majority are getting less of the food they need. Food security must be measured by how close a country is to achieving sound nutrition for all. It must also be measured in how reliable, how resilient, and how self-contained the agricultural system is. On each of those counts the Green Revolution approach means less food security for us all.

14 : The Mechanization of Farming

Of course being a primitive Luddite – against all machinery per se – is absurd. But in countries with an abundant potential labour supply but limited land, productivity per *acre* is what counts. And increasing productivity per acre is often not a matter of a 'modern' machine but of intensive and careful farming by people who have a living stake in the production. According to an International Rice Research Institute (IRRI) study of lowland rice farming, there is no significant difference in yields between farms using a tractor and those using a water buffalo. Even more striking was the conclusion that in Japan, in 1960, highly mechanized farms had no higher yields than those farmed with a hoe. (And no one has ever accused the IRRI of romanticizing the hoe!) The striking rise in rice yields in agrarian-reform Japan before 1960 was not due to mechanization but in part to the small farmers' use of improved seeds, fertilizer, water pumps, better animal-drawn ploughs and harrows, and simple revolving weeders and pedal threshers. This is hardly high technology – but it worked.[1]

Proponents of large-scale mechanization have one case, however, that they feel is airtight. The faster growing seeds of the Green Revolution make it possible for two and sometimes more crops to be grown successively in the same field in one year. Those promoting tractors and harvesters claim there is often a labour bottleneck during planting and harvesting time due to the extra work required to get each crop planted and harvested quickly so that the next one can be planted.

But who is defining the term 'bottleneck'? A bottleneck to a landlord may mean that time of year when he has to pay higher wages because the greater demand for labour gives labourers some bargaining power. The same period the landlord calls a bottleneck may be the time of year the labourer depends on to earn the extra rupees or pesos to survive throughout the rest of the year, when jobs are scarce and wages even lower.

In any case, large-scale mechanization is not the only solution to the problem of peak periods of labour needs. Small-scale improved techniques can help, as we will show below. Moreover, the need for labour can be spread more evenly throughout the year by, for instance, improving irrigation facilities to make planting less dependent on weather and staggering harvests by using seed varieties and crops of varying maturation periods.[2]

Light industry and services can also be integrated into the life of the countryside, an approach that has been successful in countries as different as Egypt and China. In many Chinese rural communes as much as 30 per cent of the population is not directly employed in agriculture but in local small-scale industry. This group represents a critical reserve labour force to help plant or harvest a crop. On the other hand, once the peak work is over, these workers are not unemployed but return to their factories and service industries. Such a plan works in China because few people look down on farming and nearly everyone has practical experience in the fields.

What must be kept in mind in all discussions of mechanization is that 'labour-saving' to the rural entrepreneur means displacing labourers from their jobs, thereby saving on his labour costs.

The Mechanization of Farming

Large landowners say that the only way they can make their new machines pay off is to reduce per acre cost by expanding their acreage. As we have already seen, expansion by the large-holders forces more and more tenants and small farmers off the land, thereby creating greater numbers of landless in search of farm work. Simultaneously, however, the machines drastically decrease the number and length of jobs available. A tractor cuts to a fifth the number of workers needed to prepare the same field with a bullock-drawn plough. The same is true of a mechanical reaper compared to a hand scythe.[3]

The net result in the Pakistani Punjab, for example, is that the amount of human labour required in the fields is 50 per cent less than in the premechanization period only a few years ago. An analysis of the trend in India concluded that 'the introduction of mechanical harvesting will eventually result in an overall decrease of about 90 million man-days of employment in the Punjab, most of it for day labourers.'[4] Labour-saving mechanization is good for the society at large only when it means saving workers from unnecessarily arduous labour and when a genuine economic evolution ensures employment for anyone displaced in other sectors of the economy.

More Appropriate Technology

Clearly large-scale mechanization is not necessary to increase production. On the other hand, technological improvements are possible that can increase production per acre, make work easier, and yet do not displace labourers as do US-style machines. Contrast, for example, a 100 horsepower tractor and a 10 horsepower rotary cultivator. A rotary cultivator is affordable and usable by small farmers; a tractor is not. While a 100 horsepower tractor *replaces* human labour, a rotary cultivator *complements* human labour.

What is needed, are machines that both make work less arduous and increase the need for human labour instead of replacing it: not a different *level* of technology but a different *kind* of technology. One that raises production while usefully involving *more* people in the production process.

The irony is that the Green Revolution seeds could have been part of such an approach. The new seeds and their need for greater care and greater application of fertilizer have the potential to create more jobs. But in most countries the forces that started the Green Revolution also initiated a process of mechanization that reduced employment. In Colombia an estimate was made of the labour requirements of modernization using high response seeds, more fertilizer, greater care in planting, and so on. *Without* mechanization these improvements would require 45 per cent more human labour per acre. With mechanization, 34 per cent *less* labour would be required.[5]

The potential for greater employment with the High Response Varieties (HRVs) is due to several factors. We have already noted that the generally faster-maturing varieties allow farmers to plant more than one crop each year – thereby increasing the need for human labour and the need to speed up all operations. But speeding up operations would not have to mean large-scale mechanization. Reducing seed bed preparation time can be accomplished by a mouldhard plough (a simple wedge-shaped instrument) and a modern harrow (an implement for breaking up the earth resembling a giant comb), that do the job in one-fifteenth the time needed using the traditional plough and plank method.[6] Threshing by hand may take too long to accommodate multiple cropping. Large-scale machines, however, are not required. A simple thresher can reduce the job from a month to only several days, making double cropping possible. (Machines do not always speed things up. On some rice fields, Chinese farmers have discovered they can squeeze in three crops if an entire team joins in to plant intensively by hand rather than relying on the slower-going rice-planting machines.)

Moreover, the introduction of certain simple machines can actually increase labour input. The rotary weeder is one example. The new seeds, with their high-response potential, make weeding even more worthwhile. And, precisely because the rotary weeder is more efficient, it makes more sense to put more labour weeding with it.[7]

We do not want to give you the impression that we are talking only of technologies recently dreamed up in some alternative technology research centre. Pascal de Pury, an indefatigable agronomist with years of experience in Africa and now working with the World Council of Churches on appropriate technology, told us that often such technology turns out to be rediscoveries of a people's traditional practices that Western arrogance caused them to be ashamed of. Over and over again he finds peasant cultures that had refined and adapted techniques over centuries to be losing them in our times. What stands to be irretrievably lost is not the quaintness of 'cultural diversity' but successful, productive techniques uniquely suited to local conditions and, by definition, controllable by the people. They will be lost if elites in these countries continue, indeed encouraged by foreign aid, to import machines in order to increase their profit margins.

The hallmark of techniques that grow out of the experience of the people is that they can be made by the people themselves. There is simply no need to depend on the transfer of technology. These basic agricultural techniques are not of complicated design. Tubewells, simple diesel engines, animal-powered ploughs and seed drills can all be manufactured at the local level by workers without the need for heavy capital equipment. For example, in the city of Daska, in the Pakistani Punjab, more than 100 small factories produce diesel engines principally from local materials.[8] In Pakistan, as in most other underdeveloped countries, this is the exception. In China it has been the rule. As mentioned earlier, each commune houses some light industry, often more like a workshop than a factory, to service agriculture. One example is the low cost pump, locally invented in 1962 through the stimulus of the *withdrawal* of Soviet technicians. It costs one-eighth as much as the Russian equipment previously used and is manufactured in thousands of rural communes.

The Forces Behind Large-Scale Mechanization

If large-scale foreign technology is not necessary to increase production, why is it being increasingly imported into underdeveloped countries? To answer that question we first have to understand *who* is introducing the machines. Mechanization is fully the business of the large landholders. The 4 per cent of Indian farmers with holdings of more than 25 acres make up 96 per cent of tractor owners in India.[9] With the breakdown of the traditional ties that have held agrarian societies together, large landholders are eager to be rid of all tenants so that they might retain a greater share of the profits. Mechanization gives them the way. Rhetoric about the efficiency of mechanization gives them the rationale.

Large landholders have seen mechanization as a way to escape minimum wage requirements, such as the Agricultural Minimum Wages Act in Kerala, India. Studies of agricultural modernization in India reveal a major reason for rapid 'tractorization' in the late 1960s was not increased efficiency but the opportunity to get rid of tenants. Getting rid of tenants is attractive to a landlord threatened by land-reform legislation that would give land to those who till it, that is, to his tenants.

Mechanization makes it possible for wealthier farmers to increase further their cultivated holdings. As long as a farm relies on labourers, there are limits to the size of the holding that a landowner can efficiently oversee. But machines can make it possible to farm land of virtually any size. Moreover, machines are more easily controlled than human beings. Landlords do not have to worry about rice being taken out of the fields to feed the hungry family of a tractor.

Who else gains from the spread of large-scale technology around the world? The people who manufacture it, of course. As Green Revolution commentator Lester Brown put it in *Seeds of Change*, 'the multinational corporation has a vested interest in the agricultural revolution along with the poor countries themselves.'[10] The thought has not been wasted on multinational agribusiness, as we found on our visits to such Green Revolution areas as northwest Mexico.

The giant agribusiness firms, their markets at home becoming saturated, began to push in the 1960s for new markets, especially in the underdeveloped countries. During the period 1968 to 1975, International Harvester built up its sales outside North America from less than one fifth to almost one third of total sales and John Deere's sales overseas jumped from 16 per cent to 23 per cent of its total. Massey-Ferguson, a farm machinery giant with head-quarters in Canada, was first to see the real growth potential abroad; 70 per cent of its sales are now outside North America.[11]

This rapid expansion has not been without the help of powerful friends. The governments of industrial countries, directly and through international lending agencies such as the World Bank, provide foreign agricultural assistance mostly in the form of credits to import machinery.

Both the United States government and the World Bank have given large loans to Pakistan for farm mechanization. The Bank has given similar loans to India, the Philippines, and Sri Lanka. In 1966, when a World Bank loan to the Philippines made cheap credit available for farm mechanization, tractor sales soared.[12] Although the Bank, observes Oxford development economist Keith Griffin, claims to be 'having second thoughts about this policy . . . the Agricultural Projects Department of the Bank remains firmly pro-tractor.'[13]

As with the problems of protecting plants from pests, the United Nations Food and Agriculture Organization, rather than help develop appropriate alternatives, is becoming a broker be-tween underdeveloped countries and multinational farm machinery firms. Its advisory Farm Mechanization Working Group includes Caterpillar Tractor, John Deere, Fiat, FMC, Massey-Ferguson, Mitsui, British Petroleum, and Shell. The FAO has joined with Massey-Ferguson to set up in Colombia the School of Agricultural Mechanization for all of Spanish-speaking Latin America. It will not take a conscious conspiracy for such a prestigious institution to overdose Latin America's rural societies with machines.

In many underdeveloped countries the value of domestic cur-rency in relation to foreign currency is kept artificially high to promote certain imports. Agricultural machinery brought from abroad is thus often 'cheaper' than it otherwise might be. This policy and other forms of subsidization in countries like Pakistan ended up making the same American tractor cost one half of what it would in Iowa, calculated in terms of wheat. In the late 1960s, the Indian government subsidized mechanization so heavily through cheap credit that in the Ludhiana district of the Punjab farmers with even less than 15 acres were encouraged to buy tractors. This was in spite of the fact that even the principal suppliers of farm machinery thought that at least 25 to 30 acres were needed to make the tractors economical.[14] The government of Iran encouraged large, mechanized farming by exempting those farms that mechanized from the Land Reform Act.[15]

Those who promote large-scale mechanization as the answer for underdeveloped countries like to throw out this challenge: 'Look at China,' they say. 'Chinese agriculture is now starting to mechanize in a big way. Isn't this a lesson for the rest of the Third World?'

This view is correct in one sense: There is an important lesson here. It is not, however, that large-scale mechanization is the answer for agriculture in the underdeveloped countries. The lesson is that mechanization is itself not the issue at all. The issue is *who* owns the machines.

Where the workers themselves own the machines, as in China, mechanization will proceed because the workers naturally wish to lighten the backbreaking toil of field labour. In China the goal is to eliminate the 'three bendings' – pulling weeds, transplanting seedlings, and harvesting. The result of mechanization will be a better life for the farmers, not unemployment. In China farm mechanization is a high priority in part because labour is needed to expand the cultivated area and to upgrade and expand the irrigation system. Farm mechanization that frees labour for such other vital work contributes to Chinese society as a whole, not to private gain. Moreover, the goal of farm mechanization must be understood in the Chinese context. By 1980, the Chinese plan to have a tractor density of one per 125 acres compared, for example, to one tractor for every 2.5 acres in Japan.[16]

Cuba now has the greatest tractor density of any country in Latin America. Yet no one is unemployed. The story of loading sugar freighters in Cuba is instructive. Traditionally Cuban raw sugar was loaded into freighters by labourers lugging a sack at a time on their backs up a gangplank and into the hold. It took over a month to fill a ship. The sugar companies tried to mechanize the operation (with conveyor belts) but they were continually thwarted by organized workers who knew that their very lives depended on keeping the machines out. But once the Cuban government expanded other sectors of the economy and guaranteed everyone a productive job, the sugar terminals were quickly mechanized. Now a ship is loaded in a little over 24 hours. Nobody objected when the conveyor belts came in; no one ever *wanted* a life of carrying sugar sacks up and down a gangplank. Cuba is also rapidly mechanizing the cutting of sugar cane, one of the most gruelling of all agricultural jobs (40 per cent of the 1979 harvest; up from one per cent in 1970). Rather than creating masses of unemployed, it will speed the development of Cuba by releasing workers for other jobs important to the economy.

The Best Appropriate Technology: A Democratic Economy.

Just as we cannot say that all large-scale mechanization is necessarily bad, neither can we say that appropriate technology itself needn't necessarily be the anwer. Even the 'right' technology cannot be imposed nor is it likely to do much good in the 'wrong' society.

Contrast, for example, the impact of biogas technology in India and China. Biogasification is a relatively simple method of fermenting organic raw materials such as crop residues and manure to produce both fuel and fertilizer. A small scale biogas plant can be built from local materials. Since the 1940s India has been developing cow-dung biogas plants, acclaimed widely as a truly 'appropriate technology'. But, in the highly stratified economic reality of rural India, this apparently beneficial technology has created even greater problems for the poorer groups, according to *New Scientist* writer, Joseph Hanlon.[17]

First, even the smallest plants require a significant investment and the dung from two cows. Thus only well-off farmers who have at least two cows and some capital to invest now control the biogas. Furthermore, the dung, which once was free, now has cash value. In areas where biogas plants operate, landless labourers can no longer pick it off the road and use it for fuel. And since the landless and other poor villagers are in no position to buy biogas, they end up with no fuel at all. In other words, their position is worsened by the introduction of biogas plants, according to A. K. N. Reddy, governor of the appropriate technology unit at the Indian Institute of Science, Bangladore.

What about biogas in China? Many visitors to China have noted the growing use of biogas in the countryside, now providing fuel and lighting for 17 million commune peasants in Szechwan, China's most populated province. In China, the biogas benefits all members of the community because plants are owned and operated collectively.

The largely methane gas produced by China's more than 4 million biogas pits is used for cooking, lighting and running farm machinery. A member of one commune noted, 'It takes only 20 minutes to cook a meal for my family of seven using marsh gas (the Chinese term for biogas). Unlike firewood or coal, marsh gas does not make the kitchen walls grimy and it has no smoke or smell'.[18] The Chinese also note that the sealed biogas pits have helped significantly reduce the incidence of parasitic diseases and eliminated breeding grounds for flies and mosquitoes.

The contrast between biogas technology in these two countries suggests that even technology theoretically appropriate to the needs of the people will *not* necessarily serve those needs. It can even exacerbate social inequalities unless a prior redistribution of social power has created structures in which all share in the control over and the use of the new technology.

Moreover, unless they really grasp the truth that any technology is appropriate only if it advances the poorest groups, many people might be taken in by the claim of multinational firms that they now have converted to 'appropriate technology.' Firestone-India provides a good example of what we mean. In 1976 the Company announced a solid rubber tyre and steel wheel that they said would increase the carrying capacity of India's 13 million bullock carts by 50 per cent. Sounds great. But there are two snags. At a price of 60 per cent more than the conventional wooden wheel, Firestone-India's wheel is beyond the means of the poor peasant. Moreover, the new wheel will put traditional wheel makers out of business. When asked why the company was introducing the new wheel, the factory director explained that the motivation was the current glut in the natural rubber market. 'Rubber tyred wheels on bullock carts will provide a large outlet for this surplus rubber.'

The source of this account, Joseph Hanlon, noted as he travelled across India: 'There is no shortage of technology, nor even of 'appropriate' technology . . . [But] the power and profits remain with those who have always had them and who have been able to exploit the new technologies as they did the old.'[19]

To repeat: even the 'right' technology cannot be imposed nor is it likely to do much good in the 'wrong' society. The truly right technology, whether it be capital- or labour-intensive, will only be the product of a profound social restructuring in which those who are doing the work decide what is right for them.

We need redistribution not of wealth but of the technology possessed by the industrial world. . . . The receiver of technology must be willing to change his way of life, and like it or not, he may have to cooperate closely with the donor of that technology during a transition training period of years. Some Third Worlders may term this 'neocolonialism,' and they are welcome to their opinions. Others might call it 'mutually beneficial cooperation.'

> Ray Vicker, *Wall St. Journal* London bureau chief, in
> *This Hungry World*

In Telukpinang, 60 miles south of Jakarta, as in other parts of Indonesia, the mill has taken over work traditionally done by women by hand – the threshing and hulling of rice stalks. Rice mills are estimated to have eliminated a million or more jobs in the fields of Java alone, the principal Indonesian island.

He [the landlord] recalled that he used to employ two women, sometimes three or four, giving them two litres of rice for every 10 they produced. But now, he said, he keeps the entire crop, paying those who help him the equivalent of about 60 cents a day plus lunch.

The mill is owned by a major general in the Indonesian army who lives in a Jakarta suburb. The villagers asked that his name not be disclosed since they fear his power.

> *New York Times*, November 30, 1975

Some past attempts to apply mechanization have also found resistance in less developed countries – especially in areas with high unemployment and a seemingly unlimited supply of low-cost labour . . . These have been temporary setbacks.

> Arthur J. Olsen, Vice-President, FMC Corporation,
> speech at 'Feeding the World's Hungry'
> Conference, 1974

PART V   THE INEFFICIENCY OF INEQUALITY

15 The Productivity of Large and Small Farms

Studies from all over the world show that contrary to popular assumption, the small farmer in most cases produces more per unit of land than the large farmer. Here are just a few examples:

- The value of output per acre in India is more than one-third higher on the smallest farms than on the larger farms.[1]
- In Thailand plots of two to four acres produce almost 60 per cent more rice per acre than farms of 140 acres and more.[2]
- In Taiwan net income per acre of farms with less than one and a quarter acres is nearly twice that of farms over five acres.[3]
- The World Bank reports an analysis of the differences in the value of output on large and small farms in Argentina, Brazil, Chile, Colombia, Ecuador, and Guatemala. The conclusion? The small farms were three to fourteen times more productive per acre than the large farms.[4]

Such comparisons go a long way toward explaining the low productivity of agriculture in underdeveloped countries when you bear in mind that, according to a study of 83 countries, only 3 per cent of all the landowners control a staggering 80 per cent of all farmland.[5] The point is that the largest landholders control most of the farmland, yet studies from all over the world show that they are the least productive.

To explain the higher productivity of the small farmer, one need not romanticize the peasant. Peasant farmers get more out of their land precisely because they need to survive on the meagre resources allowed to them. Studies show that smallholders plant more carefully than a machine would, mix and rotate complementary crops, choose a combination of cultivation and livestock that is labour-intensive and, above all, work their perceptibly limited resources (especially themselves) to the fullest. Farming for the peasant family is not an abstract calculation of profit to be weighed against other investments. It is a matter of life and death.

As we showed in focusing on Bangladesh early in the book, small farmers often cannot get ahead more because their initiatives are actively obstructed by the landed elite, threatened by any advance that would make the village's small farmers less dependent on them.

Moreover, necessities such as fertilizer and water do not reach small farmers because they have neither the cash nor the credit to buy them. Quite often loans from government agencies stipulate a minimum holding that cuts out the small farmer. In Pakistan, for example, to get a loan for a tubewell from the Agricultural Development Bank, a peasant must have at least 12.5 acres. This single stipulation excludes over 80 per cent of Pakistan's farmers.[6] One estimate is that only about 5 per cent of Africa's farmers have access to institutional credit – and it is not hard to guess which 5 per cent![7]

Sudhir Sen, Indian economist and commentator on the Green Revolution, has estimated that roughly one half of India's small farmers lack any recorded right to the land, without which they are unable to obtain crop loans from credit institutions.[8] Perhaps even more important, small farmers are reluctant to use their land for loan collateral anyway. Poor farmers quite sensibly decide that they do not want to risk losing their land.

Largely excluded from institutional credit, smallholders are left dependent on private moneylenders and merchants who charge usurious rates of interest, ranging from 50 per cent to 200 per cent. In one area of the Philippines 15 per cent of the borrowers paid an interest rate of over 200 per cent while 20 per cent of the borrowers paid only 16 per cent. Moreover, merchant-creditors can increase the interest by underpricing farm products used to repay loans and overpricing the goods that debtors buy from them.[9] By contrast, the large operator may pay no interest, or even come out ahead by borrowing money. When the nominal rates of interest on credit available to large operators from commercial institutions are adjusted for inflation, the real rate of interest is often negative.[10]

Obligations of Moneylenders and Landlords

Earlier we described the debt bondage that keeps so many peasant farmers in a form of perpetual vassalage. As agricultural economist Keith Griffin so aptly puts it, 'The *campesinos* of Latin America have suffered not from insecurity of tenure but from excessively secure tenure.' Debt bondage, he points out, has been used to tie peasants to the land to assure landowners that labour would be available, particularly in labour-scarce economies in Latin America.[11] What is the impact on production? Inevitably, motivation to increase production is stifled because the trapped peasants know that higher yields will never benefit them, only the landowner or moneylender. 'The constantly indebted peasant is virtually bound by contract to sell his produce at prices set by the private moneylender-cum-trader, as no effective marketing co-operatives exist to safeguard his interests,' explain Erich and Charlotte Jacoby in their classic *Man and Land*.[12] Debt bondage can mean that the peasant farmer must work off the debt by tending the fields of the creditor. The peasant's own plot then suffers neglect. Unable to work his land adequately, the peasant farmer often has no choice but to give it up.

Consider sharecroppers who represent a significant portion of the rural population in many underdeveloped countries. Although in many cases they must provide all of the inputs, they get only a share of the crop. Why then make the investments necessary to increase production? In Bangladesh, while owner-cultivators need the prospect of a 2 to 1 advantage in order to take the risk of adopting a new technology, sharecroppers need the prospect of a 4 to 1 advantage since they get only half the crop.[13]

Insecure tenancies result in inefficiencies. Tenants, in constant indebtedness and unsure of whether or not they will be on the same plot next year, can hardly be expected to protect the soil fertility by rotating crops and leaving fields fallow.

Without a certain minimum landholding, security of tenure, credit at a reasonable rate, and control over what is produced, farmers make the realistic assessment that it is not in their best interest to buy inputs to increase production or to take steps to preserve the soil fertility. Thus it is not the alleged 'backwardness' of the peasant farmers that keeps them from buying fertilizer and other modern inputs but hard economic sense.

The Waste of Wealth

Continuing to pin hopes for genuine development on the contribution of the large landowners overlooks another critical question: What happens to the profit made by the large landowner? Is this profit as likely to be productively invested in agriculture as would the same profit spread among many smaller farmers or collectively controlled?

Concentrating the profits from agricultural modernization into a few hands has meant that much of what might have been returned to agricultural improvements goes instead for luxury items to satisfy the conspicuous consumption impulse of the rural *nouveaux riches*. Around the world the new agricultural entrepreneurs can be found 'investing' surplus profits in tourist resorts, bars, taxi fleets, movie houses and travel agencies.

On our research visits to the 'Green Revolution' areas of Mexico we found obviously frivolous expenditures by a few amid the equally obvious poverty of the majority: tasteless, sprawling ranch-style houses, swimming pools, multiple imported luxury automobiles, periodic shopping sprees across the border, Las Vegas junkets, private planes, and children in American boarding schools.

Large farmers are often the *least* reliable credit recipients. The World Bank reports that large farmers actually have *poorer* repayment records than small farmers in countries as diverse as Bangladesh, Colombia, Costa Rica, and Ethiopia.[14] Similarly, the US Department of Agriculture tells us that rates of delinquency and foreclosure in the United States are greater on big loans for large-scale farm units than on smaller loans for family farms.[15]

Another factor to weigh is the literal waste of valuable land by large landholding interests. Plantations have always been noted for acquiring more land than they would ever use. But a recent study of land use in Central America tells us that the historic pattern holds true today: farmers who own up to 10 acres cultivate 72 per cent of their land, but farmers with over 86 acres cultivate only 14 per cent of their land. They use 49 per cent for pasture, and leave 37 per cent idle.[16] Similarly a 1968 study of Ecuador showed that farmers with less than 25 acres farmed about 80 per cent of their land while the largest farmers with more than 2500 acres generally cultivated little more than a quarter of their land.[17] Since large landowners are the *most* wasteful of the land, what makes people now believe that they are the last best hope for agricultural development?

Inequality Thwarts Co-operation

The motivation of people to co-operate toward a common goal is ultimately what all development depends upon. But a social system that gives preferential access to land, agricultural inputs, and government programmes to a few, undercuts any possibility for co-operation and shared learning. It was thought, for example, that focusing the new seeds and other inputs on the large farmer would have such a powerful 'demonstration effect' that all the smaller producers would seek to emulate the large landholder. The much-touted demonstration effect has been just the opposite of that intended. The simple fact that the large landowner is successful with the new approach is often enough to convince the smallholder that he himself could *not* be.

Finally, the suggestion that we simply cannot afford greater equality if we want to increase production ignores the most fundamental brake on production within a market system: the lack of buyers with the cash to pay for the increased production. One too often forgets that hunger alone is not enough to stimulate production in a market system. Only paying customers stimulate production and in most market economies today, their number is growing very slowly, if at all.

The suggestion implies that 'a little inequality is a good thing' or at least a necessary evil. In times of supposed scarcity it becomes even easier to accept the idea that we should turn to those who are 'on top.' The facts have, however, forced us to conclude that this is exactly the wrong approach. The very power of the large landowners makes them less compelled to try to increase production, especially of locally needed food; they divert resources out of agriculture into unnecessary consumption and unproductive investments; they underutilize the land; and finally, the constraints poverty places on motivation and consumption are the greatest blocks to increased production. Economic justice and economic progress are inseparable.

The logical conclusion to our argument on the efficiency of the small farmer would be to channel more credit, equipment, seeds, fertilizers and irrigation to them. But to focus on the small farmer is to miss entirely a large portion – in many countries 70 to 90 per cent – of the rural labour force. A recent study from Cornell University[18] concludes that the landless and near landless constitute a majority of the rural labour force in Asia, approaching 90 per cent in Java, Bangladesh, and Pakistan. In Latin America the landless and near-landless make up a majority in every country studied, exceeding 80 per cent in Bolivia, El Salvador, Guatemala, and the Dominican Republic.

Nor should one make the mistake of believing that the small farm is inherently more productive than the large. We have found that the size of the parcel of land matters less than the relationship of the people to it.

Small farms can be very productive – as in Japan – where the people working the land know that the productivity will benefit them. And there can be exactly the opposite: small farms with low productivity when credit, debt, and tenancy arrangements deny those who work the fields the fruits of their labours.

Likewise with large farming units. They can be productive where those working the land know that their labour will benefit them. Thai Binh in North Vietnam is one example. Since 1965 a single co-operative involving 4,000 people produces rice, small animals, such as ducks and geese, as well as fish in over 100 acres of village-controlled fish ponds. Harvesting two or even three rice crops annually, Thai Binh can produce almost 80 per cent more than the annual production of the less-than-five acre plot characteristic of India, for example. But large units are not necessarily productive. We have just documented the inefficiencies of many privately owned, largeholder operations. Exchange these private landowners for antidemocratic bureaucrats and productivity will still remain low, as developments in Soviet agriculture have amply demonstrated.

16: Land Reform versus Production?

Historically, genuine land reforms have led to greater agricultural production because they have redressed the 'inefficiencies of inequality' that thwart production – those just discussed. To illustrate the point we'll focus on the actual post-reform experiences in Vietnam, China, Cuba, and Portugal.

In 1945, over half of the farmland in Vietnam was held not by peasants but by landlords and French colonists. The rents they extracted from the peasants amounted to as much as three-quarters of the harvest. After the defeat of the French in 1954, land reform in North Vietnam was immediately undertaken. By the end of 1957, about 45 per cent of the North's arable land had been redistributed, with 77 per cent of the rural households benefiting.[1]

Thoroughly distributing control over resources helped to make possible production advances even during the height of the war with the United States. According to the FAO's Sixth Report on Land Reform, yields in North Vietnam were going up and irrigation was extended from 20 per cent of the cultivated area in the mid-fifties to nearly 60 per cent in the mid-sixties. Between 1960 and 1970, yields of rice went up 20 per cent and other crops by 50 per cent.[2]

China also demonstrates that national production advances follow once land reform has made control over the land more equal and democratic. After having progressed through four stages since the initiation of reforms in 1950, the ownership of land in China is vested in the production brigade, equal to one large village or several smaller ones. In practice, the production brigade turns over the land for cultivation to the village labour force, called the production team. Except where large tractors or combine harvesters are involved, the village production team is responsible for its own field management and accounting. Income is distributed according to a mutually agreed upon work-point system, and everyone is assured of the basic foodgrains and other essential items.

The share of production appropriated by the central government in taxes is small – only one to seven per cent. These taxes are fixed rates based upon the income expected, considering the soil and climatic conditions of the commune. A commune with especially fertile land would have to allocate seven per cent of its production to the central government, whereas a commune with poor natural resources like the famed Tachai would have to contribute only one per cent. This percentage does *not* rise even if the commune prospers beyond the expectations based on its natural endowment.[3] The greater the production, therefore, the greater the benefits to those who work the fields.

China's national production figures reflect these changes. By 1975 China was producing over 1700 pounds of grain per acre, 60 per cent above corresponding per acre production in India[4] and almost double the yield per acre in China before the Revolution. According to Cornell's China watcher Dr Benedict Stavis, compared to India, China feeds 50 per cent more people, 20 per cent better with 30 per cent less cultivated land (comparing per capita figures for grains and bean-type crops.) Moreover, precisely because of China's far greater equality of access to productive resources, its per capita statistics much more accurately reflect the reality of food distribution.

The experience of land reform in Cuba is also instructive.[5] It demonstrates the real post-land reform problems that take time to overcome – the heritage of the old order – as well as the necessity for workers to participate in decision-making in order for production to rise.

Cuba's basic land reform was completed by 1963, having created over 100,000 new independent landowners and having placed 60 per cent of the country's agricultural land in public hands. Some economists studying Cuba have concluded that its agrarian reform 'caused no major drop in production'.[6] Others have pointed to the short term production setbacks as the reorganization of agriculture was taking place.[7] In the years 1963 and 1964, the index of agricultural production dropped to 86 and 93 respectively, as compared to 100 in 1952-56. Although Cuba's overall agricultural progress during the 1960s was disapointing to Cuban planners, we should not lose sight of the fact that compared to levels before the beginning of the Revolution, the production of important foods did rise: by 1971 rice had risen four times, fruit three and one half times, egg production four and one half times, and potatoes by 42 per cent.[8]

Why did Cuba's agriculture progress more slowly than had been hoped during the 1960s?[9] Cubans attempted to rapidly diversify production away from sugar without the necessary skilled human resources, having inherited widespread illiteracy and a large labour force whose only skill was sugar harvesting. Thus investments in agriculture, such as more tractors, were largely wasted. In 1970 only one quarter of the tractor capacity was in use, due to unrepaired breakdowns and administrative failures to get the tractors to where they were needed. The US-imposed trade embargo also cut off the supply of spare parts. Moreover, Cuban agriculture experienced a labour shortage, especially in the gruelling work of cane cutting, as other jobs opened up in the society. Perhaps more critical, during the 1960s decision-making appears to have been overcentralized; thus investments were not based enough on calculations made at a local level.

Cuba, during the 1960s, attempted greater equality through land reform and other means of controlling income differential. Greater equality is certainly one prerequisite for greater productivity, as we have already stated, but Cuba had not yet sufficiently followed through on the second prerequisite; that is, participation in policy decision-making by the Cuban people on a local level.

By the 1970s this had begun to change. Illiteracy had been almost wiped out through a national mobilization. Primary schools were graduating four times more students in 1970 than at the time of the revolution. This basic education was an important ingredient of the more effective organization of work and decentralized participation that began to emerge in the 1970s. Mass organizations – labour unions, farmers' associations, and neighbourhood clubs – widened their roles in the 1970s, not simply to carry out policy but to help formulate it. Although problems still remain in the agricultural sector, the increased participation in decision-making was reflected in increased production. Between 1970 and 1974, non-sugarcane agricultural output grew at an annual rate of 8.4 per cent, surpassing all previous years.

Portugal's recent land reform illustrates still other key productive advances resulting from land redistribution.[10] Following the overthrow of fascism in Portugal in 1974, agricultural labourers seized almost 3 million acres of land held by huge estates in southern Alentejo. The expropriation of these big estates was then legalized by the new constitution. But, in 1977, in violation of the Constitution, the Soares government passed a law dissolving the Collective Units of Production (UCP's) set up by the farm labourers and small farmers on the expropriated land and returning the land to its former owners. In the face of attack by specially-trained police using electric nightsticks, water cannons, machine guns and helicopters, the peasants refused to give up the land. As of mid-1978, the government has abandoned its efforts to disband the UCP's.

Members of the UCP's take their wages out of the sale of produce. Profits are then directed into social benefits such as shops, playgrounds, and daycare facilities by the General Assembly which is made up of all members. Managers of the UCP's are elected.

This spontaneous land redistribution has meant that in two years, acreage actually under cultivation almost tripled in Alentejo. Even more significantly, many new jobs were created in an area previously plagued with chronic unemployment. The number of people fully employed in agriculture jumped fourfold after land reform. The new owners of the land supply 50 per cent of all of Portugal's wheat and one-fifth to one-quarter of the meat for the domestic market.

Studying the actual experience of land reform in countries as different as Vietnam, China, Cuba, and Portugal, one consistent lesson emerges: rather than leading to a fall-off in production, genuine land reform can be a first step in longterm production advances.

Underestimating the Effectiveness of Land Reform

Why do so many believe that land reform undercuts production?
• First, deliberately half-hearted and ineffective land reform laws in countries like the Philippines, Pakistan, and India have obscured the potential productive returns from thoroughgoing land reform of the type carried out in three of the countries just discussed. On pp. 216ff, we describe several features of these fake land reforms.
• Second, most official measures of production commonly include only grain entering the national market. Yet, focusing solely on official production figures may seriously underestimate agricultural advances in societies undergoing genuine agrarian reform. When millions of formerly landless gain control over their own land, there is great likelihood – and FAO officials we queried concur – that a greater proportion of food production is consumed by the people who produce it. Thus it never enters into the national

production figures used, for example, by the United Nations system.

• A third factor causing an underestimation of post-reform gains is that progress is often measured in grain production *alone*. In countries undergoing basic restructuring of control, people realize that they need not live 'by grain alone'. Although, for example, grain production per capita in China went up 19 per cent between 1962 and 1975, this does not convey a complete picture of nutritional improvements according to a report from the US Congressional Research Service of the Library of Congress.[11] People now eat more fruit, meat and vegetables. 'On the average, every Chinese eats half a kilo (just over a pound) of vegetables per day,' the report notes. And the same can be said of Vietnam. Focusing on grain production ignores 'a very important point in the strategy of food self-reliance of the Vietnamese', according to Vietnamese scholar Ngo Vinh Long. Under the French, rice alone occupied over 95 per cent of the cultivated land, but by 1970 over 18 per cent of the land was growing crops other than rice – corn, sweet potatoes, sesame seeds, and fruit.[12]

• A fourth factor reinforcing the myth that land reform equals scarcity is simply our lack of familiarity with any system other than our own. Terms such as 'rationing' are misunderstood. 'Rationing' for most people implies the scarcities of World War Two. When outsiders learn of rationing in Cuba, they assume that there is less food available now – since they never heard of rationing before the revolution. Rationing, however, can best be understood in Cuba as a mechanism for insuring the minimal supply of basic food to all, as well as the means of channelling more food selectively to those with special needs – children, pregnant women, and the elderly. Ordinary Cubans we've spoken with feel that it benefits more people than our rationing system: money.

PART VI THE TRADE GAME

17: Doing What Comes Naturally

One of the most oppressive food myths is that underdeveloped countries can grow only 'tropical crops,' and they should exploit this natural advantage by exporting them.

In reality they can grow an incredible diversity of crops – grains, high-protein legumes, vegetables, and fruits. There is nothing 'natural' about the underdeveloped countries' concentration on a few, largely nonnutritious crops. And there's no 'advantage' either.

Most underdeveloped countries now depend for 50 to 90 per cent of their export earnings on only one or two crops. Bananas in the period 1970-1972 accounted for 58 per cent of the total export earnings of Panama, 48 per cent of Honduras, and 31 per cent of Somalia's.[1] Coffee has become crucially important for eleven countries that depend on it for 25 per cent or more of their foreign earnings. In 1972, coffee brought in 53 per cent of Colombia's foreign exchange; 78 per cent of Burundi's; 50 per cent of Rwanda's; 50 per cent of Ethiopia's; and 61 per cent of Uganda's.[2]

Concentration on a limited number of crops creates vulnerability that characterizes underdeveloped countries. Vulnerability means an inability to control one's own destiny.

In addition to the vulnerability to market changes inherent in being dependent on very few crops, there is the larger question of the overall decline in the value of the agricultural commodities most underdeveloped countries export. In fact, the total loss of foreign exchange earnings to Africa due to falling prices, particularly in agricultural products, in the two decades following World War II *exceeded* all foreign funds invested, loaned, or granted to Africa during the same period.[3] Bananas, the most important fresh fruit in international trade, serve as a good illustration of what this means. The price of bananas has fallen about 30 per cent in the last twenty years while the price of manufactured goods has gone up. In 1960, three tons of bananas could buy a tractor. In 1970, that same tractor costs the equivalent of eleven tons of bananas.[4] (It is quite a treadmill if you have run almost four times as fast just to stay in the same place!)

Unreliable Prices for Export Crops

But as much as the declining export income hurts the economies of underdeveloped countries, fluctuations in price are the real nemesis of economic planning. The high prices of one year can lure economic planners and farmers into continued reliance on a given crop, even to expand production. Wild price swings then wreak havoc with long-term development plans. Not only can prices fluctuate sharply from year to year but from week to week and even from day to day.

The colonizing powers chose those crops that did not require frequent planting. That was all well and good for the colonizer who wanted to minimize dependence on labour. But for those former colonies that now have their entire economies locked into coffee, palm oil, or bananas, the results can be disastrous. A coffee tree takes five years to mature; palm oil trees require three to four years. Likewise, you can't just go in and out of banana production in response to price changes, as an American farmer might with wheat and oats. A banana tree does not reach its full potential until two years after planting and even then the payoff, if any, comes over its next five to twenty years of yields. With cocoa trees you have to sit tight for a decade or more before your first harvest.

What happens then if you are encouraged by high current prices to rush into new coffee planting? By the time your first harvest of such crops is ready you might find the bottom has dropped out of the market. And it probably will have, since producers in your country and others will also have planted to meet the demand at the same time you did. The likely result is over-production once the new trees begin to bear more than the consumers are willing to buy even with a drop in price. (Remember a ten per cent drop in the retail price that General Foods charges you for Maxwell House is likely to represent a far greater price drop for the grower. And still, you probably won't drink more coffee.) There have been several coffee busts. In the Depression coffee prices fell by 80 per cent. The Brazilian government tried unsuccessfully to bolster prices by burning 80 million bags (weighing 132 lbs. each!), or the equivalent of two years' total world consumption.[5]

Speculative activities are a major cause of extreme fluctuations in price. Take the case of cocoa. Most of the raw cocoa exported (about four fifths of the total production is exported raw) is sold through dealers and specialized firms in New York, London, Paris, Amsterdam, and Hamburg on the basis of prices determined by bids and offers on the cocoa futures markets. What causes price swings on the cocoa futures market? Perhaps a meeting of cocoa producers has been called. That alone might be taken as bullish by the hard-core cocoa traders, thus inflating cocoa prices for a period as short as a day or as long as a month.[6] Rumours of a political change in the government of a major cocoa producer or a single report of some obscure cocoa pest can have the same instantaneous effect.

The point is that the range of price fluctuations due, say, to weather-caused variations in supply, are greatly magnified by a small number of people who usually have nothing to do with growing the crop. Their 'business' is gambling. Their interest is in an actively fluctuating fast-changing market, since by playing it correctly one can make money whether prices go up or down. As an official of the Chicago Board of Trade told an agribusiness executives seminar in 1975, 'Stability, gentlemen, is the only thing we can't deal with.' Unlike fluctuations in stock market quotes that have no impact on the earnings of the corporations traded, speculation on the futures market directly hits the producers' earnings and the *predictability* of earnings.

'All Your Eggs in Two Baskets'

What can a national planner in Ghana do given that over half of his country's arable land is now planted with cocoa trees? In the late 1950s when cocoa prices were high, Ghana decided to double its production. Development plans were drawn that counted on the increased foreign exchange earnings. But, as the prices that Ghana had to pay for its imports rose steadily, the price it could get for cocoa seesawed. Up to about $1000 per ton one year and down to less than $400 another; up to $1000 again and down to less than $600 later.[7] The overall decline from the mid-fifties peak has been estimated at 80 per cent.[8] You can imagine what became of Ghana's development scheme. Income from sisal has been no more reliable. Tanzania's first five-year plan anticipated a minimum world sisal price of 90 pounds. Soon after, the price dropped to 60 pounds. In late 1976, Cuba announced that the collapse of sugar prices (from 64 cents to 6 cents a pound in eighteen months) would make it necessary to revamp its five-year development plan.

Several years ago the government of Malaysia, in one of the most ambitious settlement schemes ever undertaken in Asia, transformed hundreds of thousands of acres of jungle into new settlements growing oil palm and rubber for export. It seemed to work. The settlers were able to improve their homes, buy some consumer items, and even save for their children's education. Then, in 1974, the entire picture changed. Recession in the industrial countries sent the price of rubber and palm oil plummeting. With no alternative crop to rely on, settlers' incomes also dropped sharply. Today none of the newly cleared land is being settled. A member of the Malaysian parliament observed that: 'All our land-development eggs have been put in two baskets—rubber and palm oil. There is no diversification, we grow too little of our own food. Everything is for cash, and when the world prices that we do not control drop, it is our people who suffer.'[9]

In addition to the vulnerability built into reliance on slow-maturing crops with highly unstable prices, the choice of crops handed down by the original colonizers contains another limitation. Many are commodities that appear to be reaching the saturation point among consumers. No matter how affluent the consumers or how low the prices drop, consumers seem to eat or drink only so much of products like cocoa, coffee, and bananas.

The 'Rewards' of Export Agriculture

The revenue from the agricultural exports of underdeveloped countries kept pace with the cost of their mounting food imports from the industrial countries – in grain alone, up now to over 50 million tons a year. Ironically, the prices of the crops sold predominantly by the industrial countries, crops like grains and soybeans, have risen much faster than the prices of the commodities exported by the underdeveloped countries.

What was originally designed by colonialists as a system to transfer wealth *out* of subjugated countries is still promoted by many as the only road to development for those very same countries. Oddly enough, most observers do not see or do not wish to see a contradiction. But the contradiction is undeniable. Today export agriculture, dominating the economies of underdeveloped countries, serves foreign interests in the same way it has for hundreds of years. As such, how could it ever be thought of as the basis for self-determined development?

18 : The Losers

Peasant producers or labourers have little to gain from increased agricultural export earnings of their country, partly because so little of the export price reaches them to begin with. Typically, in Guatemala, where 75 per cent of all children under the age of five are underfed, migrant workers on the coffee plantations earn approximately $1 a day.[1] Like many other commodities, coffee boomed in 1973. Brazil's earnings shot up to $1,343,048,000. How much of that went to a worker on a typical coffee estate? About $58 a month. (Yet in 'coffeeland' itself it takes $1.66 to buy a single pound of roasted coffee.) In 1975, Sri Lanka's tea exports amounted to $860 million and were produced by 650,000 workers on recently nationalized plantations. The maximum a male worker could earn was $14 a month; a woman, $11.40.[2]

In Mali, peasants are contracted to grow peanuts by a French multinational firm. They contribute the land and their labour and yet receive only the same amount per pound of peanuts as the profit per pound made by the corporation that merely sells the peanuts abroad.[3] The same pattern exists for peasants growing peanuts in Senegal. One Senegalese official reported that the net profit to the state exceeds the total amount the state co-operatives pay to the producers of peanuts.

A slight increase in income, that peasant farmers in underdeveloped countries might acquire from a rising world price for their commodity, has to be weighted against the increased threat of displacement by land-grabbing commercial farmers or corporations that see the higher prices as new grounds for profit.

Increases in the world price for a commodity may not translate into an increase in the price paid to peasant producers. A recent United Nations report on the 'least developed countries' notes that while international coffee prices have advanced 58 per cent from 1968 to 1973, producer prices in Rwanda have remained fixed.[4]

In fact, an increase in the world price for a commodity might actually mean less income for the plantation worker or the peasant producer. When the world price for peanuts went up in 1968-1969, the Senegalese government's price to farmers actually fell.[5] In the

Ivory Coast the pattern is the same: between 1960 and 1971 the export price rose 11 per cent while the price paid to producers dropped 6 per cent.[6] When the price of sugar on the world market increased severalfold a few years ago, the real wage of a cane cutter in the Dominican Republic fell to less than it was 10 years earlier; even more significantly, it was not enough to buy an adequate amount of food.

Government policy makers everywhere push for greater production whenever the world's price for an exported commodity goes up. What at first surprised us, however, is that some government marketing boards in Africa do so by paying peasant producers *less* for each unit produced. The reasoning is that the peasants will then have to produce even more just to maintain their incomes at the same level.

Moreover, in an economy dominated by the earnings of a single export commodity, a sudden international price boom for that commodity can trigger domestic inflation that will inevitably hurt the poor. During the 1977-1978 period of unprecedented cocoa earnings in Ghana, for example, the price of a box of sugar shot up to $7.00 and a yam up to $4.00. Tomatoes, used in all traditional dishes for the last 500 years, were going for $1.00 each and were often unattainable.

Export crop production often directly undermines the local food supply. Not only does it monopolize the best land, but the demands of export crop production can interfere with the cultivation of food.

In Kenya, for instance, much effort was put into the production of a more productive variety of cotton. The seed strain finally developed was more productive but unfortunately less hardy. Food crops could no longer be planted in the same field with cotton, as was the tradition; the new cotton could not take the competition. So while cotton exports have gone up, we wonder what has been the impact on the diets of the people. In Upper Volta's drier regions the planting season is short. Where farmers are obliged by the government to grow a certain acreage of cotton, they have to find a crop that can be planted later but can still be squeezed into the planting season. Sorghum and millet, the traditional food crops, just cannot fit this schedule, but cassava, a much less nutritious food, will. Low-nutrition cassava is also taking the place of more nutritious food crops in Tanzania because of the need for labour in tobacco production during certain seasons; cassava requires less labour than other food crops.[7] Agricultural economist Ingrid Palmer has also noted an alarming increase in per capita cassava output in Latin America.[8]

World Bank rural economist Uma Lele writes of the substantial substitution of food crops with cash crops such as cotton, tea, and tobacco in Kenya and Tanzania. In one decade the acreage per family planted in tea increased more than two and a half times in Kenya. In Tanzania cotton acreage per family increased fivefold. Government resources allocated to developing agricultural extension techniques and incentive systems for cash crops have rarely been transferred to the production of traditional food crops. And the drop in food production in the cash-crop areas of those countries has not been matched by expansion elsewhere of food crops.[9]

In an effort to make Brazil a leading soybean exporter, soya production there has massively displaced the cultivation of black beans, the traditional staple of the people. By October 1976, stores serving Rio de Janeiro's poor simply ran out of black beans. In desperation the poor rioted, only to be suppressed by the police. Scarce black beans were available only on the black market. To buy one pound, however, would require a half day's labour at the minimum wage.[10] Doubly tragic is that now Brazil has begun to import black beans from Chile, where the government is also willing to sacrifice the nutritional well-being of the local people in order to earn foreign exchange.

Finally, giving priority to cash cropping means that a farming family's very survival through the year depends on the cash received only once or twice a year at harvest time. But such lump sum payments turn peasants into open targets for predatory merchants peddling gadgets and costly packaged foods. Diversified food cropping is the only guarantee of year-round food security for the rural family. In self-reliant China it is said that when peasants step outside their front door they see from where their next meal is coming.

19: The Winners

The fixation on export agriculture continues because while harmful to most, it is highly advantageous to a few. The first beneficiaries are large producers and plantation owners.

The second group to benefit is the small class of better-off urban dwellers. Much of the foreign exchange earned ultimately gets spent on their food and consumer 'needs.' Zaire is a typical case. There, export agriculture has led to the decline of food production to such an extent that 30 per cent of Zaire's foreign exchange now goes to buy imported foodstuffs. The staple foods of the people are in very short supply, but imported meat is still available for those who can pay. It comes from South Africa for the Zaire elite.[1]

Finally, export agriculture benefits those associated with the multinational corporations in their country and government officials who get paid for managing the export system.

By rewarding these elite groups, a small fraction of the entire population, export agriculture compounds the inequalities in wealth and well-being. A recent report from the United Nations confirms that.

Gains from foreign trade . . . and particularly from sharply increased export prices frequently tend to be concentrated among upper income groups to a much greater extent than is income from domestic production.[2]

Tending the Goose
If a government becomes convinced that export earnings are the sine qua non of development, export industries, whether domestic or foreign, appear as the salvation of the country. As political economist Cheryl Payer points out, the government will certainly refrain from 'killing the goose that lays the golden eggs' and will tend the goose with a great deal of care.[3] But looking at their country with the interests of the goose in mind is hardly the same as keeping the interests of the people foremost, for what export agriculture most needs is cheap and docile labour and the control over large tracts of land with no requirement to invest in their conservation.

The myth that export agriculture is the path to development makes it possible for plantation owners, multinational corporations, and state marketing boards in underdeveloped countries to claim that they must keep wages of agricultural labourers low so that their products can compete in the international market. In 1974 the disclosure by the 'World in Action' television programme of the appalling living conditions of Sri Lanka's tea estate workers met with protests from the government and the foreign estate owners. Improving the living conditions of the 650,000 workers and increasing their meagre wages ranging from 36 to 48 cents a day would, they claimed, price Sri Lanka tea out of the market.[4]

Making similar excuses, governments have excluded large land-owners from land-reform schemes. They argue that dividing up the large, cash-crop-producing estates would endanger the country's trade and monetary position. In the Philippines, for example, any land put to growing export crops, including over seven million acres with such crops as sugar and coconut, was exempted from land-reform legislation.[5] Government officials who make such decisions are themselves, of course, often large land-owners.

Export Crops Expand

Given that multinational agribusiness and local elites benefit by the continuation of a focus on export agriculture and that export agriculture continues to be reinforced by international lending agencies, it is not surprising that export crop production is growing at a much faster rate than food crop production.

From the mid-fifties to the mid-sixties, the growth rate of export crops was 2.2 times faster than the total agricultural growth rate in the underdeveloped countries. In specific countries this trend was even more marked. Coffee production in Africa has increased more than fourfold in the last twenty years, tea production sixfold, sugar cane production has trebled, while cocoa and cotton production have doubled.[6] Between 1952 and 1967, the cotton acreage in Nicaragua increased fourfold while the area in basic grains was cut in half.[7]

Elite-controlled governments have encouraged this trend. In Colombia in 1965, 90 per cent of all agricultural credit went to cash crops – coffee, cotton, and sugar.[8] As we found in the Sahel, many governments continue to use the techniques of past colonial regimes to enforce the production of cash crops. In East Java the government requires that as much as 30 per cent of the land grow sugar cane.[9] Even in countries like Tanzania that have directed a large proportion of their resources to rural development and have talked of self-reliance, colonial laws have been reactivated specifying minimum acreages for export crops.[10] The rhetoric of many development planners about diversification of agriculture becomes in reality diversification among export crops.

'Hooked' on Exports

Once set out along the export agriculture path, the 'export crop trap' is like drug addiction. Once 'hooked,' it is terribly painful to get off.[11] Farmers growing export crops might want to compensate for sharply reduced income from falling crop prices by shifting to food crops for their families, but if they have gone into debt to obtain the inputs to grow export crops, they may no longer have that choice. They may be obliged to earn a cash income to repay their debts or face the possibility of losing their lands to a creditor.

Similarly, on a national level, when an underdeveloped country receives 'aid' from abroad, even if the borrowed money does help to increase the country's production capacity, the debt cannot be paid back until the country has exported enough to earn the needed foreign exchange. Pesos and rupees do not help. Most so-called aid has to be repaid in the same currency in which it was given. The country is likely to be on a treadmill. If exports are not sufficient to acquire the needed foreign currency to pay back debts and to pay for necessary imports, the only immediate solution appears to be to seek yet another loan. This, of course, means only a greater push for export crops to pay back an even greater debt!

What we must remember is that this pattern continues not because the governments of the underdeveloped countries do not *understand* the nature of their trap. It continues because, as we have seen, export agriculture serves the interests of the elite land-holding, government, and consumer groups in underdeveloped countries and the interests of multinational agribusiness and international lending agencies like the World Bank.

Thus, promoting trade justice must not lend credence to the idea that export agriculture can be the foundation for development. To do so would be to equate the country's balance of payments and its economic growth with the welfare of the people. Until fundamental restructuring occurs within the underdeveloped nations, higher prices and better export deals for their commodities are likely to work against the interests of the poor majority.

20: Changing the Game

Agricultural exports from a country where many go hungry is largely a *reflection* of the problem, not the problem itself. Even if all agricultural exports stopped, there still would be hungry people – those who continue to be excluded from genuine control over their country's food-producing resources.

An export focus in countries where many go hungry reflects the impoverishment of much of the local population and the interests of the elite. An export focus is nonetheless an *active* force. Where productive assets are controlled by a few, export agriculture further exacerbates the deteriorating position of the majority. To sum up what we have said in the preceding pages, in such countries export agriculture:

—makes it possible for the local elite to be unconcerned about the poverty at home that greatly limits the buying power of the local people. Export agriculture means the elite can profit anyway by finding buyers in foreign high-paying markets.

—provides the incentive to local and foreign elites to tighten their control over productive resources from which export profits are made and to resist firmly any attempts at redistribution of control over productive assets.

—necessitates miserable working conditions and wages. Under-developed countries can compete in export markets only by exploiting labour, especially women and children. Owners and export oriented governments will stop at nothing to crush workers' efforts to organize themselves.

—throws the local population into competition with foreign consumers for the products of their own land, thus raising local prices and reducing the real income of the majority. (In Part VIII we discuss more fully this 'Global Supermarket' phenomenon.)

A contrast between two countries in the Caribbean reveals why export agriculture itself is not the real enemy. In both Cuba and the Dominican Republic, a large portion of agricultural land produces sugar and other exports. Both countries rely on agricultural exports for foreign exchange and both import significant amounts of grain. Yet today, in the Dominican Republic at least 75 per cent of the people are undernourished, while in Cuba, there is virtually no malnutrition. What accounts for the difference?

First, the foreign exchange earned from sugar exports is controlled very differently in the two countries. In Cuba all the foreign exchange belongs to the public and is put to work implementing the country's development plans. Thus it is used to import productive goods that generate meaningful jobs such as building schools and homes and manufacturing basic home appliances and machinery. In the Dominican Republic a large part of the foreign exchange from sugar exports is treated as profit of private corporations such as Gulf and Western. Much of it is returned to the United States or wasted on projects such as G & W's tourist enclave. The few jobs created in such an enclave do not relate to the long-term development of the country but simply cater to the white man's colonial fantasies (chambermaids are dressed like Aunt Jemima). Such projects even represent an ongoing foreign exchange drain, for example, importing processed foods from home that tourists 'need'.

A second contrast can be drawn in terms of the employment impact of sugar. The Dominican Republic suffers from a 30 to 40 per cent unemployment rate. Seventy-five per cent of all who work in agriculture have less than 135 workdays a year.[1] In addition, Dominican workers' interests are further jeopardized by the sugar growers' importation of Haitian labourers, who now make up over half of the cane-cutting work force. The intensive seasonal labour demand of sugar cane (which spoils if not cut and milled within a short period of time) has created high population densities in cane monoculture areas and yet few year-round jobs.

With mechanization of cane harvesting, unemployment in the Dominican Republic deepens still further. Mechanization of the Cuban sugar harvest, expected to be completed by 1985, does not mean unemployment; instead farm mechanization in Cuba releases human labour from the backbreaking job of cane cutting for jobs in agriculture and other vital areas of the economy. The development of an economy oriented toward fulfilling basic social needs has meant that in Cuba there is no shortage of employment for the 180,000 cane cutters (nearly half the total) already freed from sugar production.[2]

Although such international trade is not itself the enemy, the real question is trade in whose interest. One crucial qualification, *basic* food needs should be met locally. Basic food self-reliance – and by this we mean adequate local supplies to prevent famine if imports of food were abruptly cut off – is the *sine qua non* of a people's security. Moreover, no country can bargain successfully in international trade as long as it is desperate to sell its products in order to import food to stave off famine. Without basic food self-reliance, much-acclaimed 'interdependence' becomes a smokescreen for food control of one country by another.

Cuba is an instructive case from which to learn about the tension between exports and such basic food self-reliance. Cuba is trying to expand sugar production while diversifying and expanding domestic food production. During the period 1971-1975 non-sugar agricultural production increased by 38 per cent.[3] In the same period vegetable production for the local population more than doubled and fruit production increased by over 60 per cent. Egg, poultry, and pork production have increased severalfold since the early sixties. There has been virtually no increase in food prices in the last 10 years.[4]

At the same time Cuba is aiming for increased sugar exports, in part to import large quantities of grain. So far success with increasing sugar production has not been as great as with food. The reasons are complex and not entirely clear; almost certainly adverse weather for sugar growing has been one factor in recent years. Long-term sales contracts with the Soviet Union and other nations (like Canada and Japan) for much of its sugar have partially saved Cuba from the economic devastation caused by extreme international market price swings, experienced by most underdeveloped countries. This exceptional arrangement with buyers of its sugar makes Cuba a less useful model for other countries.

There are, then, tensions and unanswered questions. Will relying on exports to pay for a significant part of the national diet be judged feasible and consonant with the goal of political self-determination? Should the policy be to count on other socialist countries to meet food import needs? It will be important to watch what the Cuban people do over the next few years.

Certainly the concept of food self-reliance does not preclude exports. Most countries people now think of as having scarce resources, such as Bangladesh, could not only meet local food needs, but also export considerable quantities of agricultural products, if that was judged desirable. Food self-reliance is not isolationist but recognizes that only *after* the redistribution of control over the resources used to produce exports would the income generated possibly serve the needs of all. Part X looks more deeply at the implications of food self-reliance.

PART VII
USA – BREADBASKET OF THE WORLD?

21 : Bountiful Uncle Sam

The United States is one of the biggest food exporters, and has been likened to the breadbasket of the world. The general impression is that much of this food goes to hungry countries in a characteristically benign and generous aid programme. But there are three gaping holes in this national image:

- First, what food *is* exported on an aid basis (that is, with long-term, low-interest financing) is only a tiny fraction of US commercial exports (6 per cent in 1975).
- Second, less than 30 per cent of agricultural exports go to the 'less developed countries.'
- Third, although the US is the world's leading food exporter, it is also one of the world's top food importers.

Keeping straight on these facts is not easy; everything one hears or reads seems to give exactly the opposite impression.

In the fiscal year 1975, the top four recipients of US agricultural exports were Japan, the Netherlands, West Germany, and Canada. Contrast exports to these countries with US exports to the underdeveloped countries listed by the United Nations as 'most seriously affected' (MSA) by the food and oil price increases of the seventies.[1] The United States exported no agricultural products to nine of the forty MSA nations in either 1973 or 1974. Thirty-six of the forty MSA's export food and other agricultural products to the US.

In both 1973 and 1974, United States agricultural exports to Canada, itself a grain exporter, were greater in value than to all the MSA countries combined or to the entire continent of Africa. In fact, in 1973, such exports to Canada were almost twice as large as those to Africa. Agricultural exports during the drought years 1973 and 1974 to four African Sahel nations – Mauritania, Mali, Niger, and Chad – were less than half (in terms of value) of those to *either* Sweden or Norway or Denmark. In 1974, the United States exported 114.5 pounds of wheat per person to Japan but only 7.5 pounds per person to India. Per person, Pakistan received only 18 per cent as much wheat from us as did the Netherlands.[2]

Contrary to popular notions, the industrial countries are the major food importers; not the underdeveloped countries. In 1974, the United States ranked third among the world's leading food importers, close behind Japan and West Germany. And over two thirds of US food imports came from underdeveloped countries.[3]

While we think of America as the world's beef capital, the United States is in reality the world's leading beef importer. The United States imports over 40 per cent of all beef in world trade. In 1973 the United States imported almost two billion pounds of meat. Often it is stressed that this is but a small amount since it represents only about 7 per cent of domestic production. The amount, however, is hardly small in relation to the needs of most other countries. It also means that a considerable portion of the food-producing resources in several countries with many hungry people go into producing beef for Americans. In international trade more meat flows from underdeveloped to industrial countries than the other way around.[4]

Who are the *real* food donors? They are many of the world's hungriest people.

22 : The American Drive for Food Power

American government officials asserted that food exports are necessary to pay for 'the imported petroleum and other goods we must import to maintain our standard of living.'[1] President Ford proclaimed 'our agricultural abundance helped open the door to 800 million people on the mainland of China. . . . It helped improve relations with the Soviets. It helped to build bridges to the developing world.'[2]

Americans are told that their food will not only alleviate hunger but will even turn hungry people toward democracy. The past president of the Colorado Cattle Feeders Association hopes that by improving diets abroad 'nations will change their political feelings and move away from Communism to a more democratic form of government.'[3]

Unfortunately the genuine good will of most Americans is being manipulated so that they do not see that the food export strategy of the seventies was not a necessary development but a promotion of certain interests at the expense of the majority.

Just what were the underlying reasons behind the American Food Power strategy in the seventies?

The Payments Crisis

By the late sixties, administration officials had decided that something had to be done about the nation's balance of payments deficits. To most Americans the balance of payments has no understandable link with their everyday well-being – certainly no connection with the price of food or the fate of the family farmer. The balance of payments is something bureaucrats have to worry about, not ordinary people.

But is this true? How does it relate to the question of the need for food exports?

The meaning of a balance of payments deficit is no great mystery. Quite simply, a country has a deficit, an unfavourable balance, when more money goes out of the country than comes in. The balancing up takes into account government, corporate, and even individual transactions.

For years the United States government had been spending billions upon billions as the standing military force of the anti-communist world. The Vietnam War alone cost the United States well over a half trillion dollars ($500,000,000,000,000).

In addition, United States-based corporations, beginning in the late fifties and throughout the sixties, made large capital investments in Western Europe and to a lesser extent in Latin America and Asia. Federal tax laws encouraged these corporations to keep their considerable earnings outside the United States since profits were not taxable until actually returned to the United States. Such corporations exacerbated the negative balance of trade by turning cheap-labour, low-tax countries like Mexico, Taiwan and Singapore into 'platforms' for exporting back to the United States consumer goods such as transistors, television sets, cameras and textiles. Ironically, then, the United States was sending dollars abroad to import products made by US-based corporations.

In the late 1960s, many British, European and Japanese firms also 'went global' and began exporting to the United States, often from low-tax, low-wage plants side by side with competing subsidiaries of American multinational corporations. Before long vast amounts of dollars were being drained out of the United States to pay for imported manufactured goods. A study in the early 1970s found that US-based multinational corporations accounted for 42 per cent of all imports, often 'buying' from their own overseas subsidiaries.[4] (In the first five months of 1978 the United States imported an alarming $14 billion more in manufactured goods than it exported.[5] The cost of these imports was more than double the cost of imported oil during the same period.) United States corporations have also become increasingly dependent on foreign sources of critical raw materials. By 1970, the United States was importing 80 per cent or more of eight basic raw materials. The trade deficit in raw materials had grown to $3.4 billion.[6]

In 1971, as a result of such capital drains, the United States experienced the first balance of payments deficit in the private sector (corporations and individuals) in a century. Thus, it was well *before* the price of imported oil increased that the balance of payments crisis developed.

The Birth of Food Power

By the late 1960s, the United States had approached the international equivalent of having its credit cards recalled. By then, other countries began to get uneasy about honouring dollars, as it was less certain whether they could always be converted. Foreign countries, furthermore, began to react to the takeover of their key industries by United States corporations using the power of good-as-gold dollars. Foreign treasuries started demanding gold instead of paper in settling balance of payments deficits. By 1970, United States gold reserves had been reduced to less than one half of what they were in 1950.

For the Nixon administration, the question was:

What exports from the United States could be stepped up in a really major way to compensate for the mounting import bill? In 1970, Nixon appointed a commission composed of corporation executives and their lawyers to come up with an answer. This Commission on International Trade and Investment Policy, known as the Williams Commission, concluded that there were only two trade categories that could earn the huge sums of foreign exchange needed to balance United States payments: high technology products and agricultural commodities.

One type of high technology thought easy to push abroad was armaments. The Vietnam War had produced new 'generations' of arms and every country just *had* to acquire the latest. American military attachés and corporate hustlers around the world doubled their efforts (and often their bribes) to compete with French and British armaments manufacturers. Vast credits were extended to underdeveloped countries. All went 'well'; soon annual sales reached the multibillions. By 1975, armament sales amounted to $4.8 billion. Moreover, boosting arms sales had no awkward domestic repercussion for the administration.

But the second recommendation of the Williams Commission – boosting agricultural exports – was another matter. How could American farmers and consumers be made to go along with a plan to vastly increase agricultural exports? Just how do you get other countries to import enough American food to offset the import expenditures that the United States was not willing to reduce? Equally crucial, how do you push up prices so that every bushel sold will do the most to help the United States balance of payments? And how do you accomplish this in countries that want to protect the livelihood of their own farmers?

This was not easy. The Nixon administration, however, thought there might be one workable strategy. First, tempt potential buyers by making their initial purchases of grain cheap and by providing ample financing. Then persuade other countries to lower their protection against US grain exports by offering, under the banner of free trade, to abolish domestic price supports for American farm products. And to ensure that prices go up, direct the Secretary of Agriculture to order cutbacks in United States crop acreage; then the final touch needed to raise grain prices would be bad weather in the major grain-producing countries.

The steps by which the Food Power strategy was actually implemented began with devaluing the dollar – first 11 per cent in December 1971 and then a further 6 per cent in early 1973. This made the United States exports less costly to foreign buyers. (Underdeveloped countries that had been encouraged to hold their reserves in dollars and to fix their currency to dollar values lost hundreds of millions overnight.)

A second way to make United States commodities more attractive was simply to offer convenient financing. In July 1972, the United States announced a $750 million credit through the government's Commodity Credit Corporation to help the Soviets purchase grain. Nixon had already courted the Soviets by rescinding the requirement that at least half of any grain sold to the Soviet Union or any Eastern European country be carried in American flag ships. And the Soviets were ready to buy. Although their grain production, somewhat exceeding that of the United States, was sufficient for direct consumption, many Soviet citizens clamoured for more meat in their diets. Kremlin economic planners decided that 19 million tons of cheap United States grain for feed on such fine terms was the solution. Bad weather, which cut their harvest by a third, further convinced them.

The next step was to get prices to shoot up. The quickest way was simply to cut production back. Secretary of Agriculture Earl Butz ordered another five million acres of wheat lands taken out of production in September 1972. This put the total acreage kept out of production at 62 million, an amount equal in size to all the cultivated land in the United Kingdom. With the Soviets buying, the dollar devalued, and acute weather problems worldwide, this acreage cutback was enough to guarantee shortages, depleted reserves, and higher prices for any additional foreign sales.

Food Power and the 'Free' Market

Still one question remained for the Nixon administration: How to make the strategy stick? The Williams Commission had concluded that the only way would be to negotiate a 'free trade' policy that would open up protected European and Japanese markets to American farm products. The free trade doctrine thus became the strong arm of Food Power. You cannot, the commission said, have one without the other.

Only under free market conditions could the United States capitalize on its 'comparative advantage' in grain and livestock feed. This meant the United States would have to prove its commitment to the 'free market' by moving to scrap government-financed minimum price supports, acreage allotments, and other programmes to regulate farm income and productive capacity.

The administration calculated it was a good moment to get hitherto reluctant farmers to support just such a move: The Soviet grain purchase had significantly reduced world grain reserves and weather conditions in many areas of the world were poor; it all added up to a very bullish market for US farm products.

It was likewise easy to persuade Congress that the agricultural support programmes were unnecessary. The 1973 farm bill virtually ended payment for land held out of production; established such low target prices (i.e. the market price below which the government would step in to help the farmer) as to be meaningless in protecting the small farmer; and, in effect, abolished government-held grain reserves. After the previous cutbacks designed to create scarcity prices, farmers were now being told that the United States government was releasing its agriculture – a significant part of the world food economy – to the speculative market where a small change in supply, indeed even a threat of such change, can set off huge price swings.

Drumming Up Customers

Between fiscal years 1970 and 1974, the quantity of American wheat exports increased about 90 per cent while the *value* increased almost 400 per cent![7] The pattern was almost as striking for feedgrains. But what would happen if widespread good harvests increased the worldwide availability of grain? To keep prices up, it was necessary to find some new customers.

In 1974, the Foreign Agricultural Service (FAS) spent over $10 million developing markets for American exports. In a recent issue of its periodical, *Foreign Agriculture*, FAS was conspicuously proud to explain how it is furthering an 'aggressive foreign market development' to beat out the 'stiff competition' in the race for increased agricultural exports.[8] An arm of the USDA, FAS is also the leading wedge for agribusiness penetration into the markets of other countries. FAS's 'co-operation' with food export industries falls into three categories called 'market intelligence,' 'trade servicing,' and 'product promotion.'

If an American corporation wants to know whether it would be profitable to enter a certain market, it turns to its friend in FAS – one of the 96 US agricultural attachés or officers in foreign countries – who jumps into action. First: Does the product meet the foreign government's import entry requirements? Second: Is it acceptable to local tastes? (Call in the 'professional taste panel'!) If the company's product makes it past steps one and two, FAS helps sponsor a market test.

In addition, FAS sponsors exhibits around the world for the benefit of US producers. One favourite exhibit is a lifelike reproduction of an American supermarket. Since the United States exports 44 per cent of all the wheat in the world trade, FAS also helps sponsor schools to teach people how to cook with wheat in areas of the world where wheat is not a traditional food. In Japan, FAS has sponsored a beef campaign, noting that it is 'aimed at better-class hotels and restaurants catering to the tourist trade.'[9] Its efforts there have also helped to account for the success of fast-food outlets like McDonald's – 90 per cent of whose ingredients are imported. Although American-style fast-food outlets only began operating in Japan in 1970, FAS predicted that by 1979 these chains would have taken 70 per cent of all such sales, displacing the traditional rice, fish, and noodle bars.[10]

American Food Power strategy thus rests, not on shipping food to a world of hungry people, but on moulding the tastes and habits of a certain class of people to make them dependent on products and styles that they had never wanted before. American policy makers are encouraging other countries to become more and more food dependent on the United States and the United States itself is becoming more and more economically dependent on food exports. Reading the FAS material, one would think that the survival of the nation rested on its success in creating one more hamburger lover in the world.

The question suggests that Food Power was born as the only possible response to the rising cost of oil imports. But the Food Power strategy predated the oil price increase response. Further-

'more, Food Power was not the *only* possible response but the choice of policy makers who wanted to protect the economic status quo. Food Power was born out of the dollar drain caused by the Vietnam War, the overseas expansion of American corporations importing cheap-labour manufactured goods back into the United States, growing corporate dependence on foreign raw materials, and United States petroleum corporations' decision to import massive quantities of oil.

Today Food Power continues to be promoted as a way to buttress the US balance of payments. Military expenditures are less of a foreign exchange drain now, in part because of increased arms sales abroad. But imports of consumer goods, largely by US multinational corporations, continue as the single most important balance of payments drain after oil and industrial raw material imports. In 1973, the United States imported $9.5 billion in manufactured products from foreign plants owned by American corporations.[11]

In addition, the United States now spends over $13 billion for agricultural imports.[12] Thus, while officials talk only of how agricultural exports bring in almost $24 billion in foreign exchange, more than half of every US dollar gained in agricultural exports is spent on agricultural *imports*! Ironically, about one-half of these agricultural imports are commodities that the United States can and does produce – meat, sugar, vegetable oil, vegetables, tobacco, wine and dairy products.

The Soviet Grain Deal: A Case Study of an 'Unfree' Market

Extreme cold combined with inadequate snow cover during the Soviet winter of 1971-1972 killed 25 million acres of wheat – or the equivalent of the entire United States wheat acreage. Despite many clear indications that the Soviets were in the market to buy in a big way and the indisputable evidence that bad weather nearly everywhere in the world meant there would be an exceptional demand for American grain, the USDA, contrary to law, did not inform the farmers. Instead USDA warned farmers there would be a big surplus even after all foreseeable sales. Only a few American government officials and grain company executives were in the know.

By early June 1972, Continental Grain, Cargill, and the other four members of the giant grain-trading US corporations rushed out to the early-harvest Southwest to buy up wheat. The farmers knew that harvests were going to be big and since they did not know about the strong foreign market prospects, they were happy to unload their wheat. They got about $1.25 a bushel. A few weeks later the same wheat would have brought $2.25 to the farmer. (In early 1973, wheat would be hard to get at $5 a bushel.)

By July 5, Clarence Palmby, Continental Grain's vice-president, helped the firm to conclude the biggest grain sale in history – three days before the official announcement of the $750 million loan to the USSR that made the deal possible and that had been negotiated by Palmby while he was an official of the USDA. Still at USDA in May Palmby had even attended meetings between Continental and the Russians and surely knew a big sale was in the offing. But Palmby and his bosses at USDA had still neglected to inform the farmers, despite their legal mandate to do so.

It was not until mid-July that the USDA informed the farmers. By then in the Southwest and the early harvest areas of the Midwest, one quarter of all the wheat had already been sold.[13] In Oklahoma alone, the withholding of information by the Department of Agriculture cost wheat farmers about $47 million. Butz's rationalization? 'Farmers didn't lose money because of early sales, they just didn't make the additional money they might have made.'[14]

The Soviets kept buying and the grain companies kept selling. While huge commitments were being made, the August 1972 USDA newsletter *Wheat Situation* did inform farmers that the Soviets were buying but said that the likely total figure would be just half what Continental Grain alone had in fact *already* sold to the Soviets in early July. While the Soviets continued to buy wheat, Secretary Butz toured the country talking about *corn* sales.

In addition to extra profits made because uninformed farmers were willing to sell cheaply, the grain companies had yet another guarantee for unprecedented gain. In order to encourage exports the government at that time subsidized the exporting companies by making up the difference between the domestic price at which they bought the wheat and the lower price at which they sold it abroad. These subsidies went as high as 47 cents a bushel. (Clearly in the Soviet case there was no need for such an additional customer incentive.) As domestic prices finally began to rise, the companies claimed ever larger subsidies even though some of the wheat they were then selling in fact had been purchased earlier at lower prices.

A subsequent Senate investigation discovered that a grain export corporation sometimes collected the subsidy on sales to its wholly owned foreign subsidiary. The investigation documented sales by Cargill to its subsidiary in Panama. This subsidiary then sold to another Cargill subsidiary in Europe, which then sold the wheat at an unknown but doubtlessly higher price to a second party. In this way, headquarters collected a multimillion dollar subsidy not considered taxable income while the profits rung up by the foreign subsidiaries were sheltered from taxation as long as they stayed abroad (and that despite this country's drive to improve its balance of payments!). These transactions were in fact all on paper; the wheat never left the ship on which it was originally loaded.

Over a mere seven weeks taxpayers handed the six grain-exporting companies $300 million in subsidies. Food Power could indeed be profitable for some.

By contrast, the subsidies to farmers moved in the opposite direction. In 1972 subsidies were still paid to farmers to make up the difference between 'parity,' a price level considered fair in relation to the cost of machinery and supplies a farmer must purchase, and the average market price over a five-month period. The catch, in 1972, was that the government figured the period to begin in July, when most farmers in the Southwest and some in the Midwest had already sold out. As news of the big grain deal spread, wheat prices rose, narrowing the difference between average market prices and parity, thus cutting into the subsidies for the farmer. The farmers' lost subsidies have been estimated at $55 million.

Cook Industries, on the other hand, increased its annual profits fifteenfold between 1972 and 1974. Cook is the only firm with publicly held stock and therefore the only one required to disclose its earnings. Dan Morgan of the *Washington Post* reports, however, that privately held firms like Cargill and Bunge have doubled or tripled their net worth since 1972, according to reliable trade sources.[15] The General Accounting Office found the big traders had profits on those hundred of millions of bushels ranging from 2 cents to 53 cents a bushel[16] whereas normally a profit of 1.6 cents per bushel is considered good.[17]

So 'free trade' and an all-out export drive worked well for the grain companies. Characteristically, Butz added insult to the farmers' injury by claiming that grain companies won and the farmers lost out in the 1972 grain sales simply because the farmers 'weren't smart enough to take advantage of the situation.' Some trading companies did make big money in the deal, he conceded, 'but that's the name of the game.'[18]

Butz is right. Big money is the name of the game. Under free trade export companies are able to extend their control and increase their profits. During the winter of 1972-1973, three of the large grain export corporations, Cargill, Continental, and Cook, were able to corner 90 per cent of the soybean harvest for $4.00 a bushel, sending soybean prices up to $10.00 a bushel only a few months later.[19]

Free trade allows speculators to drive up prices out of all relation to actual supply. Speaking of food prices in 1973, Donald Paarlberg, then USDA's chief economist, said that his staff could account for only one half to two thirds of the sudden price rise. 'The rest is psychological and speculative activity and these are not in our models,' he explained.[20] But how real is any model of the free market that does not include speculation?

What free trade really does is free private multibillion dollar corporations to manipulate prices and supply to their advantage. When we say 'private' we mean very private – with no room for public scrutiny. Five of the six largest grain conglomerates are closely held, private firms owned by a few individuals or families. None publish any detailed financial information. When Dan Morgan wondered why grain trade lobbyists are hard to find in Washington, one former grain trade lobbyist explained it to him this way: the grain companies 'don't need to have powerful lobbyists – for they have no regulation.'[21]

Hoping to avoid a repeat of the infamous 'Russian grain deal', the Department of Agriculture soon began requiring the reporting of large grain sales. Exempted from the reporting requirement are subsidiaries of US grain trading corporations located in other countries. In order to capitalize on this loophole, the Russians bought only through such subsidiaries when prices were most depressed in 1977. They made a killing before news of their buying pushed prices up. The USDA's crop estimators had sorely overgauged the Russian crop. Again the primary losers were US farmers who, assuming a low purchase by the USSR, had already sold their crop.[22]

US Food Power's Domestic Victims

As part of its free market strategy, the administration encouraged farmers to plant 'fence to fence,' assuring them that the 'hungry world' would take all the grain the US could produce. With more acres in production than at any time in recent history, farmers did produce record harvests with record prices. Indeed Food Power looked good to many farmers in 1973 and 1974. The annual income per farm doubled between 1971 and 1973; even adjusting for inflation, income was up 60 per cent.[23] But not every farm benefited equally. Gains in earnings accrued overwhelmingly to large farm operators. The nation's largest farms, representing only 4 per cent of all farms, increased their average annual net farm income two and one-third times between 1971 and 1974, from $36,000 to over $84,000.[24] (This top 4 per cent had gained control of 46 per cent of all farm-produce sales even as early as 1973.[25]) But the majority of all farmers, those with sales of $20,000 or less, were able to increase their average net farm income only about 20 per cent – from about $2000 in 1971 to less than $2500 in 1974.[26] Increases in the incomes of small-farm families have come only through off-farm jobs. This alone says a lot about the impact of the Food Power strategy.

In hopes of prospering on the new export markets – after a long period of stagnation – many farmers invested in more land and new machinery. To do this, most farmers had to take out big loans, especially since land and machinery costs were soaring. (A tractor equivalent to one costing $9000 in 1966 cost $32,000 in the early 1970's.)[27]

Then with farmers having gone out on a limb on the promise of Food Power's unlimited markets, markets became saturated. Farm prices started to plummet. Compared to 1973, net farm income dropped 65 per cent by 1977.[28] Farmers were still increasing their borrowing, now not for expansion but just to keep afloat. Farm debt (sum debts of all farmers) had doubled compared to 1971. By 1978 interest payments on an enormous $119 billion farm debt were eating up half of the farmers' shrunken income. 'Such ratios of farm debt to farm income have no precedent in this century,' observed a Federal Reserve economist.[29]

Food Power's production push and export strategy, moreover, set off a virtual land rush in the United States. In the four years following 1972, land values more than doubled. Just as we have seen in underdeveloped countries, those manoeuvring to profit on the agricultural boom were not all farmers. Non-farm investors and even foreign investors began to perceive US farmland investments as the best hedge against inflation. A Brussels investment consulting firm established that foreign investors bought up $800 million worth of US farmland in 1977 alone. The Commerce Department notes that this figure, if correct, would amount to 30 per cent of all direct foreign investment in the United States. A Commerce Department official told *Business Week*: 'We simply cannot get a handle on farmland since ownership is disguised through the extensive use of trusts, partnerships, and corporations headquartered off shore.' Foreign purchasers of US farmland often buy through corporations headquartered in countries like the Dutch Antilles, for example, that levy little or no taxes.[30]

In part because of the pressure of non-farm and foreign investment, even when farm incomes began dropping in 1975, farmland prices kept on climbing steeply, slackening slightly only in 1977. Few people realize that 38 per cent of all US farmland is rented out.[31] The rising cost of land is particularly hard on farmers who rent their lands. As land prices rise, so do rents.

So, then, who has gained? In 1976 the US farm population dropped at the fastest rate in 13 years. In Iowa that year 166 farms were going out of business each week.[32] Food Power strategies were thus accelerating the trend toward increasing concentration of control over the nation's farmland.

What Is Being Lost

The USDA obviously does not seek to prevent this increasing concentration of farm ownership. In the eyes of USDA, the decline of the small farmer is a fait accompli. Speculating on what American agriculture will look like in the future, USDA's Director of Agricultural Economics predicted a 'highly co-ordinated industry of large farms very likely . . . operat[ing] in much the same fashion as nonfarm manufacturing industries.'[13] Never mind that USDA has shown in its own studies that there are no economies of scale above the one-or-two-operator farm,[34] and that the greatest value per acre is produced on family-size farms.[35]

Often supporters of family farms are viewed as romantics who are yearning for the good old days that never really existed. Is it just nostalgia that makes many want to revitalize small-farm America? What is the difference between a rural America dominated by a few large-holders and corporations and a rural America dominated by family and cooperatives?

In 1944 a remarkable piece of sociological work was done in California. A researcher with the USDA selected two towns, Arvin and Dinuba, similar in the dollar value of production yet different in the average farm size – one with a few large farms and the other with many small farms. The differences between these two communities tell us a lot about the future of America if the present direction toward concentration of control is not reversed.

By every measure the quality of life in the small farm community turned out to be significantly richer than in the large farm community. The 'quality of life,' generally a vague term, was quantified by this study. For example, Dinuba, the small-farm community, supported:

- about 20 per cent more people and at a higher level of income;
- a working population that was mostly self-employed in contrast to the large-farm community where less than 20 per cent were self-employed (and nearly two-thirds were agricultural wage labourers);
- many more democratic decision-making organizations and much broader representation in them;
- better schools, parks, newspapers, civic groups, churches, and public services;
- twice the number of small businesses and 61 per cent more retail business.

Researcher Walter Goldschmidt had intended to continue the study by comparing other farm communities. He never got the chance. The implications of this study were so 'hot' for the Department of Agriculture that Goldschmidt was ordered to stop his investigations. Then, in 1977 California officials visited Arvin and Dinuba to find that the contrasts in family income recorded by Goldschmidt in 1946 had only continued to grow in the ensuing 31 years. In 1945 the median family income in the small-farm community Dinuba was 12 per cent greater than the big-farm town Arvin; by 1970 the difference had grown to 28 per cent. In recent testimony before a Senate committee on land monopoly in California, Goldschmidt stated: 'The vision of the future under increased corporate control of the land is the vision of Arvins rather than Dinubas – indeed of super-Arvins.'[36]

Food Power versus Food First

The most serious criticism of Food Power is that it moves the United States in the opposite direction from Food First. Just as in many underdeveloped countries where so many are hungry, agriculture is increasingly seen in the US as a prime arena for speculative investment and as the way to earn foreign exchange to ease an economic crisis the roots of which are unrelated to agriculture. Food Power has not been a solution to a problem; it has been a way to avoid the solution. Relying on Food Power to earn foreign exchange has been a way out for a government unwilling to touch the power and profits of the large grain-trading and other corporations moving abroad in search of new markets and cheap land and labour. Indeed, a Food Power-free trade strategy reinforces the power of large corporations both directly and indirectly: by undercutting small farmers who cannot survive extreme market fluctuations; and by increasing the price swings on which speculative companies thrive. Moreover, foreign exchange earned with agricultural exports is used to import agricultural and manufactured goods produced abroad often by American corporations – items that could have been produced at home. Finally, Food Power is a way to pay for a costly United States anti-people strategy that puts American military presence in every corner of the world to preserve 'law and order.'

By contrast a Food First agricultural economy in the United States would unite agricultural production with the development of viable rural communities and the long term protection of the soil and water resources. It would look at food production, not as a source of speculative investment nor as merely a source of foreign exchange, but rather as a source of livelihood for millions of farmers and the basic necessity of life for all.

Every new regulation that hampers agricultural production – every new bit of legislation that interferes with the individual farmer's management decisions, every new economic control that erodes his profit incentive – drives another nail into the collective coffin of mankind.

Earl Butz
Secretary of Agriculture
1968-1976

In one breath, an assistant secretary of agriculture told a farm group that in the new order of things each farmer must respond to signals of demand from world markets, that only their own forward-thinking management would protect them from the 'ups and downs' of the market place. In the very next breath, this public servant told farmers that markets were changing on a daily basis, with doors opening and closing so fast that 'what might happen next, no one can tell.' Good luck, and good-bye.

Jim Hightower, *Eat Your Heart Out*

PART VIII   WORLD HUNGER AS BIG BUSINESS

23 : Multinational Food Companies and Feeding the Hungry

We are living in the era of the worldwide penetration of agribusiness, the linking up of underdeveloped countries' farms with global food markets: a Global Farm supplying a Global Supermarket.

The world's hungry people are being thrown into even more direct competition with the well-fed and the over-fed. The fact that a food is grown in abundance right where they live, that their own country's natural and financial resources were consumed in producing it, or even that they themselves toiled to grow it will no longer mean that they will be likely to eat it. Rather, it will go to an emerging Global Supermarket where everyone in the world, poor or rich, must reach for it on the same shelf. Every item has a price and that price, in large part, is determined by what the world's better-off customers are willing to pay. None without money will be able to move through the check-out line. Even our pet dogs and cats can outbid most of the world's hungry people. This emerging Global Supermarket will be the culmination of food 'interdependence' in a world of unequals.

As much as agribusiness firms talk of producing food in underdeveloped countries, they are not talking about the basic staples – beans, corn, rice, wheat, and millet – needed by the hungry. Instead they are referring to 'luxury crops': asparagus, cucumbers, strawberries, tomatoes, pineapples, mangoes, beef, chicken, even flowers, where there is an affluent market that can afford to buy these products.

Palm oil is one such story. We heard about a producers' entente for palm oil and looked into it to see how it might help underdeveloped countries that export palm oil. The producers' entente was, in effect, none other than the Anglo-Dutch multinational company, Unilever, one of the first corporations profiting on tropical agriculture, and now the ninth biggest company in the world. Unilever now controls 80 per cent of the international oil seed market. The producers' entente has six members, but Zaire-Palm, an arm of Unilever in Zaire, exports over 80 per cent of the group's total. When the world market price for palm oil dips, the local government and the peasant producers suffer, not Unilever. The company simply 'slows down their activities when the price goes down and appeals to the State for multiple tax and other exemptions.' Unilever thus buffers itself from the vagaries of the international palm oil market. A nice arrangement – for Unilever.

Furthermore, agribusiness 'expertise' is not so much in producing as in marketing. They know who and where the world's affluent shoppers are – a small group in the underdeveloped world's urban centres such as Mexico City, Nairobi, Delhi, and Rio and a much larger group in New York, Tokyo, London, and Stockholm. And agribusiness knows what they 'demand'.

Del Monte is but one example of agribusiness creating a Global Farm to service a Global Supermarket. Del Monte operates farms, fisheries, and processing plants in more than two dozen countries. Board Chairman Alfred Eames, Jr., wrote glowingly in a recent annual report: 'Our business isn't just canning, it's feeding people.' But which people? Del Monte is operating Philippine plantations to feed the banana-starved Japanese; contracting with Mexican growers to feed asparagus-cravers in France, Denmark, and Switzerland; and opening a new plantation in Kenya so that the British need not go without their jet-fresh pineapple.

Del Monte finds that pineapple that would bring only 8 cents in the Philippines (still a significant portion of a worker's pay) can bring $1.50 in Tokyo. No wonder that Del Monte exports 90 per cent of its Philippine production. Yet the average Filipino has virtually the same inadequate calorie intake as the average Bangladeshi and serious protein-calorie undernutrition affects an estimated half of all Filipino children under four – one of the highest rates in the world.

There is nothing really new in food being grown for those who can afford to buy it. What is new is the agribusiness notion that *all* the world can be one Global Farm. Production of many low-nutrition crops that can fetch premium prices for the seller is being shifted out of the countries where most of the buyers live. These overseas production sites, in many countries with vast under-nourished populations, are becoming mere extensions of the agricultural systems of western countries. In fact, the corporations themselves regularly refer to their farms and processing plants in underdeveloped countries as 'offshore production units' – a revealing terminology.

The Mexican Connection

In Mexico the rush to link up with the Global Supermarket is far advanced. Traditionally, the American sunbelt and more northern greenhouses have supplied the United States with vegetables during the winter and early spring. But now agribusiness giants such as Del Monte, General Foods, and Campbell's, as well as numerous southwest-based 'food brokers' and contracting supermarket chains such as Safeway and Grand Union, are changing all that.

Take the asparagus industry. Up until a few years ago you could bet the asparagus that was exported from the United States to Europe was grown in central California. But now a significant part of production has been shifted to Irapuato, 150 miles north-west of Mexico City.[1] Since 1975, for instance, white asparagus is no longer grown in California. In Mexico, two firms control over 90 per cent of asparagus production. One of them is Del Monte. In 1973, Del Monte paid American asparagus farmers 23 cents a pound for their crop; Mexican Del Monte contractors got 10 cents a pound.[2] The Mexican contractors pay the seasonal workers a mere 23 cents an hour.[3] Since labour costs account for up to 70 per cent of the cost of growing vegetables, Del Monte translates cheap labour into bigger profit margins.[4]

Mexican soil and labour are already supplying one half to two thirds of the United States market for many winter and early spring vegetables.[5] The rate of increase has been phenomenal.

Here are a few examples of the shift in Mexico from cultivation for local consumption to production for the United States.[6] Most are operations contracted and financed by American firms. From 1960 to 1974, onion imports from Mexico to the United States increased over five times to 95 million pounds. From 1960 to 1976, cucumber imports soared from under 9 million to over 196 million pounds. From 1960 to 1972, eggplant imports multiplied ten times, and squash imports multiplied forty-three times. Frozen strawberries and cantaloupe from Mexico now supply a third of United States annual consumption. The National Bank of Mexico notes that domestic strawberry consumption depends on 'what's left over after exports.'[7] About half of all the tomatoes sold in the wintertime in the United States come from Mexico, or, more precisely from some 50 growers in the state of Sinaloa who in 1976 sold about 600 million pounds of tomatoes to the US West and Midwest.

The shift is so far advanced that Ray Goldberg, of the Harvard Business School, in his 1974 study *Agribusiness Management for*

Developing Countries notes, 'If the recent rates of growth of imports from Mexico continue, in a relatively short time Mexico will account for almost the entire winter supply of most of these fruits and vegetables.' The same study goes so far as to recommend that Mexico 'seek further expansion' of vegetable exports.[8]

Multinational agribusiness is radically altering the availability of food for Mexico's poor, but in the wrong direction. Only a few years ago the national production of many fruits and vegetables was sufficient to keep prices low enough for lower-income families to eat some of these local products, at least occasionally. But now luxury crops grown for the Global Supermarket often crowd out more nutritious crops for local consumption,[9] taking over land that previously had grown up to twelve local food crops.[10] The land that is now contracted by Del Monte once grew corn, wheat, and sunflower seeds for local consumption. (Significantly, crops for the Global Supermarket monopolize the funds and services of government agriculture programmes.) As obvious as it may sound, we must remind ourselves that land growing crops for the Global Supermarket is land the local people cannot use to grow food crops for themselves. Higher prices of basic staples due to distortion of production priorities are making even beans a luxury Mexico's poor can no longer afford.

A Cucumber Republic?

In order to play off both US and Mexican producers, agribusiness has started contracting with Central American businessmen-farmers for alternative sources for a wide variety of fresh fruits and vegetables. While banana exports barely increased, the volume of other fresh fruits and vegetables (such as cucumber, cantaloupe, honeydew, and okra) entering the United States from Central America rose thirteenfold between 1964 and 1972. Focusing narrowly on gross production and revenue figures without asking who benefits and who loses, agricultural economists and international aid and lending agencies have applauded this diversification into 'nontraditional' fruits and vegetables. ('Nontraditional' is in contrast to the great 'tradition' of bananas, coffee, and cotton.)

Enthusiasts see this sharp increase as only the beginning for Central America. According to Goldberg, such nontraditional exports could jump from 18 million pounds weight in 1972 to over 100 million pounds per year by 1980. They could become a *new* tradition! Already by 1969 over 19 per cent of the total crop area of Central America was planted with nontraditional fruits and vegetables.[11] If we combine this 19 per cent with the 29 per cent of the crop-land devoted to coffee, cotton, and sugar exports[12] – not to mention untold acres for banana and cattle exports – we begin to understand why so many people in these countries are undernourished.

The utter inability of the Global Farm to meet the needs of the majority of the people – the absurdity of the whole scheme – came home to us in one fact, so calmly stated in the Harvard Business School study already mentioned: At least 65 per cent of the fruits and vegetables produced in Central America for export is 'literally dumped or, where feasible, used as animal feed'[13] because it either confronts an oversupplied market in the United States or does not meet the 'beauty' standards of consumers there, while at home, where it is produced, people are too poor to buy it.

Strawberry Fields Forever?

In only fifteen years whole areas of Mexico have been turned into strawberry fiefdoms by US-based suppliers to the Global Market: Pet Milk, Ocean Garden, Imperial Frozen Foods, Griffin and Brand, and Better Food Sales. Already by 1970 over 150 million pounds, three-quarters frozen, were being exported to the United States annually.

For two years Dr Ernest Feder, formerly an FAO specialist on peasants in Latin America, painstakingly investigated the strawberry industry in Mexico. He was not particularly fascinated with strawberries – in fact, he is allergic to them – but he believed the industry would show how agribusiness affects rural people in an underdeveloped country.[14]

Dr Feder's research makes clear that, first of all, we should not speak of the *Mexican* strawberry industry but of the US strawberry industry located in Mexico. Officially, Mexican growers produce the berries and even own some of the processing facilities. The real control, however, remains with the American investors and food wholesalers. Using production contacts and credit facilities, these American firms make all the important decisions: the quantity, quality, types, and prices of inputs; how and when the crop will be cultivated; the marketing processes, including prices for the producers; the transportation and the distribution; and the returns on capital investments. US marketing control is so powerful that, despite efforts by the Mexican government to develop markets in

Europe, all Mexican strawberries pass through American exporters even when ultimately retailed in a third country such as Canada or France.

Even more revealing of this control, all strawberry plants come from nurseries in the United States. After fifteen years of commercial strawberry growing, Mexico does not yet have its own source of high-grade strawberry seedlings based on varieties best adapted to conditions in Mexico. Only two varieties are sold to Mexican producers; and they are not necessarily those best adapted to Mexico but the ones that meet the preferences of American consumers.

Although competition among strawberry producers might appear as a war between Mexican and Californian producers, in fact the rivalry is between two American groups, with different production sites. And the only way the Mexican production site can compete with the Californian one (where inputs and careful management give high yields per worker and per acre) is by keeping production costs extremely low. First, wages *must* be kept miserably low. Wages average only one seventh of those in California, even taking into account the higher cost of living in the United States. Feder is convinced that the very enforcement of Mexican minimum wage laws would 'tend to drive the US strawberry industry located in Mexico back to the US or into some other Latin American country.'

Second, the US strawberry industry's interest in Mexico is strongly linked to cheap land and water. Water is 'cheap' to the investors since its cost is largely paid for by federally funded irrigation schemes.

Third, the investors, Feder observes, bring in only enough technology to keep production going without raising costs. If they were to put in the type of money that would give yields comparable to those in California, they might as well stay in the United States.

Finally, the attraction of Mexico is that land obtained cheaply can be treated cheaply. Rather than requiring careful farming and applying inputs to increase yields, more land is ploughed. The land, according to Feder, is 'plundered': bad plants, destructive use of irrigation, bad farming, and misuse of pesticides are in many places ruining the soils. But agribusiness knows that it can just move on to new land, eventually even into another country, where the whole process can be started again.

Because such an agricultural system is not oriented to the needs of the domestic population, it is, by that very fact, thrown into competition with production centres in other countries. To compete commercial agriculture in Mexico must maintain underdevelopment (cheap wages and land) even at serious jeopardy to the longer term future. It is a vicious circle: this maintenance of underdevelopment ensures the continuing absence of a strong domestic market that alone could orient production toward local consumption.

The Desert May Bloom . . . but for Whom?

It takes a lot of freight to fill a DC-10 jumbo jet. Yet three times a week from early December until May a chartered DC-10 cargo jet takes off from Senegal's dusty Dakar airport loaded with green beans, melons, tomatoes, aubergines, strawberries, and paprika. Ironically these food airlifts began just as the drought in Senegal was beginning and they dramatically increased even as it was getting worse.[15]

In the late 1960s, certain agribusiness firms circled Africa's semiarid regions on their world maps. Were they concerned about hunger there? No. What they saw in the Sahel was not hunger but low-cost production sites from which they might profit, given the European demand for fresh winter produce.

In 1971, Fritz Marschall, an executive of the European affiliate of the world-ranging Bud Antle Inc., now a subsidiary of Castle and Cooke Dole, visited Senegal. Marschall was struck by the similarity of the climate of Senegal to that of southern California, where only two generations ago United States government irrigation projects had made the desert bloom. Why couldn't Senegal, he mused, replace California as his company's source of vegetables for the high-priced European winter market? As a confidential World Bank report noted, 'Senegal is the closest country to the European market where vegetables can be cultivated in the open, without glass or plastic protection during the winter.' By February of the following year, Marschall had set up Bud Senegal as an affiliate of Bud Antle's Brussels affiliate, the House of Bud.

Today, Bud Senegal operates giant garden plantations, using nothing but the latest technology. Israeli, Dutch, and American engineers have set up a drip irrigation system with miles of perforated plastic tubing. The water for this system comes over some distance from northern Senegal through pipelines installed at government expense. In order to make way for mechanized production, Bud uprooted scores of centuries-old baobab trees, To remove baobab, sometimes as much as thirty-feet in diameter, required the power of two or even three Caterpillars. The local villagers explained to us the value of these unusual trees: Not only do they protect the soil, but they provide the local people with material for making everything from rope to houses.

Since the undertaking is billed as 'development,' Bud has had to come up with virtually none of its own capital. Major stockholders and soft-term creditors include the Senegalese government, the House of Bud, the World Bank, and the German Development Bank. The Senegalese government also helped by removing villagers from land that was to become Bud's plantations. Even four members of the Peace Corps helped develop the vegetable plantations for marketing through Bud.

Despite the rhetoric about development and the reality of widespread undernourishment in Senegal, all the production is geared to feeding consumers in the European Common Market. This, in spite of the fact that in 1974 alone European taxpayers spent $53 million to destroy ('withdraw from the market') European-produced vegetables in order to keep prices up. One year green bean prices in Europe went lower than the costs of picking, packing, and air freighting Bud's big crop in Senegal. Did that mean more food for hungry Senegalese? Hardly. As the director of Bud Holland, Paul van Pelt, admitted 'since the Senegalese are not familiar with green beans and don't eat them, we had to destroy them.'

From May to December, European tariffs make it unprofitable to export any vegetables. Does Bud Senegal let its plantations lie fallow or allow the local people to grow food for themselves during those months? Again, no. Bud's better idea is to grow feed for livestock.

In July 1977, the Senegalese government fully nationalized Bud Senegal reportedly because the government thought the income was not being fully accounted for. The House of Bud, however, continues to handle the marketing of the plantation's vegetables in Europe – invariably the most profitable part of the operation. Visiting the Sahel in late 1977, we learned that Bud is breaking ground or planning to do so in nine other African countries.

American Foods Share Co, a multinational corporation owned by two Swedish shipping firms, also has its eyes on Africa. President Robert F. Zwarthuis states 'Anyone who says that "we go to

Ethiopia in order to help those poor things" is lying.' The company is now 'trying out' countries such as the Ivory Coast, Egypt, Kenya, and Ethiopia as production sites for supplying Europe. Investments in Africa, he estimates, can expect a yield on capital two to two-and-one-half times those in Sweden.[16]

Zwarthuis admits that the need for a 'continuous supply' makes him favour countries like Egypt 'which do not have any local market for these products.' He foresees that 'Africa is going to become the world's biggest producer of vegetables, not only to Europe but also to America.' Recent World Bank reports on Senegal and Mauritania also see the region's future in mango, aubergines, and avocado exports.

Why is Africa so attractive to agribusiness? Not only is it close to high-paying consumers in the Middle East and Western Europe but many African countries offer the prospect of unutilized land. Take the case of Ethiopia, where, notwithstanding the recent severe famines, *most* of the arable land, held in large estates was not utilized. The existence of large, uncultivated royal and church estates was an open invitation to agribusiness looking for cheap production sites. In the early 1970s, the government of Haile Selassie granted a concession to the Italian firm MAESCO to produce alfalfa to feed livestock in Japan. Ethiopia's climate makes possible several cuttings of alfalfa a year, compared to only two or three in the United States. MAESCO's plantation is in the area where thousands of people, evicted by such commercial plantations from their best grazing lands, starved to death in 1973 along with their herds of camels, sheep, cattle, and goats. That year MAESCO started to raise cattle and sheep for export.[17]

Exporting the Steak Religion

United States firms have set out with missionary zeal to spread the American steak religion to the world. Yet, we ask, who benefits? Is the meat going to the hungry? Or does it merely mean low cost imports for fast-food chains in the United States?

From one third to one half of total meat production in Central America and the Dominican Republic is exported – principally to the United States. Alan Berg, in his Brookings Institution study of world nutrition, notes that, despite dramatic gains in per capita meat production in Central America, the meat is 'ending up not in Latin American stomachs but in franchised restaurant hamburgers in the United States.'[18] Central America has become the chosen site for investment in meat export operations, first because it is so close to the United States and, second, because it is free from foot-and-mouth disease, not true of Argentina and Brazil whose fresh and chilled meat imports are not allowed into the United States. Should Central America consider itself fortunate?

In 1975, Costa Rica, with a population of 2 million, sent 60 million pounds weight of beef to the United States. Per capita beef consumption declined in Costa Rica from almost 49 pounds in 1950 to 33 pounds in 1971. If the 60 million pounds exported had stayed in Costa Rica, local meat consumption would have doubled.

Per capita consumption figures, however, are deceptive. Many Costa Ricans – those without land or jobs to earn money – can never afford meat no matter how much is available. One half of the country's children do not get enough food to eat, much less meat. True, however, to the Global Supermarket phenomenon, a few well-off Costa Ricans can afford to get some Costa Rican beef just like Americans – at one of the three McDonald's in San José. ('El Big Mac' is now in every Central American capital.)

The export market for beef has lured farmers, in countries like Costa Rica and Guatemala, away from raising dairy cows. The result has been sharp increases in the price of milk, putting it out of reach of most families.

We might think that, even though most of the meat gets exported because people are too poor to buy it, at least local folk are the ones who make money on these exports. But are we really talking about Central American small-time producers making good in the big-country market?

Not exactly. Those profiting in the meat export market are the traditional oligarchs as well as former United States diplomats (e.g., the ex-ambassadors to Nicaragua and British Honduras), a former Peace Corps director in Costa Rica, big western ranchers (including the lawyer for the country-sized King Ranch in Texas), and giant processors like United Brands' meat subsidiary John Morrell Co.[19] Even industrial multinational corporations like Volkswagen are getting into the beef business. As one Volkswagen executive pointed out, 'You get a lot more for a pound of sirloin than a pound of beetle in Tokyo.'

The World Bank, regional banks, and agribusiness corporations, working in projects costing several billion dollars, seem as committed as ever to increasing cattle production for export from Latin America and Africa. Several studies indicate it may be only the beginning.[20] The growth rate for world demand for beef has been higher than that for any other agricultural item.

Those who demand meat with every meal are capable of being coaxed on to a higher and higher price to get it. The American steak religion has already caught on in Japan and Western Europe and is becoming the 'in' thing in Eastern Europe, the Soviet Union, and the oil-producing Middle East. In many Asian countries, a taste for grain-fed meat is being developed. But why is cattle production shifting to the underdeveloped countries? First, big US ranchers have turned away from the higher land and labour costs of the United States. As one rancher put it: 'Here's what it boils down to – $95 per cow per year in Montana, $25 in Costa Rica.'[21]

Second, to avoid the rising costs of feedgrains, the beef industry is searching for areas where grazing is economical. Moreover, multinational conglomerates have recently taken over the major meat-processing firms. (Now Armour is really Greyhound, Wilson is LTV, Swift is Esmark, and Morrell is, as we just saw, another way of saying United Brands.) As meatcutters in the United States and Europe are just beginning to realize, these firms will now try to transfer labour-intensive meat preparation (boning, prepacking) right to the new production sites in cheap-labour countries. Finally, giant agribusiness firms do not want the bother of purchasing from several independent suppliers and competing among themselves for those supplies. Thus, United Brands is integrating backwards to ranching subsidiaries, especially attractive due to cheap labour, government incentives, and available development funds, in countries like Honduras. The Global Ranch is but a variant of the Global Farm.

Another impetus behind shifting the beef industry abroad is the US government and corporate drive to build markets for American grain and soybean exports. Meat production may yet become the equivalent of the 1960s 'screwdriver' industries for many Third World countries. Just as in the sixties underdeveloped countries began assembling consumer items that were machined in industrial countries for shipment *back* to industrial markets, cattle operations controlled by multinational corporations commonly import American grain to be fed to animals that then get shipped to the United States.

In their drive to increase exports to Western Europe, Japan, and the United States, many governments in underdeveloped countries have enacted a whole series of measures to *de*crease domestic beef consumption at home. Several Latin American countries, including even Argentina and Uruguay, have even decreed days and weeks of the year during which no beef can be sold. (The principal impact has been that the well-off suddenly decide it is time to buy a freezer!)

Africa has many of the same attractive features for livestock investors as Latin America. European corporations are reportedly considering numerous ranching projects in Kenya and the Sudan – some of the finest and cheapest grazing land near Europe. According to one FAO officer who is afraid to be quoted, the plan is to use Green Revolution inputs on fully mechanized farms to raise feed grains. This feed would fatten the animals brought in from ranches. The goal is export.

A Chicken in Every Pot?

We tend to think of chicken as a true 'people's food' compared to meat. Promoting chicken in the underdeveloped countries might sound like a good idea: Isn't a low-cost source of protein just what they need?

But that is not how Ralston Purina sees it. Ralston Purina considered creating a poultry industry in Colombia, not so that the poor would have more chicken in their diet, but to create a need for its chief product, concentrated feeds. Experience had taught multinational feed companies like Purina that promoting poultry production was the fastest way to create customers for concentrated feed. The poultry business requires less initial capital and land than the cattle-feeding operation. Moreover, poultry feeds are among the most profitable for the feed companies.

First, Purina offered credit to commercial farmers to buy baby chicks and feed. Soon there were more chicks than could be supplied by feedgrain. So the company offered credit to other commercial farmers to grow feed crops and encouraged the government and private creditors to do the same. Traditional food crops like corn gave way to sorghum for feed. A portion of the corn crop that had been for human consumption now brought a higher price as grist for Purina's mill. Beans, another staple of the poor, gave way to soybeans for feed. Between 1958 and 1968, the acreage planted with the traditional beans was halved while soybean plantings – all grown for animal feed – jumped sixfold.

The plight of the poor is compounded by the nature of the

market. As livestock feed production takes up land that once grew beans and grain for human consumption, the prices of these staples go up.

Ralston Purina still likes to talk about how it was a prime mover in the production of new sources of protein: chicken and eggs. It is true that Colombia, an egg importer in 1957, was by 1961 no longer importing eggs. From 1966 to 1971, annual broiler production doubled from 11 million to 22 million. Yet, as the excellent Consumers' Union-sponsored study notes, 'The displacement of cropland from pulses [beans] to feed crops did not simply replace a cheap source of protein with an expensive one. It also reduced the total availability of protein in the country, because animal sources of protein are less efficient to produce than are vegetable sources.'[22]

A plot of land used to grow beans and corn can satisfy the protein requirements of significantly more people than when it is used for animal feed crops. Based on actual experience in the Valle region of Colombia, the Universidad del Valle arrived at the following estimates: One acre of land growing feed crops for chickens provides only one-third the amount of protein for people that the same land could provide if it grew corn or beans; if the acre grew soybeans for human consumption, it could provide sixteen times more protein than is produced by using that land to grow chicken feed.[23] Using the feed to produce eggs instead of chicken reduces these differences somewhat. But according to calculations based on Colombian government statistics for 1970, a dozen eggs would cost more than an entire week's earnings for over a quarter of the population.

Ralston Purina and the other feed companies in Colombia like to cite figures showing increases in per capita egg consumption. But, as usual, per capita figures are misleading. Higher averages merely reflect the increased consumption of eggs by the small middle- and upper-income groups, directly or in processed items such as snack foods and mayonnaise. For all the additional eggs Ralston Purina can count on a national basis, there is evidence that Colombia's protein gap is growing eight times faster than the population.[24]

Thus what looked like just the way to create a needed source of cheap protein for Colombians turns out to undermine the only accessible protein sources of the people. Ralston Purina helps teach us, as discussed earlier in Part V, that 'modern' techniques and production skills in themselves mean nothing. We must always ask: For what? For whom? At the cost of what alternatives? The answer to these questions will be determined by who is in charge of the production: the people themselves or multinational corporations.

Where Have All the Flowers Gone?

Another 'know-how' that agribusiness is eager to bring to underdeveloped countries is the production of 'ornamental crops' – the academic name for cut flowers and foliage.

If the local peasants cannot afford chicken or eggs, perhaps they can brighten their shacks with cut flowers. Since 1966 the value of cut flowers and foliage imported into the United States has increased over sixty times to over $20 million in 1975 – over 90 per cent coming from Latin America.[25] Some experts feel that by 1980 it will no longer be 'feasible' to produce cut flowers in many current production areas in the United States.

The favoured country so far is Colombia, where cut flowers are now a $17-million-a-year business. In 1973, a Colombian government economist estimated for us that one hectare planted with carnations brings in a million pesos a year; planted with wheat or corn, the same hectare would bring only 12,500.[26] Given that at least 70 per cent of Colombia's agricultural land is controlled by a small group of wealthy farmers who need not think of land in terms of growing food to live by, it is not at all surprising that ornamental crops join feedgrain and cattle on their list of priority crops.

Ecuador and Guatemala, and to a lesser extent Mexico, are also being transformed into major flower production sites for the Global Supermarket. Already in 1972, Guatemala was supplying the United States with 159,278,421 – the USDA counts them! – chrysanthemums, roses, pompoms, daisies, chamaedorea, and statice.

Agribusiness's shifting of flower production to underdeveloped countries to supply the Global Supermarket follows the twofold pattern we have seen with other crops.[27] First is the search for lower-cost production sites (land preparation costs for flower cultivation in Central America have been estimated to be less than 10 per cent of comparable costs in Florida). Second is the corporate effort to integrate operations from the seed to the flower shop. The US flower business has historically consisted of large numbers of independent enterprises: small growers, larger grower-shippers, and tens of thousands of retail shops. But certain agri-business firm such as Sears, Green Giant, Pillsbury, and United Brands and the supermarket chains are beginning to eye the profits to be made by linking the retailing to low-cost foreign production sites[28] – an integration process that is a little out of the reach of your neighbourhood florist. United Brands is known already to have production operations of several hundred acres in Central America and plans for major expansion. They will market the flowers through supermarket chains and franchised stores ('Flowers from Sears' and Backman's European Flower Markets, a subsidiary of Pillsbury). Neighbourhood florist shops could well go the way of tens of thousands of other corner shops – out of business.

So agribusiness firms are doing exactly what the question suggests: bringing their production know-how to the countries where many go without food. But what are they growing? Asparagus, cucumbers, strawberries, aubergines, beef, and flowers – 'luxury crops.' And for whom? For the well-fed to whom it is profitable to sell. More and more of the prime agricultural resources that the hungry people abroad need for their food get channelled into supplying well-fed foreigners.

The corporations described are not the worst. They are run by managers, probably no better or more ill-intentioned than any others. But there is one fundamental obstacle: corporations must sell for a profit. You say that agribusiness firms cannot afford not to be successful. You are right. 'The bottom line is what counts,' James McKee, chief executive of CPC International, told us in an interview. 'If we lose sight of that, no matter how much good we were doing, we wouldn't be around long.' But that is exactly the reason they cannot help the hungry. No matter how many hungry people there are, as long as they are being impoverished, hungry people just do not add up to a market.

Help for the Local Economy

To find out whether multinational corporations help Third World countries by providing local jobs and income, we must look at how they operate overseas. Traditionally, foreign agricultural investment in an underdeveloped country meant owning and operating plantations. This is changing. Due to risk of 'expropriation, revolution or insurrection' plantations are a 'poor risk' says the

Overseas Private Investment Corporation (OPIC),[29] the United States government agency insuring American firms against just such risks. Direct ownership of production, moreover, is not attractive to a corporation seeking to tie up as little capital as possible.

Contract Farming

By 1965 agribusiness investment in direct land ownership abroad was half the value of a decade earlier.[30] Nevertheless this decline has come at a time of a stepped up interest in investment in Third World agriculture. Is this a contradiction? Not really: Many agribusiness firms are shifting from the plantation mode to that of 'contract farming.' Exceptions are found where military dictatorships make foreign corporations feel totally secure and when firms find that they must produce directly in order to control quality.

Instead of owning land and farming directly, contract farming means that the corporation gets local producers to sign a contract committing them to use certain inputs to produce a stipulated amount of specified products with the date of delivery to the corporation and the price fixed. The corporation obviously still maintains the control it requires, with little capital invested – and, best of all, there is nothing that can be nationalized.

As a food corporation, Nestlé is second only to the Anglo-Dutch conglomerate Unilever in size. Over 50 per cent of their turnover derives from products using milk, cocoa or coffee as raw materials[31] and yet Nestlé owns not a single cow nor an acre of coffee nor cocoa producing estates. It doesn't need to. It can control production more effectively and with less risk by dominating the local commodity markets and by monopolising supplies to the producers.

For example, dairy farmers in Brazil sow their pastures with seeds selected by Nestlé's Brazil research station. Loans are given to farmers for the purchase of these seeds as well as cattle fodder, vaccines and farm machinery. Nestlé then buys the farmers' milk output and deducts from its payment an amount for loan repayment. It is unlikely that either small or large farmers would be in a position to refuse such loans – being unwilling to risk offending perhaps the only customer for the milk.[32] For Nestlé it is ideal (no pun intended on one of their best known brands). They can control the quantity and quality of the milk. No money is tied up in farming. The farmers take all the risks and pay interest to Nestlé on the loans they have taken.

Being in such a powerful position enables Nestlé to get the commodities at a bargain price, too. In Ghana, Nestlé paid an average of $1135 per tonne for cocoa in 1974 (when the world price was $2163). They paid the Ivory Coast $393 per tonne for coffee (less than one-third of the world price) and sugar producers throughout the world 57 per cent of the going rate.[33]

Nestlé finds the Third World a valuable supplier of another essential commodity – labour. Throughout the world Nestlé's wage bill comes to about 16 per cent of turnover whereas in Africa it is one tenth of this and in Asia accounts for only 2.8 per cent of turnover.[34]

We might suppose that the Third World tax collectors would reap a tidy sum from the profits of Nestlé subsidiaries in their countries. Not one bit. The latest records show that in Latin America as a whole – where the Nestlé turnover is more than £500m per year – they actually make a loss. Bad management? Unlikely. Nestlé is known for its rigorous training of managerial staff.

More to the point is the art of 'transfer pricing', whereby profits are shifted from one country to another where taxes are lower. Funds lent to an overseas subsidiary by the parent corporation at a high rate of interest,[35] or generous payments by the subsidiary to the parent for the privilege of using a well-known brand name,[36] are two such techniques.

Transfer pricing is not just used in the Third World, either. It helps to explain why Nestlé's $650m US operations (where taxes are about 40 per cent) makes a loss,[37] as does the enormous UK subsidiary. However the Swiss subsidiary (where Nestlé on average pays a mere 5 per cent of its profits in taxes[38]) declares over £300m in profits.

United Brands (who markets Fyffe's bananas in the UK) pioneered the way to get out of direct ownership and still maintain control. It saw the light in 1960 when the Cuban government nationalized 271,000 acres.[39]

The company began to develop its 'Associate Producer Programme,' which allowed it to sell much of its land. In Central America alone UB's direct ownership has fallen from close to two million acres in 1954 to a third of that by 1971. In Ecuador the company sold all its extensive holdings by the mid-sixties. But in every case UB maintained total control.

An associate producer is a local person who buys or leases land from the plantation company. Such an individual is hardly a struggling small farmer. In Guatemala Del Monte's one associate producer, formerly contracting with United Fruit, has over 3,000 acres.[40] A United Nations study found that Del Monte's thirteen associate producers in Costa Rica own an average of 612 acres each.[41] The associate producers contract to buy their inputs and technical assistance from the company and to sell their entire production to it. If the company believes an associate is politically well placed, he or she might also receive a company loan to get started. The company splits the difference between the total cost of production and the purchase price *the company sets*. In addition, the company nets a further profit marketing the produce in what *Business Week* calls 'the big, well-heeled market.'[42] There are two additional bonuses to such contracting for the foreign companies: one economic and the other political. When the foreign market is booming, the companies rely on the associate producers to supplement their own direct plantation production. But when an oversupply might depress prices, the companies simply raise quality standards so as to reduce purchases from their associate producers. Politically, the system gives foreign companies an influential bloc of nationals who identify their welfare with that of the companies – the best insurance against nationalization of the remaining holdings or against national tax reforms, as the banana companies proved in 1974.

The corporation may not be called United Fruit anymore and soon there may be no more company plantations, yet little has changed for the ordinary people. The best lands still grow fruits like bananas and vegetables for the world's well-fed. Still the best that rural inhabitants can hope for are low-wage, seasonal jobs in an associate producer's field. Most of the value produced still goes to UB.

Former US Secretary of Agriculture Orville Freeman, a leading agribusiness spokesperson, thinks this type of contract farming holds a bright future for Third World agriculture. He is now president of Business International and of a company called Multinational Agribusiness Systems, Inc. At a United Nations-organized conference on agribusiness and world hunger,[43] he shared his vision with other multinational executives of 'a kind of contract farming' he prefers to call 'satellite farming.' He foresees 'many agribusiness companies' – he named Del Monte, FMC, International Systems and Controls, the Hawaiian super companies, and

Nestlé – with 'the experience, technology and the management know-how' cultivating a 'core-producing unit of optimum size, using the most modern technology,' and providing 'supervisory services' to 'hundreds of adjacent small farmers' and contracting their production.

Such a vision is not new. Contract farming was not invented by agribusiness for underdeveloped countries. It is an already proven tool of agribusiness in gaining control over food production in western countries too.

The food business in Europe is tightly controlled, but nowhere more than in the UK. Stemming from colonial days with a traditional dependence on imported food, Britain has developed a highly centralized food industry – whose companies on the whole dwarf its European counterpart. So 14 UK food companies have turnovers exceeding £100m p.a. whereas the original six members of the EEC put together can only muster 4 such companies.[44] Out of the top 200 European companies recorded in 'Vision', 12 are British food companies, only 6 are food companies from elsewhere.

This sort of agglomeration of power inevitably brings with it a near monopoly of the raw materials market. For instance, Unilever (who own Birds Eye and Batchelors) has almost complete control of the pea market of East Anglia without owning a single acre of farmland itself. They not only tell the farmer what particular variety of pea to grow, but also when to plant, what fertilizer to apply, when to harvest and what price they will pay.[45] Unilever shoulders no risk. If there is a glut, or if for some reason the peas turn out too hard, they don't have the problem of finding another customer.

No examination of contract farming is complete without looking at the American poultry industry: the first in the United States with contract operations on a large scale.

The production contract was the tool by which corporations like Ralston Purina, Cargill, Pillsbury, and Continental Grain took control of chicken production in the United States beginning in the late 1950s. Since at that time prices were only a few pennies a pound, an offer of credit from the corporation was one a hard up independent farmer could hardly refuse. These same corporations controlled the feedgrain market and, sure enough, the contract required the farmer to use only his creditor's feed.

Within ten years the percentage of United States chicken production under contract went from 4 per cent to 92 per cent.[46]

These contracted farmers are in reality little more than hired hands in a corporate factory. Only there is one big difference. It is they who must go into debt to build the 'factory' and put in new equipment. As an official of the Mississippi Farm Bureau told USDA researchers, 'Today a Mississippi farmer could not sell broilers in the market if he wanted to produce them. Farmers do not own the birds. They furnish only the labour and the houses. They do exactly what they are told.'[47]

George Anthan, a first-rate investigative reporter for the *Des Moines Register*, described a recent visit to a poultry area in Northern Alabama after the 'integrators' came in:

For farmers to get a contract, certain 'improvements' specified by the corporation had to be made on their farms. These investments were financed by the farmers through local banks. Failure to meet the specifications would result in the contract being withdrawn, leaving the farmer virtually without a market. The integrators did not offer long-term contracts in exchange for the farmers making the changes the companies insisted upon. The farmers I talked to said that every time it looked like they were going to get the loan paid off, the integrators would come up with a new 'improvement' like gas heaters, insulated chicken houses, and automatic feeding equipment. Once in debt, the farmers had to stay in business, but to stay in business they had to get deeper in debt. One of the farmers described himself and other poultry farmers as the 'new slaves.'
Most of the farmers had to take jobs in town to supplement their incomes and usually had a wife or daughter working in the local poultry processing plant for minimum wages. Farmers were getting about 2c a pound for their chicken. I didn't find a single farmer making more per pound than they made five to ten years ago, but their costs had doubled.[48]

According to Harrison Wellford in the chapter 'Poultry Peonage' of his pioneering study *Sowing the Wind*,[49] a USDA economist found Alabama chicken growers making minus 36 cents an hour for their service to the corporations. The same USDA study in 1967 concluded chicken farmers were pauperized because of their lack of bargaining strength in dealing with the corporations. In 1962, some poultry growers in Arkansas under contract to processing companies tried to organize an association. The companies blacklisted the growers and ruined them by making certain that they could never again receive a contract.[50]

Growers do not dare speak out against the unfair trade practices for fear of being blacklisted. This fear was dramatized in an interview with a contracting chicken grower in Alabama on ABC-TV in 1973.[51] The woman so feared reprisals that she would not allow her face to be shown or any mention of the corporation for which she raised chickens. At the end, the interviewer asked, 'Why do you stay in the business of chicken raising?' The reply: 'We have to! We'll lose our house mortgaged to pay $29,600 for the chicken houses. Our farm. Everything we've worked for.'

In 1958, Earl Butz, just having left the post of Assistant Secretary of Agriculture to become both Dean of Agriculture at Purdue and a director of Ralston Purina, wrote a widely disseminated article directed at American farmers titled, 'Don't Be Afraid of Integration' (certainly an eye-catching title in the South in 1958). Today agribusiness, the United States government, and the World Bank would have farmers in underdeveloped countries trust the corporate hand, hoping they have not heard of the fate of small American chicken farmers.

Tens of thousands of American farmers, hardly naïve to the ways of the modern world and living in a country with an array of antimonopoly and fair trade laws as well as regulatory agencies, have not been able to protect their interests against a few powerful poultry supply and marketing corporations. What then is the likelihood that farmers, even the better off, in countries like Pakistan, Mexico, Colombia, and Thailand will fare any better?

Agribusiness and the Peasant

What is the real life condition of those who labour to supply the Global Supermarket? Has the coming of agribusiness meant decent jobs, income for adequate food and a secure foundation for development? Certainly not in the case of the thriving strawberry industry in Mexico studied in-depth by Ernest Feder in his book *Strawberry Imperialism: An Enquiry into the Mechanisms of Dependency in Mexican Agriculture.*

As Feder relates, in the mid 1960s, before the strawberry boom hit the Zamora Valley, Zamora and the neighbouring Jacona were small towns. Today Zamora has 100,000 inhabitants and Jacona 30,000. Thousands more come to the valley in search of work and return to their villages at night or sleep in the streets, since the cost of transportation for some represents 30 per cent of their daily wage even if they find work. Over three quarters of the population lives in half-mile wide carton-shack slums that ring the towns. No sanitation, no running water, little electricity. All and all, a classic case of 'overpopulation'.

Yet in the Zamora valley you can also find the ranch-style houses of the new 'strawberry millionaires.' As employers, these few individuals and their American partners directly benefit from the desperate misery of the majority. Since the number seeking work far exceeds the number of jobs, the growers are able to hold wages down. Some growers, despite the large numbers of unemployed already in Zamora, send recruiter trucks to outlying villages because the peasants there are willing to work for still less.

In Zamora, during the four months of peak field work you can find over 5,000 would-be workers gathering at 5.30 am next to the railroad station. Guarded by the military armed with submachine guns, they wait for the growers or their agents to come in trucks. The largest growers come to pick up several hundred workers at a time. Still, many do not find a job. They must walk back to their villages only to return the next day hoping for better luck.

Those who do get hired get somewhat under the legal minimum wage of $3 per day. This is particularly true for women and children who, despite the law on equal wages for equal work, have to be content with two thirds of the wages paid to men. The employers say they prefer women and children 'because they do not have to stoop so far,' but fortunes have been made on such thoughtfulness. Like fieldhands in the fruit and vegetable industry in the United States (where the orange crate alone sells for more than the labour to fill it), a family must field every member including young children, if it is to survive.

When the trucks do come, no workers dare to ask how much they would be paid, for, according to Feder, they would simply be told: 'There is no work for you.' The workers climb on board the truck without the slightest idea of where they will be taken, how much they will be paid, or whether they will have work the next day. As one worker put it, 'In order not to starve, we don't ask any questions.'

Employers are known to use a variety of tactics to boost their profit on each worker such as shortening the lunch break and working the labourers overtime and seven days a week without extra pay. Everyday exposure to pesticides results in vomiting, fainting spells, severe headaches, and even death. Efforts to organize for better working conditions have always met with employer violence.

And what about the strawberry-processing and freezing factories? Do they through their famed 'transfer of technology' develop new skills and provide decent employment?

The strawberry factories are geared to just one thing – strawberries. Since strawberries are harvested less than half the year, the factories lie idle six to seven months, employing no one. Despite this wasteful use of capital equipment, owning a factory can be quite lucrative. Feder reports that some companies have recovered their capital investment in a single year. During a few peak weeks the freezing factories in Zamora (most with United States capital) employ 10,000 to 12,000 women and girls, mostly between fourteen and twenty-five years of age. But the work for most is very short-term since the factories operate way below capacity during the beginning and end of the harvest.

Although child labour is illegal, Feder reports that in plants controlled by American capital he found up to sixty children working. The work is monotonous and the conditions are unconscionable. The workers must stand all day even though, during the peak season, that means standing up to eighteen hours a day, at 40 to 50 cents an hour. In some plants supervisors make extra money selling the obligatory white uniforms that cost four to five days' wages.

What about the small farmers in the region – can't they at least profit from growing strawberries? Only in theory. First of all, government permits, aimed at preventing massive overproduction, regulate who can plant how many acres. Since there is money to be made, those with political and economic influence make sure they get the permits.

In one *ejido* land-reform community, 19 out of 220 families received permits. Each recipient had a clear power connection. None actually worked on the land.

The processing factories, according to Feder's research, further narrow down the number of growers. Production contracts favour the larger suppliers, giving them priority and better terms in distribution of inputs and the purchase of their output.

Some larger growers use their influence literally to pocket the key to the watergates of the irrigation system. They can then use water in excess of the legal limit while the small producers are left to fight over the remaining water that trickles down to them. The district's small farmers growing food crops find they have less and less water. Mainly because of the flooding of the strawberry fields, the area irrigated by the Zamora system has actually shrunk. Strawberries use up 75 per cent of the water on only 20 to 30 per cent of the total area under cultivation.

In contrast to the agribusiness-controlled monoculture of today's Zamora, a peasant-controlled agriculture would naturally build on mixed cropping. Mixed cropping is not only environmentally sound (as already discussed in chapter thirteen), but also means year-round food supply and work. Furthermore, when the rural population individually or collectively owns and controls the agricultural resources, it is likely to use its spare time to improve the agricultural resources – drainage, irrigation, terracing, tree planting, storage, and so on. By contrast, in Zamora today, most of the population can obtain at best only part-time seasonal work. The control of the valley's agricultural resources by an export-oriented industry with a pronounced seasonal peak and unstable export markets results in mostly part-time, insecure jobs and a plundering approach to the land.

In Zamora a single system produces millionaires and paupers. It adds up to a stunning waste of human life, as well as agricultural resources and even the vast underutilization of investment capital. Hardly a foundation for development.

Counter Land Reform

Much of what we have learned points to one truth: People must control their agricultural resources if they are to free themselves from hunger. Yet supposed land redistribution programmes in such countries as Brazil, Colombia, Central America, the Shah's Iran, and the Philippines have exempted agribusiness land, even though it is often the best land.

The Philippines, a country with an estimated 3,000,000 landless peasants, is a recent clear example. A 'sweeping' land reform programme – sometimes presented in the media as the justification for the martial law suspension of all human rights – exempted fully two thirds of the country's agricultural land because it has been put into production for the Global Supermarket.

In the Bukidnon region Del Monte is attempting to coerce self-provisioning smallholders to lease their land to the company.

Armed company agents have fenced off and driven cattle onto the cultivated fields of those who refuse to lease.[52] An American priest, arrested for helping the peasants resist, described Del Monte's landgrabbing: 'They bulldozed people right off the land. Now they're using aerial sprays, harming farm animals and giving people terrible rashes.'[53]

Iran is also a prime example: a country where equating agricultural development with agribusiness investment has spelled the *reversal* of land reform. Consequences for the rural population have been disastrous, and are an important cause of the social unrest which swept the Shah from power in February 1979.

In 1962 the Shah of Iran declared a substantial land reform that irrevocably broke the political power of the large landowners. 'Land to the tiller,' however, was taken literally. If a family was not well-off enough to own a plough and a draught animal – and many were not – they could not qualify for the broken-up estates.[54]

Throughout Iran, farmers who did receive land began to produce food. In the Khuzestan province, bordering on Iraq and the Persian Gulf, the farmers' productivity was extraordinary, especially considering the lack of technical assistance and irrigation and the 98 per cent illiteracy. Traditional farming methods provided ample work for all.

Also during the 1960s, the government began to construct several large dams under the supervision of David Lilienthal, Roosevelt's designer of the Tennessee Valley Authority. The largest dam is on the Dez River in Khuzestan. It offered the prospect to the small farmers of over 200,000 acres of irrigated land. It sounded promising. Then, just when the dam was being completed, the Shah and his elite advisors decided that what Khuzestan needed was foreign agribusiness corporations.

Until the overthrow of the Shah, the farmers in Khuzestan could no longer speak of land reform. Nor did they wait for the waters of the Dez to reach their parched lands. Irrigation channels, built for only *one fifth* of the potential irrigated area, took water to the 'farms' managed by such firms as Hawaiian Agronomics, the Diamond A. Cattle Co, Mitsui, Chase Manhattan, Transworld Agricultural Development Corp, Bank of America, Dow Chemical, John Deere & Co, Shell, Mitchell Cotts, and Hashem Naraghi (an Iranian émigré who became a major Californian grower).[55] For most of these firms, Khuzestan was but the latest venture of the Global Farm. Hawaiian Agronomics, for instance, is a subsidiary of C. Brewer – known in most western countries by its C and H brand line – which in 1974 netted $3.8 million from agribusiness operations in Iran, Indonesia, Ecuador, and Guadalcanal.

Khuzestan, instead of being an area of many small family farms utilizing the new irrigation, became a province dominated by large-scale (12,000 to 50,000 acres), highly mechanized, capital-intensive, cash crop units. Some 17,000 Iranians have been pushed off their lands.[56] Hawaiian Agronomics has boasted, 'Land Barren for 23 Centuries Now Producing Food, Supporting Livestock.'[57] The fact that peasants produced food there before the coming of agribusiness has been ignored. Even more significantly, it was the massive irrigation system installed at public expense *before* agribusiness moved in that really made the parched lands productive. As one agribusiness executive remarked, 'they develop the water first and we come in and farm it. It's an attractive arrangement.'[58]

And how have the people of rural Khuzestan been doing? Most are landless and jobless. Some saw no alternative but to flee to the already overcrowded urban slums. They would gladly have farmed if they had their own plots; their real skills were those of small rice farmers. The government did not even train them for semiskilled jobs as construction workers, truck drivers, and machinists in Iran's candyfloss 'boom' economy. While urban unemployment soared, the government *imported* workers – 80,000 South Koreans and innumerable Pakistanis – for such jobs. No wonder so many Iranians were willing to risk all in the year-long demonstrations and riots prior to the Shah's overthrow.

Sweet Corn

Of course not all contract agribusiness projects are export-oriented. At a symposium on world hunger in September 1975, CPC International presented the history of its investment in Pakistan to show what a positive contribution a foreign enterprise can make to a country's food supply. CPC International (known to Americans by its Thomas' English muffins, Skippy Peanut Butter, and Mazola Corn Oil) is no newcomer in underdeveloped countries and therefore can be taken as a significant example of what agribusiness has to offer.

There are two ways of reading the CPC case study the company presented. The intended victory-over-hunger version is roughly as follows: In 1962, CPC International purchased control of Rafhan Maize Products, the largest corn grinding and processing company in Pakistan. By the late 1960s, Rafhan had expanded with loans from US AID and the Pakistani government. But its mills just could not get hold of enough corn. So in January 1970 Rafhan 'launched a corn development programme.' CPC decided it would use the agricultural expertise of its associated companies and brought in its subsidiary from the United States, the Funk Seed Company, to design a high-yielding hybrid. CPC has, the company notes, 'people with know-how.'

Rafhan worked out a contract system with the leading farmers whereby the company would supply on credit the right seed, pesticides, and fertilizers, to be deducted at harvest from the contract price. 'The contract farmers obtained average yields of more than twice the national average.' Rafhan also built 'modern facilities to shell, dry, and store the grain.' So successful was Rafhan that it decided to expand yet further its processing plant.

Sounds good. But let's give it a second, more careful reading. Why was CPC not getting enough corn to its mills? According to the company:

Historically in Pakistan corn has been a food crop consumed by the underprivileged [sic] in the country and in the villages. It has been a popular food commodity because it was nearly always plentifully available during about six months of the year. . . . The price has been lower than the alternative food grains – wheat and rice. Corn has also been used for barter by farmers in the rural areas.[59]

In the 1960s, once CPC moved in, corn prices did increase and some better-off farms expanded total corn production. But still, according to the company, 'the supply of corn available to the processors increased very little.' The company sees three reasons for this: First, corn farmers 'ate too much of their corn' or 'bartered it for [other] food.' Second, as the numbers of the poor grew rapidly they collectively 'consumed increased quantities of corn as food.' Third, the growing poultry industry was competing for the supply of corn.

In order to insure the corn supply it needed, Rafhan introduced a contract system that 'completely changed the pattern of corn production.' Corn farming is no longer the subsistence crop of the small farmer. CPC notes, 'Corn had been cultivated on very small areas – not more than five acres for each farmer – now it was planted in larger fields.'

As for storing the harvest, CPC states 'there were two alternative methods.' One was for the farmers to build narrow corn cribs where the air could circulate between the unshelled ears 'preventing moulding – *until the farmers wanted to sell*' [emphasis ours]. Rafhan, however, chose the other alternative: 'Purchase the corn from farmers at the time of harvest, dry it in mechanical dryers and store it in [the company's] silos.' Why? According to CPC, 'the alternative of helping farmers obtain and own their corn cribs had two weaknesses.' First, Rafhan 'needs' corn, not cobs, and 'the farmer-owned or community-owned shelling equipment is small, slow and inefficient.' Second, when farmers store corn in their own cribs, there was always the chance that they might let family or friends consume the grain; or the farmers might sell or barter it to someone else!

Rafhan *will* have its corn. CPC indirectly notes an added advantage for the company, namely, that by buying up at harvest, rather than 'when the farmers wanted to sell,' the company is likely to get more and get it cheaper since the large supplies at harvest depress the price.

" Improved' corn farming has come to Pakistan. Once a subsistence crop, corn is now grown by large farmers as just one link in a process controlled from seed to bin by CPC's Rafhan.

And what is it all for? To make 'corn sweetener' as a sugar substitute in the fast-growing market for soft drinks and other snack foods among Pakistan's better-off classes.

Foreign corporations in an underdeveloped country's agriculture, then, are no help to the hungry, the landless or the small farmers. Natural resources like land and water, human resources and great sums of capital are spent on making profits for the corporations and their few local partners. The hungry do not benefit. It is not they who eat the food (if indeed it is food that is grown). It is not they who sell the products. Their wages must remain miserably low if production is to compete in the Global Supermarket. Their jobs, relatively few and seasonal compared to what could be the alternatives, are fundamentally insecure. Foods once relatively inexpensive become commercialized at prices affordable only by the world's well-fed. Agribusiness, furthermore, reverses and dooms agrarian reform.

Once a country's elite has opted to make agribusiness the engine of development, government must cater to agribusiness. The government is increasingly deprived of the capacity for independent economic and social planning. The interest of the state becomes indistinguishable from the interests of the multinational agribusiness firms within its territory. 'Fiscal encouragements' lead to more 'fiscal encouragements.' There is the corporation's ever-present threat of pulling up stakes or turning to another country's supply.

Multinational agribusiness, often building a colonial inheritance, is elite-controlled export agriculture under another name.

Among the most important reasons for the internationalization of the multinational corporation is to increase its utility in the developing world of Latin America, Asia and Africa. Its role in the development process becomes more urgently clear every day, as we witness the limitations and handicaps of local governments . . . even if local governments were strong and assistance to them plentiful, the fact is that the enormous complexities of the development process require abilities and attributes which are as natural to the multinational corporation as they are unnatural to government.

Herbert C. Cornuelle, United Fruit Company
Annual Report, 1968, Boston

We find ourselves in the right business at the right time. Agriculture and the food industry will have top priority in a world of shortages. Rises in population and income will create unprecedented demand. Food will be the growth industry for at least the remainder of the century.

Heinz management, 1975

I was sitting at a table beside the swimming pool of the Biltmore Hotel in Guatemala City writing up my log of the day's interviews, when I became aware that six men at the next table were discussing development plans for Guatemala.

When I went over later and introduced myself, I learned that the advisor of the group was the former executive director of a foundation whose effectiveness in providing overseas assistance had been endorsed by Presidents Kennedy, Johnson, and Nixon. Two of the men in the group were wealthy businessmen from upstate New York who had generously decided to contribute

money and time to set up their own programme to help feed the
people of at least one hungry nation.

The sincerity of the men in the group and their basic Christian
goodwill are also typical, and I urge that their conversation not
be interpreted as a caricature of naivete. On the contrary, they
were too highly motivated for that.

'What are the crops they raise here?'

'Don't know, but we can ask AID or the (US) Department of
Agriculture.'

'World's going to starve to death in 1976, so we don't have
much time.'

'How much time do we have?'

'Two year.'

'Let's work on that basis.'

'That means we've got to have a crash programme.'

'How do they plant corn? Anyone here ever planted corn?'
(Silence)

'Hell, the Dept. of Agriculture can tell us that. What we need to
know is how to change the system here. It's bound to be lousy.'

'You mean we don't have a contract to do this yet? How do
we get one?'

'That's what we're talking about now. We've got to get a
plan first.'

'Right.That's what we need, a contract and a plan. The plan,
I guess comes first.'

'These people (the Guatemalans) don't even know how to
use a screwdriver. You can't imagine how easy it would be to
double their food production once you get them to accept our
ideas.'

'What ideas do you mean?'

'You know, modern machinery. That's what they need.'

'Right. Think what a tractor would do here!'

'How about strawberries? Hell, they use a lot of strawberries
in the states.'

'That's a great idea!'

'Strawberries grow ten months of the year, and all you do is
plant them and cultivate. Wonder why they don't raise them
here.'

'Personally, I think this coconut idea is worth looking into. Of
course, you can't use them all, but how about 15 or 20 million
coconuts?'

'There ought to be a market for that many.'

'Why not go into the cattle business or raise pigs? We could feed the coconuts to the pigs. We'll get the natives to harvest the coconuts to feed to the pigs.'

W Paddock and E Paddock,
We Don't Know How, pp. 61–64

24: Changing Traditional Diets

The beans and corn diet of Latin America, the lentils and rice of India, and the soybean and rice diet of China appear to most of us in the West as starchy and nutrient poor. In fact, they are not. Such diets evolved because they *work*. As basic dietetic staples, these combinations are, in fact, quite ingenious. In each case the two items together give more biologically usable protein than if each were eaten separately.[1] Therefore, when we consider the problem of world hunger, we should always keep in mind that the traditional diet is adequate – *when* you can get enough of it. The problem is usually not quality. The problem is quantity.

What, then, do the food companies have in mind for 'improving the food of the poor'?

Until several years ago the involvement of foreign firms in food processing in the underdeveloped countries was insignificant. With markets burgeoning at home and with so few urbanized consumer markets in the underdeveloped countries, there seemed little reason to bother. But suddenly multinational food processors have begun to take another look. The top 10 to 20 per cent of the population in the underdeveloped countries constitute an emerging consumer class – but one lacking the servants who once made 'convenience foods' unnecessary. At the same time the market in industrial countries for highly processed, more expensive, convenience items has become 'saturated.'

A 1973 *Business Week* article, 'Starving for Profits,' published a survey indicating that US food processing companies had reported the lowest annual rate of domestic sales growth (5 per cent) of any industry surveyed.[2] Each new dollar invested in advertising to get you to buy this or that exciting new convenience food was meeting with fewer and fewer market results. Population growth had plummeted. The middle classes in the industrial countries were unlikely to ever consume more than their 1700 to 2000 pounds a year of grain per person.

But perhaps the 'worse' sign for food processors, according to Joseph Winski of the *Wall Street Journal*, is that 'After years of looking for the quick and easy way, Americans are returning to the basics in their food consumption.' With more sandwich-box lunches, more vegetable gardening and bottling, more homebaking and cooking 'from scratch,' convenience food sales have been plummeting. According to one estimate, unit sales of canned goods are down from 25 per cent to 60 per cent depending on the item. One large supermarket chain reported its frozen prepared food volume fell by 16 per cent in one year alone. As its chairman Donald S. Perkins commented, 'Today's consumers are willing to do it themselves.' Even more disheartening to food-processing executives is that their own surveys show that the slump in the highly profitable convenience foods is not just a passing phase attributable to the recession. A *Better Homes and Gardens* survey revealed that 63 per cent of the respondents agreed with the proposition that they were making 'important and lasting changes' in the way they shop and the foods they eat regularly.[3]

Britain has not yet started to see a movement away from convenience foods – quite the opposite in most cases. Many big dairy companies such as Nestlé and Unilever are moving out of the liquid milk and semi-processed dairy product field into the more lucrative highly processed convenience food market.[4] More than 60 per cent of food expenditure in the UK is now on processed foods[5] and 35-40 per cent of the UK grocery trade is controlled by Tesco, Allied Supplies, Fine Fare, Sainsbury's and the Co-op.[6]

In this respect Britain leads the European field. The UK frozen food sector, for example, is 16 times bigger than that of the French.[7]

In some fields, however, a 'back to nature' trend is very apparent. The consumption of bread from the big modern bakeries for instance, is tailing off steadily[8] in spite of the £4m annual advertising budget[9] by the two bread company giants Rank Hovis McDougall and Associated British Foods. Consumers are rediscovering the pleasure of fresh wholesome crusty bread through hot bread kitchens, supermarkets' 'in store bakeries', and through home baking.

The most thorough integration of a food product perhaps is by the three flour and bread giants (Rank Hovis McDougall, Spillers and Associated British Foods) who have moved back along the food chain to control huge agricultural suppliers, and, through property companies, own land. At the consumer end of the food chain they own caterers, wholesalers, restaurants and supermarkets (e.g. Fine Fare). They produce many other goods on the super-market shelves (such as pet foods, tea, salt, biscuits, crisps, cakes, pasta, eggs, meat pies) and use milling by-products as the basis of a huge animal feed sector (which in turn leads to big interests in meat, poultry and dairying[10]). Nowhere else do we find such a logical and complete example of corporate integration, though other food companies have expanded in ways all of their own which are no less interesting.

Who would have thought that Nestlé – the coffee people – also produce Findus frozen foods, Branston pickle, Ideal milk, toffee and – wait for it – the wide range of Oreal Cosmetics?

More unexpected diversity comes from Booker McConnell the vast health food company. Their sidelines are sugar and spirits (particularly rum) – frowned on no doubt by most of their health food customers. Booker's list of subsidiaries also includes chemist shops (for those not cured by health foods), shipping lines and, would you believe . . . a majority shareholding of the copyright royalties on Agatha Christie, Harold Pinter, and Ian Fleming.

First prize for diversity though, must go to Grand Metropolitan. Besides owning Express Dairies (the second largest milk and dairy product company in Britain) they also own 55 hotels throughout Europe, 500 restaurants, 10,000 pubs and off licences, Watney Mann, Truman, Peter Dominic, Berni Inns, Radio Bingo (of the Isle of Man), the Mecca Empire, Luncheon Vouchers Ltd., the World Poker Federation, an amusement park, industrial catering contracts (including the North Sea oil rigs and Saudi Arabia's school meal programme), 8 casinos, City Tote, International Distillers and Vintners (including J & B whisky), Chicken Inns, Directors Wine Club, Olympia Cleaning Services, Coca-Cola rights in UK, the World Dancing Championships, Carlsberg lager rights, and Holstein and Pils.

On top of this is the diversity of interests of the company directors. Former chairman and present director of the £587m a year turnover Booker-McConnell Empire is Sir George Bishop who also happens to be chairman of the Agricultural Mortgage company and on the board of Barclays Bank, Barclays International and Rank Hovis McDougall. To round it off, he is also chairman of the Overseas Development Institute. It's a small world when you are at the top!

For the executive of a world ranging food company, under-developed countries are not to be thought of in terms of the number of inhabitants, let alone the number of the malnourished. Countries *are* markets.

Peter Drucker, prolific corporate theologian, advises executives not to be put off by India's obvious poverty but to keep in mind that 'within the vast mass of poverty that is India' there is 'a sizeable modern economy, comprising 10 per cent of the Indian population, or 50,000,000 who can consume on the level with most Americans and Western Europeans.'[11] When we discussed the future of Nabisco in the underdeveloped world with Lee Bickmore, then chief executive of the corporation, he told us of his enthusiasm for the initial surveys indicating that Brazil could mean 20 million potential Ritz munchers, even though an estimated half of its 100 million people are so poor that they *never* handle money. In Mexico, considered one of the largest and most dynamic markets for food processing companies, less than one third of the population has the means to buy some type of canned foods – as compared with 90 per cent in the United States.[12]

André van Dam, who plans strategies for Hellmann's mayonnaise, Skippy's peanut butter, Knorr soup cubes and other CPC products to 'penetrate' Latin American markets, is quite aware what a large portion of the population is outside his industry's net. But he is not discouraged. With such large total populations van Dam is excited by the absolute numbers who could be made into customers. In a 1975 speech to top executives of food companies in Latin America he estimated the potential customers:

Within ten years . . . Latin America will have 444 million inhabitants. . . . Of this number, a fifth will be able to buy, through their economic power, almost all the products which the gentlemen industrialists here presently manufacture, while a third will be able to buy some of these products only very infrequently. The rest of the population, about half of the total, are not customers except for the most simple and basic products and probably will continue on a subsistence basis. The potential market varies from country to country, from product to product, but those who have a continental vision realize that the potential market of 1985 in Latin America will double compared to today.[13]

No doubt Mr van Dam would like to be concerned about the hungry. But with the 'continental vision' of 89 million affluent Latin Americans ready to buy, he hardly need worry about those 208 million so miserably poor they could never buy a jar of Hellmann's mayonnaise or Skippy's peanut butter.

The *Financial Times* waxed lyrical on the markets for semi-processed foods in Africa describing the type of operation involved: 'New markets for British made ice cream, sausages and frozen foods are being pioneered by Unilever Export in up-country regions of Sierra Leone and Liberia. In the present situation it is possible to establish conservator deep-freezes at retail outlets in villages, replenished by van from refrigerated supplies shipped from Liverpool or London. Another development of the frozen foods market involves consignments which arrive at the Zaire port of Matadi. Arrangements have been made for Birds Eye and Walls products to be sent in containers via roll-on, roll-off ferries to Antwerp. The containers are shipped to Matadi and then railed 400 km up country to Kinshasa. Some of the goods are then distributed to other regions by insulated containers carried in aircraft.'[14]

At Home Away from Home

Are the food companies bringing in a better food system away from home?

Corporations, like people, behave much the same away from home as they do at home.[15] If anything, away from home there are fewer inhibitions. At home, firms have become giants not by offering a better product and greater efficiency but by a one-two punch of local takeovers and advertising expertise. And that is exactly how the multinational food companies are expanding throughout the underdeveloped world.

Rather than starting from scratch, the food companies gain an initial foothold by buying out a local firm that is already in at least one of the same product lines. Nabisco has taken over local biscuit and cracker companies in countries like Venezuela, Mexico, Iraq, Brazil, Nicaragua, and Puerto Rico. Wall's, the Unilever ice-cream and sausage subsidiary, took over Eldorado ice-cream in 1968, Sol-Is-A-S, a Danish manufacturer in 1971, Hughes Bros Ice-Cream of Ireland in 1973 and Alnasa, a Brazilian ice-cream company, in 1974. Pepsico, big in the United States snack market since its acquisition of Frito-Lay, has taken over an established Venezuelan bakery company. Borden bought out the largest maker of pastas in Brazil. In 1966, W. R. Grace, a conglomerate with an historical base in guano (fertilizer from bird droppings) and shipping in Latin America, bought Alimentos Korn in Guatemala. Grace developed it into a frozen-foods line. By 1969, Grace claimed to control 60 per cent of the Central American market for packaged processed foods with sales increasing at the rate of 70 per cent a year.[16]

General Foods is a star acquisition operator. Former president C. W. Cook reflected on the lessons of the company's experience. 'With the rapid progress we made in England through acquiring Alfred Bird and Sons, we concluded that where possible we would find an ongoing business with a management that knew the country, the trade, the banking facilities, the governments and the people.' He observed that 'starting from scratch' in Germany had proven a 'difficult experience.' So the question was – where could profitable takeovers still be made? 'When we looked around, Europe was pretty well combed over.' Latin America, however, offered excellent prospects.[17]

In 1956, General Foods acquired La India, the largest chocolate processor and the best-known seafood processor in Venezuela. In 1960, it took over Kibon, the largest ice cream manufacturer in Brazil. Other acquisitions gave General Foods two thirds of Brazil's chewing gum market. General Foods already had the gum market wrapped up in Europe through takeovers there (Hollywood and Maple Leaf). In Mexico, in the 1960s, General Foods acquired several coffee and soup manufacturers.

Expanding through acquisitions has advantages. Starting costs are minimized. In addition General Foods requires each new subsidiary to finance itself through retained earnings and local loans. With such a low-cost-to-headquarters strategy, a big food company can enter several country markets almost simultaneously. Politically there is an advantage, too. The new subsidiary can be a 'low profile' foreign multinational company, not raising the patriotic hackles of local consumers whilst being sure of US or British government investment insurance and diplomatic support if need be.

What is Agribusiness Offering?

The food companies expanding overseas are those whose western operations are concentrated in high-advertising products. 'In investing abroad, these firms have sought out the faster growing, convenience foods where advertising, rather than price cutting, is the instrument of competition.'[18]

The underdeveloped countries are thus getting our worst, not our best. They are getting those corporations *least* likely to fill real needs or to be useful models. Underdeveloped countries are but the latest markets to conquer for those corporations that have made it big and are getting bigger because they have hit upon a formula for large profit margins, maximum processing, and advertising. Is this what either we or the underdeveloped countries need?

At least 92 per cent of the 'research and development' costs of these big food companies goes to develop quick preparation and consumer appeal or what the National Science Foundation calls 'motivational research and product promotion.'[19] 'Quick preparation,' 'convenience' foods mean prewashed, prepeeled, precooked, premashed, premixed – almost pre-eaten foods! Take the common potato, a staple in human diets for centuries – and not just because it fills you up. It actually contains such a wide array of vitamins, minerals, and protein that you could practically live on the potato alone. This applies to the potato as it comes out of the ground: a cheap, nutritious food that you can eat for about 9 cents a pound. The more a potato gets processed, however, the more its price goes up and its nutritional value goes down (i.e. you get much more fat and chemicals per unit of real potato).

The shop price for potatoes in the UK is 8-10p per pound (1979). Dehydrated and powdered as Cadbury's 'Smash' the price is equivalent to almost 24p per pound. As Birds Eye (Unilever) crinkle cut chips they work out at 53p per pound, and ordinary potato crisps work out at about £1.30 per pound. The winner at over £2 per pound are new fangled snacks such as Frazzles (Smiths) – specially shaped crisps made from reconstituted dehydrated potato. Each processing step offers a new opportunity for profits.

Of course, the potato is just one example of a basic inexpensive low-profit staple turned into an expensive, high-profit 'modern' food.

Big profits are made in the British food industry by the domination of two or three companies of the retail market for certain production. In the confectionery industry, three companies – Cadbury Schweppes, Rowntree Mackintosh and Mars – divide up 80 per cent of sales. Two companies – Walls (Unilever) and Lyons – have a virtual ice cream monopoly. Likewise Findus (Nestlé) and Birds Eye (Unilever) control frozen foods in the UK. Tate and Lyle and British Sugar Corporation sell 85 per cent of the nation's sugar; and over 60 per cent of the coffee drunk in the UK comes from Maxwell House (General Foods) and Nestlé.[20]

As British food researcher Chris Wardle has pointed out 'In every major food product area one, two and sometimes three companies account for the major share of retail sales. In the case of margarine, consumers in the UK might think they have five different brands from which to choose; Blue Band, Stork, Summer County, Echo and Imperial. How many of them know that all these brands are made by one company (Unilever) whose sales account for 70 per cent of the retail market?

'The inherent danger of a small number of companies dominating any given product area is that the goals of both efficiency and equity might suffer. Lack of competition can encourage inefficiency. It can also tempt companies in a given product area to collude in a manner running counter to the public's interest. The recent disclosure that the three big bread companies who control 70 per cent of the £450 million UK market [reduced to two companies in 1978 – ed. note] operated a total of 77 restrictive practices between 1968 and 1974 is an example of what can happen.'[21]

In highly processed foods, freshness, colour, shape, and texture are frequently chemically induced. This makes it possible for big processors to get by with cheaper grades of farm products. In 1971 Alfred Eames, Jr, chairman of Del Monte, cited its pudding cup desserts as an example of a 'continuing shift' to 'higher-profit formulated or "manufactured" products.' 'What do they have to offer?' he asked. 'Among other things, above-average profit margins and little or no dependence on agricultural commodity prices.'[22]

Ironically, according to a Federal Trade Commission study, most of the processing technologies were developed with public funds – many through Pentagon contracts – reminiscent of Napoleon's awarding of the first contract for canned food in 1810 for his far-travelling army. It was tax dollars that bought the research for frozen concentrated juices, prepared mixes, low-calorie foods and drinks, baby foods, dried milk products, instant beverages, frozen poultry, and refrigerated biscuits.[23]

Advertising is the other part of the growth formula of the giants. In product lines dominated by only three or four corporations, advertising allows each company to increase its sales volume without lowering its price below a competitor's – an unsporting act that would narrow the comfortable profit margins of all 'club' members.

In 1973 the UK food industry spent £88 million on the promotion of its products (£1.50 for every man, woman and child in the country). This was more than a fifth of all the advertising expenditure in Britain, and more than that spent on any other single product category.[24] And by far the largest proportion of food advertising expenditure – 88 per cent – was spent on advertising on television.

It is precisely these giant food companies, which have succeeded by maximum processing and all-out advertising, that have been expanding abroad – first into Canada, Latin America, Western Europe, and South Africa, then into the Far East, and now even into Africa.

Branded Consciousness

The immediate goal of a food company is brand consciousness: making consumers conscious of supposed differences between its product and Brand X. You can be sure you have brand consciousness if you reach for the brand-name product even though it seems identical (and probably is) with the one having the private label of the supermarket chain. It is the development of this brand loyalty, not feeding people, that is the goal of multinational companies in underdeveloped countries. The former chairman of Nabisco, Lee Bickmore, told us that his yardstick for measuring success of his company in Brazil would be whether people no longer ask for crackers but instead ask for Ritz. 'That's what I call consumer demand,' he said.

What a global food company, then, has to offer underdeveloped countries is not good food but good advertising. And as a multinational operator, it can repeat the same performance with each new audience – recycling a successful advertising campaign based on research originally paid for by sales in the American market.

The costs of designing such a campaign could never be afforded by a local firm. As Robert Ledogar in his well-documented probe of American food and drug companies in Latin America observes, 'Translating this success [of a US advertising campaign] into another language is so much easier for a multinational firm than developing new products to meet specific local needs.'[25]

General Foods brought in marketing and advertising experts when it acquired Kibon, its Brazilian ice cream subsidiary.[26] Why not, they reasoned, promote Kibon products in rural areas by offering toys made of ice lolly sticks? But the real problem was how to get urban Brazilians to eat ice cream in the winter rainy season. One bright idea was 'lucky visits': A Kibon representative

might some evening call at your house and award you a gift certi-
ficate if you had a pint of Kibon's ice cream in the refrigerator.
(The suspense was undercut for millions since they are too poor
to have refrigerators.)

In Mexico, General Foods took over a dried-soup company
to serve as its launching vehicle for Jell-O. It relied on a tried and
true promotional gimmick: Put on the back of each three-pack
carton a plastic Walt Disney figure (costing 6 cents each) and then
saturate the media encouraging kids to aspire to be 'the first to
collect all 24.' In one test market Jell-O sales jumped 1000 per
cent in one week. (Jell-O has virtually *no* nutritional value.)

Also in Mexico, General Foods masterminded a way to get
Mexicans to pay more for one of their most traditional food items
– chilli powder. It added a few herbs like oregano and marjoram,
figured out how small the packets had to be to get the cost within
the reach of lower-income buyers (50 centavos each) and shaped
the envelopes, called *triangulitos*, to imitate a locally popular stew
flavouring. General Foods then topped it all off with a huge advertising campaign complete with a singing jingle, display signs in
thousands of small shops throughout the countryside, and promotional gimmicks like a lottery and a TV contest.

Beechams have explored some ingenious ways of building up a
market for Horlicks in India and elsewhere in Asia. First of all
they claimed their product to be 'twice as good as milk' but the
Indian government clamped down on this. Their replacement
slogans dwelt on the energy-giving properties of the drink – the
life and vitality it gives (yes – the same drink that is sold in Britain
to send you to sleep!). Important too is to develop its prestige
value, think Beechams, so they also advertise it as 'recommended
by doctors'. Most worrying perhaps are the film adverts (Indians
are avid filmgoers with entrance fees so low they can be afforded by
most). In these a mother takes a sick child into a doctor's surgery
and receives a prescription for Horlicks.[27]

Soft Drinks – Something for Everyone?

Although most multinational food processors aim their products
at small upper-income groups, some are determined to market
something to the poor – even to the very poor. But is it possible
to find a product that the poor will want and that can be priced
within the reach of millions while still producing a profit large
enough to support the big advertising budget necessary to make

the poor want it? Nothing fits this description better than soft drinks. The ingredients cost little – they're basically sugar and water. Yet the poor can be made to think of soft drinks as symbols of the good life.

The most extensive dietary impact of foreign corporations in the underdeveloped world is unquestionably coming from soft drinks. In many underdeveloped countries, as diverse culturally as Iran and Venezuela, the jump in sugar consumption is attributed largely to increased soft drink sales. Mexicans go through well over a staggering 14 billion bottles a year, or nearly five bottles per man, woman and child *every week.*[28]

With such volume markets, even a small profit on each bottle translates into big advertising budgets and big profits. According to Albert Stridsberg, writing in *Advertising Age*, it is saturation advertising that makes the difference. He notes with satisfaction that 'in the poorest regions of Mexico where soft drinks play a functional role in the diet [whatever that means!] it is the international brands – Coke and Pepsi – not local off-brands, which dominate.' Coke, having taken over several local bottlers' brands, has 'captured' 42 per cent of the Mexican market. Stridsberg evidently thinks that Coca-Cola's advertisers should be commended that 'a Palestinian refugee urchin, shining shoes in Beirut, saves his piastres for a real Coca-Cola, at twice the price of a local cola.'[29]

To appreciate how deeply soft drinks can penetrate into the most remote regions of an underdeveloped country, we would like to quote from a letter written by a Mexican priest, Father Florencio, in June 1974:

It seems that soft drinks are a very important factor in the development of villages. I have heard some people say they can't live one day without drinking a soft drink. Other people, in order to display social status, must have soft drinks with every meal, especially if there are guests. . . .

Near the larger towns where daily salaries are a little higher, soft drinks are cheaper. But in the very remote villages where people earn much less, and where soft drinks have to be transported in by animals, soft drinks cost in many places up to twice as much. The typical family in Metlatonoc can't earn more than 1,200 to 2,000 pesos a year. But even the little they receive each year they spend drinking soft drinks. In the richest village in this area, Olinala, where the majority of people are artisans and earn from 25 to 70 pesos a day [$2.00 to $5.60], about 4,000 bottles of soft drinks are consumed each day. Olinala has 6,000 inhabitants.

The great majority of people are convinced that soft drinks must be consumed every day. This is mainly due to extensive advertising, especially on the radio which is so widespread in the mountains. . . . In the meantime, in these same villages, natural products such as fruit are consumed less – in some families just once a week. Other families sell their own natural products in order to buy soft drinks. . . .[30]

Robert Ledogar found Coca-Cola has also been busy in Brazil. Coca-Cola's competition came from a local popular soft drink with stimulant properties, made from the guaraná fruit grown by small farmers in the Amazon basin. Unlike Coke, the caffeine in guaraná is a natural ingredient, extracted from the seeds of the guaraná tree. Because it is pasteurized it avoids several controversial additives used by Coca-Cola (and Pepsi Cola) products. In 1972, Coca-Cola decided to undercut the popular local drink once and for all. It began to produce Guaraná Fanta. It is entirely artificial, however; hardly the 'real thing.'

Fanta Orange is Coca Cola's biggest seller in Brazil after Coke itself. Despite its name Fanta Orange contains no orange juice. Yet Brazil is the world's largest exporter of orange juice. Brazil sells almost all of its orange crop to foreigners, mostly to the United States where Coca-Cola is one of the prime buyers for its Snow Crop and Minute Maid orange juice brands. Brazilian consumption of oranges is very low and many Brazilians suffer from a vitamin C deficiency. A study in 1969-1970 of working-class families in populous Sao Paulo found that poor working-class families obtained only about half of the minimum daily requirement of vitamin C.

Ledogar comments in his study that the companies are 'anxious to avoid adding costly nutritious [natural] ingredients to their products' that might force them out of an expanding 'poor' market. Fanta-Uva ('Grape') has not a drop of grape juice. Yet in southern Brazil there is a chronic 'surplus' of grapes – sometimes over 200,000 tons – that necessitates government-support programmes.

Another strategy is to reach a younger and younger market of new consumers. Brazilian Robert Orsi who is in charge of Pepsi's million-dollar advertising account adapted Pepsi's American advertising campaign to the 'needs' of the Brazilian market. The 'Pepsi Generation' became the 'Pepsi Revolution.' Orsi explains the choice:

> In this country the young don't have protest channels; the present generation didn't receive any political or social education. So we provide them with a mechanism for protest. It is protest through consumption; the teenager changes from the old-fashioned Coca-Cola and adopts Pepsi, the Pepsi with a young and new image, and he is happy, because he is young and young people drink Pepsi.

The seduction of the youth market begins right at school. The cola companies provide or finance refrigerators and other appliances and provide free soft drinks at school events in exchange for permission to sell in the schools. Dr Anne Dias of the Nutrition Institute in Rio de Janeiro surveyed six- to fourteen-year-old school children. She found high levels of consumption of Coke, Fanta, and Pepsi (one to two bottles per day) by all but the very poor with family incomes under $80 monthly. Dr Dias also found vitamin deficiencies even in the diets of the rich children (who were the highest soft-drink consumers). Middle-class children showed symptoms of protein malnutrition as well as vitamin deficiency. The children of poor families, of course, suffered from both protein-calorie malnutrition and vitamin-deficiencies. Virtually none of the children drank milk.

In Zambia the *New Internationalist* magazine reported that babies have become malnourished because their mothers fed them Coke and Fanta, believing it is the best thing they can give their children. In the area of the country that produces much of the world's copper, Dr Stevens, the only paediatrician on the Zambian copperbelt, reports that 54 per cent of the seriously malnourished children admitted to the Children's Hospital at Ndola had 'Fanta Baby' written on the progress charts at the foot of their beds. The Zambian government now has reportedly banned Fanta advertisements 'because of their influence on the poor.'[31]

Canned Pineapple by the Slice

Besides soft drinks, some of the least nutritious foods the companies have been able to devise are now reaching the poor. While frozen foods and aerosol cans clearly can never be sold to the poor, there are other products that can reach them by being divided up into smaller units. A smaller saleable unit means a smaller price – but, of course, higher cost per volume.

Just visit many of the shacklike stores in poor neighbourhoods and rural areas throughout the Third World. You will see chewing gum sold by the stick and even the half stick; Ritz crackers counted out one by one; Kellogg's Frosted Flakes scooped out of regular boxes and sold by the cup; cigarettes sold singly; a pack of two ITT's Hostess Twinkies cupcakes split open to sell separately. In pineapple-rich Mexico, you even find stores selling Del Monte's canned pineapple by the slice.

As we have seen, the strength of the multinational food company is not food, but advertising and marketing strategies. Advertising reaches into the most remote villages of the underdeveloped world. Mr V. G. Rajadhyaksha, former chairman of the Anglo-Dutch multinational company Unilever (Bird's Eye frozen foods, Lever Brothers, Wall's Ice Cream, MacFisheries) in India is enthusiastic about the 'new and exciting challenge' of 'penetrating rural markets.'[32] His goal is to sell Unilever's products in 565,000 Indian villages. Unilever has been persuading 'dealers' in the larger towns to open branches, particularly in those villages where they have relatives. No promotional vehicle is beyond consideration, including cinema vans with advertising films, puppet shows, clowns, wall paintings, and sales personnel on stilts. Radio advertising is possible in the so-called well-to-do rural villages where 30 to 50 per cent of the people have transistors. In any Third World country, go into the smallest shop in the most remote village and you will have a good chance of finding a placard for Nestlé or for Coca-Cola.

Lee Bickmore, the former Nabisco chairman quoted earlier, long ago saw the connection between media advertising and getting Ritz crackers into the smallest stores:

> Why, we plan someday to advertise all over the world. We might spend, say, $8 million for an advertisement on a communications satellite system. It might reach 359 million people. So what we are doing now is establishing the availability of our products in retail outlets all over the world.[33]

With this advertising effort, even those with very little money are reached. It persuades them that food in a package has special powers. Its subtle message is that their traditional diets of beans, corn, millet, and rice are worthless compared to what westerners eat.

Mexican nutritionist Joaquin Cravioto has studied the changing food habits in Mexican villages. He told us that the *campesinos* are switching from traditional corn tortillas to white breads like Pan Bimbo (ITT's name for Wonder Bread south of the border). ITT might argue that it has more vitamins ('enriched') but the reality is that a poor family's few pesos could buy much more nourishment if they were used to buy tortillas. As nutritionist Alan Berg notes, 'Industrial processing inevitably elevates a product's cost beyond that of an equal quantity of the staple.'[34] Berg, working for several years in India, found that 'saturation food advertising convinced many low-income families they *must* buy certain high-priced nutritious products to keep their children well and alert.' As a result, Berg found low-income families 'seduced into spending a disproportionate amount of their income on canned baby foods and similar items *at the expense* of more needed staples.'

If people in the west insist on processed, branded food, they simply end up by spending more of the family income on food. Nobody starves, although nutrition suffers. But in underdeveloped countries where it is common for families to have to spend 80 per cent of their income on food, the impact of shifting to more costly but less nutritious food is grave.

How often we see in developing countries that the poorer the economic outlook, the more important the small luxury of a flavoured soft drink or smoke . . . to the dismay of many would-be benefactors, the poorer the malnourished are, the more likely they are to spend a disproportionate amount of whatever they have on some luxury rather than on what they need. . . . Observe, study, learn [how to sell in rapidly changing rural societies]. We try to do it at IFF. It seems to pay off for us. Perhaps it will for you too.

H. Walter, Chairman of the Board, International
Flavours and Fragrances, 'Marketing in
Developing Countries,' *Columbia Journal
of World Business*, Winter 1974

Lack of effective media in developing communities inhibits demand stimulation activities. Creative, adaptive applications of demand stimulating techniques are needed for the developing communities.

> Charles C. Slater, 'Foreign Agribusiness
> Contribution to Marketing Agricultural
> Products,' May 1972

What is it that GFC can contribute to a foreign subsidiary? Well, first we have more than 10 per cent of all the food researchers in private industry in this country, and therefore we have a capability in food technology to contribute. Our Dream Whip and Gainsburger dog food products, for example, were technical achievements.

> President, General Foods

25 : The Baby Food Scandal

When the birth rate in industrial countries started to decline in the 1960s, articles in business magazines proclaimed the crisis: 'The Baby Bust' and 'The Bad News in Babyland.'[1] One response of baby food corporations was to diversify into other products. Another was to market to the fast-growing population of infants in underdeveloped countries.

Sales of milk powder for babies in underdeveloped countries by Wyeth Labs (SMA), Nestlé, Unigate (Cow & Gate), and Bristol Myers (through its Mead Johnson Division) began to increase faster than sales at home. Nestlé, with 81 plants in 27 underdeveloped countries and 728 sales centres throughout the world, intensively promotes its Lactogen, Nan, and Cerelac. Glaxo and Carnation are also in on the growing business.

It was the *New Internationalist* magazine in 1973 which first broke the scandal that companies promoting baby foods in underdeveloped countries, far from helping infant nutrition, were contributing to severe malnutrition and a significant increase in baby deaths. The article was based on interviews with two leading professors of child health who had worked in hospitals and dispensaries in Africa for a total of more than thirty years. Soon the magazine was swamped with calls and letters from doctors, nurses, volunteers and missionaries in the Third World corroborating and extending the evidence against the Western Baby Food Manufacturers.

In 1974 the overseas charity, War on Want, followed up the *New Internationalist* exposé with an extensively researched pamphlet, 'The Baby Killers.'[2] It was translated into German as 'Nestlé Kills Babies,' Nestlé sought $5 million in damages in the Swiss courts. Nestlé charged that the accusations in the pamphlet – that its efforts were unethical and immoral, that its marketing techniques resulted in infant death, and that it disguised its representatives as medical personnel – were all defamatory. At the last minute Nestlé decided to drop these three claims of defamation. The only charge which Nestlé pressed was that the pamphlet's title 'Nestlé Kills Babies' was defamatory. Although the judge ruled in favour of Nestlé on this count, he declared, 'This verdict is no acquittal [of Nestlé].'

The issue has now generated more than a thousand articles in the popular press, been the subject of a number of television and United Nations reports and provided the fuel for probably the most intensive and angry campaign against multinational food companies' activities in the Third World ever. Why?

In underdeveloped countries the mortality rate for bottle-fed infants is about double that of breast-fed. A recent Inter-American Investigation of Mortality in Childhood, checking on the causes of 35,000 infant deaths, has determined that 'nutritional deficiency' as an underlying or associated cause of death was 'less frequent in infants breast fed and never weaned than in infants who were never breast fed or only for limited periods.'[3] In rural Punjab, India, according to a 1974 report in the medical journal, *The Lancet*, 'in the study population virtually all infants died who did not receive breast milk in the first months of life.'[4] Two decades ago when breast-feeding was widespread among the poor, severe malnutrition was usually held off beyond the absolutely crucial first year of a child's life. But now, according to World Bank nutritionist Alan Berg, the rapid decline in breast-feeding over the past two decades has caused the average age of the onset of malnutrition to drop from eighteen months to a more critical eight months in several countries studied.[5]

Dried baby formula milk displaces mother's milk. But because, as scientific research indicates, mother's milk has changed and evolved along with the human race, it, like nothing else, can sustain the new-born. It contains not the 'highest amounts' but the *proper* amounts of proteins and fats for the human baby. Human milk contains only 1.3 per cent protein; cow's milk, 3.5 per cent.[6] The protein, mineral and fat levels in mother's milk, notes Dr Hugh Jolly, a prominent London paediatrician writing in *The Times*,[7] suits the capacity of a human baby's kidney perfectly. Calves need and can handle more protein because they grow much faster. A six-week calf is, after all, already a small cow.

Mothers' milk is not only properly balanced in proteins and fats but comes complete with infection immunizers for humans, especially critical in unsanitary living conditions.[8] Scientists hypothesize that the immunity probably results from the initial dose of antibodies in the colostrum (the yellowish fluid that comes from the mother's breast a few days after birth). Apparently colostrum protects the child against locally common infections, particularly those of the intestinal tract, and against food allergies. 'This might explain why allergies are more common in artificially fed babies,' comments Dr Alan Berg. 'Gastroenteritis is almost unknown in breast-fed babies, whereas it may be lethal in those fed on cow's milk, especially where sterilization of bottles may be impossible,' notes Dr Jolly.[9] Diarrhoea, which can prevent the absorption of any nutrients at all, is rare among breast-fed babies.[10] A mother can adequately feed her infant for at least six months. Even mothers who are themselves malnourished can adequately breast-feed – although partially at the expense of their own tissues. Physiologists agree that the first months of life are crucial for normal brain development. The negative effects of later malnutrition, though highly undesirable, are far more remediable.

Actually a child can be well nourished on breast milk for two years or more if a few other foods are added – and they certainly need not be from a tin of dried milk. In some cultures children are breast fed much longer. As recently as forty years ago, Chinese and Japanese mothers nursed their children as long as five and six years; Caroline Islanders up to ten years; and Eskimoes up to fifteen years.

Several multinational companies, however, have not been satisfied with nature – or at least, not satisfied that nature seemed to leave no room for commercial exploitation. But to create a market where none seemed to exist, multinational corporations found they could play upon another aspect of human nature – the natural desire of parents to ensure a healthy baby. Exposed to countless billboards, newspaper advertisements, and colour posters, parents in underdeveloped countries come to equate a happy, healthy baby with a bottle or tin of Lactogen. They learn that educated and upper-class families use feeding bottles. They, too, want the best for their baby. The tragic irony, however, is that for most parents in underdeveloped countries, formula feeding actually endangers their baby's life.

First, most families simply cannot afford to buy the necessary amount. To feed one four-month-old infant in Guatemala would require almost 80 per cent of the per capita income. To feed such a baby in Lima, Peru, adequately by bottle would take almost 50 per cent.[11]

These cost estimates do not include bottles, artificial nipples, cooking utensils, refrigeration, fuel, and medical care (often ten times more needed for the formula-fed than for the breast-fed child). How can a family devote over half or more of its income to food for their youngest and totally unproductive member? The answer is that it cannot.

The seeming solution is to 'stretch' the formula with water. Reports of dilution are commonplace. A 1969 survey in Barbados found that 82 per cent of the families using formula as the sole food for two- or three-month-old babies were making a four-day can last five days to three weeks.[12] Dr Adewale Omololu, a professor of nutrition in Nigeria, reported treating a severely malnourished baby whose mother had switched from breast-feeding to a bottle. For a month the child had nothing but water from the bottle because there was only enough money for the *bottle;* it took a month to save up to buy the can of formula!

On diluted formula, a baby loses weight and deteriorates progressively into the malnourished condition called marasmus. The child becomes increasingly susceptible to infection, a problem compounded by bottle-feeding, as we will see.

Second, formula-feeding requires clean water and conditions for sanitary preparation that often do not exist even for the middle classes in underdeveloped countries. 'Wash your hands thoroughly with soap each time you have to prepare a meal for baby,' reads the Nestlé's *Mother Book* distributed by the company in Malawi.[13] But 66 per cent of the households even in the capital city have no washing facilities. 'Place bottle and lid in a saucepan of water with sufficient water to cover them. Bring to the boil and allow to boil for 10 minutes,' is the counsel of the Cow and Gate Company in its Babycare Booklet for West Africa. The text is accompanied by a photo of a gleaming aluminium saucepan on an electric stove. But you have to go far to find an electric stove in West Africa. Most West African mothers have to cope with a 'three-stone' kitchen, that is, three stones supporting a pot above a wood fire. There is only one pot. One pot for sterilizing the baby's bottle and for cooking the family meal. To the mother's eye, putting the bottle in boiling water doesn't seem to do much, anyway; so sterilizing is probably forgotten.

The bottle, the nipple, and the formula are invariably found in the context of illiteracy, a contaminated water supply and the lack of washing, refrigeration, or cooling facilities, and household hygiene. The combination, then, of malnutrition and exposure to bacteria sets up a vicious circle. The infant gets chronic diarrhoea and therefore is unable to assimilate even the diluted formula. The infant's nutritional state worsens and it becomes even more vulnerable to respiratory infection and gastroenteritis. This is the state of millions of children who could have been adequately nourished by their mother's milk.

The companies like to argue that they are *fulfilling* and not creating a need. 'Just think what the situation would be if we were to say, all right, we think these people [the critics] are right. What would the result be?' asks Ian Barter of Cow and Gate Company.[14] 'It would be the death of thousands of children because there are tens of thousands of mothers in these countries who have got to have some substitute for their milk in order to feed their babies.'

Let's look at the facts. Nutritionists recognize that there are some women who cannot feed for physiological reasons. But even the companies admit that at most such mothers are fewer than 5 per cent.[15] Dr David Morley surveyed a rural Nigerian village and found less than 1 per cent of mothers had serious breast-feeding problems.[16] Moreover, many societies have devised 'wet nurse' arrangements to meet the needs of a newborn whose mother could not nurse it.

Indeed, confidence – lack of anxiety – seems to be the key to breast-feeding without difficulties. Several doctors now believe that the typical company advertising does more than anything else to undermine the mother's confidence. By just mentioning 'women who do not have milk' and 'poor quality' milk, the companies place not so subtle doubts in a mother's mind about her ability to breast-feed.

The companies also stress that their products are needed by women who work. In fact, the percentage of Third World women who work away from their families is very low. (Countries where there is far greater employment for women, such as the Soviet Union and Cuba, provide extensive paid maternity leaves and day care centres at the workplace, which allow working mothers to breast-feed several times a day.)

But even if there is a need for artificial feeding, does it follow that a country needs a half dozen profit-oriented multinational firms? Is this the only alternative that you, say, as a minister of health, could think of for your country? Is the technology of making an equivalent baby food really so difficult? The United Nations Protein Advisory Group has recommended that underdeveloped countries come up with a product *better* than the expensive, easily contaminated products of the world's largest companies.[17] Various nutritionists have designed, for mothers who cannot breast-feed, nourishing artificial feeding regimes suitable to low-income homes with minimum hygiene, no refrigeration, and limited cooking facilities – and several would cost only a quarter of the current high-priced formulas.[18]

Finally, the companies try to defend themselves by claiming that they really aim their products only at the rich. According to Ross Laboratories' president David O. Cox, only 'coincidentally' do his company's promotional activities reach the poor.[19]

This claim again does not fit the facts. The companies have actually devised sophisticated and often ingenious promotion strategies specifically for expanding sales down the income ladder. To begin with, coloured wall posters of a healthy baby clutching a feeding bottle greet women, both rich and poor, who enter hospitals and clinics. The companies also employ milk nurses, women who commonly are fully trained nurses. In Nigeria 96 per cent of mothers who used bottle-feeding thought they had been so advised by impartial medical personnel, mainly nurses. In fact, these nurses were company representatives. Nestlé employs 4000 to 5000 such 'mothercraft advisors' in underdeveloped countries. Dressed in crisp white uniforms, they visit new mothers, no matter what their income level is. In many countries these nurses are allowed to enter maternity wards. Often they receive a commission in addition to salary. Moreover, higher pay offered by the companies diverts nurses trained at public expense from basic full-time health work.

In addition, the companies provide free samples, often through the hospitals. Surveys have shown that just as many illiterate mothers as literate ones receive samples, indicating there was no attempt to select mothers who were able to afford the product.[20] Companies often supply hospitals with free formula supplies, hoping that mothers will feel they must keep on using the products. Abbott Laboratories recently sold $300,000 worth of Similac to the New York City hospitals for only $100,000. A city spokesperson said, 'For the company, it's an investment. They hope to get the future business.'[21]

Another device clearly aimed at the poor are 'milk banks,'[22] usually in hospitals and clinics. They sell the commercial formulas at discount prices to mothers who can prove they are really poor. In this way they can expand sales among the really poor without lowering the price in the normal commercial market. Milk banks in their hospitals just serve to convince women that they need something that they really don't. But even at discount prices (usually 30 to 40 per cent), the formulas are too expensive for parents to buy enough. In Guatemala City, fifty mothers buying at a milk bank were questioned. Despite the discount, they could not afford enough so they 'prepared the bottles with less milk and more water and in this way the milk lasted longer.' Tea or chocolate drink is often substituted.

Radio is also an advertising vehicle to reach the poor. A typical day in Sierra Leone sees fifteen 30-second radio advertisements for Nestlé: 'Now Lactogen a better food cos it don get more protein and iron, all de important things dat go make pikin strong and well. . . . Lactogen and Love.' The use of the common dialect of the poor makes it hard for Nestlé to convince us that they are directing their advertising at only those who can afford it.[23]

Under the pressure of unfavourable publicity, the companies say they have modified their advertisements.[24] Now the commercial product is pushed as 'the next best thing to mother's milk,' for cases in which 'you find you need a substitute or a supplement to breast milk.' Nestlé now recommends 'an occasional bottle-feed – if you cannot breast-feed Baby entirely yourself.'

The tactic is ingenious. As a Consumers' Union-funded study comments, 'By openly recommending breast feeding, the companies can earn their public relations credits. At the same time, the companies can undermine breast feeding by implying repeatedly that a mother may not have enough milk and may need supplementary bottles of formula.'[25] La Leche League International, an organization devoted to helping women breast-feed, comments, 'The "supplementary" formula is one of the greatest deterrents to establishing a good milk supply, and frequent nursing is one of the greatest helps.'[26]

The companies can also put off would-be breast feeding mothers by persuading them that their own milk is inadequate for nursing or that their living conditions are too unhygeinic.

A booklet that Nestlé produces and gives free to mothers in the Third World tells them that 'you should bathe your breasts daily, wiping the nipples with cotton wool dipped in mixture of spirits and glycerine' (available perhaps at their local pharmacist?).

Later the booklet advises on diet. Breast feeding mothers, says Nestlé, must eat 3,500 calories a day – a large proportion of which must come from protein rich foods such as milk, meat, fish, poultry and eggs. Most readers of this pamphlet would consider the occasional piece of meat a luxury and would be persuaded that they couldn't afford to breast feed. What's the alternative? You can be sure that the pamphlet tells you!

Such ingenious modification of tactics serves to emphasize how the solution to this grave situation is not simply another 'code of conduct' for the companies. One such code, already drawn up, would have company milk nurses wear the company insignia on their uniform. The companies must really think their critics are simple-minded! All the codes condone the use of medical facilities to market their products.[27]

Nestlé hoped to get some public relations mileage out of its claim that it no longer would dress its salespeople in white uniforms. White uniforms obviously gave the impression of medical authority. What Nestlé neglected to say is that its salespeople now are wearing blue and yellow uniforms. Now really. Doesn't a uniform, any uniform, still carry authority?

Not only is the decline in breast-feeding a personal tragedy for babies who suffer malnutrition and disease, but it can be calculated as a loss to the natural resources of the country. In Kenya, notes Alan Berg, 'The estimated $11.5 million annual loss in breast milk is equivalent to two-thirds of the national health budget, or one-fifth of the average annual economic aid.'[28] In the Philippines $17 million was wasted on imported milk in 1958; by 1968, the number of mothers breast-feeding their babies dropped by 31 per cent, and the national dollar loss had doubled. As breast-feeding declined sharply in the 1960s, Colombian milk imports soared; in 1968 they were seven times greater than the 1964-1967 average. Berg concludes that 'losses to the developing countries more likely are in the billions.'

An attack on the bottle-baby tragedy is now underway in some underdeveloped countries. Here are only a few examples. In Papua, New Guinea, the director of public health is enlisting the support of all health workers to persuade storekeepers not to display formula company advertisements.[29] Dar es Salaam University in Tanzania has put out a new guide on baby care for paramedical workers warning of the dangers of formula feeding. In Segbwena, Sierra Leone, a Nutrition Rehabilitation Unit is feeding malnourished children on locally available foods and showing mothers how to prepare well-balanced and inexpensive meals for their families.[30] The Nairobi City Council, Kenya, has banned milk nurses. Some African governments have even instructed rural health workers to destroy formula ads wherever they find them.

In contrast to the private multinational companies, a state-owned company in Zambia announces on its can of milk: 'Breast Feed Your Child.' The label goes on to persuade the potential buyer not to buy the product unless the purchaser can afford to buy enough for many months.

Public action in the industrial countries to halt the ongoing tragedy did not stop with the Nestlé trial in the summer of 1976. Later that summer groups from eight countries working on infant formula malnutrition met in Berne to plan and co-ordinate their efforts. That fall in New York the Sisters of the Precious Blood, working with the Interfaith Centre for Corporate Responsibility (ICCR), brought suit against Bristol Myers. The Sisters charged Bristol Myers with committing fraud in its proxy statement to shareholders. In its statement Bristol Myers claims to have been 'totally responsive' to the concerns of the earlier stockholder resolution. Moreover, the company claims that it does not promote its products to people who cannot afford to use them safely, that it does not sell directly to the consumer at all but only through professional medical personnel. The Sisters, working with ICCR, gathered over 1000 pages of testimony and other evidence from around the world that directly contradict these claims. This documentation demonstrated that Bristol Myers does use many techniques to reach the poor, including selling its products in poor people's stores, distributing free samples through health clinics, and using sales personnel dressed as nurses.

Even though the suit was not successful – the Sisters' appeal was dismissed by the US District Court in 1977 – the publicity of the suit, combined with the earlier Nestlé trial, launched the concern over infant formula malnutrition into an international campaign. The Infant Formula Action Coalition (INFACT, 1701 University Avenue, SE, Minneapolis, Minn. 55414) formed to co-ordinate the campaign. Its first move was to launch a boycott of Nestlé until the corporation agrees to stop all promotion on infant formula in the Third World. Many groups such as Clergy and Laity Concerned and Church Women United immediately backed INFACT and the Nestlé boycott. In addition, a Senate subcommittee held hearings on the problem in May of 1978. Thus news of the bottle baby tragedy is spreading rapidly. Church and community groups around the country are educating their constituencies using the film, 'Bottle Babies,' (available from INFACT). The crisis of infant formula malnutrition is thus becoming for more and more people an example of how corporate economic motives not only can fail to serve the interests of people, but can directly contribute to their suffering.

We hope that by now we have given you an understanding of what the judge in the Swiss trial meant when, after ruling in favour of Nestlé, he added: 'This verdict is no acquittal [of Nestlé].'

In an interview on West German radio in 1975 a paediatrician on the staff of Nairobi's Kenyatta National Hospital, Dr Elizabeth Hillman, told this story:

A short while ago . . . the Nestlé's representatives came to visit us at Nairobi's hospital to ask if we had any opinion about the publication 'Nestlé Kills Babies.' They really wanted us to say that Nestlé did not kill babies.

We discussed this at length with them and were not able to say of course that Nestlé either does kill or does not kill, statistically speaking. But, to illustrate the point, I mentioned that there was a child over in our emergency ward . . . who was very near to death, because the mother was bottle-feeding with the Nestlé's product (Lactogen, a milk preparation), and out of interest I asked whether they would like to see the baby. I took the two representatives over into our emergency ward and as we walked in the door the baby collapsed and died. I had to leave these two non-medical gentlemen for a moment . . . and help with the resuscitation procedure. It was unsuccessful. And, after the baby was pronounced dead, we all watched the mother turn away from the dead baby and put the can of Nestlé's milk in her bag before she left the ward. . . . In a sense . . . it was a vivid demonstration of what bottle-feeding can do because this mother was perfectly capable of breast-feeding. The two gentlemen walked out of that room, very pale, shaken and quiet and there was no need to say anything more.'[31]

Its broad geographical and product diversification, its involvement with the population explosion in backward countries, where it makes cheap baby food, and finally, the fact that it keeps its cash in solid Swiss francs, make Nestlé *shares good insurance against depression, inflation, or revolution.*

Barrons, May 20, 1968

PART IX   THE HELPING HANDOUT: AID FOR WHOM?

26 : Triage

The term originated from the mass-slaughter of the Great War of 1914-1918. It was used to describe the system of administering medical aid in the field hospitals of the Somme and Ypres. The wounded were divided into three groups – those who would live to fight again without medical aid, those who would not recover even with medical aid, and those for whom medical aid would make the difference. The analogy with selecting which underdeveloped countries to give aid, is all too apparent.

The whole of *Food First* is an answer to this cruel theory of triage. For the triage metaphor doesn't hold water when compared with the reality of world food production and distribution we have described.

• First, the triage concept is misleading because it implies that we have been giving aid according to some soft-hearted notion of need and that now we must be realistic, selecting recipients according to who is most likely to make it. But no one who has seriously looked at United States aid policies could accuse the country of being softhearted! As one member of the National Security Council put it, 'To give food aid to countries just because people are starving is a pretty weak reason.' No, overseas aid is already highly selective, going to serve the narrow political and economic interests of certain groups in the west.

• Second, triage assumes that the underdeveloped countries are on the receiving end only, when, in fact, many underdeveloped countries are net food exporters, particularly of high protein foods such as meat, seafood, and legumes. It reinforces the idea that these countries are the greatest burden because they have too many people. In fact, as we have shown in Chapter 2, it is the industrial countries that are the major food importers. Between 1970 and 1974, four of the highest GNP countries – Japan, the United Kingdom, Italy, and West Germany – imported six times more grain than China and India, although these four countries have only a quarter of the population of China and India.[1]

• Third, triage is built on the scare notion that we are entering an era of absolute scarcity. According to the theory, food must be allocated judiciously to ensure the survival of – let's face it – ourselves.

Another analogy is suggested by Garrett Hardin, Professor of Human Ecology at the University of California: that of the lifeboat. If we let everyone on board our lifeboat, we will all drown. But as we have seen throughout this book, the world has hardly reached this point. We have discussed what we call the 'inefficiency of inequality' – that the main constraint on food production is the gross inequities in control over the earth's food producing resources. The hungry have increasingly less control over the production process. The result? Tremendous waste: the underutilization of land, the expansion of nonfood and luxury crops to feed the already well-fed, and the feeding of over one third of all the world's grain and at least one quarter of the world's fish catch to livestock. As long as we have a system that is actively *creating* scarcity out of plenty, to say we are reaching natural limits is worse than merely misleading. The suggestion allows the present scarcity-generating system to go on unrecognized for what it is. Meanwhile people are manipulated with fear-evoking images of 'shortages' and 'overpopulation.' Metaphors like triage thus work in the interests of those few who have seized power and wealth for themselves – forces that are steadily undermining the welfare of people both here and in underdeveloped countries.

27: The Debt Trap

When western aid-giving countries publish figures of their yearly commitment to help the poor world, they tend to maximize their generosity. But more than half our aid is not given, but *lent* with interest. We all know a loan is not a gift even if the interest rates are low. Low interest rates on such 'aid' have not prevented the debt obligation of the underdeveloped countries from becoming an increasingly unbearable burden. Between 1967 and 1976 the total debt burden of the non-oil producing underdeveloped countries, both public and private, increased over fourfold, from $43.7 billion to about $180 billion.[1]

Each year an even greater portion of aid coming in must go out again just to repay loans received in previous years. By 1973, almost 40 per cent of all loans and grants from foreign governments received by underdeveloped countries was spent on debt service payments on such past 'aid.'[2] But if debt service payments on loans from private lenders are also considered, by 1978 the sum paid out by non-oil exporting underdeveloped countries – over $13 billion – approached the *total* development assistance coming in from government sources in the industrial countries. In fact, according to AID official Abelardo L. Valdez, lenders in the industrial countries in some cases now receive more in loan repayments than they lend. In 1977, says Valdez, the US government received $150 million more in loan repayments from Latin American countries than it had provided in the form of AID and Export-Import Bank loans.[3]

Moreover, the debt service payments are growing faster than the rate of increases in aid. Between the mid-sixties and the end of the decade, the gross flows of external aid to Pakistan rose by 5 per cent; but the debt service payments rose by 91 per cent! (For many countries the level of aid is decreasing, not increasing.) Debt service payments are also going up twice as fast as the export earnings that bring in foreign exchange to repay the loan.[4] In some countries such as Bangladesh almost a quarter of export earnings must go out again just to pay off past debts. The percentage is growing rapidly. And a quarter is already far greater than the bankers consider tolerable.[5]

It is obviously a no-win situation for the underdeveloped countries. But many of us are made to go on believing that all we can do to help is to increase aid. Not only will more aid of this type only compound the debt burden, but it will also force a destructive all-out push for exports. The only way to get the foreign exchange to repay debts is to sell in the international market-place. Internal development (building sanitation facilities, schools, and clinics, for example) based on local production and local currency does not count; it does not earn foreign exchange. Thus for most countries debt obligations lead right into the trade trap we discussed in part VI.

In any discussion of development assistance these facts should never be forgotten: 'Assistance' is often loans and the debt they create can itself be the ultimate roadblock on the path to self-reliance. Debt takes an increasing bite out of development resources and ensures that a country's economic choices will be determined by foreign markets, foreign banks and foreign development agencies often opposed to the internal needs of the country.

28 : The World Bank's 'Assault On Poverty?'

The World Bank cannot be taken lightly. It has rapidly emerged as the leading institution for development financing, with lending commitments for 1979 projected at $9.8 billion. President Carter asked American taxpayers to virtually double their contribution to the Bank. Our $2.2 billion in fiscal 1979, we were told, would help the Bank further its 'assault on poverty.'[1]

Putting on the Blinders

Important insights into the World Bank's battleplan can come from reading any of its confidential rural project planning documents ('grey covers').[2] Here the Bank staff seems to follow a ritual formula – one apparently unaffected by the Bank's 'basic needs' rhetoric of the past five years.

Technical and statistical data are paraded forth. Poverty is quantified. Despite the stress on 'participation' in publicly-touted policy papers (for example, 'The rural poor must participate in designing and operating a programme which involves so many of them'),[3] poor people, project documents imply, can be reached from the top down. The poor are rarely seen as the participants, much less the instigators, of their own development. In para-military language, the poor become the 'target population.'

Project proposals, nominally written by the local government, are in most cases ghost-written by Bank 'missions' that fly in – at no small expense – from Washington for a few days.

The presumption throughout project design is that development can be achieved only by bringing in external resources. Foreign investment is thought of as essential. Everything should be done, therefore, to develop a favourable climate for foreign banks and corporations. That a project design includes ongoing reliance on imports is not seen as a problem.

The project implementations section of the grey covers amounts to a series of best-of-all-worlds projections. Statement of goals plus money equals success. Poverty is simply *there* with no hint that forces are at work creating and sustaining it. A project plan is an exercise in economics divorced from political, sociological and cultural factors. On the rare occasion that conflicts of interest are recognized, their implications for the implementation of a project are ignored. Government and other actors are all presumed to be working together to eliminate poverty. Results of projects are measured only in statistics, not in the impact on the lives of real people.

It is no surprise to learn, then, that US Senate investigators were told by one Treasury department official that '10 per cent of all Bank projects have "crippling problems" and 50 per cent have "major or serious" problems during implementation.'[4]

'Going to the Big Boys'

With the Bank's project designs opting to ignore the social roots of poverty, is it surprising that they seem time after time to achieve the reverse of stated goals?

Take the Bank's credit to the government of Bangladesh to fund 3000 tubewells.[5] Each tubewell has the capacity to irrigate 60 acres, making possible an extra crop of rice during the dry winter season in northwestern Bangladesh. According to a Bank press release, each well would serve between 25 to 50 farmers joined together in a cooperative irrigation group. But independent researchers Betsy Hartmann and James Boyce who lived for nine months in one of the villages covered by the project found what was no secret to anyone in the village: the tubewell in reality has wound up as the property of one man, the richest landlord in the village. And the vaunted co-operative irrigation group amounted to a few signatures the landlord had collected on a scrap of paper.

The World Bank (in reality the Bangladesh government) paid $12,000 for each well; and this landowner paid less than $300 for his and that mostly in bribes to local officials. The landowner *will* allow smaller farmers tilling adjacent plots to use 'his' water – but at his price, an hourly rate so high that few are interested.

Was the Hartmann and Boyce experience atypical? Apparently not at all. They expressed their shock to a foreign expert working on the Bank project. He told them,

I no longer ask who is getting the well. I know what the answer will be and I don't want to hear it. One hundred per cent of these wells are going to the 'big boys'. First priority goes to those with the most power and influence: the judges, the magistrates, the members of Parliament, the union chairmen. If any tubewells are left over, the local authorities auction them off. The big landlords compete and whoever offers the biggest bribe gets the tubewell.[6]

But should the Bank have known this in advance? Are we just proving that hindsight is often clearer than foresight? Not at all. An evaluation carried out for the Swedish International Development Authority (SIDA) (that joined the Bank in financing the tubewell project) examined 270 tubewells and concluded:

It is not surprising that the tubewells have been situated on the land of the well-to-do farmers, or that it is the same well-to-do farmers who are the chairmen and managers of the irrigation groups. It (would have) been more surprising if the tubewells had not been located on their land, with the existing rural power structure, maintained largely because of the unequal distribution of the land.[7]

The Bank nonetheless will tell the world that the tubewell project is a success. The World Bank expert who told Hartmann and Boyce that the wells would only go to the 'big boys' added:

On paper it all sounds quite nice. Here are the peasants organizing to avail themselves of this wonderful resource. When the officials fly in from Washington for a three-day visit to Dacca, they look at these papers. They don't know what is happening out here in the field, and no one is going to tell them.[8]

And since the amount of land owned by the rich landowner is only half the area that the tubewell is minimally capable of irrigating, the tubewell will be greatly underutilized. (It is, in fact, this prevalent tubewell underutilization that most troubles World Bank technocrats.)

World Bank officials who find themselves forced to admit the failure of such a project invariably do not question its premises. 'More managers' they say, are what is needed.

But what is the real tragedy here? That tens of millions of dollars (in reality loans that must be repaid by the work of the people of Bangladesh) have been wasted? That a resource has been grossly underutilized? That poor farmers have not been helped? Yes, all of these things, but much more.

The Bank's impact should not be understood as simply a failure to help the 'target' group. By enriching their enemies, such a project actually *undercuts* those it is supposed to help. In the villages studied, the large landowner – like his counterparts in other villages – is reported to 'already have an eye on the plots nearest his tubewell.' Thanks to his new income from the World Bank tubewell, he will be better positioned to buy out the smaller farmers when hard times befall, thus driving them into the growing ranks of the landless.

Not Neighbours, But Rivals

We ourselves investigated another Bank rural development programme in Bangladesh, a major 'pilot' programme called RD-1 (Rural Development Phase One). The stated goal of the $16 million RD-1 is 'to reduce the domination of rural institutions by more prosperous and politically influential farmers and to make farm credits and agricultural inputs . . . available to the small farmers through the co-operative system.'[9]

The Bank thus first of all presupposes that there could be a co-operative system in which the well-off participate but do not dominate. People in each village we visited, however, told us that the so-called co-operatives were for the well-off – generally the top 10 per cent owning six acres or more – who controlled the records and determined who could join and get credit. For the rest of the villagers, especially the half owning one acre or less, not only are the repayment terms too stringent but even the membership fees are too high. And without land, coming up with collateral is virtually impossible. 'Even if I did come up with a scheme to pay back a loan,' one landless villager complained, 'the co-operative would still not give me credit.'

For us, the SIDA evaluation of the aid-funded village co-operative programmes rang true: 'Democratically functioning co-operatives never can work, if land holdings continue to be as unevenly distributed as they are today. To try to keep the big landowners outside the co-operatives . . . is nothing but wishful thinking.'[10]

Projects dreamed up in a social vacuum must nevertheless play themselves out in the real world of injustice and conflict. As one FAO agronomist with 15 years experience in Bangladesh told us, 'The thing to remember about the villages is that the people are not neighbours but rivals.'[11] Similarly, an anthropologist[12] studying a disparate group of Bangladesh villages told us that the fundamental social reality is struggle over land: the well-off do everything possible to get their smaller neighbours in debt to them in order to foreclose on their land; the poor farmers do everything possible to hold on to the little land they have, even hiring out wives and daughters for demeaning servant's work. Not only do the well-off landowners not want the small farmers or landless labourers to prosper, they want them to become more *dependent*, more indebted to them.

Thus the rural elite who usurp the tubewell – or the new machine or the extension worker's guidance or whatever the Bank projects supposedly earmark for the small farmer – will make sure the poor will not benefit. This is true even if it means vastly underutilizing the new input. Ignoring this constant economic warfare, World Bank projects not only fail in narrow production terms (production in the RD-1 villages of Bangladesh, for example is no higher than elsewhere) but also strengthen the oppressors of the already desperate small farmers and the landless.

Don't Rock the Boat

A 1975 Bank policy paper on rural development explains how projects should deal with 'the existing social system.' The paper states: 'In many countries, avoiding opposition from powerful and influential sections of the rural community is essential if the Bank's programme is not to be subverted from within.'[13]

Bank President Robert McNamara tells us that the Bank's agricultural programme 'will put primary emphasis not on the redistribution of income and wealth – as necessary as they might be in many of our member countries – but rather on increasing the productivity of the poor, thereby providing for a more equitable sharing of the benefits of growth.'[14]

But will increasing their output benefit the poor if merchants, moneylenders and other exploiters continue to siphon off the lion's share? Will not Bank programmes to improve the productivity of the land of a region (for example, by a dam-irrigation project) in a society structured against the poor only heighten the chances that smallholders will be bought out, tricked or otherwise forced off the land?

That the Bank is committed to 'avoiding opposition from the powerful' is also clear when we discover that many of its rural programmes do not even make the pretence of aiding poor smallholders. In *Assault on World Poverty* the Bank states that it is allocating almost half of its rural credit to small farmers.[15] Sounds good. But wait. This means then that more than half of the Bank's rural credit will still be going to medium and large farmers who at most constitute only 20 per cent of all landholders in the underdeveloped countries.[16]

Moreover, closer examination of project appraisals has taught us to be on the alert about even the 'almost half' supposedly going to 'small farmers.' For whether or not World Bank credit is getting to the rural poor depends, in part, on how the Bank defines 'small.' In Guatemala, for instance, a joint FAO/World Bank farm credit programme would allocate one-half of the credit to the top three per cent of the landholders, those owning 112 acres or more. The other half would go to what the Bank calls 'small farmers,' those owning less than 112 acres. To an American, 112 acres sounds small. But this cut-off point hardly separates out the rural poor in Guatemala where a full 97 per cent of all farmers have less than 112 acres. With such a guideline, the Bank's project could bypass totally the real poor majority in Guatemala – farmers with less than even one acre and, of course, the many with no land at all. The size of the subloans provides another clue as to whom such projects are directed. In the 'small farm' category the maximum would be $10,000. But what kind of collateral could the truly small farmers and the landless put up to qualify for loans on the scale suggested by such a figure?

Even where the stated purpose is to benefit truly smallholders, the Bank acknowledges that the credits go through national agricultural and development banks, primarily winding up in the hands of largeholders.[17] In the Philippines, for example, the World Bank made two loans to rural banks that were partially governmentowned. Although the stated purpose was to help small farmers, smallholders with less than seven acres (who comprise 73 per cent of all farmers in the area) actually received less than one per cent of the credit extended.[18]

The Landless

And if the Bank is serious about attacking rural poverty what does it offer the millions of landless in countries where a few monopolize the land? Even in the Bank's own conservative estimate, the landless make up 40 to 60 per cent of the population in many Third World Countries. Here the Bank unabashedly revives the supposedly discredited 'trickle down': we are told, for example, that millions of dollars for an irrigation dam will generate more farm employment – a boon to the landless. But, as Hartmann and Boyce ask, 'Is giving aid to the rich so they can hire more poor at subsistence wages really the way to best help the poor?'[19]

As an utterly rare exception the Bank did design a programme in Bangladesh to benefit landless villagers directly. Within the RD-1 project in Bangladesh, there is provision for a landless co-op in a single village. But even in that one village the programme excludes two-thirds of the landless and does nothing to confront the structures that generate their poverty. The programme has made available a meagre $4,000 loan and a pond for cultivating fish plus three acres of government land. (There is much more government land in the village but the well-off have usurped it.) Since the workers' income is still such that they must also work for the village landowners to survive, this pathetic programme amounts to a wage subsidy for the rich landowners.

In visiting this single project for the landless, we could not avoid the feeling that it was consciously or not being used as a showcase. In signing the co-op's visitors book we noticed we had been preceded by visitors from several European countries and Canada. Were the poor people we met there being underpaid for the unwitting service to the Bank's image?

The Bank goes out of its way not to rock the boat even in cases of outright corruption by elites. In Bangladesh the price tag on pumpsets for the Bank's deep tubewell project jumped from $9 to $12 million simply to meet the demand for super profits by the pumpset manufacturer, Bangladesh's richest citizen. According to the *Far Eastern Economic Review*, an effort by the resident Bank mission to cancel the contract was overruled by Bank headquarters in Washington:

World Bank officials were apparently told that the highest Government authorities in Dacca were involved in placing the contract, and to cancel the whole scheme now would create embarrassing political problems in an area where the Bank hoped to have increasing influence in years to come.[20]

A Bank is a Bank

While 'feeding the hungry' might warm the heart of the Bank's president Robert McNamara, there is no column headed 'full stomachs' on his ledger sheets. Hungry people who grow food so that they can eat better do not produce much money and foreign exchange. Only if they grow enough to sell, that is, a 'marketable surplus,' will loans get repaid with interest. And that is what the Bank is concerned about.

The World Bank, like any other bank, seeks to minimize its risk. The Bank itself notes, 'Lending only to those with investment opportunities sufficient to produce a significant marketable surplus is perhaps the best way to reduce the level of default.'[21] 'Those with investment opportunities' is a euphemism for the larger farmer. It is rough to try to be a bank and a saviour of the world at the same time!

Besides betting on the large farmer, the Bank also provides credit for non-food crops, thus ensuring a marketable surplus. Indeed, with crops like rubber and cotton, all of their production will go to market; it can't possibly be eaten by the producer. Furthermore, as the Bank notes. 'Delinquencies (in loan repayments) have also been reduced when repayment has been co-ordinated with the marketing of crops that are centrally processed, for example, tobacco, cotton, cocoa, tea, and coffee.'[22]

In 1978, in response to a newspaper article by the Institute, the World Bank denied that it had provided any loans for nonfood export crops since 1973, the year the Bank marks as the beginning of its focus on the poor. You can imagine our disbelief. In 1978 alone the World Bank's annual report lists $258.5 million for loans for crops such as tea, tobacco, jute and rubber. In addition, loans focused on food crops such as vegetables, sugar, and cashews explicitly designed as going for export promotion – amounted to $221 million.[23]

Livestock is another 'crop' that might be seen as a nutritious food. It is certainly one sector highly favoured by Bank loans. Yet what Bank loans support is primarily commercial ranching, serving the local elite's and foreign consumers' growing taste for meat. As late as 1975, the Bank announced that 'livestock loans constitute nearly one-third of all agricultural credit projects and over 70 per cent of those in Latin America'.[24] Since then, new Bank commitments for livestock schemes have lessened, although the largest single 'Agricultural and Rural Development' loan in 1978 went to a $200 million livestock production project in Mexico.[25]

A large Bank-financed livestock project in Kenya currently allocates credits in the following manner: 54 per cent for a few commercial ranchers; 33 per cent for a few company ranches; 9 per cent for 42 individual ranches; and 4 per cent of the loans for 25 group ranches supporting 1500 ranchers. Bank economist Uma Lele notes that even the 'employment potential is low.'[26] She gives a classic Bank rationalization for so much money for the benefit of so few: 'The tax revenues generated from these ranches are expected to help the government provide rural services to other needy areas.' (Another example of how 'trickle down' theory is still believed in at the Bank.)

Cane sugar has become another Bank favourite. Visiting Indonesia, we learned that the Bank is bankrolling (so far to the tune of $50 million) the rebuilding of the sugar mills built by the Dutch colonizers. Unfortunately, local farmers do not want to raise sugar, in part because they say they can make twice as much cultivating rice. According to the *Wall Street Journal*, the sugar mill officials are 'forcing the unhappy farmers to grow cane at gunpoint.'[27]

Similarly, the World Bank decided that what new settlers in Way Abung, Sumatra (Indonesia) needed was rubber trees.[28] But the farmers resisted. What are their reasons?

'I'll make more money growing rice.'

'I've never worked with rubber and I don't understand it.'

'I want to plant food, not something I can't eat.'

'The price of rubber fluctuates too much.'

'There is no factory nearby so transportation costs will be too high.'

'If I spend time each day tapping rubber, I won't have time for other crops.'

As a crop in addition to rice, farmers and officials much prefer coconut to rubber. Coconut oil is needed for cooking, husks become fuel and leaves are used in roofing and making walls. Coconut meat and milk are food. If cash is needed, the market is local, not requiring costly transportation.

Rubber prevailed, however. One reason, we were told, was simply that the World Bank expert on the scene was a rubber not a coconut specialist. Farmers now refuse to give up their land to the rubber scheme. At the last count only 11 per cent of the rubber area had been planted. As one confidential Bank review of the project noted, such problems result 'when the development strategy overlooks the basic economy of the settlers themselves.'[29]

Besides focusing on the large landholders and ranchers and on non-food crops, yet another way to insure that the marketable surplus does not get eaten is to send out 'supervisors' to make sure it does not happen. Again we quote the Bank itself: 'Supervision is designed to help the farmer but also to prevent loan funds from

being misused for financing consumption and to ensure repayment
. . . *But supervision can never completely eliminate increases in
consumption* following the receipt of loans, even when credit is
provided in kind' (emphasis added).[30] Even the World Bank can't
always prevent people from eating what they grow!

We are not saying that agricultural exports are necessarily bad.
But they tend to strengthen the mechanisms that cause hunger.
To weigh the impact of export agriculture, one has to ask: Who is
in control of the return from those export earnings? Does the
decision to focus on exports represent a choice of the rural people
themselves who have already achieved basic food security and who
can deal with the uncertainties of the export market? And how does
the conversion of small, self-provisioning farmers into commercial
producers take into account the interests of the many more who
have been deprived of land? Given the present powerlessness of
the poor whom the World Bank says it is 'targeting,' is it realistic
to think that they could genuinely participate in such choices? Not
without prior mobilization and organization by the rural people –
a development which World Bank-style projects stand directly
against, as we have seen in the preceding examples.

Agriculture Only a Quarter of the Pie

In all our discussion of agricultural development we fear that
we may leave you with a false impression. Because World Bank
speechmakers talk so much about helping the hungry, one might
forget that almost three-quarters of its loans go not to agriculture
but to commercial development – electric power, railroads, highways, hotels, ports, telecommunications, mining and manufacturing installations. These investments – most of which reinforce the
economy's export orientation – are just what the local elites and
foreign corporations need to make their own investments profitable.
They're, of course, only too happy to have the World Bank foot the
bill. Such Bank loans also aid corporations in industrial countries
by financing their capital goods exports to the Third World. Even
when these large projects claim to be part of rural development, it
is those already in control of the productive assets who gain by
them.

All this is not to say that the Bank should loan more to agriculture but to point out yet another aspect of how the reality of the
Bank's function contrasts with its 'basic needs' rhetoric. What we
have had to conclude is that since the Bank's strategy for develop-

ment is counter-productive, encouraging the Bank to 'live up to' its rhetoric is dangerous. Less, not more, of the World Bank is what is needed.

Pushing Money

We repeatedly hear in our investigations that the Bank is a 'money pusher.' What does that mean?

First of all, within the Bank target loans quotas are established for each country. Project officers are judged on how well they find project outlets to fill those quotas.

Their complaint often is that there are not enough good projects. Focusing on scoring up outlets for huge sums of money isn't exactly conducive to Bank officers reflecting on the social consequences of their projects. 'Anyone who stops to raise questions,' we were told by one Bank consultant who has worked with every department of the Bank, 'is considered an obstructionist – not a good team man.' (There are even repeated accounts of the Bank plunging ahead so fast that crucial technical and other implementation aspects are overlooked until it is too late.)

This 'excess of funds syndrome,' as those in the field speak of it, launches premature large-scale projects when smaller scale, slower-germinating projects would be at least less undesirable. Moreover, it lends itself to the perpetuation of extreme corruption in government. The *Wall Street Journal* reports that in Indonesia it is 'authoritatively estimated' that 10 to 15 per cent of the total cost of bank-financed projects (now running at over $500 million a year) is dissipated through 'leakage.'[31]

As the largest single lender in most countries, the Bank also can undermine the efforts of smaller official and voluntary agencies that try to circumvent corrupt and exploitative structures by placing tight conditions on aid. Why would a government bother with such agencies when the Bank is ready to lend large sums with no effective strings attached? In Bangladesh we learned of one aid agency labouring for four years to design a $4.5 million funding to the Agricultural Research Institute and then, at the last minute, the World Bank coming along and dumping in a additional $10 million to 'beef up' the Institute. The aid agency officers were horrified; they feared that this sort of sudden money would be bad for the Institute. Indeed, they argued, had more money been in order, they themselves would have arranged it. The Bank, we have often been told, tends to be a 'reckless donor.'

In Tanzania, a major part of the funds in a World Bank urban garden project went to an outside contractor for building a storage unit. It cost four times as much per square foot, we were told by a community worker close to the project, as a comparable structure built by the participants themselves in a similar project nearby. The community worker also told us that the Bank this year has channelled into the project twice the amount of money needed. 'The excess,' she stressed, 'leads to waste and inefficiency.'

The Bank is pushing money, yes, but not giving it away. Loans must eventually be repaid – and with foreign exchange earned as we have seen, largely by the labour of the rural population producing for export. At best the Bank through its IDA operation, waives the interest charge, charges only .75 per cent yearly service charge, and allows 40 to 50 years for repayment. Much of these loans, however, merely serve to create the cash flow that makes it possible to make payments on previous regular Bank loans.

Nor should we overlook that Bank projects invariably require the local government to put up 'counterpart funds' amounting to 20 to 60 per cent of the costs of the projects. Thus scarce financial resources – and human ones, too – are tied up by Bank projects.

Repaying mounting debts puts a country under even greater pressure to orient every aspect of the economy towards exports. The 'debt trap' pushes countries away from building a basis of self-reliance, the only foundation for a new international economic order.

Financing Exports

The World Bank was chartered at the close of World War II to stimulate and finance capital goods exports from countries like the United States. In mid-1978 the US State Department estimated that for every dollar Washington had paid into the Bank, $2 has been spent in the US economy – which should lead some to ask who is aiding whom.[82] 'Development' then inevitably gets defined as things that cost large sums of money and must be imported – buildings, high-salary foreign technicians and the vehicles they need, dams, roads, laboratories, audio-visual equipment, and so forth. Thus it is not unusual that at least 50 per cent of a Bank nutrition project in Indonesia goes to bricks and mortar and fancy equipment for fancy buildings, as one American technician working for the UN in Indonesia told us. Even under the heading of agriculture and rural development, World Bank loans go overwhelmingly to build infrastructures – from roads to dams – that enrich local and foreign contractors and consultants. Such projects leave intact or reinforce the economic stranglehold of the elites that prevents true agricultural progress and causes rural poverty.

Looking at some of the Bank's confidential planning documents, we found shockingly inflated prices for goods to be imported for projects. In a 1977 agricultural extension project in Thailand,[33] sophisticated audiovisual equipment and other electronic hardware, largely imported, make up over $1,000,000 out of the total budget. Sounds more like a Harvard graduate course in mass media than a rural development project in Asia!

Here are some of the Bank's 'bargains' to be obtained for the project by 'international competitive bidding': 420 hand calculators at $50 each; 30 desk calculators at $160 each; 30 16mm movie projectors at $1200 each; twelve 21-in colour televisions at $1050 each; and on and on.

The World Bank and Agribusiness

Sometimes World Bank projects aid private corporations much more directly than just through creating a demand for pesticides, fertilizers, tractors, roadgraders, desk calculators and so on. Part of the World Bank since 1964, the International Finance Corporation (IFC) was created to 'act as a catalyst, to bring together private foreign and domestic capital and investment opportunities, and to facilitate investment with its own funds.'[34] IFC provides loans for hotels and other profit-making ventures as well as for agribusiness.

Recall the story of Bud Senegal's export vegetable operations from the African Sahel? IFC helped Bud get started. In fact, IFC granted three loans to Bud Senegal. Other loans have gone to food processors and export crop estates, largely in Latin America and Africa.

In addition, the IDA, the soft-loan arm of the World Bank that is supposedly reserved for the 'needy' governments, has apparently found some needy corporations. A 1978 loan, for instance, to rehabilitate commercial oil palm plantations in Zaire will, according to the Bank, 'benefit three companies' – a subsidiary of the giant firm of Unilever (known in the United States as Lever Bros) and two subsidiaries of the Belgian holding company Compagnie Generale.[35]

And benefit they will, in notable contrast to their Zairian employees. The plantation workers (3,500 jobs theoretically to be created by the project) will earn about $200 a year, which breaks down to $4.00 a week, low even for Third World plantation work. The net annual income of the participating companies, however, is expected to be $3 million at the time of the loan's maturity in 1987.[36]

In discussing its fears that the project's profitability might be reduced if unable to secure labour, the Bank's secret grey cover report on the project points out that better housing and social services for workers will be provided to 'reduce the risk of labour shortage.' Thus, while the World Bank talks publicly of its humanitarian motives, apparently a better life for the poor is a goal when it serves the economic interests of the real beneficiaries, in this case multinational corporations.

Finally, it would seem at this point almost gratuitous to point out that the project completely overlooks the needs of Zaire's three to four million traditional small family farms. The rehabilitation of commercial oil palm plantations was selected instead because, the Bank says, it 'offers the best prospect for future production increases at the least cost.'[37] Growth maybe, development no. –

More Than a Bank

The World Bank is not simply a provider of development loans. Over the past few years it has become a major force shaping the economic policies of various countries. In the Bank's own words:

> IDA's (part of the World Bank Group) borrowers, in particular, would be unlikely to obtain finance on terms as satisfactory as IDA's from any other source; they are therefore unlikely to disregard the kind of advice they may be given by Bank IDA missions whose periodic surveys of their economics include assessments of the soundness of their economic policies.[38]

The Bank has started establishing permanent missions in underdeveloped countries, often locating them right within national planning ministries and central banks. In an increasing number of countries the Bank puts together and chairs a consortium of the principal bilateral and multilateral lenders to co-ordinate donor contributions and policies. In many countries such as Bangladesh, the Bank is quietly placing and leading the funds for advisors in key ministries of the government. One trump card of the Bank is that it determines the government's international credit rating.

The Bank, in short, is increasingly spoken of as *the* power in many Third World countries we have visited.

A 1975 article in the *Guardian* gives some notion of what that power is used for in a country like Bangladesh:

> . . . devaluation is only the most dramatic measure in the World Bank programme, which to be successful must be accompanied by fiscal and other changes which will restore monetary stability. An integral part of the programme is the creation of a 'favourable investment climate' . . . In spite of the clinically neutral language . . . the stabilization programme is not simply a technical exercise in monetary management. It amounts to imposing lower real incomes mainly on the urban and other working classes.[39]

We should not be surprised then that loans go increasingly to the world's most repressive regimes, those willing to implement measures dictated by the Bank that penalize the working people with higher price and wage controls. Thus four countries that have undergone military takeovers or martial law since the early 1970s – Argentina, Chile, the Philippines and Uruguay – received a sevenfold increase in World Bank lending by 1979. Loans to all other borrowers increased only three times.[40]

The World Bank, the United States and the Human Rights Campaign

The US government has been congratulated for trying to alter the trend of Bank loans going increasingly to the most repressive regimes. Since the Harkin 'human rights' amendment to the International Financial Institutions Act of 1977, US representatives in the international banks are required to oppose loans to governments that engage in 'a consistent pattern of gross violations of internationally recognized human rights.' Exempt from this law, however, are loans for projects that address 'basic human needs.'

Those who congratulate the United States for adhering to the Harkin amendment base their support on the fact that in the first year after enactment, US representatives abstained on 17 votes and voted 'no' only twice on World Bank loans to 12 countries officially recognized as 'human rights violators' during that period.

(In other international lending agencies, the US representatives voted 'no' 7 times and abstained 4 times.)[41]

Most of these loans were approved anyway; 'abstention' is not very effective opposition. But the uselessness of this record in providing that the administration is serious about forcing the Bank to stop supporting repressive regimes is revealed in one basic fact: During the first post-Harkin amendment year (FY 1978), a full quarter of all new World Bank (including IDA) loans went to just four countries, all well known for denying the economic and political rights of their people – Brazil, Indonesia, South Korea and the Philippines.[42]

How can this record of loans occur when the administration claims to adhere to the Harkin guidelines? First of all, the Harkin amendment loses much of its meaning when one realizes that the administration can decide which countries are 'gross violators' and what are 'internationally recognized' human rights, as well as which loans address 'basic human needs' and are therefore exempt. Obviously there is great latitude for the administration to support loans to just about whichever government it wishes. As James Morrell of the Center for International Policy points out,[43] the administration can always refrain from employing the exact language in the legislation and instead simply state that a country has 'serious human rights problems.' In this way the administration can look sensitive to the issue but avoid invoking the Harkin amendment.

Secondly, such 'human rights' legislation unfortunately allows the criteria for judging who is and who is no longer a 'human rights violator' to be narrowed down to the number of political prisoners being taken or released that week. Thus when martial law governments like those of the Philippines, Argentina, Chile and South Korea release some political prisoners, it is said that their human rights situation has improved. Pressure exerted by the United States through such stipulations as the Harkin human rights amendment is credited. But has the only true measure of human rights enforcement with lasting meaning been obscured? That is, whether or not a government's economic policies are denying the majority the 'human right' to survive?

Finally, there are at least two false assumptions behind the efforts such as the Harkin amendment as ways to help the poor abroad. The amendment assumes World Bank projects claiming to serve 'basic human needs' *can* actually further the interests of the poor majority instead of strengthening the mechanisms that make the poor poor. Throughout these chapters on aid we have questioned this assumption.

Efforts such as the Harkin amendment also assume that the US government will and can be a global 'social worker,' pressuring 'wayward governments' to 'go straight.' The reality, however, is that every administration – and the Carter administration is clearly no exception – will ignore even the most ruthless violations of elementary human rights whenever it is seeking to keep in power a government that is subservient to the needs and demands of US corporate and military interests. It will go to great lengths to preserve an elite-controlled economy that does not present a threatening contrast to the concentration of the economic power within the United States itself.

Mobutu's Zaire is just one case in point.[44] President Mobutu was installed in power with western connivance in 1965, following the Belgian-inspired murder of the popular Patrice Lumumba. He has kept Zaire (formerly the Congo) wide open for multinational corporation mineral exploitation. A full 45 per cent of the cobalt used in the US, for instance, is taken from Zaire.[45]

Despite Zaire's enormous mineral wealth, Mobutu's elitist, corrupt, and pro-foreign investment policies have generated even more widespread poverty and its inevitable partner – brutal repression – for 20 million peasants. Hundreds of thousands of the rural poor have sought refuge in nearby countries. In January 1978, 700 to 1000 villagers – men, women and children – were massacred in the Bandundu province.[46] Yet only a couple of months later the White House proclaimed the Mobutu regime a 'moderate government'[47] and President Carter rushed in US military planes to transport Belgian and French troops to crush a revolt against Mobutu. At about the same time the World Bank, with US support, approved yet another World Bank loan, this time for the palm oil plantation already discussed. World Bank and other international loans have come forth so readily to Mobutu that already by 1977 the servicing of those debts and tumbling copper prices combined to make the country virtually bankrupt.[48]

But only when the brutal policies of a government cause the American government to fear that a revolutionary change will bring about a government no longer willing to serve US corporate and military interests does it finally move to cut off aid. Such, for instance, is the case of the Carter administration's policy toward the Nicaraguan dictatorship of Anastasio Somoza, which we discuss later.

No Accountability

The Bank is in no sense a democratic or even broadly representative institution. It is accountable to no one but itself. And it would be naïve to expect that such a powerful institution can or will effectively monitor itself.

Bank documents are secret. The Bank is virtually unstudied even by social scientists; there are fewer than a dozen articles and books analysing this powerful institution. No staff member will testify before any congressional or parliamentary hearings. Only recently has the Bank begun to go through the motions of evaluations (secret, of course) of all the projects it funds. Those who have seen some reports of the Bank's operations Evaluation Department tell us that they were greatly 'sanitized' when they were later summarized for public release.

Evaluations are sometimes commissioned of outside consultants; but how independent are they, given that their next contract might come from the Bank? One such major evaluation we heard of was critical. It has been suppressed and the author was ordered to do a 're-write.' Public reports, we are told, must be upbeat in order to gain support in the congresses and parliaments of donor countries.

While in Bangladesh we learned from informed foreign sources that recently a mission had flown in from Washington and pronounced the RD-1 programme we discussed earlier a success 'because it is based on sound principles' and that it should be expanded. Yet only the day before a Bangladesh government official had shown us an internal Bank memorandum indicting every aspect of the implementation of the project and concluding that the co-op system operates 'excessively in favour of the more wealthy farmers.'

Moreover, many local government negotiators of Bank loans often aspire to a position with the Bank in Washington. Are they about to question a Bank project? As we were told in Sri Lanka, a country now taking on massive Bank loans for a dam irrigation project, government elites in the capital are already expectant about 'having a whisky' with all the foreign experts who come with such a project. In all, a fairly closed circuit.

Accountable to no one, the Bank is free to make whatever grandiose claims it wishes about the number of people who benefit from its projects. Mr McNamara, for instance, would have us believe the Bank's agricultural and rural development programme will 'reach' 60 million in the 'poverty target group' by lending during 1975-1979. The Bank, you see, likes to count beneficiaries by totalling up the number of people living in the area where a Bank project is to take place. This is equivalent to arguing that a dam in Paluba, California, benefits the population of California which is 20 million – and therefore the 4 million of those who live below the poverty line. Soon the Bank's calculations of the total number of poor beneficiaries is likely to be more than the total number of poor people in the world.

Although the World Bank is blatantly unaccountable, this does not mean that responsibility cannot be assigned. The United Kingdom has 9 per cent of the voting power.[49] British taxpayers have directly contributed 12 per cent of the funds to the 'soft loan' section of the Bank – the International Development Association. Moreover, although the strictly commercial arm of the Bank does not get its capital from government subscriptions but from the public sale of bonds (many undoubtedly held by universities, pension funds and churches), the fact that governments back up these bonds is an important factor making them attractive to private investors.

The more we learn about the World Bank, the more astonished we are that the Bank has been so successful in convincing so many that it is promoting the interests of the poor and hungry. Since we as citizens are directly connected through our governments to the World Bank, it is we who must take responsibility for revealing the true impact of World Bank programmes and ending them. We must make it clear that the World Bank is still a bank; its concern is with the stability of current elite-controlled economies; its clientele will never be the world's hungry. Indeed, by strengthening the enemies of the hungry, World Bank programmes are further undercutting the very poor they claim to be helping.

. . . perhaps more than any other institution in the world, (the World Bank) is helping large numbers of people move out of absolute poverty toward a more decent life.

Robert S. McNamara
President World Bank
New York Times, April 2, 1978

. . . filling (of the reservoir) began on schedule, and initially went according to plan, except that for a short period, the rise of the reservoir had to be slowed to allow some of the 80,000 people who had been slow to move out of the reservoir area, to get away from the rising waters.

From World Bank Report on
Tarbela Dam Project (Pakistan)
July-August, 1975
quoted in Susan George,
How the Other Half Dies

Rural Development is a new thing; it's only a few years old.
Acting chief of World Bank mission, Bangladesh

What isn't generally recognized and what I want to emphasize is that the salaries of the staff of the Bank are not paid for either in whole or in part by United States taxpayers but rather by the developing countries we serve.

Robert S. McNamara
President World Bank
New York Times, April 2, 1978

29 : The Value of Food Aid

EEC and Food Aid:

The EEC food aid programme was launched in 1967. By 1978 it was the largest donor of food aid in the world, contributing 30 per cent of all cereals, 50 per cent of skimmed milk powder (SMP), and 95 per cent of the butter at a cost of L490 million a year. Each year the EEC now sends overseas 150,000 tons of SMP and 45,000 tons of butter.[1]

In trying to sell its food aid programme, the EEC has made clear to Europeans that it is they who stand to benefit most: the EEC baldly stated that food aid shipments 'should not be regarded as a simple act of charity.' The costs of food aid must, the EEC pointed out, be weighed against the costs of 'alternative measures of satisfactorily dealing with unsaleable supplies,'[2] referring, as we shall see, to their use as animal feed. Mr Lardinois, former EEC Commissioner for Agriculture, has declared, 'the best way to dispose of SMP surpluses is to use them extensively for food aid.'[3]

Food aid provides, then, a way for the EEC to dispose of surplus commodities – its chronic headache. Agricultural oversupply is a product of the EEC's Common Agricultural Policy (CAP) which consumes some 70 per cent of all its spending on price supports and related programmes to protect the income of European farmers. CAP's guaranteed prices for farm products are calculated to bring the earnings of even relatively small-scale farmers up to a level comparable with industrial earnings. The prices are high – often two or three times the world market price. Such payments are incentives to farmers to convert to ever more intensive methods in order to increase their output – particularly of the livestock products for which the prices are most favourable. The result is overproduction – sometimes chronic – of many basic farm products.

EEC's biggest headache is the dairy sector. At present approximately one pint of milk in six is produced surplus to requirements. In a year the weight of surplus milk produced is greater than the aggregate weight of the entire population of the EEC – all 260 million people!

In order to achieve these bumper dairy yields, cows need a rich diet, high in protein and calories – a diet now supplied largely by imported grain and soya. Such feed has historically come primarily from the United States. Increasingly, however, foods such as groundnuts and cassava from tropical and semi-tropical countries are finding their way into Europe's animal feed. Thailand's top agricultural export is now cassava for feed; its exports to Europe having multiplied threefold since 1971.[4] (Until recently cassava has been only a source of cheap calories for millions of the world's poorest.) Senegal's exports of groundnut cake – particularly to France – increased 125 per cent from 1971 to 1974 in spite of the estimated 300,000 ton deficit of cereals for human consumption each year in that country.[5]

The cost of the dairy surplus on this imported feed is about 40 per cent of CAP spending – about £180 per cow – and is a very real source of political and economic embarrassment.

What to Do With the Surplus

Milk doesn't keep. The first problem is to convert surplus milk into products that can be stored – butter and skimmed milk which can then be dried into skimmed milk powder (SMP). The second problem is to find a customer for them. At double or triple the world price, they are too expensive for commercial sale either within the community or without. This is where EEC subsidized sales come in, although not all subsidized sales meet with public approval. Sales of butter to the USSR in 1974 received bitter criticism in the press and elsewhere. ('If we've got to pay for it to be sold off, why not pay for it to be sold to old age pensioners' etc. In fact, subsidized sales to the elderly would result in their not buying the full price butter and so would not reduce the surplus proportionally). Such sales as those to the USSR still occur but are generally of smaller magnitude.

Less politically sensitive, it seems, than subsidies to Russian butter eaters are subsidies for cattle producers. The bulk of the skimmed milk and SMP produced goes into animal feed. Being high in protein, SMP makes an ideal substitute for soya meal.

But feeding milk to cows does not quite solve the problem. Cheap sales of a highly nutritious food for animal feeds create higher yields of animal products – more surpluses – and so we start again! The United States, moreover, is not very happy with the scheme. They think subsidizing skim milk as an animal feed is unfair to their soya exporters. The United States threatened legal action when tariffs on soya imports were introduced.[6]

Indeed, to the EEC Commission there seemed to be only one way to get rid of our surpluses that surely no one could object to: give them to the poor countries as food aid. As an estimated 10 million people starve to death every year in the Third World, it would be a cruel person indeed who would object to the EEC sending some of its unwanted surplus to the needy.

Unfortunately, it's not as simple as it sounds.

Half the dairy aid given is SMP for reconstitution as milk and is sold within the recipient country. Theoretically it then brings in funds for development projects[7] – particularly the building up of indigenous dairy industries. But can imported milk truly help build up a local industry? In Bangladesh a high proportion of the funds generated by milk sales went to a project to increase local milk production. In fact the lower price of milk, caused by the newly abundant European supply, has so depressed prices that Bangladeshi farmers are producing less milk, not more.[8]

And some would question whether or not dairy development in the Third World is a good thing to promote anyway? Milk production in much of the Third World represents a much less efficient use of agricultural land than, say, growing grain and beans. But the assumption is that since milk is a high protein food, it should be encouraged. Overlooked is that the grain and legume (peas, beans or lentils) diets of most traditional cultures are in fact sound in their nutritional composition. What is lacking is quantity.[9] Greater availability of the present diet is the prescription – not protein rich foods.

There is another pitfall. Food aid can lead to an acquired taste for new foods and therefore a dependence on imports when the aid runs out. This has certainly happened in Sri Lanka where wheat aid has led to a taste for bread – replacing rice as a staple in many homes.[10] Likewise in Taiwan and South Korea as we discuss later in this chapter.

Finally, many nutritionists argue that milk is a particularly dubious food for distribution in the Third World in any case because many non-Caucasians are unable to digest the milk sugar. This intolerance for milk has been estimated as high as 60 per cent among non-Caucasians. It can lead to chronic diarrhoea and a loss, not gain, of nutrients.[11] The effects are particularly acute for children. The EEC has thus been asked to keep a watchful eye on the use of powdered milk in baby foods.[12]

The White Revolution: Lessons from India

All of these reservations notwithstanding, the White Revolution – a term coined to describe ambitious dairy development projects in the Third World – is being encouraged by development planners. India – principal host for the Green Revolution, described in earlier chapters – is now the scene of the world's most ambitious programme. As in the Green Revolution, the driving force is western agricultural machinery and methods. The success of the project – better known as Operation Flood – rests on the building of big modern dairies, rapidly developing dairy farming in the rural areas, and the capturing of the urban dairy market. The project's aim is to provide a steady supply of hygienic milk in the cities to replace the dirty, often diluted milk sold by the traditional milk vendors.

In specially built dairies, butter and SMP imported as food aid are reconstituted into milk and other dairy products. The food aid, then, primes the pump. Once the dairy establishes its market, it can then start buying milk from farmers in surrounding rural areas. Funds generated from the dairies can also be used to form village milk co-operatives so that the farmers can by-pass the middlemen and get a better deal. Funds can be used to build new dairies elsewhere and to resettle in rural areas the old-fashioned, inefficient urban cow-keepers who will have lost their market and livelihood to Flood. Funds can also be employed through the co-operatives to boost the present inefficient yields of milk and also to improve social, health, transport and education facilities in the villages. The scheme is designed to evolve into a 'national milkgrid' distribution system, linking some 10 million producer families with 150 million consumers in 142 towns and cities.[13]

The origins of Operation Flood go back to 1946 when an experimental dairy producers' co-operative was launched in Kaira district, Gujarat state. The co-operative was successful and spread like wildfire throughout the district. Twenty years later they boasted the most advanced dairy processing plant in India and supplied Bombay with much of its milk and most of its butter. It had over 500 village co-ops and became a model for other parts of India.

The take-off point for Operation Flood, ironically, arose out of a fear that the rumoured gift of 20,000 tons of EEC butter to India was going to kill the co-op's butter market.[14] Plans were drawn up for a project, modelled on their own success, but aimed at providing milk through a modern dairy in the four main cities in the state. The World Food Programme (agent for about 25 per cent of EEC food aid) agreed to supply the needed quantities of butter and SMP starting in 1970. The four city dairies were built, food aid poured in and Operation Flood was born.

In the eyes of the EEC, the World Bank (who lent money to the programme) and the large dairy multinationals, the scheme has been an unqualified success. The chairman of Unilever even applauded Flood in his annual report of 1978. It should be borne in mind, however, that a by-product of Flood is the escalating Indian demand for animal feed. And India's major supplier of feed is a firm called Hindustan Lever – a subsidiary of Unilever.

According to the World Bank, Operation Flood is 'helping to promote a technology most appropriate to Indian conditions.'[15] But just how appropriate is it really?

Critics of the programme argue first that milk and other dairy products (including butter, cheese, chocolate) are entirely for the elite market. Although a stated aim is to improve the diets of the urban poor, in reality the milk is priced out of this market.[16]

Second, the displaced traditional milk sellers are not being helped to resettle in the countryside. Instead of the 15 per cent of the budget allocated for this sector only 0.3 per cent is being used for resettlement.[17] Urban employment is being additionally threatened by the rapidly spreading use of automatic milk vending machines – a bizarre innovation in a country where labour is so cheap and unemployment so rife.

A third criticism is that dairies are becoming increasingly dependent on imports of butter and SMP, not on local procurement, as was intended. It is difficult to get accurate information but there is evidence that at least in some areas indigenous production is actually decreasing. In Delhi, for instance, the daily procurement actually dropped 40 per cent from 1976 to 1977.[18]

Indian imports of butter and SMP increased by more than 50 per cent from 1974 to 1976.[19] The sophisticated milk plants themselves are largely imported or built by multinational corporations operating in India. Once established the plants are fed with imported butter and SMP. It's no wonder that companies like Unilever like the scheme!

A fourth criticism of Flood is that it is more relevant to the richer farmer, one who can afford the cattle feed and higher yielding breeds of cow, than to the poorer farmer. Only 10 per cent of the members of the Kaira co-operative are landless peasants.[20]

Finally, the programme encourages farmers to use their land to grow fodder for cows rather than food for local consumption, potentially worsening nutritional standards in the rural areas.

Schemes such as Operation Flood complete the cycle of 'surplus' and export created because those who really need food cannot afford to buy it. In other words, a large part of the surplus livestock products that represent such a headache to EEC agricultural planners are themselves produced on feed imported from the Third World – where it might have stayed, had those who are hungry been able to buy it. Once in Europe as feed, these Third World foods help create the surplus that then must be dumped back into the Third World in the form of milk products – foods much less appropriate to local needs than the indigenous foods shipped out as feed. In this bewildering pattern of export, surplus and re-export, only one thing *is* clear. It is not the poor of the world who benefit. State marketing boards, trading corporations, some European producers and consumers plus the better off in the Third World are the only winners.

From the United States

Historically the United States has been the largest food aid donor. Since 1950 it has given over $25 billion in food aid, but at no time was its primary aim to feed the hungry. In fact, it was not until 1966 that humanitarian intent was even written into the food aid law. Food aid has been an extension of US foreign policy and business interests, which in most cases are mutually supportive.

To understand the origins of food aid you have to look no farther than an interview with the co-ordinator of United States food aid in the Ford administration, Robert R. Spitzer. After recounting how, in the early 1950s, farmers' organizations were calling for something to be done with the mounting surpluses threatening their incomes and how 'humanitarians' hated to see food wasted, Spitzer continues:

There were other people who realized that there was a great potential for the products of the American agricultural community, and that perhaps by wisely placing some of these foods in certain countries, we would develop buyers for future commodities. Then we weren't thinking too much of oil, but I think some of our advanced thinkers were beginning to realize that we were not independent so far as many of the trace minerals are concerned. So someone had to do some thinking. Okay, what do we have to ship out? So the Public Law (480) [food aid] was passed.[21]

Spitzer touched on virtually all the motives for food aid: the farmers' interest in unloading potentially price-depressing surpluses, the interest of agribusiness corporations in creating markets, and the potential of food as a weapon in assuring access to strategic materials. The only motive he neglected to mention was the use of food aid in support of United States military intervention, one of its principal functions during the Vietnam War.

Not unlike EEC food aid, PL 480 aid, later also named 'Food for Peace', itself resulted from the crisis of oversupply. American farmers grew too much food. During the 1940s, grain production in the United States had increased by about 50 per cent, while domestic consumption lagged well behind, increasing only by about 30 per cent. Productivity increases, based on more fertilizers and pesticides, plus better seeds, and price supports for farmers, created enormous surpluses that were costing taxpayers $1 million a day just for storage.

These surpluses represented a terrible dilemma. The farm lobby would not allow them to be put on the domestic market. And if dumped on the world market, grain prices would drop by a dollar a bushel. US grain corporations were opposed to such a disruption of their international commercial market. In 1952, at their national convention, the American Farm Bureau, a group representing large- and medium-sized farmers, proposed a solution: Create a secondary foreign market by allowing food-deficit countries to pay for American food imports in their own currencies instead of in dollars. That is what PL 480 did. PL 480, then, was seen as a way to help low-income countries, which otherwise would not constitute a market at all, to buy surplus American food while keeping the commercial dollar price up for higher-income countries. PL 480 meant the United States would have its cake and eat it too.

Such are the origins of food aid. But, most important, has food aid gotten to the hungry who have needed it?

Food to the hungry

Over the last several years our Institute has received letters and other reports from many countries around the world revealing that food aid does anything but reach the hungry. Bangladesh, however, is a useful country on which to focus because it is a principal recipient of food aid and because most people think that food aid to such a needy country surely must be helping. Unfortunately, the story of food aid and the hungry in Bangladesh is by no means unique.

Today Bangladesh receives a full third of its food aid from the United States. Since 1974, 92 per cent of US food aid has been under Title I. Title I – dollar credits to buy food on a low-interest, long term basis – gives the local government total control over what is done with the food.

The Bangladesh government sells most of the Title I food through its ration system that allows cardholders to buy a portion of their food at 50 per cent subsidy. Bangladesh researchers James Boyce and Betsy Hartmann point out that most of this food goes to those who could have afforded the market price: the urban middle class.[22] In 1976, 90 per cent of the food aid was sold to this middle class.[23] Conservative World Bank figures[24] are revealing: 27 per cent of the food aid goes to the police, military and civil service; another 30 per cent goes to the predominantly middle-class cardholders in the six major cities. (In 1975 the government revoked all of the few ration cards held by the marginally employed living in Dacca's slums.)[25] Yet another 8 per cent is supplied to mills for grinding flour for urban bakeries.[26]

While 85 to 90 per cent of the people of Bangladesh live in rural areas and many of them are undernourished, a mere one-third of the ration cards are allotted to rural families. In theory, these cards allow for the purchase of half the amount of subsidized food allotted to an urban cardholder. In practice, rural cardholders can buy even less. First of all, fulfilment of their allotment depends on there being something left over after urban allotments are covered. Moreover, rural ration dealers sell a good part of the food on the black market, pocketing the cash. (Getting a dealership is a coveted political favour.)

The government's concentrating food aid on the urban middle class is deliberate. The ration system is designed, in the words of a 1976 US Embassy cable, 'to keep potentially active Dacca dwellers supplied with low-priced foodgrains.'[27] 'Active,' of course, means politically active. (This use of food aid to keep middle class urban dwellers from wanting to revolt is a story often repeated around the world. In Upper Volta at least 75 per cent of the relief aid during the drought – and during the political 'unrest' – was distributed to the better-off dwellers in the capital city and the largest provincial towns, leaving very little for the hard-hit rural areas.[28])

Food aid not only does not feed Bangladesh's hungry now but it also helps perpetuate hunger. Food aid is fundamental to the neglect of any serious efforts at increasing food production. The US embassy in Dacca acknowledged in a 1976 cable to Washington that 'The incentive for Bangladesh government leaders to devote attention, resources and talent to the problem of increasing domestic foodgrain production is reduced by the security provided by US and other donors' food assistance.'[29] This reduced incentive is welcomed, to say the least, by the government because in fact it is widely understood that meaningful production increases – and ensuring that everyone has access to the food produced – would require not so much the 'attention, resources and talent' of government bureaucrats as a thorough restructuring of control over productive resources. And that this is the last thing the government wants was amply demonstrated when in 1975 in the face of widespread and serious uprisings in the countryside the government imposed martial law.

Part of the ten per cent of food aid to Bangladesh that winds up in the countryside is earmarked for a few rural works programmes. Such seasonal 'food-for-work' projects are certainly no long term solution to the unemployment at the root of hunger. Moreover, in the opinion of some observers we spoke with, their main function is to take the edge off a potentially explosive rural situation by providing a few jobs during the slack agricultural season. And a recent study by the FAO stressed that food-for-work programmes 'lend themselves to misappropriation of grain, misuse of funds, false reporting of works, creation of a class of profiteers, poor quality construction, etc.'[30]

But most crucially such rural works almost exclusively benefit the already better-off part of the rural population, primarily the bigger landholders. According to an AID-sponsored study:

Such projects (eg, the building of a farm to market road) provide income to rural workers for a specified period, but do nothing generally to change the fundamental economic conditions that produced unemployment in the first place. At the same time, such projects tend to provide long-term benefits to landholders who, in this example, use the road to gain access to local markets.'[31]

While preparing this response, we happened to receive, independently of each other, two letters from missionaries in Haiti. Both described food-for-work programmes using US food aid. One wrote: 'Haitian local leaders very quickly learn what kinds of projects are being approved for food-for-work and quickly come up with that kind of project. They then take control of the food, do as little work as possible, give the workers as little food as they can get away with and sell the rest. Numerous examples could be given.'

Market Development

In the first five years after it was passed, PL 480 succeeded in unloading abroad over $5 billion worth of American grain or 28 per cent of total American agricultural exports. But even this was not enough to unload US grain surpluses. By 1959 the United States held its highest stocks in history. Merely responding to food aid requests was not enough. Policy makers decided they had to take an active role in *creating* markets. The goal spelled out in the preamble to PL 480 included these words: 'to develop and expand export markets for United States agricultural commodities.' The goal was clear; the question was how to achieve it.

The answer was 'development.' PL 480, by allowing countries to import food *without* using dollars, made it more likely that poor governments would have dollars available to import American capital goods for light industrialization. Assistant Secretary of State W. L. Clayton testified that the World Bank financing for such capital goods 'would certainly be a very good one for US agricultural exports, because as you help develop them industrially, you will shift their economy to an industrial economy, so that I think in the end you would create more markets for your agricultural products.'[32]

In 1957, the US government agreed to accept the local currency generated by its PL 480 food sales as repayment of aid loans. This lasted until 1972. This local currency modification of PL 480 was then turned into a direct aid to US corporation investment.

Up to 25 per cent of the local currency accepted in exchange for food could be loaned at very low interest rates to US corporations investing in those countries.

Thus, US food surpluses were to be sold on credit to a foreign government that in turn sold the food for local currency. That local currency then in part financed American companies that would, it was hoped, generate the need to import yet more food. 419 subsidiaries of American firms in 31 countries established or expanded their operations at very low cost. In India alone, such loans have gone to Wyeth Labs, Union Carbide, Otis Elevator, Sylvania, Rockwell International, Goodyear, CPC International, Sunshine Farms, First National City Bank, the Bank of America, and American Express, among others.

In addition, the Department of Agriculture uses food loan repayments to promote feedgrain livestock and poultry industries throughout the underdeveloped world.[33]

Building a Wheat Market

PL 480 has succeeded in creating markets for wheat among the world's original rice lovers. PL 480 'was the best thing that ever happened to the wheat industry.' observed one market development specialist, pointing to the tremendous increase in wheat consumption in such countries as Japan, Taiwan, and Korea. Wheat aid credits to the Taiwanese government allowed it to export the people's staple, rice, while it exhorted the population to embrace the new diet by such slogans as 'eating wheat is patriotic.'[34] South Korea now has 7000 bakeries, and Koreans eat Italian-style noodles made from wheat flour.[35] 'We taught people to eat wheat who did not eat it before,' bragged an official of the US Department of Agriculture.[36]

PL 480 has perhaps proved that people like what they eat rather than eat what they like. At any rate American corporations have taught them to eat what they have to sell. This achievement was lauded, in 1974, in testimony before the Senate Foreign Relations Committee by former Secretary of Agriculture Orville Freeman, now president of Business International. Freeman noted that, 'In the last seven years, our agricultural exports to Taiwan have climbed by 531 per cent and those to [South] Korea by 643 per cent because we created a market.' PL 480 'makes very good sense,' he added.

Yet does it make good sense for South Korea?

Food Aid, Strings Attached

In a 1975 article entitled, 'PL 480 – Humanitarian Effort Helps Build Markets,' USDA congratulates itself for helping to stimulate food sales abroad. 'Many countries,' it says, 'have "graduated" from PL 480 status.'[37] Besides helping American corporations build import-demanding industries abroad, PL 480 created yet another method for helping countries 'graduate' to commercial purchases. In order to receive food aid, the potential recipient had to accept one condition: agreement to purchase in the future on commercial terms American agricultural commodities. In 1973, the US government made food credit to the Dominican Republic conditional upon much larger commercial purchases. In 1975, PL 480 loans to Egypt for wheat and to South Korea for rice were tied to additional commercial purchases of these commodities.

The United States applies this stipulation regularly for all commodities except wheat and reserves the right to apply it to wheat also. 'The US takes this seriously,' emphasizes one American official. 'If a country hasn't met its commercial requirements by the end of the year, the requirement is added on to the next year.'[38] Apparently the compassion of the United States government is limited to future customers.

Food Aid and Local Production

South Korea has been the second largest recipient of American food aid and has purchased more US agricultural goods than any other underdeveloped country. What has been the impact on South Korea's own agriculture? United States grain imported into Korea has allowed the government to maintain a 'cheap food' policy, undercutting Korean farmers. Prices that the government paid to rice producers barely approached the costs of production throughout the sixties. Pressure from farmers led to some increase in the government rice purchase price in the 1970s but, according to the Korean Catholic Farmer's Association, prices are still below farmers' costs.[39] Not surprisingly then, the rural population fell from one-half to slightly more than one-third of the total population between 1963 and 1976 as farm people sought their livelihood in the cities, often with no success, as evidenced by the rising unemployment. Moreover, South Korea, 92 per cent self sufficient in grain in 1961, now must import one-third of its grain.

The basic purpose of US food aid, along with the more than $13 billion in direct economic and Security Supporting Assistance to Seoul since the Korean War, has been to maintain a low-paid disciplined labour force for use by export-oriented, multinational companies that dominate the Korean economy. Former Assistant Secretary of Agriculture Clayton Yeutter, however, claimed 'South Korea is the great success story worldwide of the Food for Peace (PL 480) programme in terms of its contribution to the growth of the nation.'[41]

Colombia is another dramatic case, showing the effects of PL 480 shipments. Between 1955 and 1971, Colombia imported over 1 million tons of wheat that could have been produced more cheaply at home.[42] The marketing agency of the Colombian government fixed the price of the imported grain so low that it undercut domestically produced wheat. This dumping resulted in 50 per cent lower prices to Colombian farmers. From 1955, the first year of PL 480 shipments, to 1971, Colombia's wheat production dropped by 69 per cent while its imports increased 800 per cent to the point that imports came to account for 90 per cent of domestic consumption.[43]

The impact of American food aid to Bolivia has been similar.[44] But an additional turn of the screw came when the United States stopped accepting payments in local currency and demanded dollars for food aid shipments, albeit on easy terms. Despite its rich agricultural potential and high rural underemployment, Bolivia had come to depend on United States imports, and local wheat production had stagnated. Millers had turned themselves primarily into flour-importing companies because importing was more profitable than milling. Thus, even after local currency was no longer accepted to repay PL 480 shipments (the final cutoff point being at the end of 1971), Bolivia had to continue to import flour. The big difference, however, was that Bolivia was forced to use up scarce foreign exchange to purchase the flour in dollars – foreign exchange that might have gone to purchase what it could *not* easily produce itself, such as productive industrial goods.

Dumping large quantities of low-priced American or Canadian or Australian grain on underdeveloped countries makes it economically *impossible* for the small domestic producers to compete – no matter how much they might want to. Unable to get a fair return for their grain, such producers are frequently forced to sell their land, becoming landless (and often jobless) labourers. A study published in an agricultural economics journal in 1969 concluded that for every pound of PL 480 cereals imported, there was a net decline in Indian domestic production over the following two years of almost one-half pound because of the reduced return to the farmer.[45]

A 1975 US government (General Accounting Office) report concludes that: 'Leading world authorities now indicate that such food assistance has hindered the developing countries in expanding their food production and thus has contributed to the critical world food situation.'[46]

Food Aid Disaster

In visiting Guatemala, we learned that even in times of natural disasters, food aid can undermine the livelihood precisely of local poor farmers. In the months after the terrible February 1976 earthquake, US food aid dramatically increased.[47]

The people in the earthquake areas were mostly smallholder farmers. who just before the earthquake had brought in exceptional harvests. Following the earthquake, what they needed was cash to help rebuild their homes and farms. To get that cash these farmers, like farmers around the world, needed to dig out and sell part of their stored corn and other grain. But the widespread and indiscriminate distribution of free food from the US (largely through CARE and Catholic Relief Services) contributed to lowering prices for locally grown food. Even when the Guatemalan government's National Emergency Committee asked voluntary agencies to stop bringing food into the country, the food aid kept pouring in.

Oxfam, the international non-government development agency, gave a special loan to an organization of farmers in earthquake-hit Chimaltenango, the Quetzal Marketing Cooperative. The loan was expressly for the purpose of trying to stabilize food markets, disrupted in part by the CARE and CRS food giveaways. The Co-op used the loan to set up a grainbank that bought crops from the farmers at a price above the depressed levels. The scheme thus helped the farmers of the area to get the cash they needed to rebuild their lives at a price that did not force them to take a severe loss. According to observers with whom we spoke, the Cooperative's scheme served as a significant stabilizing element, counterbalancing the impact of the food handouts.

William Rudell, who has worked with a Guatemalan highlands co-operative since 1971, and Roland Bunch, who has worked with rural co-operatives in Guatemala through World Neighbours and

Oxfam since 1968, told us that even where there was a need for food for the first days following the earthquake, before stored food could be recovered from the rubble, the food should have been brought from areas in Guatemala not affected by the earthquake. Such purchases could have been a boost to farmers in those villages. Moreover, purchases within the country could be more easily curtailed when farmers in the recipient villages had dug out their stored harvests. As Bunch commented, 'if the Guatemalans were sending wheat into the United States this year as their own version of a PL 480 donation and giving it out to American consumers, American farmers would be screaming bloody murder about it.'

Disasters that massively destroy crops might present a somewhat different situation. Still, the principle that emerges for us is that even for genuine short-term emergencies the effort should be to purchase the relief food as locally as possible and from peasant producers whose families' livelihood depends on selling its grain. A principle at least if we are serious about helping the needy.

Food as a Weapon

The political and military use of US food aid is not a new story. In this century, immediately following World War I, future President Herbert Hoover put his support behind a food aid programme for Germany to avert the danger of hungry Germans voting socialist (as well as to solve the American food surplus problem generated by the wartime agricultural effort).

In 1943, forty-three nations created what would become the United States-dominated United Nations Relief and Rehabilitation Administration (UNRRA) to give food aid to war victims. The aid was 'not to be used as a political weapon and no discrimination was to be made in distribution for racial, religious or political reasons.'[48] Despite this explicit provision, American food aid went to fascist forces in Greece and to Chiang Kai-shek in China. India received no help following the great famine of 1943 in which 4 million Indians died, nor in the 1946-1947 famine.[49] India, at that time, did not qualify as a priority anticommunist front zone, according to the Secretary of State Dean Acheson.

Following World War II, over one quarter of all United States funds on food aid was spent under the Marshall Plan. Enormous quantities of grain on credit flowed into Italy and France to help keep the impoverished working class from voting against capitalism.

Marshall himself stated at the time: 'Food is a vital factor in our foreign policy.'

In 1959, Senator Humphrey criticized those who would have food aid serve only as a surplus disposal mechanism. He saw food as a potent political weapon:

> We have been told repeatedly that this is a worldwide struggle between the forces of evil and the forces of decency. . . . We all know we are engaged in the struggle for men's minds, for their loyalties. There is a struggle between ways of life, a system of values. Our values are different from those of the totalitarians. If it is a worldwide struggle, it would seem to me we would want to mobilize all the resources we possibly can in order to win it. And in a world of want and hunger what is more powerful than food and fibre?'[50]

Since we have been told China, North Vietnam, and North Korea are 'the forces of evil,' naturally most of our food aid has gone to the bordering countries: India, South Vietnam, during the Vietnam War Cambodia, South Korea, and Taiwan. By 1973, almost *half* of all US food aid was going to South Vietnam and Cambodia. *Between 1968 and 1973, South Vietnam alone received twenty times the value of food aid that the five African countries most seriously affected by drought received during that same period.*[51]

The withdrawal of food aid can also be a powerful political weapon. Aid to Chile was abruptly discontinued when a government was elected that threatened American corporate interest, as we will discuss later. Because US policymakers see food aid as a political tool, they do not like to contribute food to international agencies where its use might be less under their control. In October, 1974, the *Washington Post* reported on an unreleased government document, part of the preparation for the World Food Conference the following month. In it the United States opposed expansion of the World Food Programme (WFP), a United Nations programme to aid famine areas. The document states that the United States has 'not been able in recent years to influence appreciably the policies and procedures on the WFP or the distribution of aid to particular destinations. There would appear to be no advantage to the US favouring a greater role and more resources for WFP.'[52] The administration clearly wanted to have nothing to do with food aid projects it could not mould to its own purpose.

Food Aid as the Perfect Guise

By 1973, with commercial sales booming, the amount of agricultural products shipped under PL 480 dropped to 3.3 million tons, one fifth of the level of the midsixties. The Department of Agriculture no longer needed PL 480 to dispose of surpluses. But the National Security Council and the State Department under Kissinger were there to pick up the food aid baton.

Congress had begun to resist efforts by the administration to continue to prop up the regimes in South Vietnam and Cambodia as well as to aid the Chilean junta, which so flagrantly disregards human rights. PL 480 provided the administration with just the funding vehicle needed to skirt congressional controls.

• First, the administration was confident that expanding food aid expenditures would be hard for Congress to oppose since so many well-meaning Americans think food aid is to feed hungry people.

• Second PL 480 country programmes are not subject to annual congressional approval. For instance, in the fiscal year 1974, Cambodia was slated to receive $30 million in food aid but in fact received $194 million.[53] In addition, the Commodity Credit Corporation (CCC), established in 1957 to expand markets for American agricultural products, has its own capacity to extend credits for agricultural purchases to favoured governments. Here, too, there is flexibility. During the course of the fiscal year 1976, the actual CCC credit sales were double the amount originally budgeted. All this gave the administration quite a bit of leeway.

• Third, food aid can easily, yet discreetly, be turned into direct support for foreign military efforts. The food can be sold locally by foreign governments, thereby generating funds for that government's military budget. In the case of certain countries the administration does not require repayment of the food aid loan. It simply authorizes the recipient government to use the proceeds from the food resale as a grant for 'common defence.' In October 1973, an agreement signed with South Vietnam allowed all proceeds to the Saigon government from PL 480 sales to go to the military budget; in Cambodia the figure was 80 per cent of food aid sales.

By 1975, $6 billion in local currencies generated by the sale of PL 480 food had been spent for military purposes; over one third of this in South Korea and South Vietnam.[54] One study showed that in 1965 over 85 per cent of South Korea's resale funds were used for military purposes.[55]

These three realities make food a handy tool indeed. In fiscal year 1974, for instance, Congress cut more than 20 per cent out of the economic aid requested for Indochina by the administration. Undaunted, the White House more than doubled the PL 480 allocation to South Vietnam and Cambodia to $499 million, giving these two countries half of all food credits that year[56]. An American reporter in Cambodia documented a refugee camp where 70 per cent of the smaller children[57] went hungry while nearby the bags of food aid were being sold to pay the troops.[57]

For fiscal year 1975, the administration was again budgeting half of all PL 480 credits for South Vietnam and Cambodia. In light of a growing image of America as indifferent to the plight of the hungry, Congress tried to balance the obvious military and political intent of US food aid with some concern for the starving. It passed an amendment requiring that 70 per cent of the food aid go to countries on the United Nations list of 'most seriously affected' countries.

In order to get the amount of military support it wanted for Cambodia and Vietnam and to give its vote of confidence to other repressive regimes in Chile, South Korea, and the Middle East, the administration merely increased the total amount of food aid available. It could then support its client regimes and still stay within the new ruling requiring 70 per cent of our food aid to go to the neediest countries, claiming to have generously acceded to the demands of the 'humanitarians' by increasing food aid from $1 billion to $1.6 billion.

In 1975, in protest against the junta's repressive policies, Congress placed a $26 million limit on economic aid to Chile (still the second-highest amount granted by the United States to any country in Latin America) and cut off military aid altogether. All that meant little. By the end of the year, Chile's share of food aid was over $60 million.

We do not claim to have all the answers about food aid. A few points have, however, become clear. First, hungry people should know that the western food donors can never be a source of food security. Indeed, food security is not something that can be given, even by a well-intentioned foreign government. Underdeveloped countries had better *assume* that western governments will use their food surpluses to help expand their commercial markets, to assist the penetration of agribusiness firms and to support the very regimes that work in direct opposition to the policies that would enable hungry people to free themselves from hunger. Let anything else be a pleasant surprise.

Second, concerned citizens should not think of aid as *the* way to help the hungry. Dwelling on the issue of overseas aid – how much and what criteria should be used – diverts attention from the *process* of how hunger is created. It allows us to forget that the overriding impact of the west on the ability of people to become food self-reliant is not through aid, but through its corporate, military, and economic involvement in their countries.

If you can't quite remember what 'starvation' is – bring in an international expert and he will tell you. It's to do with 'groups of the population which, because of insufficient income or for other reasons, were previously prevented from translating an inherent need for food into actual consumption'; and why is this such a bad thing? 'besides being undesirable in itself and a major cause of mortality, malnutrition entails long-term economic costs to individuals and to the economy.'

G N Vogel,
Executive Director of UN's World Food Programme

I have heard . . . that people may become dependent on us for food. I know that was not supposed to be good news. To me, that was good news, because before people can do anything they have got to eat. And if you are looking for a way to get people to lean on you and to be dependent on you, in terms of their cooperation with you, it seems to me that food dependence would be terrific.

Senator Hubert H. Humphrey, 1957

On only one occasion did we have the opportunity to see food aid reaching needy people. While visiting an adjacent area affected by floods, we saw a union council member handing out cornmeal biscuits from a tin dated 1963 and labelled, 'Office of Civil Defense, US Department of Defense.' The biscuits had evidently been produced for American fallout shelters during the days of the bomb scares. After more than a decade, the US government decided to dispose of them. They were reportedly on their way to Cambodia when Phnom Penh fell, at which point they were redirected to Bangladesh. Each villager received

one rather stale biscuit. 'The only reason these weren't sold on
the black market is that no one would buy them,' remarked a
village elder.

Betsy Hartmann and James Boyce
reporting on 9 months in a
Bangladesh village

PART X FOOD SELF RELIANCE

30: Working Toward Food Self-Reliance

Food self-reliance is not a new concept; it is as old as humanity itself. Throughout history, people have assumed that producing their food was the basis of their survival. Recognizing this fact at a 1976 conference of Asian students, one participant explained, 'When we are affirming the struggle for self-reliance in Asia today, we are not affirming a foreign ideology. Self-reliance as a law of social and political existence has always been there. . . .'[1]

Not Necessarily Self-Sufficiency

Food self-reliance does not necessarily mean producing everything the nation eats but producing enough of its basic foods to be independent of outside forces. Food self-reliance calls for the maximum utilization of local resources – physical and human – before seeking out foreign resources. While food self-reliance is not necessarily food self-sufficiency, it does imply the ability to become self-sufficient enough to survive a sudden cut-off of imports. No people should allow themselves to be vulnerable to the disruption of their food supply due to natural disasters or wars elsewhere or to the political manipulation of food exports by foreign governments.

It is crucial not to confuse food self-reliance with simply a sufficient per capita production of basic food. Today both India and the Philippines, countries where many suffer chronic malnutrition, claim self-sufficiency in basic grain. In fact, the Philippines became a rice exporter in 1977. And India now has bufferstocks of at least 22 million tons of grain stored on old World War II airstrips. Soldiers parade around it with orders to shoot anybody who comes to steal the grain ... even as the grain rots for the lack of adequate tarpaulin cover.

Thus food self-reliance is measured not in terms of production totals. The real criterion of self-reliance must rather always be: Do all the people have access to an adequate amount of food?

Fundamentals of Food Self-Reliance

Keeping this meaning of food self-reliance in mind, we have

learned that re-achieving food self-reliance involves at least eight fundamentals. These fundamentals are not speculative points. They have proven to be crucial in countries that have achieved or are well on the way toward achieving food self-reliance – countries, we should not forget, that contain over 40 per cent of all people living in the underdeveloped world.

1. Food self-reliance requires the allocation of control over agricultural resources to local, democratically organized units.

Since food self-reliance involves not only adequate production but adequate consumption realized by everyone, a society will never achieve food self-reliance unless the control of agricultural resources is shared democratically. A re-allocation of control over productive assets is crucial for the redistribution of purchasing power; this alone will insure that agricultural (and industrial) production benefits the local population instead of just local and foreign elites. For only by sharing in control of productive assets will the local majority make up the priority market toward which production is oriented.

Land Reform Part of the re-allocation of control is land reform. But many so-called land reforms in the last thirty years have actually tended to 'consolidate the prevailing social order,' notes economist J. B. W. Kuitenbrouwer.[2] Loopholes have been commonplace. In several states in India, for example, reform legislation did not apply to fruit cultivation. A landowner with several hundred acres of rice cultivation could plant six mango trees in his rice field and – bingo – his land was exempt.[3] Reforms have often affected only a small fraction of the land. Over five years after the land reform decree in the Philippines, less than one per cent of the cropped land has been 'redistributed' – and then only to tenants who must meet the payments of a 15-year mortgage.[4] The plight of the landless has been ignored by land reform laws in countries like the Philippines, Pakistan, India and Egypt.

Many land reform laws have aimed explicitly at promoting tenant security by granting permanent lease rights to tenants who cultivate a given piece of land over a certain period of years. But they have often had just the opposite impact. Afraid of eventually losing their land to their tenants under such laws, landlords change tenants every year or switch to day labourers.

Even when some of their land is taken away, the largeholders can still be the real beneficiaries of the 'reforms.' A 1959 land reform in Pakistan compensated landlords handsomely for poor, unirrigated land that had previously brought them little or no income.[5]

As a report published by the Christian Conference of Asia concludes, 'Land reforms of this type have been adopted chiefly to pacify the countryside so that the government could concentrate all its efforts on the urban sector and on industrialization.' Such fake reforms obscure an appreciation of what the effects of real distribution could be. Production advances have not been sacrificed in countries that have authentically redistributed the land and other food-producing resources, countries as different as Japan, Cuba, Taiwan, China, and North Vietnam. Indeed, just the contrary, people who own the land they work, either individually or as a group, naturally invest more time, labour and money in it than do nonowners. In Japan in 1940, only about 31 per cent of the landholdings were worked by people who owned the land. By 1960, over 75 per cent of the holdings were operated by owner farmers.[6] This shift goes a long way toward explaining why recent yields per acre of foodgrains in Japan were as much as 60 per cent greater than in the United States.[7]

However, *land redistribution in itself will not prevent a regression to old inequalities.* But some might logically ask: how could land redistribution fail to redistribute power if considerable power rests in land ownership itself? Part of the answer is that power also rests in control of all the resources from water to fertilizer to credit that makes the land produce, as well as in access to markets that make that production profitable. The South Korean reform ended tenancy, at least in theory, by giving small amounts of land to former tenants. But rich peasants illegally retained large holdings. Moreover, credit systems, marketing and irrigation were not reorganized co-operatively to meet the needs of the new small holders. There existed no built-in mechanism for the poorer peasants to overcome the privileges clung to by the rural elites. Twenty years later the results are predictable: by 1970, 54 per cent of those farmers who had received land under the land reform had become tenants again.[8]

Moreover, landowners who are compensated for their land through land reform programmes can invest that gain in urban consumer and export industries. Money that might have gone into rural development instead goes into other sectors, further exacerbating the pre-existing urban export bias. Such 'reform' in no way mitigates the concentration of wealth.

Fake and partial land reform cannot therefore lead to food self-reliance. But two fears seem to haunt many western experts in any discussion of a thorough-going land redistribution – the 'wholesale slaughter' of the land-owning elite and 'forced collectivization.' Neither generalization captures the lessons to be gained from the many land reforms carried out in this century.

During land reforms, retribution against individual landlords by outraged peasants has occurred, especially when those landlords fought to hold onto their privileges. Some landlords, in Cuba for example, have been brought to trial for particular crimes such as the murder of tenants. When not convicted of severe crimes against those previously under their control, however, former landlords have often been integrated into the new social order. Many have received regular compensatory payments from the state. (In countries where the land is tightly held, the number of individuals who actually must give up land because of redistribution is relatively small. Moreover, many landlords, precisely because of their economic resources, are able to flee into exile.) Rarely have land redistributions triggered the wholesale liquidation of a landlord class.

Nowhere has forced collectivization worked successfully. Where attempted, it has often later been reversed.[9] By the early 1950s, Yugoslavia and Poland abandoned a top-down approach to creating agricultural co-operatives. For one thing, the agricultural machinery – that could have increased production and lightened work on the larger co-operative units and thus compensated the peasant farmers for the felt loss of owning their own land – was simply not in adequate supply. Farming in both countries is now mainly by small holdings served by extensive networks of co-operatives for sharing machinery and for marketing. Both countries have protected these small holdings by setting a ceiling on farm size – a maximum of 37 acres and 248 acres (less on good soils) in Yugoslavia and Poland respectively.

Where a forced or top-down approach to collectivization has continued, development has suffered. Production stagnation on the state farms in the Soviet Union, as compared to the obvious productivity of private garden plots, can be seen as peasant resistance to a system in which they are mere employees of the state – and underpaid at that.

By contrast, successful collective agricultural development has been the result of a transition through progressive stages in which people can come to appreciate the advantages to themselves of co-operative work.

In China, the first stage was the 'mutual aid team' in which families shared tools and labour – a traditional practice in much of the world. The organization of rural life has now moved in China to the three-tiered commune in which effective control of the land resides in the production team comprised of 20 to 30 families. An FAO report referred to the production team as 'an extended family farm.'[10] Everyone is expected to contribute and the rewards are determined by the entire 'family,' based on work done – with a guarantee of the basic food requirements to all.

Likewise, in Vietnam (formerly North Vietnam) co-operative control of the land was not brought about in one fell swoop but step by step.[11] The 1953 reform act distributed land primarily to the landless and small peasant households; by the end of 1957, 77 per cent of the rural households had benefited from the distribution of 2 million acres. The movement toward collective work built on the tradition of individuals joining together to construct and maintain dykes.

Collective models of work were reinforced by the war. By 1956, half of the peasants belonged to labour-pooling groups and mutual aid groups. The movement toward collective control passed through four stages of organization. It was not until the mid-sixties that most co-operatives actually pooled land and determined the individual's income by his or her work. By 1967, 90 per cent of the cropland was worked co-operatively.[11]

The advantage of co-operative development of the land in contrast to individually worked plots depends also on the size of the plots in question. And this factor varies greatly. Many who have studied Asian agriculture have concluded that in countries such as Bangladesh, where the typical holding is less than two acres, co-operative agriculture is the only hope of lightening labour and increasing production. Even small-scale power tillers and tubewells are beyond the capacity of many individual small farmers. Pre-existing cultural patterns of co-operative work, particularly in Asia, play a part too, as we see in China and Vietnam.

Participation A final point remains. Rural people must not only control the land they work but effectively participate in wielding national political and economic power. They must exercise a strong voice through their co-operatives and political organizations in the control of credit and marketing institutions. As part of this taking charge, they will need to acquire the knowledge and skills to manage their own affairs. Thus literacy and basic education for *all* men and women must be a high priority to help make and keep their organizations democratic. While including bookkeeping and administrative skills, this basic education should not be seen merely as a means of increasing people's productivity. Education is the process by which the rural majority can develop co-operative values and discover their own range of capacities.

Effective *campesino* (peasant) organization was becoming a reality in Chile during the Popular Unity government before its overthrow by the military in September, 1973. The government promoted democratically elected *campesino* councils for each county and province as well as for the nation as a whole. Jointly with the state, these councils were beginning to plan and carry out agrarian programmes such as credit and marketing. Pressured by many *campesinos*, the government also actively encouraged *campesino*-controlled unions and co-operatives.

Only the redistribution of control of the land and the participation by farmers in national political and economic power can create a new kind of farmers, able to co-operate as equals and to face difficult challenges, no longer afraid of bosses, moneylenders and landlords.

2. Food self-reliance depends on the initiative of the people, not on government directives.

Only when the transformation of the agrarian structure takes place under the overwhelming pressure of organized peasants will the changes favour them. Mass initiative is the opposite of government-managed 'development.' If food self-reliance is managed from above, people feel they are working 'for the government,' not for themselves. People become 'clients,' not the motive force.

A government policy of simply parcelling out land to the peasants is not, for example, self-reliant development. Land reform must involve the people themselves who deliberate to decide how the resources are to be used and how disputes are to be resolved. Land reform must not only redistribute land but must be the first step in the creation of real democracy. The *process* of land reform is as important as the reform itself.

'Bureaucratic devices may be able to crush the landlord's power, but they will not be able to help the peasant establish his own power,' observes China scholar Yu-Hsi Chen.[12] During Taiwan's land redistribution (1949-53), the peasants remained passive recipients while the government acted as the insulating agent between the landlords and the peasants. The land reform did not give birth to independent peasant organizations able to look out for their own interests. The post-reform era, therefore, left Taiwanese peasants at the mercy of their new exploiter – the state. Twelve years after the reform, the land tax more than tripled while the price of rice increased less than 20 per cent.[13]

Even progressive Tanzania has, in part, fallen into the trap of trying to 'manage' self-reliance. Political economist P. L. Raikes, in his detailed study of *ujamaa* villages in Tanzania,[14] finds that bureaucratic, external interventions have thwarted release of the enthusiasm and productive energy of the peasants. Under urban- and foreign-oriented administrators, the peasants treat the communal lands as if they were government farms. The use of coercion leads to passive resistance. Raikes notes, for example, that all too often administrators present villagers with a plan that is primarily a set of production targets. The allocation of needed farming inputs and social services is made to depend upon acceptance of this plan. The villagers know that to question its merits will probably displease the bureaucrat, thus reducing the likelihood of their getting any assistance.

Since the development of any society is based entirely on the development of the individuals within it, the programme of redistribution must break the pattern of dependency. It must initiate a process of people themselves taking more and more control over their own lives. Only when the people are in control is there hope of preventing a fall back into hierarchical patterns.

The *process* of land reform is therefore as important as the reform itself. The people must together deliberate and decide how they want to distribute the land and resolve any conflicting claims that arise. The experience of land reform will then be one of a valuable social education, training the people for the new task of collective administration. Such is the conclusion of a group of Asian rural economists reflecting upon what the Chinese experience has to teach. Their report observes: 'Land reform through mass . . . action also gives an opportunity for other dominance-dependence relations to be shaken up: women and youth, the low castes, even the children, will be in the thick of this experience which will shock them emotionally and help remove deep-seated inhibitions in their minds as well.'[15]

3. Food self-reliance based on popular initiative presupposes group solidarity and therefore, equality.

Popular initiative is not simply the sum total of individual self-seeking. It rests in awakening the confidence of the people that their natural self-interest and the goals of co-operative struggle are not in conflict but, indeed, share common ground.

Current dependency relationships that tie the poor to the rich – as tenant, labourer, debtor – engender disunity among the poor. Competition for survival means that the poor often see each other, rather than the elite classes, as the threats. The struggle for self-reliant development must therefore begin with co-operative activities that reduce the dependency of the poor on the rich and allow the oppressed to grasp how solidarity can benefit them.

People have proved themselves willing to sacrifice and work hard for future reward when they can see that all are sacrificing equally. Thus, equality is a necessary prerequisite for popular initiative. (In countries with great inequalities in wealth and income, appeals for national sacrifice are correctly perceived by the poor majority as a way for the controlling elite to extract yet more wealth through the extra exertion of the people.)

What does equality mean? How is it achieved? And, once achieved, how is it maintained? We do not claim to have the answers. But we do believe that now, perhaps more than at any time in human history, people are struggling with these questions, questions that may never be definitively answered.

It is these questions that the Chinese are tackling, perhaps more seriously than any other people. Within 5 or 6 years of the 1949 land redistribution in China, the old rural inequalities were re-appearing. In direct response came the initiative for collective control of both the land and needed farm inputs. Collective control was thus an attempt to prevent the re-emergence of an elite-controlled economy. But what about the inequalities among geographic regions, as well as differences in human resources? Given these differences, why would not one co-operative organization tend to move ahead of another? Attempts to enlarge the size of the accounting unit so as to even out these differences as much as possible were tried – and resisted by peasants who felt it unjust that they should have to share their hard-earned success with the less well-endowed – and tried again as the wealth base has increased.[16]

Even by the early mid-sixties, the gap between the richest 20 per cent and the poorest 20 per cent was one-third what it was before the revolution began. Today in China you find spirited debate over such issues as the size of the accounting unit and the use of material incentives. Although not all Chinese agree on the role of material incentives, reductions in inequalities have played a notable role on the path of the Chinese people to development.

4. With food self-reliance, trade becomes an organic outgrowth of development, not the fragile hinge on which survival hangs.

To our surprise one of the most controversial propositions in our writing has been that trade is not universally positive. Trade *can* play a positive role, but dependency on imports for basic survival puts whole populations at risk of famine and makes national self-determination an illusion.

Perhaps most of us are unaware of how totally we accept the notion that 'free trade' is by definition 'progressive' and that anti-trade sentiment could only throw us 'back to the stone age.' With only partial tongue in cheek, economist Samir Amin claims that if one were to follow prevailing attitudes of the world powers, 'one would have to add to the Charter of the United Nations a new crime of aggression against civilization: the refusal to trade.'[17]

We are not against trade; we only question whether trade can be accepted as a universal good. Agricultural exports should come only after the agricultural resources are in the hands of people first meeting their own food needs. No country can hope to 'win' in the game of international trade, as we explained in Part VI, as long as its very survival depends on selling its one or two products every year. A country simply cannot hold out for just prices for its exports if it is desperate for foreign exchange with which to import food. When the basic needs are met, however, trade can become a healthy extension of *domestic need* instead of being determined strictly by *foreign demand*.

Such trade – trade that would supplement domestic production with items needed by the majority for their own development – is a far cry from the trade-oriented economies of most Third World countries today. In elite-dominated economies, a fixation on trade as the road to development represents an option against the creation of a domestic market – for that would require the elimination of mass poverty. Theories of 'comparative trade advantage' (exporting cocoa, for example, theoretically to import basic foods), end up being an advantage to the domestic elite and a disadvantage to the majority of the people.

A people working for basic self-reliance is thus the only context in which trade can play a positive role. Only then will trade help to broaden people's choices rather than, as is so often the case now, help to concentrate economic power in the hands of the few.

Moreover, only when all avenues for local production have been tried should imports be sought. This principle will lead to diversity, giving rise to unique models for unique localities. As development economist Johan Galtung notes, any loss in efficiency that might result from reinventing something already invented somewhere else 'is more than offset by the gain in self-confidence in accepting the challenge of being the innovator.[18]

5. Food self-reliance means reuniting agriculture and nutrition.

If colonialism's plantations first converted food into a mere commodity, production contracted by multinational agribusiness for the Global Supermarket completes the divorce of agriculture and nutrition. Self-reliance would make the central question not 'What crop might have a few cents edge on the world market months or even years hence?' but 'How can the people best feed themselves with this piece of land?'

As obvious as it may seem, the policy basing land use on nutritional output is practised in only a few countries today. For these countries food is no longer just a commodity. As a necessary of life, it is considered as precious as life itself.

With Food First self-reliance, industrial crops (like cotton and rubber), livestock feed crops, and luxury fruits and vegetables are planted *after* meeting the basic needs of all the people.

6. Food self-reliance makes agriculture an end, not a means.

In countries where so much of the population today is hungry, agriculture has been seen, since the onslaught of colonialism, as the sector from which to extract wealth to serve urban, industrial, and foreign interests. Theoretically things have changed. But have they really?

In most underdeveloped countries the terms of trade between agriculture and industry continue to be biased in favour of industry. The government controls the price of the main farm products – either directly or through food imports – while the prices of industrial goods inflate. An elite-controlled government is pleased if this means that industrial wages can be kept low, but the result for farmers is declining real income and mounting debt. The process is particularly pronounced in countries with export-oriented industrial policies.

Although agriculture in underdeveloped countries ordinarily generates most of the national product and foreign exchange, a recent survey found that, on the average, agriculture receives only 11 per cent of all investment. On the other hand, mining and manufacture receive over one quarter of all investment.[19] A United Nations study of Africa notes that although agriculture contributes 20 to 50 per cent of the GNP, it receives only 10 to 30 per cent of the public investment.[20]

The Chinese people have chosen a different path. They have decided quite deliberately to reject the Soviet approach of squeezing peasant producers through low prices for their products and high prices for consumer goods and farm inputs. They have chosen a policy of relatively high and slowly increasing prices for agricultural commodities along with low prices for farm supplies. Between 1950 and 1970, the exchange power of a given amount of agricultural goods increased 68 per cent.[21] In addition, the farm taxation rate has been effectively cut in half.[22] Rather than extracting a surplus from agriculture, the rest of the society contributes 23 per cent in excess of what it receives from agriculture.[23]

With food self-reliant policies, the goal of agricultural progress is first and foremost rural development, not the draining of surplus to subsidize the industrial sector.

7. *With food self-reliant policies, industry will serve agriculture; town and country will meet.*

If the majority of people are in command – and their income growing – invention and production will be based on their *needs*. A rural, dispersed, small-scale industrial network will grow to fill the need for fertilizer, farming equipment, and other simple manufactures. We are not talking about dumping factories that produce for urban markets in the middle of a rice field just for the sake of 'decentralization', but of developing industry as an organic outgrowth of the needs of labour-intensive agriculture and those of the local population.

In India decentralization of industry became official policy but with no understanding of the process. Clock and radio factories were established in rural areas. But since both the production materials and the market for the finished product were in the cities, a lot of money was spent shipping springs to the country and clocks to the city. The problem was that a clock factory did nothing to stimulate the growth of agriculture and that agricultural growth did not give impetus to the clock factory.

Moreover, Food First self-reliance will halt, even reverse, the flow of landless refugees who daily migrate to cities in hope of work. The wide gap in income between rural and urban workers will begin to close. Rural life will no longer be looked upon as backward. The Cuban people, for example, understood the need to bring to rural areas the health, educational, and cultural facilities – dance, film, library, theatre – invariably associated, especially by the young, with city life. Over the past several years more than 500 boarding high schools have been constructed in the countryside for students from both rural and urban areas. These schools are among the country's finest and offer not only a regular high school education but also daily work in food production. Through such schools in the countryside tens of thousands of young people come to appreciate the difficulties and rewards of rural work and to realize that they too can contribute to their country's development.

Not only can urban dwellers go to the countryside but the countryside can come to the city. In Cuba a substantial area around each large city is reserved for agricultural and livestock production. Root crops, vegetables and coffee are cultivated by volunteer workers and school children from near-by cities. Surrounding pastures graze cows that provide milk for the cities.

Sending students to the countryside, as is the policy in countries like Cuba, Somalia, and China, has often appeared to Western observers as a form of anti-intellectualism. Rather it is the recognition that the entire population, and especially the young, must appreciate the importance of agriculture. If not, rural development will likely be sacrificed by urbanized, white-collar bureaucrats who go on believing that agriculture should be the handmaiden to other sectors and to the needs of an elite (including themselves).

8. Food self-reliance requires co-ordinated social planning.

Social planning need not mean authoritarian rule from the top. In fact, effective social planning can only result from the decentralization of authority that allows each region to work out appropriate solutions. As Johan Galtung suggests, self-reliance does not exclude planning but uses it in a way that 'sets into motion a process of diagnosis . . . by local people formulating practical proposals for action.'[24]

First, planning is not a mere technical activity. Effective planning is not simply establishing quotas, targets and tasks; it is the organization of a sensitive and flexible structure of communication between government bodies and communities. This structure of communication serves optimum feedback and agreement on joint action – which then provides the basis for planning as a technical activity.[25]

The Chinese call this 'from the people to the people' social planning. Food self-reliance starts with the nutritional needs of all the people and translates them into a national agricultural plan. A Canadian report on agriculture and nutrition in Cuba describes how local farmers participate in this translation: 'Meetings take place with all the farm workers and small farmers at the local level to discuss the plan and the production quotas allocated to their area. Suggestions for revisions or changes are made. This feedback process is very important because it is the local farmers and workers who know best what crops will grow in their area.'[26]

Such planning presupposes common goals among the communities and the government. It substitutes conscious intervention and co-operation for the free market. This does not mean that social planning precludes the market altogether. The difference is that in a society whose conscious goal is to meet the needs of the people, social planning can 'utilize the market instead of being governed by it,' observes UN development analyst J. B. W. Kuitenbrouwer.[27] With social planning, prices of necessary items might be fixed to guarantee their availability to all; and the production of key industrial and consumer goods might be subsidized out of the profits from other lines of production, all with an eye to maximally stimulating both economic and social progress.

Planning for self-reliance, however, may well require both a short-term as well as a long-term strategy. The fundamental principles of self-reliance we have so far outlined represent the long-term thrust that appears to be necessary for self-determination and food security. Real life, however, does not often leave every policy option open. Countries now working genuinely toward food self-reliance often find they face immediate crises presented both by the inheritance of the old colonial order (see Part III) and the collapse of its structures.

Vietnam and Mozambique are good examples. The Vietnam war forced the abandonment of about 2.5 million acres of cultivated land – or between 20 and 25 per cent of all arable land throughout Vietnam. Reclaiming agricultural land, the Vietnamese faced the threat of unexploded mines and bombs still in the fields. At the end of the war several million tons of American explosives still lay unexploded. The task of agricultural reconstruction could not happen overnight. Thus in the early years, Vietnam asked urgently for food aid (which the United States refused to contribute), not, as in so many countries, to avoid agricultural restructuring but in order to sustain people while they worked at carrying out their development plans.

Mozambique, having won its independence from Portugal in 1975, also faced staggering agricultural problems. Portuguese settlers had been the main suppliers of food to the capital city. After independence most of these Portuguese fled the country, but not without first sabotaging farm machines and irrigation equipment. Thus, although the stated policies of the new Mozambican government stressed the development of co-operative villages, the immediate policy was to focus first on state farms as the only quick way to bring into production the abandoned land that had been feeding the cities. Moreover, the new government imported wheat and beef primarily so that the food habits of the city dwellers would not be overly altered. It was feared that those who lived in the city, because they had not, for the most part, experienced the liberation struggle directly, would be less willing to accept any sacrifices. Moreover, there continued to be many in the cities whose support for the new government was only marginal but whose skills Mozambique felt it could not afford to lose, at least in the early years. (The colonial system had so blocked the education of Mozambicans that the flight of Portuguese left the new country bereft of many essential technical skills.) Thus the focus on feeding the cities was a carefully weighed political choice. Only in 1978 was the government in a position to turn its attention to the working out of a national structure to promote the development of co-operative villages. However, from the beginning a national literacy and health campaign reached deep into the countryside, helping to establish the prerequisites for building productive and self-reliant villages.

For such countries, struggling first for their survival, the challenge is to be able to make short-term compromises demanded by the exigencies of immediate crises without losing sight of the long term strategy for democratic, equitable, and self-reliant development.

The Food Self-Reliance Bandwagon

As forced food dependency continues to translate into food shortages and rising prices for people throughout the world, national politicians will increasingly call for food self-reliance. They will claim that their new agricultural policies will make their countries independent. But the food self-reliant policies we have described simply cannot be implemented by the present governments of most underdeveloped countries. Why not? Simply because these policies directly counter the self-interest of the propertied elite now in power. Food First, then, is not a simple call to put food into hungry mouths. It is the recognition that, if enabling people to feed themselves is to be the priority, then all social relationships must be reconstructed.

If present governments will not implement Food First policies, what, then, is the value of this prescription for food self-reliance? Its value, we think, lies in showing what is possible – in giving evidence to groups struggling for self-determination that food self-reliance is a *viable* alternative. A prescription for food self-reliance and a continuing effort to garner the proof of experience that it is possible will serve to discredit all governments that now rationalize continuing dependency as necessary for survival. Indeed the strongest weapon of oppression is the belief, by oppressor and oppressed alike, that while dependency may not be desirable, it is better than starvation. Food self-reliance is the cornerstone of genuine self-determination and it is possible for every country in the world.

Food Self-Reliance and the Industrial Countries

How would food self-reliance in the underdeveloped countries affect those of us in the industrial countries? Many might assume that the citizens of the industrial countries benefit by the continued dependency of the underdeveloped countries.

The answer, we have seen, is an emphatic no. Self-reliance for the now dependent countries would strike at the heart of the Global Supermarket phenomenon, that is, the collaboration of elites in both industrial and underdeveloped countries to profit from the land and people of underdeveloped countries by supplying those locally and abroad who can afford to pay the most. Although citizens of the industrial countries might be told by the apologists of agribusiness that the Global Supermarket exists to serve them, it does not. We have already seen, in Part VIII, that it serves only its creators.

The prescription for food self-reliance presented here is not simply what 'those poor, hungry countries,' should do. Redistribution of control over food-producing resources is the only path toward true self-reliance for the industrial countries as well. By understanding the parallels, the majority in the industrial countries will come to see that the hungry masses they are often made to fear are, in reality, their natural allies. We are all in a common struggle for control over the most basic human need – food.

31 : But Where Would Funds for Development Come From?

If you truly examine the 'what is' now in underdeveloped countries, you will soon realize that no one could devise a system with *less* chance for accumulating wealth.

Capital accumulation is not simply money in the bank. Most workers in every underdeveloped country, no matter how poor and undernourished the majority of its population, produce more than they consume. This surplus generated by their work is the root of wealth. The real question is who will control the accumulated goods and the means to produce more.

In most underdeveloped countries the surplus is not available to the majority of the people who produce it, for it is drained off by landlords, moneylenders, merchants, industrialists, state bureaucrats, and foreign corporations. Traditionally it is argued that unequal control over the surplus is 'good' for a society because only the rich will save the surplus and invest in a society's future. Recently, however, respected economists studying underdeveloped countries have independently concluded that in reality such a rationalization of unequal control simply does not hold up.[1] They find that in the countryside, the landlords, moneylenders, and merchants who appropriate so much of the surplus generally do *not* reinvest it; rather, they tend to spend it on imported luxury goods and expensive consumer items manufactured in foreign-style factories that use up large amounts of capital and provide little employment. Even when they do invest, as we noted in Part V, it is invariably abroad or nonproductively, for instance, in hotels, bars, restaurants, rental property, taxis and the like.

One of us lived for several months in a village in the remote southern Yucatan jungle of Mexico. The Indians were poor farmers – former chicle gatherers for Wrigley's chewing gum until Wrigley came up with a synthetic gum – who were gravely exploited by the village's general storeowner and moneylender. We will call him Don Eziquiel. One day Don Eziquiel used his accumulated profits to import what had been his heart's desire since the day he saw an ad in a newspaper – a Ford Galaxie – and there wasn't even a single paved road in the jungle!

What About Foreign Investment Capital?

Foreign corporations like to claim that underdeveloped countries need them because they need investment funds. But numerous studies[2] now have demonstrated that a multinational corporation usually brings in precious little initial investment funds to those countries. Why should a corporation bother when it finds it can tap the local savings since everyone wants to lend to, say, General Foods. Often a large part of the equity contribution by a foreign corporation to a joint venture with a local partner or the state consists not of money, but of technical and marketing 'know-how.' In addition, all or part of the profit is frequently not re-invested but is 'repatriated,' that is, returned to the home country.

We have seen that agribusiness corporations, whether operating plantations or through contracts, appropriate the lion's share of the value of produce through their monopoly hold on foreign marketing. All types of foreign corporations regularly siphon off foreign exchange (in addition to declared profits) through untaxed royalties, debt payments, and inflated charges by headquarters for management advice, research, and the like. All the devices open to them rely on the marvels of modern corporate accounting (recently defined by one accountant as a subdivision of creative writing).

It is doubtful if even a country like the United Kingdom has enough skilled civil servants to monitor the accounting alchemies of the multinational corporations operating across its borders. Certainly no underdeveloped country can even come close to doing so. The chief accounting alchemies are overpricing imports from headquarters (including depreciated machinery) and under-pricing exports to another subsidiary of the same company. These devices enable the local subsidiary to claim it is losing money. It can then threaten to pull up stakes if it does not receive even more subsidies, 'tax holidays,' no-striking guarantees, free roads, water, and so on.

Some governments are finally realizing therefore that a foreign 'investor' is often a net drain on funds. Ironically, one such government is that of Brazil. We say 'ironically' because the military government of Brazil since 1964 has sought above all to provide the proper 'climate' for foreign investment. An official study late in 1975 showed that the eleven most important foreign firms have remitted more out of Brazil than they have brought in. Since 1965, the giant agribusiness firm, Anderson Clayton, for example, has brought $1.6 million in foreign exchange into Brazil. By 1975, it had generated a surplus 32 times greater, $16.8 million of which was sent abroad in the form of profits and dividends.[3]

Plastic Shoes for Development?

Nonagribusiness firms also can appropriate the surplus that the peasants produce and perpetuate a distortion of the country's potential food resources. A good example of this was sent to us by a missionary in the Cameroon. The Bata Shoe Company, a ubiquitous Canadian-based multinational corporation, a few years ago started manufacturing plastic shoes in the coastal town of Douala. The shoes are heavily advertised throughout the predominantly rural country and they have become one of those symbols of status that poor people buy. Tourists in Douala seek out traditional hand-crafted shoes while the peasants save up money from the export of their cocoa, peanuts, and cotton to buy plastic shoes. With such 'incentives' the peasants expand their production of export crops (thereby often lowering market prices) on land well suited for food crops, despite serious rural undernutrition. The Bata Shoe Company (and similar multinationals) therefore are in fact recouping part of the foreign exchange paid to the Cameroon for its agricultural exports – foreign exchange that theoretically goes for development needs. At the same time several thousand village shoemakers, perfectly capable of meeting the country's needs, are being put out of work and will likely go hungry. The plastic shoe factory itself, the missionary noted, employs all of thirty workers.

Over the past few years European textile firms have been moving south to central Africa to avoid labour unions and higher labour costs. The first impact, already dramatic in countries like Mali and Chad, is an increased push for cotton production at the expense of food staples. In addition, through the firm's repatriations and remittances for machinery, loans and service fees, much of the foreign exchange earned by the export of agricultural products and textiles leaves the country. In other words, foreign exchange is not being spent on the type of development that decreases poverty, unemployment, inequality, and hunger. Tens of thousands of local craftspeople, formerly tailors, makers of cotton and wool thread and cloth, are being put out of work. Such companies perpetuate underdevelopment by sopping up, displacing and mis-channelling the country's actual and potential wealth.

Wealth Begins with Land and People

In a Food First economy people would mobilize the potential wealth of their labour power and of underutilized land. Vast tracts of underused land exist on large estates, monocultural plantations, and mechanized farms that employ capital to displace people.

Moreover, the redistribution of income that is the product of the Food First economy we described in 'Working toward Food Self-Reliance' can mean greater savings for investment, not less. We have seen, in Part VI, that even under present conditions poor farmers, especially if they have some land, often turn out to be better savers than the rich. And if poor peasants are given reason to believe that their savings will benefit them, they can save at impressive rates. After the Chinese revolution the net savings ratio in China rose from 1 to 2 per cent in 1949 to 20 per cent in 1953.[4]

The Chinese people have learned through their own struggle to overcome hunger that neither money nor the natural geographic endowment of an area are the determining factors.

In the 1950s, Tachai and Wu Chai-Ping were two neighbouring villages with very disparate natural qualities. Wu Chai-Ping wanted to separate itself from Tachai because it felt that the potential of its superior natural endowment would be held back by its neighbour, the resource-poor Tachai. They did split up. But Tachai, through intensive collective work has more than made up for its inferior natural resources. Tachai now produces better harvests and enjoys a considerably higher income than the other village. The people of Tachai overcame an extremely hostile environment *without outside material support.*[5]

The point is that where people are organized, share in the decision-making, and know that their work will benefit them, resources will be available which before were siphoned off. Kathleen Gough, author of *Ten Times More Beautiful* and an anthropologist with 30 years' experience in the field, compared in some detail two geographically comparable rice growing regions of Asia – one in southeast India, Thanjavur, and one in the Red River region of Vietnam, Thai Binh.[6]

In Thanjavur, land ownership is tightly concentrated, and in some areas as much as three-quarters of the land is controlled by absentee owners. Gough estimates that under these conditions one-half to three-fourths of the value of agricultural production is drained off by landowners and merchants for personal consumption and investment outside of agriculture.

In a typical village in Thai Binh, however, where the agricultural land is co-operatively worked, 45 per cent of the harvests and a good portion of the livestock products and crafts goods are bought by the national distribution system. The money received plus the remaining 55 per cent of the production, is divided up among the villagers. Seventy per cent goes for wages and running expenses such as hand tools; 20 per cent is spent on engineering projects and machinery and fertilizer, and 10 per cent on social welfare, including housing and medical care. Thus all of what is produced goes to the development of the village.

If people are working cooperatively toward mutually agreed-upon goals, the resources that do exist can be put to much greater use than where most resources are controlled by a few. In Vu Thang, a Vietnamese village in the Thai Binh area visited by Gough, 12 irrigation pumpsets irrigated 300 acres whereas a typical Indian village in Thanjavur needed 18 pumpsets to cover only 175 acres of rice land – that is 50 per cent more pumpsets to irrigate 42 per cent less land.

Vu Thang's pumps were more efficiently used in part because their location was determined by the co-operative, based on maximum irrigation potential. By contrast, the privately owned pumps in Thanjavur were located to benefit only the owners, who often diverted water from others into their own fields. Moreover, irrigation is a delicate and sophisticated operation, needing continual maintenance. But in Thanjavur, Indian agricultural officials find it difficult, according to Gough, 'to move an embankment or channel even one foot in order to improve irrigation because they cannot obtain permission from the numerous village owners.' Just as came clear in Part V, 'The Inefficiency of Inequality,' the co-operation essential to development is not possible where a few control the resources, forcing the majority into competition and dependency.

But what about resources that don't now exist in the villages or even in the underdeveloped countries? Don't development needs such as fertilizer have to be imported? Local resources that are there all the time but unused and even unrecognized *can* be mobilized for development – if a co-operative organization of the people turns that development into a priority.

Take fertilizer. First of all we must keep in mind that shifting from monoculture to a variety of crops and instituting crop rotation will, as first steps, reduce the needs for fertilizer. More important, however, the local potential for producing fertilizer from indigenous waste material is estimated to represent six to eight times the amount of nutrients in costly, largely imported, chemical fertilizers actually used by the underdeveloped countries.[7] This energy and fertilizer potential can be tapped right at the village level, using materials that are often wasted.

Biogasification, mentioned in Part IV, is a simple method of fermenting organic raw material such as crop residues and manure to produce methane (for fuel) and a nutrient-rich effluent (for fertilizer). The fertilizer produced through the biogas technique is many times richer in nutrients than the waste products that went into it. By fermenting the village wastes of 500 human beings and 250 cattle, a biogas 'plant' can supply the average cropped land of a typical Asian village with two and one half times the present nitrogen applied in the form of chemical fertilizers. Moreover, it can supply almost double the present daily energy needs of the village for cooking, water pumping, electricity, and industries.[8]

Again, a comparison of villages in Vietnam and India is useful. In the Vietnamese village studied by Gough, every scrap of human and animal excrement is collected for fertilizer. Moreover, 46 hectares of bomb craters are used not only for fish breeding but for growing algae for fertilizer. Trees are planted around the co-operatives to provide fuel, shelter for crops and green manure. In Thanjavur, India, however, excrement is not a fertilizer resource. Dropped haphazardly it is instead a health hazard. Cowdung is burned as fuel instead of being fermented to produce much more potential fertilizer and fuel in the form of methane gas.

Both villages studied by Gough would be considered by many to be without adequate resources – both in need of outside sources of funds for development. Yet in both, wealth currently exists, not to mention the much greater potential. The questions are: how is that potential to be mobilized? And how is the wealth to be used? The answers to both depend entirely on the social system. Is the social system used to drain off the wealth produced by the villagers? Or is it used to channel that wealth to the villagers themselves (thus promoting their well-being and their willingness to co-operate and to work) as well as to the development needs (irrigation, schools, clinics) of the community as a whole?

But a social system based on collective control over resources and on co-operative work may seem unreal in a culture such as ours – or in most underdeveloped countries today for that matter. What could *make* people work to mobilize the potential resources at hand, many would find themselves wondering. And how could people ever be made to work co-operatively?

Such reservations in part reflect our experience of seeing people's reaction when they are called upon to 'sacrifice for the sake of their country.'

People sense intuitively and correctly that in a highly inequitable society such calls are usually a convenient way for the rich to blind the nonrich to the fact that only *they* are being made to give up something. In the Vietnamese village of Vu Thang we have been discussing, the income gap between the lowest and the highest paid peasant is only about 20 per cent. Contrast this with the 1000 to 8000 fold difference between the income of the rich landowner in Thanjavur, India, and that of a landless labourer there. Thus in the first village, appeals to eschew selfishness for co-operative work makes sense because all gain relatively equally. But in Thanjavur, peasants know that the wealth they produce will principally benefit others.

The next time you hear or read a discussion on the lack of aid, poor terms of trade or the poor natural endowment of the underdeveloped countries, don't conclude that such are the causes of underdevelopment. Lack of development funds is really not the problem. The fundamental problem is the unjust social structures that block the development of the great potential wealth that does exist – structures of control described throughout this book that prevent the poor majority from mobilizing that potential for their own benefit.

32 : The Passive Peasantry – Too Oppressed to Change

Bombarded with pictures showing the poor as weak and hungry, we should not lose sight of the obvious fact that they often must exert themselves tremendously just to stay alive – travelling long distances and working 10 to 14 hours a day. In that sense, the poor are hardly passive. They represent great potential energy that, once released, can be applied to their own development.

Moreover, those living and working with the poor in under-developed countries have found that they comprehend quite well the forces oppressing them. In a report for the UN Asian Development Institute, the four Asian authors with much experience in organizing with the rural poor concluded that the poor 'have an understanding of the working of the economic system and can describe in detail the processes (wage exploitation, money lending, bribery and price discrimination) through which exploitation takes place.'

Those with direct experience working with poor peasants also counter the notion that it is mainly superstitious religious beliefs that keep the poor down. Lasse and Lisa Berg, writing of their experiences in India, in their book *Face to Face* observe that, while reasoning based in religious beliefs might characterize India's middle class, the poor almost never cite religion to explain their daily actions. 'If asked why they do not revolt,' note the Bergs, 'they do not answer that they want to be reborn to a better position; they answer that they are afraid of the landowner or the government or the police.'[1]

But stressing both the powerful structure of control over the lives of the poor and their understandable fear can cause us to ignore the fact that *in every country in the world where people are hungry there is a struggle going on right now over who controls food-producing resources* – in Mexico, the Philippines, South Africa, Brazil, Chad, the United States, El Salvador, Bangladesh, Thailand and we could go on and on. Those standing up to resist are the very people who have been perceived by so many as 'too oppressed ever to change.'

Moreover, many who would question what peasants can do seem unaware that there are countries such as Vietnam, Mozambique,

Guinea Bissau and Angola where, after decades of intense struggle, mainly by peasant-based organizations, independence has recently been won. Now these people are turning their energies into eradicating hunger and building the basis of genuine food security. Neither must one forget that since only the early 1950s, over 40 per cent of the population of the underdeveloped world have freed themselves from the fear of famine through their own efforts.

Because of the selective way news is transmitted to us, we are often unaware of the courageous struggles of millions of people everywhere to gain control over food-producing resources rightfully theirs.

Events often come to us filtered through a lens that causes us to identify not with people like us, but with the governing elites in underdeveloped countries. We once read, for example, a news account of the depressed economy of Senegal, ruined by a fall-off in production of the main export crop, peanuts. Simply presented this way, our natural response was to ask: What can be done to spur the lagging production of this crop? How can we help to get the economy rolling again? We thus were made to identify with the export economy of Senegal, not with the people.

The real story was that many Senegalese peasants had purposefully spurned cash-cropping in order to grow food for themselves, particularly millet and sorghum. This shift was interpreted by some as the reaction of tradition-bound peasants. On the contrary, this example of peasant resistance can be seen as a positive break away from tradition, if being traditional means doing what the political and social hierarchy has always demanded. These lessons are seldom, if ever, drawn for us; such is the power of selective news that reinforces the notion of the passivity of the world's disenfranchised.

To counter the myth of the passive poor we must find sources of news that go behind the selective, filtered information offered us by most of the media. At the end of this book we therefore include a list of some of the publications and organizations that provide news and analysis of the struggles of ordinary people in countries around the world for their food rights. We find these sources invaluable in uprooting the myth of the passive poor and the companion myth, that of our own powerlessness.

33 : Food Versus Freedom

Many people are troubled by what they view as a trade-off between freedom and ending hunger. They are distressed by charges that societies that have eliminated hunger have done so only by denying people's rights.

Such changes raise critical questions that must be grappled with. But a clear grasp of those questions is clouded by the multiple distortions contained in the 'food versus freedom' formulation.

First it implies that societies that are not making structural changes to end hunger at least have more freedom. Even in terms of *theoretical* freedoms, this is often false. People in countries with widespread hunger and other forms of poverty, like the Philippines, Chile, or Nicaragua do not have even the theoretical freedom of free assembly or to vote.

Moreover, learning more about countries where many, often the majority, face hunger has forced us to confront the difference between theoretical freedoms and effective freedoms. In countries like India or Mexico, more and more people are losing control of their land. Still more find it hard to get any kind of job, even at slow starvation 'wages'. In such countries people have the theoretical freedom to organize and to vote. But do they effectively have the freedom? Given the violent reaction of elite threatened by any mobilization of the poor, we doubt it. And while perhaps the most basic freedom is the freedom to achieve security for one's self and one's loved ones, in such countries – now the majority of the world's countries – life is increasingly insecure.

In other words, with absolutely no share in control over their country's productive assets, how much *effective* freedom do people have? This contradiction between theoretical freedom and effective freedom applies in the so-called western democracies as well.

Second, the myth seems to suggest that in eliminating hunger, countries have moved from a state of 'more freedom' to less freedom. But when we study societies in which the majority are achieving greater food, job and old-age security – as in China or Cuba, for example – we find, of course, that most people have not moved from a state of freedom to a state of repression in the process of achieving that security. No, the political and economic structures that preceded the present ones were among the most repressive in the world.

Studying these societies today, we find many problems – including the incredible difficulties resulting from hundreds of years of internal and external exploitation. Their problems are not only physical but human – how people can transform their consciousness of themselves in order to make true self-government possible. We also find the drive for greater self-government accompanied by some restrictions on people's individual choices. For many this might seem an untenable contradiction. But perhaps is not. Perhaps it is rather an inevitable tension in societies attempting to create structures to meet the needs of all.

In such an attempt the legal definition of what is socially harmful might have to be enlarged. In our system we allow speculation in land and food that ensures that some persons go hungry while others profiteer and many over-consume. In a system attempting deliberately to plan for the needs of all, hoarding and speculation are not accepted. (Most important, of course, most people seem not so motivated to hoard and speculate when their basic needs for a job and food are assured.) Moreover, individual choices may sometimes have to be adjusted in order to fulfil the community's needs. At least during the primary period of overcoming underdevelopment some may not be able to choose whatever job or location they prefer. (We must keep in mind of course that few even supposedly free market societies have such absolute freedom.) Clearly, every society places limits upon the individual's choices. The real issues then are these: How can those restrictions be made fairly? Are they restrictions imposed by an elite for their benefit or imposed by the community for the good of all? Is the goal to achieve a society in which the individual's legitimate self-interest and the community's needs are more and more complementary?

Freedom for critical expression is also of pivotal concern. In countries that choose to break with the private control over productive assets this issue is made considerably more problematic by the denunciation, aggressive posturing, and even subversive intervention of foreign powers like the United States. Such external hostility creates the worst possible environment for the fostering of internal critical expression (and individual variety). Americans should know this all too well from the years following Pearl Harbor. Any individual or grouping of individuals differing with the commonly held view runs the risk of being labelled a collaborator of the foreign enemy. The challenge for a society in the difficult period of restructuring is both to recognize the vulnerability caused by a lack of unity, and yet to develop effective means for constructive critical thinking. Critical thinking must be encouraged, thinking that can speak out and be heard *even* when at first few acknowledge the very existence of an issue, as with nuclear power or sexism.

Thus, instead of the simplistic notion that 'freedom' must be sacrificed to eliminate hunger, we find tremendous complexity. But we also find grounds for hope. While no people on earth have achieved a model society which ideally melds individual and community needs, we do have much to learn from people engaged in the *process* of attempting that goal. Some of the most critical lessons we have discussed in Chapter 30.

We wish to underline that these lessons represent a *process* and not simply goals that are achieved once and for all. And within this process are profound tensions – the tensions between the individual's wishes and the community needs; the tension between democratic, participatory decision-making and the need for leadership based on specialized skills, knowledge and experience; the tension between a focus on agriculture and the need to build up industry as necessary to increase agricultural productivity.

These are just a few of what we have come to believe are *necessary* tensions in creating a social, economic, and political system designed to maximize both individual fulfilment and community progress. The trouble with a 'freedom versus food trade-off' is that by over-simplifying and distorting it frightens people, preventing them from being able to learn from the concrete experience of their counterparts in other countries.

34: Postscript – The Possibilities for Change

After a talk we gave while writing this book, students asked: But what makes you think people can change – that anything can change? You say that your position counters the fatalistic over-population and weather theories of hunger; that it puts control of our fate back into the hands of the people. But aren't the forces of concentrated wealth and power just as hard to confront, or more so?

First, the very phrasing of the students' questions reflects their sense that the elites dominating the food economy both here and in the underdeveloped countries have completely taken charge. Yet we have seen over and over again that the dominant groups are constantly on the defensive, trying to protect their power as more and more of us become aware of our worsening position. The mechanization of agriculture, can be seen, in part, as a defensive move. Large landowners, for instance, mechanize in order to no longer have to deal with the legitimate, militant demands of labourers and tenants.

The phenomenon of the Global Supermarket – international food companies supplying us with the produce of the underdeveloped world – can also be seen in part as a reflection of the effort of multinational firms to deal with the strength of farm labour movements in the industrial countries demanding decent wages for their work. Even the considerable expenditures by corporations on advertisements portraying themselves as helping to solve world hunger mean that they themselves are worried. They recognize that the power of corporations is beginning to be questioned. Perhaps those who control the food economy appreciate the power of the awakening people more than we ourselves do.

Second, we believe that anyone who is privileged enough to become aware must make a choice. We either choose to be observers of history, thereby lending our weight to the forces now in control or we choose to be participants, actively building a new culture based on human values. Put this way, do we really have a choice?

Human society is, after all, only a product of the collective struggle of all people. If we say that *we* have no power to change things, who does?

If we answer that the power is in the hands of an elite who alone are making the decisions, we will be doing exactly what the established forces of power want of us. We will have folded our arms in defeat, saying that we prefer to build shells to protect ourselves from reality, to keep out the bad news.

Based on our own experience we have come to believe that people prefer a protective shell only because they are overwhelmed with negative information that they cannot integrate. They cannot integrate facts into useful action because they are made to feel guilty about and fearful of the hungry. Too often, the problem of hunger gets turned into a contest between them and us – all of us in the rich world versus all of them in the poor. In fact, the majority of the people of the industrialized countries are *not* pitted against the hungry people; these are not the battle lines of the hunger struggle. The struggle is against a system that increasingly concentrates wealth and power. The struggle is against a system profiting on hunger in the Philippines or Brazil just as it is in Europe. The real forces creating hunger span almost all nations in the world. Once the lines of struggle are clear we can no longer be manipulated by profferers of guilt and fear.

But some would say that our choices, if we do indeed have them, are limited – that since people are basically self-centred, all we can do is build on that trait. What we are saying is that this belief in human selfishness directly serves the interests of those who have taken power. It is a view of human nature that neatly fits with the status quo. But the economic system we have here today is not God-given; it represents a choice to build on certain human traits – to play on human insecurities. It in no way tells us what is *possible*.

New systems of human organization *are* being dared, systems that assume people can co-operate and work to provide opportunities for everyone to have a fulfilling life. There is no more important work today than explaining this to people in countries like our own. Before they would work for change they have to believe that change is possible, that a culture fixated on individual profit-seeking is not 'natural.' The tragedy is that we have had to reach the point where so many people are hungry and malnourished, including those here at home, before we could begin to see that our system – a system built on the vulnerabilities of the human personality instead of its strengths – can never create a humane society.

Finally, we must not allow our appropriate sense of urgency to lead to frustration and despair. It took centuries to create the structures that cause the worldwide deprivation we now witness. It will take time to construct a human world. That does not belittle our task; that makes it all the more important. We must come to understand today's struggle in light of the entire scope of human history. What we see today may tell us little about what our children and their children are capable of creating.

When we say that we are learning through studying hunger where our own self-interest really lies, we are not saying simply that we are learning how our lives are limited by the same forces exploiting the hungry peasant in Africa or India. We are also saying that understanding the forces that generate hunger is in our own self-interest because through this understanding we are made freer. The more we grasp the system we are part of, the more able we are to make conscious choices to alter it.

We want you to join us, not simply because of the urgent struggle to construct a just and life-giving society, but because through our own experience we have become certain that none of us can live fully today as long as we are overwhelmed by a false view of the world and a false view of human nature to buttress it. Learning how a system can cause hunger then becomes, not a lesson in misery and deprivation, but a vehicle for a great awakening in our own lives.

What We Can Do

by Dexter Tiranti, Co-editor, *New Internationalist*

I believe we have just read an extraordinary book – one of the most challenging of the decade. But it is very easy for us to throw up our hands in the air, roll our eyes and with a resigned shrug turn away from the enormity of the problems. The authors would be horrified. Their purpose was not simply to explode conventional myths, not just to log the interests and the mechanisms which create hunger. It was to do more – to provoke action for change. New systems are being dared, new ideas are being shared and many of them hinge on the issue of food.

For the subject is intimately part of our lives. We are involved through our Sunday roast; our week's shopping; our countryside and our farms; our jobs provided by the food companies; our bank, pension fund or insurance company investments in the agribusiness concerns; and not least by the policies of our government – from food subsidies to overseas aid, from the international trade and tariff conferences to the Common Agricultural Policy of the EEC.

People everywhere can take up some of the issues tackled in this book. Students, environmentalists, active Christians, trade unionists, teachers, shoppers – all can help to dispel the myths that are part of our national culture, and act to change the sad reality. For 'authoritative opinion' couches its answers to the problems of world hunger in the tired old ways, despite annual proof that the well-fed are becoming too well-fed and the hungry stay hungry. We are given the same inadequate explanations and answers: too many people, harsh climate, ignorance, laziness, not enough incentives to allow our companies to do the job.

However, there is an enormous fund of sympathy and goodwill in all manner of organizations. After all, everyone is human. Not even the hardest hearted corporation executives would like to think that their work stops people feeding themselves, that every time they make a corporate decision they swell the ranks of the starving. So there *is* the potential for changing minds and policies – it is up to us to work on it.

But one of the first lessons so effectively demonstrated by Frances Moore Lappé and Joe Collins is that acting out of ignorance can strengthen the very interests that are most harmful. Focusing on the small farmer sounds good until we realize that in many countries up to 90 per cent of the rural families have no land. Focusing on increasing production sounds good until we ask how the hungry will ever find the wherewithal to buy the larger harvests. Introducing modern machines sounds like progress until we ask who is being made redundant. Giving food aid sounds good until we look at the impact on the local farmers. Business claims to feed the hungry sound good until we remember their primary obligation is to their shareholders, and to make a profit – and there is no market in the impoverished.

Not only do such 'answers' have to be challenged, but we should look to clearing the obstacles originating in our countries that deny the hungry the means to feed themselves. For another lesson of *Food First* is that the poor don't have to be helped to feed themselves, we just have to restrain the forces that make it so difficult for them.

Above all, any action that will achieve a positive change must be founded on an understanding of the need for a redistribution of power. Nothing is achieved by promoting changes in production – from cash crops to food crops, from adulterated, chemically treated groceries to organically grown cereals, from a meat-centred to a vegetarian diet – unless there are radical changes in the power structure. This means the poor and the marginalized have to have an effective say in how they will lead their lives, and power in the market place to buy the more than ample stocks of food in the world. This issue, the redistribution of wealth, must be brought out from the shadowy wings of the stage where it has been consigned by those who want to ignore the awkward questions. It has to be spotlit, stage centre, as *the* important prerequisite for the world's people to be adequately nourished.

There is no perfect series of answers – written on tablets of stone – which can accomplish this. Putting genuine *Food First* policies forward will depend on where you live, what you do, what type of organization you are working with and who you are trying to reach. Most of all, it will depend on you. It is impossible to be effective until you *feel* effective and positive in your efforts for change. Here are some ideas.

Exploding the Myths

Glib, mistaken assumptions and views are continually being made in the local press, on radio and television. Start a media-watch group and pick up the distortions and fallacies. Write to the newspaper, or phone in to the radio station and point out the errors. One admirable media group in Australia have repeatedly badgered the *Sydney Morning Herald* with corrections to stories and readers' letters. Now the journalist responsible for the correspondence columns telephones them *before* he prints any letter on the underdeveloped countries. But beware of firing from the hip. That same group bitterly attacked one of the newspaper's leading feature writers about a supposed racist story. Their facts were wrong, and a journalist who could have been a sympathetic friend has become totally hostile. So write and explain politely what was wrong and why. Never make it a personal attack, never exaggerate to sharpen your point, and never indulge in hyperbole – for credibility is easily dissolved in the acid bath of editorial cynicism.

There's no need just to be re-active. Button-hole reporters or radio producers (local radio stations are crying out for material), persuade them to give the *Food First* answers an airing. Pirate this book, pillage it for the arguments and evidence to write something yourself. You probably receive numerous newsletters, house newspapers or parish magazines – most would be happy to print short clearly set-out articles from readers.

False assumptions and exaggerated nutrition claims are particularly apparent in the advertising of food products. Indeed, more advertising money is spent on promoting particular food brands – 25 per cent of total advertising in the UK – than on any other type of product.[1] If the advertising claims do not appear to you to be 'truthful, legal, decent and honest' write to the Advertising Standards Authority. They are meant to police such activity, but cannot take any action until a complaint has been filed. Sadly, they will take no responsibility for British food companies advertising activities in the underdeveloped countries. Charles Medawar's excellent recent study, 'Insult or Inquiry? An enquiry into the marketing and advertising of British Food and Drug Products in the Third World' – see Appendix B – documents the advertising claims about the beneficial qualities of such products as Horlicks (a Beecham product), Bovril, Guinness stout, Bournvita (a Cadbury-Schweppes product) and Flora margarine (a Unilever product) in countries like Nigeria, Kenya, India, Bangladesh and Malaysia. Write to the parent company about their subsidiaries' advertising claims and publicize such activities. Company executives *do* become embarrassed when quizzed about unethical promotional activity and *do* change their policies under such pressure.

It can become quite an art to ride on the back of publicity vehicles which already deliver to a wider public – such as the newspapers or radio stations. There is another ready-made constituency to be tapped through the hundred and one groups and societies which hold regular meetings to talk about social problems. It can be a Church gathering, a union meeting, a civic society or a women's group . . . they all have interested audiences. Ask the organizer if you can talk or lead a discussion about some aspects of *Food First* ideas. From personal experience with local branches of the Labour Party, National Childbirth Trust and National Housewives Register, I have been surprised by how positively such audiences will respond.

There is plenty of room for action in our educational structure, particularly the secondary schools. Myths abound in the classroom: how we brought 'civilization' to Africa, why the natives are lazy, how our way is the only way to develop. Look at your children's textbooks and tackle the teachers about them. The schools are not a closed shop, and there is generally a sympathetic educationalist struggling on a current affairs course who would be happy for some fresh ideas. Tactfully suggest different topics for the curriculum. There are plenty of action groups recommended in Appendix A who would be happy to send you some of the alternative educational material that is being developed on Third World issues.

And where do our political parties stand on this subject? Pan through the detritus of rhetoric and cant they pour out, find the nuggets of truth. Once you have established which is the most sympathetic party, join it and work from the inside. Lobby for the adoption of views and policies that give power back to people and help create a more sane, safe and less hungry world.

Clear the Obstacles

The British food industry is a fascinating animal to study. More than half our food is imported. We spend more on it than any other type of product (a fifth of our total expenditure). And the gross output of the manufacturing side of the food industry is more than that of any other manufacturing industry in the country. The supposed cut-throat competition between different food products in reality disguises one of the most monopoly-ridden industries in the country. Kelloggs and Weetabix have more than 70 per cent of the breakfast cereal market, Tate and Lyle and British Sugar Corporation retail more than 80 per cent of the sugar sold, Heinz and Crosse and Blackwell more than 70 per cent of the canned soups, Unilever and Nestlé 94 per cent of the frozen vegetables and so the list goes on[2].

Investigating who owns what, where, is an enlightening way to understand the power structure around us. Some of the most active groups studying the food industry are the BSSR Agri-Capital Group and the Earth Resources Research Centre. The Agri-Capital Group in particular would welcome help.

Research need not confine itself to our foods, it can be illuminating to trace the accumulation of wealth and power in our country. The well known sociologist, Tony Atkinson, has estimated that 'as much as three quarters (of the wealth in Britain) belongs to the top 10 per cent.'[3] Such figures are startling for people who accept the belief that the rich have been taxed out of existence, and we need more incentives and inequality to ensure our country flourishes again. The prescription of 'more of the same' can hardly help an ailing patient. For more information on the distribution of wealth, contact the Child Poverty Action Group.

A fairer distribution of power in the UK, however, has to mean more than an exclusive commitment to a shake-down of money. Taking responsibility for our lives means not being passive responders to decisions being made in the City or Whitehall, the boardroom or the town hall. We should try and make the effort to become more active agents, by participating in the institutions and decisions which mould our lives . . . from parent teachers associations to industrial democracy.

Specific Campaigns

There are a number of food campaigns aimed at clearing the obstacles blocking Third World people's road to food self-reliance They include:

* Boycotting imports from countries where the rural people are grossly malnourished, the government is grossly repressive

and where there have been specific requests for boycott action from the local people. The Anti-Apartheid Movement is active in a consumer campaign to end fruit imports from South Africa. Oranges, for instance, can usually be distinguished by the brand name 'Outspan'. The boycott extends to tinned fruit, but is hampered by sloppy legislation on labelling. So the country of origin is not always clearly printed on the can.

• A number of trade unionists have been active boycotting any imports or exports from and to Chile. Liverpool dockers refused to unload food imports from a regime infamous for its persecution of unionists and domestic 'food last' policies. And unionists in Scotland blocked the export of aero-engines for Chilean fighters for more than four years. The Chilean Solidarity Campaign is one of the main co-ordinating groups for action against the Junta.

• Policing the baby food recommendations made at the World Health Organisation meeting in October 1979. Here, Corporation representatives agreed to recommendations that there should be 'no sales promotion, including promotional advertising, to the public of products to be used as breast milk substitutes or bottle-fed supplements and feeding bottles.' At face value it looks as though powdered babymilk advertising in the Third World is going to stop. But the recommendations have plenty of loopholes – not least that they are 'recommendations'. And what is the difference between 'sales promotion' and 'educational advertising', which will still continue? A British action group based on War On Want[4] is anxious to hear from anyone who would like to ensure the ending of such corporation activity in the Third World. An additional bonus for potential activists is a full-length film, speakers and an excellent publication, *The Baby Killer Scandal*, all available through contacting War on Want.

• Auditing government action on food issues. Ministries are often unaccountable for decisions which have great repercussions on vulnerable rural economies overseas. It is up to us to take up this auditing job and hold accountable the relevant Ministers, Under-Secretary, civil servants and our own MP. We should explain to them the harmful effects of such policies and publicize the response. And we shouldn't be fobbed off and discouraged by the short, bald official answer. Follow up the reply and explain the faults in the argument.

A Cabinet Minister in the Heath Government of 1970-1974

once said, 'If an MP gets five letters a week on the subject he takes notice; if he gets ten letters – he gets worried.' Discussions with civil servants bear this out. Both they and their masters act pragmatically, moving under pressure. There is plenty of lobbying by the chemical fertilizer, agricultural machinery and agribusiness corporations. Pressure from another direction would be a change. Often the decisionmakers are totally unaware of the revelations of *Food First* or if they already have nasty suspicions, would welcome lobbying by food activists.

One of the main groups that works in this area, and has a number of successes under its collective belt, is the World Development Movement.

The most obvious auditing work should be of the official aid programme administered by the Overseas Development Administration. Some of the policies to be tackled are:

1. The tying of aid money to goods and services bought in the UK. The Ministry even boasts that two-thirds of the aid budget never leaves the country. What the recipients are forced to buy is often inappropriate or overpriced. If Her Majesty's Government wants to subsidize British industry then it should say so. But it shouldn't call this 'aid' and make it at the expense of the poor world.

2. What are the priority countries for our aid? We should work to make them those like Tanzania, Mozambique and Vietnam which are putting Food First policies into practice.

3. The projects supported in the Ministry announcements should be carefully scrutinized. For instance the contract given a few years ago to a Leicestershire firm to supply air conditioning equipment to Bangladesh, is hardly of great help to the Bangladeshi peasant. Even more curious, from the office of the Minister who made a priority of the needs of the poorest in the rural areas, was the announcement to fund the building of a fertilizer factory and the provision of cargo ships to India. The repercussions of the Green Revolution and international trade on the hungry have been well documented in this book – they hardly help the rural poor.

We could also be scrutinizing Britain's role in the Common Agricultural Policy, and the EEC food aid programme. So far Brussels has had it far too easy from food action groups. This is probably because of the seeming imperviousness of the supranational bureaucracy and the complicated intricacies of the decisions made. But we now have Euro-MP's and can use them as our pressure point. Whether it is 'mountains' of butter and dried milk or 'lakes' of wine and olive oil, the geographical features of the Common Agricultural Policies are becoming monotonous. The public and press are likely to be very sympathetic to action which redesigns this landscape!

Campaigns against the EEC can be successful; the World Development Movement was very active in countering pressure for the United Kingdom to fall in line with the Common Agricultural Policy on sugar. The European demand was for regional self-reliance, the replacement of sugarcane imports from the Third World by sugarbeet from France, Italy and Belgium. What would have been the national and international effects of such policies on the powerless and underprivileged? Domestically, it would bring a bonus to our own farmers and the conversion of more land to the crop. But by and large British farmers are not the poorest of our society and they could, and do, grow other crops. Of course it would also benefit the European sugarbeet farmers who are generally smaller and less well-off. So who would lose? The British consumer would lose, for prices would be significantly higher for this staple foodstuff (because the EEC intervention agencies fix a considerably higher price to pay for European sugarbeet than the world price for sugarcane). The refinery workers would lose, for there would be the closure of the sugarcane refinery plants like that of Tate and Lyle in Liverpool – a city with notoriously high unemployment rates. And the sugarcane exporters would lose. Jamaica is one of our biggest suppliers, an island whose plantation economy was shaped by the imperialist's sweet tooth.

The country is rare amongst the hungry nations in having a popularly elected government which is working for a society where everyone would be adequately fed. Blocking the market for one of its major exports would disrupt the economy to the disadvantage of all Jamaicans. World Development Movement in conjunction with the trade unions of the refinery workers successfully campaigned to ensure the British government resisted EEC demands and maintained our traditional sugarcane suppliers.

The Tools of the Trade

Some of the tools of the trade that we can use include:

• Working together. It is essential to have the support of like-minds; a sympathetic milieu to discuss ideas, educate ourselves and encourage us when we face the inevitable disappointments and setbacks. For there is a continual drip, drip, from the conventional tap of ideas which erode away the sentiments and principles of a better way to order our world. Find others within your community who have a similar outlook, collect the names and addresses of those who are sympathetic at any meeting you call, and pull together a small group.

If you would rather plug into a group that is already working for change, then the addresses of all the action groups referred to in this chapter can be found in Appendix A.

• The bread and butter of campaign groups can often be the writing of letters to newspapers, representatives, companies and government departments. Prepare a stencilled briefing paper on the issue so that all the correspondents have something to work from. Why not do the writing together, report back the answers, discuss them and fire off another volley?

• Outside speakers, slide and film shows are further staples of an action group. There are a number of 'how to' action guides listed in Appendix A which give hints on where you can borrow a projector, who has relevant films and so on. Incidentally, plan your action for the next six months or a year. The mechanics of meetings take time to arrange. And think of using a telephone instead of writing to make arrangements. It might cost more, and be more inconvenient as it has to be done in work hours, but it greatly increases effectiveness. Often speakers cannot make a specific date, but a quick discussion can fix a mutually suitable alternative – and it is hard to refuse someone on the telephone.

• Look carefully at the investment portfolio of your Church, University or pension fund to see whether the institution is investing in companies that are exacerbating the problems of world hunger. Work through the institution's shareholding to press for a change in company policy, or work to sell the shares. It is surprising how omnipresent is our involvement with the machinery of food deprivation. It was some time after the *Guardian* newspaper first began to campaign to expose British companies that paid less wages than the Poverty Datum Line in South Africa that the staff found their own pension fund held large blocs of shares in those same companies. And the pressure on immoral investments can be effective. In late 1978, the Ivy League College of Yale sold more than a million dollars worth of securities in a New York bank which was lending to South Africa. The reason for this headline grabbing action against injustice by the Yale trustees was pressure on staff from student activists.

• Sharebuying is a recent tactic, much the same as the non-violent sit-ins belonged to the 1960s. Essentially it involves buying a minimum shareholding from the company whose actions you want to publicise and change. This entitles you to a copy of the annual report and an invitation to the annual shareholders meeting with the board of directors. Few shareholders turn up to such tedious tokens of company democracy. But activist shareholders can and have used such meetings to debate the morality of the company's policy and ask awkward questions of the board. It forces the directors to bone up on the more unsavoury actions of the company for which they are responsible. It reminds other shareholders that because of such policies, they have their dividend cheque. And it's a god-send to the press. The City Editor is obliged to print something about the corporation annual returns. And the controversial questions, lively discussion that follows and perhaps, the demonstration outside the meeting all make for a good story. National publicity, highly embarrassing for the company, is the result. Such tactics have been used to great effect by such organisations as the End Loans to Southern Africa group and the Anti-Apartheid Movement.

• Commodity campaigns are another recent phenomenon. Action on Sri Lankan tea, sparked off by the World in Action television report (described in Chapter 19), has involved not only the World Development Movement but Action for World Development in Australia and Trade Aid in New Zealand. The Australians and New Zealanders import the tea at above market prices, pack it in straw plaited bags with an information label and retail it. People have been quite happy to pay over the odds for their tea, and swallow a *Food First* message with their cuppa.

Perhaps the most successful British commodity campaign has been based on the importation of coffee from Tanzania. Campaign Co-operative was the originator of the idea. Their purpose was to promote some understanding amongst consumers of the inter-national commodity market, to stimulate interest in Tanzanian agrarian policies and to provide some token help to a country whose economy had been disrupted by fluctuating primary product prices. The most important educational part of the campaign was the labelling of the coffee package. Great care and attention was given to the design and message. The result was a very polished presentation of the international trading system which works against the producers. At the time of writing, the Co-operative is poised to re-launch the campaign.

The Role of Voluntary Agencies

Direct aid to organizations in the Third World working to establish *Food First* policies is often best achieved through supporting our voluntary agencies that fund such projects. The British have a long tradition of raising money for such agencies – our colonial history has given us a myriad of interests and connections with Africa, Asia and Latin America. The voluntary agencies annually raise significant sums of money to fund development projects. And one of our activities might well be to help swell those funds by raising money. But hold back a moment. The type of projects supported by the different agencies vary enormously. Frances Moore Lappé and Joe Collins have documented so many instances of well-intentioned action that worsen the distribution of wealth and power in the underdeveloped world, that they suggest we ask some very hard questions about where the money is being spent, before deciding which agency to help.[5]

Seven Questions to Ask an Aid Project

1. Whose project *is* it? Is it the donor agency's?
      or
   Does it originate with the people involved?
2. Does the project diagnose the problem to be tackled as a technical or physical deficiency (e.g. poor farming methods or depleted soils) that can be overcome with the right technique and skills?
      or
   Is the physical or technical problem seen as only a reflection of social and political relationships that need to be altered?
3. Does it reinforce the economic and political power of a certain group which then becomes more resistant to change that might abolish privileges?
      or
   Does it generate a shift in power to the powerless?
4. Does it, through the intervention of outside experts, take away local initiative?
      or
   Does it generate a process of democratic decision-making

and a thrust toward self-reliance that can carry over to future projects?

5. Does it reinforce dependence on outside sources of material and skills?

or

Does it use local ingenuity, local labour, and local materials, and can it be maintained with local skills?

6. Does it merely help individuals adjust to their exploitation by such external forces as the national government or the international market?

or

Does it encourage an understanding of that exploitation and a resistance to it?

7. Will success only be measured by the achievement of the pre-set plans of outsiders?

or

Is the project open-ended, with success measured by the local people as the project progresses?

The Politics Behind the Voluntary Agencies

What about the argument: 'All aid is destructive, it placates the people and delays the revolution.' It is a version of the 'reform or revolution' chestnut. In response, a couple of points that badly char the chestnut. First, there is something strangely contradictory about such fanatical commitment to humanitarian ends which denies all humanitarian needs along the way. And voluntary agency supported projects which answer the Lappé/Collins questions are helping those needs. Second, most historical changes where people have seized their own destiny, have not been by gaunt half-starved skeletons. The initiative has been taken by those who understand the forces that oppress them and have the strength of hope and will for a change to the better. The right projects can only encourage such initiative and comprehension.

One test of the direction of the voluntary agency, and the grasp of development issues by its personnel, is whether they believe any of their work is political. Frances Moore Lappé and Joe Collins[6] quote the director of one of the largest American agencies CARE as saying:

By remaining apolitical and by fostering projects whose primary goal is to make it possible for low-income people to attain dignity, a subtle depolarizing process seems to take place – alienation between rich and poor, governments and the people, tribal groups, and even between countries can be reduced.[7]

They go on to point out:

'Remaining apolitical means not being involved in the shift of power from an elite propertied class to the majority. Concentrating on "apolitical" projects can only mean choosing projects that reinforce the present distribution of power, creating perhaps a new class of entrepreneurs. But such a choice will inevitably only serve the interests of those already in power by providing yet another layer of comparatively well-off individuals who then also have a stake in the status quo.

In the UK such agencies can only qualify as 'charities', and hence receive substantial tax exemptions from the Treasury, if they abide by the Charity Laws. The definition of what is a charity is vague and woolly, dating from statutes of Queen Elizabeth I. The commissioners who watch over the charities believe that all political activity, as they understand it, is illegal. But of course 'apolitical' Third World projects can be highly political—by maintaining or reinforcing the structures that divert food from the mouths of the hungry. In practice, some agencies are prepared to risk the Commissioners' wrath and sail more closely to the legal winds than others. Possibly these are the agencies *Food First* activists would like to support when raising funds.

What About Ourselves and our Lifestyles?

Educating ourselves has to be the basis of informed action and there are many reading suggestions in Appendix B that can be followed up. The self-education by you or your study group might like to focus on something more specific than world hunger. It could tackle the production and trading of *one* commodity, the activities of *one* food company, the causes of hunger in *one* country. Scratch around and dig out all the material on the subject. Remember the interests of those who are publishing the material, and note the yawning gaps between the claims of the public relations personnel and the actuality of disinterested research work. Flesh out your study by contacting people with first-hand experience. Read personal accounts. Look out for the involvement of the British government. See what groups are working in the chosen study area, and keep a weather eye cocked for what your group can do to help.

One way of more closely understanding the nutrition problems overseas, is by personally visiting such countries. Being a concerned tourist however, has the major drawback of lack of time. Far better to volunteer to live and work in the Third World. Unfortunately some volunteers can represent the worst of our Coca-cola culture. And the volunteer work itself can have little to do with *Food First* principles. But it is wrong to be too discouraging about such personal action, working in underdeveloped countries can be an extraordinary educational experience.

Another personal action which is very worthwhile, is the commitment to tax oneself. It involves giving a percentage of income to an action group or movement that is pursuing some of the principles of this book. The mechanism for such a self-tax is simple enough. You instruct your bank, via a covenant or standing order form, to make a regular payment to the chosen agency of whatever sum you can afford. Nearly all groups listed in Appendix A have such forms available on request.

More active ways of opting out of the food-for-profit system can involve:
- Joining bulk-buying organizations. The economics of scale are

continually being dinned into us, so it is self-evident that teaming up with like-minded people to buy food means a bigger pool of cash for bulk purchases. The buying unit can tap whole-sale outlets, avoiding the fancy wrapping and extra processing of supermarket products. A simple example of such a group in Dallas, Texas, was a neighbourhood where every family tossed five dollars into a kitty every week. Responsibility for the collection of the money and the bulk buying rotated regularly. The purchasing family would go to the downtown wholesale fruit and vegetable market where the local farmers brought their produce, to sell from the back of their pickups. The evening of the market day each family called on the purchasers to collect their share. Everyone was happy. Tips on how such projects can work in the UK can be found in 'Food Co-ops – How to save money by getting together and buying in bulk' published by Friends of the Earth.

• Growing your own vegetables. If your garden is too small then apply for an allotment from your local council. The usual fear of people thinking of doing this is whether they will have enough time to look after the plot. If you work the allotment *communally*, the problem dwindles. There has been a run on 'lotties' in the last few years and waiting lists in some areas can be long. Friends of the Earth are campaigning to increase the amount of land devoted to allotments by local authorities. They are particularly incensed by the 150,000 acres of officially designated waste land in the cities, and the unofficial figures of up to ten times this acreage unused in the UK. As the land is only needed for six to nine months to produce a harvest, tem-porary allotments would also help to allow people to become more self-reliant. A useful small book 'Economic Growth – The Allotments Campaign Guide' has recently been produced by FOE.

• Eating less grainfed meat. This book has shown us how protein foods like groundnuts, dried skimmed milk and cereals are fed back to beef and dairy cattle. It is the preferred way of dis-posing of protein-rich foods in a world where those who need the protein are too poor to buy it. Thus meat is pushed on us. The butchers' advertisement, 'No proper meal is complete with-out it' strikes a sympathetic chord when we are planning the next dinner. However, many of us consume far too much pro-tein; obesity, heart attacks and coronaries are assiduously promoted by such overrich diets. And some meatless days every week would be useful for both our bodies and our purses.

• Living more communally. Whether shopping, gardening, studying, campaigning or simply living, sharing resources, enthusiasms and ideals can be a great regenerating source of strength and fulfilment. Explore the ways you and your family can work more closely with other people in your community.

One final reminder when talking about changing our lifestyle for the better. Consuming less, wasting less, growing our own foods and living more simply are all constructives for ourselves. It is certainly worthwhile. It loosens the grip of our consumerist environment upon us. But there is no magic mechanism which transfers what we have saved to those who are hungry and powerless. What they ultimately need are the effective means that will give them a voice in the global market place.

If you agree that the arguments of *Food First* carry weight, that the discoveries of the authors are convincing, then we are beholden to act upon them. It is not because of some philosophical point of knowledge of the food structure bringing complicity, nor is it a point of duty to God or humanity. It is because we owe it to ourselves. Ultimately our lives are not shaped by the books we read, but by our own actions. That – not fine sentiments – defines who we are. And that, when it comes to the reckoning, defines the world around us.

APPENDIX A

RECOMMENDED ACTION GROUPS

United Kingdom
Australia
New Zealand

RECOMMENDED VOLUNTEER ORGANIZATIONS

United Kingdom

Recommended Action Groups

United Kingdom

Britain – Tanzania Society. J. Roger Carter, Battle Hill, Austwick, Lancaster LA2 8BW
Aims to provide information and support to a country working for food self-reliance.

British Society for Social Responsibility in Science (And the Agri-Capital Group), 9 Poland Street, London W.1. Tel: 01 437 2728.
Active in research into the British food industry.

Campaign Co-operative, 172 Lavender Hill, London S.W.11. Tel: 01 228 7877.
Imports and sells coffee from Tanzania as part of a campaign to highlight the injustices of world trade.

Catholic Institute for International Relations, 1 Cambridge Terrace, London N.W.1. Tel: 01 487 4431.
Is the centre of a lot of Third World action campaigns, particularly on Latin American issues.
Produces publications on commodities and countries.

Central Bureau for Educational Visits and Exchanges, 43-45 Dorset Street, London W.1. Tel: 01 486 5101.
Provides advice and information on volunteering and studying abroad.

Centre for Alternative Industrial and Technological Systems, North East London Polytechnic, Longbridge Road, Dagenham, Essex. Tel: 01 599 5141.
Based on the Lucas Aerospace Combine Shop Stewards Committee, the centre does research on alternative and socially constructive work by business corporations.

Centre for World Development Education, 25 Wilton Road, London SW1V 1JS. Tel: 01 828 7611.

Main British development education centre, particularly useful for providing teaching materials on world hunger.

Child Poverty Action Group, 1 Macklin Street, London W.C.2. Tel: 01 242 3225.
Energetic lobbying and research group on maldistribution of wealth in the UK.

Christian Aid, P.O. Box 1, London S.W.9. Tel: 01 733 5500
Largest Christian aid agency. Has an active education department with books, films and pamphlets.

Contemporary Archive on Latin America, 1 Cambridge Terrace, London N.W.1. 4JL. Tel: 01 487 5277.
Good source of material for research on Latin America.

Counter Information Service, 9 Poland Street, London W.1. Tel: 01 439 3764.
Research group producing regular anti-reports on British and multinational corporations.

Earth Resources Research Centre, 40 James St, London W.1. Tel: 01 487 4185.
Research group on all aspects of food production and consumption in the UK.

Friends of the Earth, 9 Poland Street, London W.1. Tel: 01 434 1684.
Action-orientated environmentalist group.

Intermediate Technology, 9 King Street, London W.C.2. Tel: 01 836 9434.
Researches use of appropriate technology, particularly in Third World rural areas.

MAGIC (*Mozambique, Angola, Guinea Information Centre*), 34 Percy Street, London W1P 9FG. Tel: 01 636 7108.
Information centre on development in the three countries since liberation.

Medical Aid Committee for Vietnam, 36 Wellington Street, London, W.C.2. Tel: 01 836 1350.
Raises funds to help Vietnam.

Oxfam, 274 Banbury Road, Oxford. Tel: 0865 56777.
Largest of the British Voluntary agencies supporting Third World

rural development projects and supplying development education materials for schools.

Scottish Education for Action and Development, 146 Lauriestan Place, Edinburgh. Tel: 031 228 1477.
Centre for voluntary agencies' education work and campaigns in Scotland.

Society for Anglo-Chinese Understanding, 152 Camden High Street, London, N.W.1. Tel: 01 485 8236.
Provides the official Chinese line. Arranges tours to China.

Third World First, 232 Cowley Road, Oxford. Tel: 0865 45678.
Student-based organization, very active on world issues.

Trade Union Committee for International Co-operation and Development, WDM, Bedford Chambers, Covent Garden, London, W.C.2. Tel: 01 836 3675.
Campaigns within the trade union movement on Third World issues.

Trade Union International Research and Education Group, Ruskin Hall, Dunstan Road, Old Headington, Oxford OX3 9BZ. Tel: 0865 58545.
Provides slide and tape representations on international trade for union events.

Uhuru, 35 Cowley Road, Oxford. Tel: 0865 48249.
Important Third World shop, can advise on how to establish a 'fair trading' and cheap health food centre.

United Nations Association, 3 Whitehall Court, London, SW1A 2EL. Tel: 01 930 2931.
Publicizes the work of the United Nations and its ideals.

War on Want, 467 Caledonian Road, London, N.7. Tel: 01 609 0211.
Voluntary aid agency with a heavy commitment to education campaigns in UK.

World Development Movement, Bedford Chambers, Covent Garden, London, W.C.2. Tel: 01 836 3672.
Most important of the action groups campaigning on Third World commodities issues and fairer trading links.

Other Useful Addresses
Advertising Standards Authority, 15 Ridgmount Street, London W.C.1. Tel: 01 580 0801.
For all complaints on whether an advertisement is 'legal, decent, truthful and honest'.

Development Studies Association, Centre for Development Studies, University College, Swansea, S. Wales.
Primarily for those 'professionally' interested in development studies.

European Economic Community Commission. UK Office: 20 Kensington Palace Gardens, London W.8. Tel: 01 727 8090.
Very helpful with information on the Common Agricultural Policy.

Farm and Food Society, 4 Willifield Way, London N.W.11. Tel: 01 455 0634.
Campaigns on farm animal welfare and chemical additives in food.

Food and Agriculture Organization, via delle Terme di Caracalla, 00100 Rome, Italy.
The best source for the most recent statistical estimates on all aspects of agriculture, food production and hunger in the world. Publish *Ceres* magazine.

Institute of Development Studies, University of Sussex, Falmer, Brighton, Sussex.
Research institute with a good library and highly sympathetic academic staff.

Overseas Development Institute, 10/11 Percy Street, London W.1.
Research institute, publishes *ODI Review.*

Overseas Development Ministry, Eland House, Stag Place, London S.W.1.
Administers the UK overseas aid programme, including funding domestic development education projects.

Australia

Australian Council for Overseas Aid, P.O. Box 1562, Canberra City ACT 2601. Tel: 062 47 4822.
Co-ordinating body for voluntary aid agencies, has an active education programme.

Australian Development Assistance Bureau, P.O. Box 887, Canberra City ACT 2601. Tel: 062 48 6644.
Administers official government aid programme.

Action for World Development, 183 Gertrude Street, Fitzroy, Victoria 3065, Tel: 03 419 5588.
Campaigns on international trade and commodity issues.

Asian Bureau, Australia, 175 Royal Parade, Parkville, Victoria 3052. Tel: 03 347 8595.
Research on South-East Asian issues.

Australian Catholic Relief, P.O. Box J124, Brickfield Hill, New South Wales 2000. Tel: 02 26 1592.
Largest Catholic overseas aid agency, also involved in domestic development education campaigns.

Australian Council of Churches – World Christian Action, c/o Rev. M. Chittleborough, 199 Clarence St, Sydney, New South Wales.
Aids agricultural schemes in Third World and is active in domestic development education issues.

Australian Freedom from Hunger Campaign, P.O. Box 395, Canberra City, ACT 2601. Tel: 062 48 0555.
Finances Third World rural development projects and domestic education programmes.

Community Aid Abroad, 75 Brunswick Street, Fitzroy, Victoria 3065. Tel: 03 419 7055.
Assists self-help development projects in Third World, and concerned to change the relationship between rich and poor countries.

Friends of the Earth, Australia, 366 Smith Street, Collingwood, Victoria 3066.
Environmentalist group with interests in Third World and food issues.

Overseas Service Bureau, 23 Clarendon Street, East Melbourne, Victoria 3002. Tel: 03 416 1788.
Sends volunteers to developing countries.

United Nations Association of Australia, 205 William Street, Melbourne, Victoria 3000. Tel: 03 602 2100.
Publicizes the work of the United Nations and its ideals.

New Zealand
Christian World Service, P.O. Box 297, Christchurch, Tel: 69274.
Anglican overseas voluntary aid agency.

CORSO, P.O. Box 9716, Wellington. Tel: 859585.
Main non-religious Third World voluntary aid agency.

Ecumenical Secretariat on Development, P.O. Box 5038, Auckland.
Tel: 774433.
Concerned with domestic action for social change.

New Zealand Catholic Overseas Aid, P.O. Box 2450, Christchurch.
Tel: 61360.
Vigorous help to social justice programmes in Asia.

Trade Aid, P.O. Box 1066, Christchurch. Tel: 796929.
Concerned with 'fair trading', with Third World shops throughout
the country.

Recommended Volunteer Organizations

Required reading for anyone thinking of voluntary work in the Third World is *Volunteering*, a short paper which discusses the implications of volunteering, from the point of view of both the volunteer and the country receiving assistance. Available from Returned Volunteer Action, 1c Cambridge Terrace, Regents Park, London N.W.1. Tel: 01 935 9447 (send sa.e.). Returned Volunteer Action, as its name suggests, is an organization of British ex-volunteers and can produce advice and suggestions on many aspects of overseas voluntary work.

The four main British agencies which send volunteers overseas are:

CATHOLIC INSTITUTE FOR INTERNATIONAL RELATIONS
Non-denominational. Covers mainly Central America, Haiti and Yemen. The pioneer of a more radical approach to volunteering, committed to work for social justice both in the Third World and the U.K. through its educational programme. 1 Cambridge Terrace, London N.W.1.

INTERNATIONAL VOLUNTARY SERVICE
British Branch of Service Civil International – a movement of people working together in peace. Also organizes internationally attended workcamps in Europe through its contacts, as well as workcamps in the UK. 53 Regent Road, Leicester LE1 64L.

UNITED NATIONAL ASSOCIATION INTERNATIONAL SERVICE
The smallest of the four agencies, therefore few opportunities. 3 Whitehall Court, London SW1A 2EL.

VOLUNTARY SERVICE OVERSEAS
The largest of the British volunteer agencies.
14 Bishops Bridge Road, London W2 6AA.

APPENDIX B

SOME RECOMMENDED PUBLICATIONS
RECOMMENDED FILMS AND SLIDES
RECOMMENDED ACTION GUIDES
RECOMMENDED PERIODICALS

Some Recommended Publications

Third World Publications, 151 Stratford Road, Birmingham B11 1AG. Tel: 021 733 6572, can provide all the British publications in print listed below. It is in particular the UK distributor of the publications of the Institute for Food and Development Policy.

Food First Resource Guide

The Institute for Food and Development Policy that produced *Food First* has created a unique tool for those who wish to learn more.

The *Food First Resource Guide* is not just a list of articles, books and other publications.

The Guide boils down *Food First* into a clear point-by-point outline of the causes of hunger. For each point it provides selected documentation from sources around the world; many are annotated.

And it provides the information you need to acquire that documentation.

The *Food First Resources Guide* is a must for students, teachers, study groups, journalists, development activists – for all those eager to dig out the true roots of needless hunger.

80 pages. Available through Third World Publications (address above).

Two other Institute publications of special interest to *Food First* readers:

World Hunger: Ten Myths

By the authors of *Food First*. By burying the ten most paralysing 'hunger myths,' *World Hunger: Ten Myths* clears the way for each of us to work in appropriate ways to end needless hunger. Now in a completely revised and updated edition, approximately 60 pages. Previous editions in 12 languages have been used by millions.

World Hunger: Ten Myths is perfect for group discussion. Available through Third World Publications (address above).

Needless Hunger: Voices from a Bangladesh Village

By Betsy Hartmann and James Boyce, fellows of the Institute for Food and Development Policy.

Many who read *Food First* find among its most shocking revelations the idea that Bangladesh is not a hopeless basketcase – neither today nor tomorrow. Indeed Bangladesh is among the agriculturally richest countries in the world.

Many want to know more: Why such hunger and poverty amongst such abundance?

To answer that question, Hartmann and Boyce, Bengali-speaking Americans who lived in Bangladesh for two years and in a single village for nine months, draw us into the daily struggles of real Bangladeshis. Hartmann and Boyce cut through the enigma of needless hunger to its economic and political roots. Moreover, we learn how we are directly linked to the very forces that generate hunger in Bangladesh.

The global analysis of *Food First* is vividly captured here in a single country – in a single village.

Approximately 75 pages with photographs and optional discussion guide.

In the Summer of 1979 the Institute completed a *Food First* slide and tape show (alternatively available in filmstrip format). Much of the essence of *Food First* in a lively 30 minute colour presentation with recorded narration and music. Comes with study and discussion guide. Highly successful in classroom and other group discussions.

For more information about this audio-visual presentation, please write to:

Institute for Food and Development Policy
2588 Mission Street
San Francisco, California 94110
USA

Further reading on Part 1 of this book, The Scarcity Scare

Arens J & J van Beurden. *Jhagrapur – Poor peasants and women in a village in Bangladesh*, Third World Publications, 151 Stratford Road, Birmingham B11 1AG.

Brookfield, Harold. *Interdependent Development*, London, Methuen & Co, 1977.

Bryan, Helen. *Fertilizer: Part of the Solution, or Part of the Problem?* War on Want, 467 Caledonian Road, London N7 9BE.

Farvar, M. Taghi and Milton, John P. eds. *Careless Technology*, Garden City, New Jersey, The Natural History Press, 1972.

Mamdani, Mahmood. *The Myth of Population Control – Family, Class and Caste in an Indian Village* Monthly Review Press, New York and London, 1972.

Tudge, Colin. *The Famine Business*, Faber & Faber, London, 1977.

New International Publications: 'Back from the Brink – Bangladesh Revisited'. *New Internationalist* magazine March 1977. 'Population Special: Birth Control and Wealth Control', *New Internationalist* magazine June 1977. 'Answering Back: The Questions People Ask About World Poverty', *New Internationalist* magazine October 1978. All available from: New Internationalist, 62a High Street, Wallingford, Oxon, OX10 0EE.

Parsons, Jack. *Population Fallacies*, Elek Pemberton, 1977.

Robbins, C & Ansari, J. *The profits of Doom*, War on Want, 467 Caledonian Road, London N7 9BE.

United Nations Research Institute for Social Development (UNRISD). *Famine Risk and Famine Prevention in the Modern World*. 1976.

On Part II, Colonial Inheritance

Beckford, George L. *Persistent Poverty – Underdevelopment in Plantation Economics of the Third World*, New York: Oxford University Press, 1972.

Caldwell, Malcolm. *The Wealth of Some Nations*, Zed Press, 57 Caledonian Road, London N1 9DN, 1978.

Feldman, David, and Lawrence, Peter. *Africa Report*, Global II Project on the Social and Economic Implications of Large-Scale Introduction of New Varieties of Foodgrains, UNDP/UNRISD, Geneva, 1975.

Gunder Frank, Andre. *Latin America: Underdevelopment or Revolution*, Monthly Review Press, New York & London, 1970.

Mende, Tibor. *From Aid to Re-Colonisation*, Pantheon, New York, 1973.

Oliver, Roland, & Fage, J. D. *A Short History of Africa*, Penguin, 1975.

Owen, R. & Sutcliffe, R. eds. *Studies in the Theory of Imperialism*, Longman, London, 1975.

Rodney, Walter. *How Europe Underdeveloped Africa*, Bogle-L'Ouverture Publications, 141 Coldershaw Road, London W.13., 1972.

Williams, Eric. *Capitalism and Slavery*, Deutsch, London, 1964.

Worsley, Peter. *The Third World*, Weidenfeld & Nicholson, London, 1967.

On Part IV, Modernization and the Green Revolution

Griffin, Keith. *Land Concentration and Rural Poverty*, Macmillan, New York, 1976.

Griffin, Keith. *The Political Economy of Agrarian Change*: Harvard University Press, Cambridge, Mass., 1974.

Matthews, William. ed. *Outer Limits and Human Needs – Resource and Environmental issues of Development Strategies*, The Dag Hammarskjöld Foundation, Uppsala, 1976.

New Internationalist Publications: 'Dancing South to South – A New Partnership in Technology – of, by and for the Third World.' *New Internationalist* magazine May 1978.

Perelman, Michael. *Farming for Profit in a Hungry World: Capital and the Crises in Agriculture*, Allanheld, Osmun & Co, Montclair, New Jersey, 1977.

Power, J, & Holenstein A. *World of Hunger*, Maurice Temple Smith, London, 1976.

Sinha, R. *Food and Poverty*, Croom Helm, London, 1976.

Tudge, Colin. *The Famine Business*, Faber & Faber, 1977.

Pearse, Andrew. *Bitter Rice*, forthcoming.

Hewitt de Alcantar, Cynthia. *Modernizing Mexican Agriculture*, United Nations Research Institute for Social Development. Geneva, 1976.

On Part VI, The Trade Game

Galeano, Eduardo. *Open Veins in Latin America: Five Centuries of Pillage of a Continent*, Monthly Review, New York, 1973.

Gallis, Marion. *Trade for Justice: Myth or Mandate?* World Council of Churches, *Geneva*, 1972.

Jonas, Susanne, and David Tobias, eds. Guatemala, North American Congress on Latin America (NACLA), New York and Berkeley, 1974.

Morton K, and Tulloch P. Trade and Developing Countries, Croom Helm/ODI, London, 1977.

New Internationalist Publications: 'The World in Your Shopping Basket – Who sells what, where and who makes the money', *New Internationalist* magazine April 1976; 'Third World Power,' *New Internationalist* magazine November 1977.

Payer, Cheryl, ed. *Commodity Trade in the Third World*, Macmillan, London, 1977.

On Part VII, USA – The Bread Basket of the World

Commoner, Barry. *'The Poverty of Power'*, Knopf, New York, 1976.

deMarco, Susan and Sechler, Susan. *The Fields Turn Brown – Four Essays on World Hunger*, Washington DC Agribusiness Accountability Project, 1975.

Hightower, Jim. *Eat your Heart Out: How Food Profiteers Victimise the Consumer*, Crown, New York, 1975.

Jones, D. *Food and interdependence: The Effect of Food and Agricultural Policies of Developed Countries on the Food Problems of the Developing Countries*, Overseas Development Institute 1976.

North American Congress on Latin America (NACLA). 'US Grain Arsenal,' *Latin America and Empire Report 9*, 7. (October 1975).

On Part VIII, World Hunger as Big Business

Barnet R, and Muller R. *Global Reach: The Power of the Multinational Corporations*, Jonathan Cape London, 1975.

Berg, Alan. *The Nutrition Factor*, The Brookings Institution, Washington DC, 1973.

Chetley, A. *The Baby Killer Scandal*, War on Want, 467 Caledonian road, London N.1.

Feder, Ernest. *Strawberry Imperialism*, distributed by America Latina, 71 Fleet Street, London.

George, Susan. *Feeding the Few: Corporate Control of Food*, Institute for Policy Studies, Paulus Potterstraat 20, Amsterdam 1007, Holland. 1979.

George, Susan. *How the Other Half Dies*, Penguin, London, 1976.

Hightower, Jim. *Eat Your Heart Out. How Food Profiteers Victimise The Consumer*, Crown, New York, 1975.

Ledogar, Robert J. *Hungry for Profits*. US Food and Drug Multinationals in Latin America, New York: IDOC 1976.

Medawar, Charles. *Insult or Injury? An Enquiry into the Marketing and Advertising of British Food and Drug Products in the Third World*. Social Audit, 9 Poland Street, London W1V 3DG, 1979.

Muller, Mike. *The Baby Killer*. War on Want, 467 Caledonian Road, London, 1975.

New International Publications: 'The Footloose Phase of Capitalism' *New Internationalist* magazine March 1976.

North American Congress on Latin America (NACLA): 'Bitter Fruits.' *Latin America and Empire Report*, Berkeley CA September 1976.

Radice, Hugo. ed. *International Firms and Modern Imperialism*, Penguin, Harmondsworth, 1975.

Turner, Louis. *Multinational Companies and the Third World*, Allen Lane, London, 1974.

CIS AntiReport II: *Unilever's World*. Counter Information Service, 9 Poland Street, London W1V 3DG, 1977.

Yost, Israel. 'The Food for Peace Arsenal' *NACLA Newsletter* 5, 3 (May-June 1971).

On Part IX, The Helping Hand: Aid for Whom?

Dumont, René. *False Start in Africa*, Sphere, London, 1968.

Hayter, Theresa. *Aid as Imperialism*, Penguin, Harmondsworth, 1973.

National Action/Research on the Military-Industrial Complex (NARMIC). *Food as a Weapon*. The Food for Peace Program, 112 South 16th St, Philadelphia, Pa., 1975.

New Internationalist Publications. 'Who's helping Who? A Radical Reassessment of Foreign Aid'. *New Internationalist* magazine, January 1976.

North American Congress on Latin America (NACLA) 'US Grain Arsenal' *Latin America and Empire Report*, 9, 7 (October 1975).

Payer, Cheryl. *The Debt Trap: The IMF and the Third World*, Penguin, Harmondsworth, 1974.

Stevens, Christopher. *Food Aid and the Developing World*, Croom Helm, London, 1979.

Wachtel, Howard. *The New Gnomes: Multinational Banks in the*

Third World. Transnational Institute, 20 Paulus Potterstraat, Amsterdam 1007, Holland, 1978.

Weissman, Steve. *The Trojan Horse: A Radical Look at Foreign Aid.* Ramparts, San Francisco, 1974.

On Part X, Food Self-Reliance

Dunman, Jack. *Agriculture: Capitalist and Socialist,* Lawrence & Wishart, London, 1975.

Food and Agriculture Organisation. *Progress in Land Reform, Sixth Report,* 1975.

Food and Agriculture Organisation. *Progress in Land Reform,* prepared by H. V. Henle, 1974.

Galtung, Johan. *Self-Reliance: Concepts, Practice and Rationale,* Ecumenical Institute, Chateau de Bossey, CH 1298, Celigny, Switzerland. April 1976.

Gough, Kathleen. *Ten Times More Beautiful: Rebuilding the Republic of Vietnam.* Monthly Review, New York, 1978.

New Internationalist Publications. 'How Can The Basic Needs of all the People in the World be Met?' *New Internationalist* magazine, August and September 1976.

ul Haq, Mahbub. *The Poverty Curtain: Choices for the Third World,* Columbia University Press, New York, 1976.

Recommended Films and Slides

Most of the voluntary agencies and development education bodies have a number of films and slide sets, including: Christian Aid, Commonwealth Institute, Centre for World Development Education, Oxfam, Third World First, Scottish Education & Action for Development, and War on Want. Unfortunately, some of the presentations are simply designed to excite pity and loosen purse strings. At least two presentations, however, are very sympathetic to the issues that *Food First* raise are:

Something More Important Than God (The United Society for the Propagation of the Gospel). This is a superbly produced three screen slide presentation on the power struggle in Latin America. USPG, 15 Tufton Street, London S.W.1. Tel: 01 222 4222.

Bottle Babies (War on Want). The film raises all the issues explored in the chapter on The Baby Food Scandal, as well as such questions as the social responsibility of investors. War on Want, 467 Caledonian Road, London N.7. Tel: 01 609 0211.

A number of commercial film distributors hold a wide range of material related to world hunger issues including:

Concord Films, 200 Felixstowe Road, Ipswich, Suffolk IP3 9BJ. Tel: Ipswich 76012. They hold all the main television documentaries that would cover the *Food First* subjects. Catalogue available.

Contemporary Films, 55 Greek Street, London W.1. Tel: 01 734 4901. This company distributes a number of the commercial films on radical issues.

A useful publication is the Third World First Film Catalogue, containing reviews and information on more than 160 films dealing with international issues.

Third World First, 232 Cowley Road, Oxford. Tel: 0865 45678.

See also page 360 for a description of *Food First* slide show and film strip.

Recommended Action Guides

A special issue of the *New Internationalist* magazine called 'Yes, But What Can I Do?', October 1976, carried more than 150 articles from Britain, Europe, America, Canada, Australia, New Zealand and Japan profiling action for change that's happening now. Not all the action or organizations would be consistent with the *'Food First'* analysis, but it is a unique sourcebook of ideas.

There are a number of other publications with useful advice on arranging meetings, running campaigns, showing films etc. They include:

Action for International Justice and Peace (Catholic Institute for International Relations), Attractively produced, this booklet although primarily intended for Catholic readers, has a general appeal. It includes sections on communications and publicity, list of publications, pamphlets, posters etc.

Guide for Groups (Third World First). Although primarily intended for students, this book again has a general appeal. It includes suggestions on how to run a craft/food stall, street theatre, film festivals, fundraising and study groups. It describes successful actions undertaken by local Third World First groups.

Into School (Third World First.) Gives advice on how to present issues like world hunger in schools.

Resources Notes (World Development Movement). These are a modest series of notes on 'how to', including sources of information and support, bookstalls, arranging meetings, lobbying government, getting local media coverage, printing and publicity.

What Can be Done? (Christian Aid). This is part of a 'One World' series of booklets on issues like lifestyle, jobs, trade, health and hunger. It contains more editorializing than most of the other guides, less on the mechanics of campaigning for change.

World Development – A Guide to Speakers, Contacts and Resources (Scottish Education & Action for Development). This is particularly intended to help Scottish activists with lists of local speakers, organizations and academic institutions on 'rich world, poor world' issues.

Recommended Periodicals

New Internationalist magazine specializes in popularizing and making intelligible development problems and attacking the myths that surround them. A free sample copy is available from: New Internationalist, 62a High Street, Wallingford, Oxfordshire OX10 0EE.

Ceres bi-monthly, P.O. Box 569, London SE1 9NH. Sponsored by the Food and Agriculture Organization, the magazine is particularly concerned with food production and aid in the Third World. The editorial content is generally very 'safe'.

Review of African Political Economy, three times a year. Enquiries to Onyx Press, 27 Clerkenwell Close, London EC1R 0AT. A Marxist-orientated academic publication often carrying very useful articles on African agrarian problems.

World Development, monthly. Enquiries to: Subscription Fulfilment Manager, Pergamon Press Ltd., Headington Hill Hall, Oxford. This is the most comprehensive British academic journal on the subject. The absurd subscription price (nearly £60 in 1979), equalling the annual income of some Third World peasants, means you have to use a University library copy.

Chapter Notes

PART I. THE SCARCITY SCARE
Chapter 1
Too Many People, Too Little Land?

1. Calculated from Food and Agriculture Organization, *Production Yearbooks*.
2. *The World Food Problem: A Report of the President's Science Advisory Committee* (Washington D.C.: Government Printing Office, 1976), Tables 7-9, p. 434; see also Leroy L. Blakeslee Earl O. Heady, and Charles F. Framingham, 'World Food Production, Demand and Trade,' Iowa State University, 1973.
3. Nelson A. Rockefeller, *Vital Resources: Critical Choices for Americans, Volume I, Reports on Energy, Food & Raw Materials*, D. C. Heath and Co., Lexington, Massachusetts, 1977, p. 101.
4. World Bank, *The Assault on World Poverty*, 1975. p. 244.
5. Keith Griffin, *Land Concentration and Rural Poverty*, Macmillan, New York, 1976, p. 135.
6. Calculations based on Food and Agriculture Organization, *Production Yearbooks*.
7. Comparisons regarding MSA countries are calculated from US Department of Agriculture, *Foreign Agricultural Trade Statistical Report*, Calendar Year 1974, May 1975.
8. Calculations based on Food and Agriculture Organization, *Production Yearbooks*.
9. Alan Riding, 'Malnutrition Taking Bigger Toll Among Mexican Children,' *The New York Times*, 6 March 1978, p. 2.
10. United States Department of Agriculture, *Foreign Agriculture*, 20 February 1978, pp. 8f.
11. *Bangkok Post*, 26 January 1978.
12. Calculated from Food and Agricultural Organization, *Production Yearbook*, vol. 28-1, 1974.
13. Ibid., *Production Yearbook*, 1975.
14. Samir Amin, 'L' Afrique sous-peuplée,' *Dévelopment et Civilisation*, nos, 47-48, March/June 1972, pp.60-61.

15. Calculated from FAO *Production Yearbook*, 1974.
16. Ibid.
17. World Bank, *World Economic and Social Indications*, 1977.
18. Steve Raymer, 'The Nightmare of Famine,' *National Geographic* July 1975.
19. *World Hunger, Health, and Refugee Problems, Summary of a Special Mission to Asia and the Middle East*, US Government Printing Office, Washington, 1976, p. 99.
20. F. T. Jannuzi and J. T. Peach, 'Report on the Hierarchy of Interests in Land in Bangladesh,' September 1977.
21. Food and Agriculture Organization, *Bangladesh: Country Development Brief*, 1973, pp. 7, 31-32.
22. United Nations Report (confidential), 'Some Notes on Agriculture in Bangladesh,' Dacca, 18 Nov. 1974, p. 4.
23. Food and Agriculture Organization, *Progress in Land Reform*, p. iii-82, (emphasis added).

Chapter 2
Are People a Liability or a Resource?

1. Robert d'A. Shaw, *Jobs and Agricultural Development*. Overseas Development Council, Washington, D.C.: 1970, Table 2, p. 10.
2. World Bank, *The Assault on World Poverty*, Johns Hopkins University Press, Baltimore, 1975, pp. 242-243.
3. Wolfgang Hein, 'Over-unemployment or Marginality,' a review of *Urban Unemployment in Developing Countries, The Nature of the Problem and Proposals for Its Solution* by Paul Bairoch ILO, Geneva, 1973, in *Ceres* May-June 1976: 61.
4. Edgar Owens and Robert Shaw, *Development Reconsidered*, Heath, Lexington, Mass: 1972, p. 54.
5. Richard Barnet and Ronald Mueller, *Global Reach*, Simon & Schuster, New York, 1974, p. 169.
6. Colin Tudge, *The Famine Business*, Faber & Faber, London, 1977, Chapter 1.
7. Robert Maurer, 'Work: Cuba,' in *Cuba: People – Questions*, ed. W. L. Kaiser Friendship Press/IDOC/North America, New York, 1975, p. 22.
8. *New York Times*, 1 November, 1970.
9. International Labour Organization, 'Agricultural Mechanisation and Employment in Latin America,' prepared by K. C.

Abercrombie, in *Mechanisation and Employment in Agriculture*, 1973, pp. 61-63.

10. Gordon Gemmill and Carl K. Eicher, 'A Framework for Research on the Economics of Farm Mechanization in Developing Countries,' African Rural Employment Research Network, paper no. 6, p. 2., 1973, Department of Agricultural Economics, Michigan State University, East Lansing, Michigan.

Chapter 3
Birth Control and Wealth Control

1. Helen Ware, 'The Sahelian Drought: Some Thoughts of the Future,' Special Sahelian Office, Food and Agriculture Organization, March 1975, p. 13. See also Ben White, 'Children: The Benefit to the Poor and the Cost to the Rich,' *New Internationalist*, No. 52, June 1977, pp. 16-17.

2. Mahmood Mamdani, *The Myth of Population Control: Family, Class and Caste in an Indian Village*, Monthly Review Press, New York and London, 1972, pp. 78, 113.

3. Mamdani, *op. cit.*

4. David Heer and David May, 'Son Survivorship Motivation and Family Size in India: A Computer Simulation,' *Population Studies* 22 (1968): 206, cited in Rich, *Smaller Families*.

5. Perdita Huston, 'Power and Pregnancy,' *New Internationalist*, No. 52, June 1977, 10-12.

6. Roger Revelle, Centre for Population Studies, Harvard University, Letters, *Science* 187 (21 March, 1975).

7. William Rich, *Smaller Families through Social and Economic Progress* Overseas Development Council, Washington, D.C.: 1973, Chapter 1.

8. Alan Berg, 'The Trouble with Triage,' *New York Times Magazine* 15 June 1975: 22ff.

9. Leo Orleans, 'China's Experience in Population Control: The Elusive Model,' *World Development* 3 (July-August 1975): 507.

10. Lester Brown, *World Population Trends*, Washington D.C.: Worldwatch Institute, 1978. Appendix B. Our estimate is also based on discussions with Leo Orleans, China scholar at the Library of Congress.

11. Leo Orleans, 'China's Experience in Population Control: The Elusive Model,' Prepared for the Committee on Foreign

Affairs, US House of Representatives by the Congressional Research Service, Library of Congress, September, 1974, GAO, Washington D.C.

Chapter 4
Population Pressure on the Environment

1. Howard E. Daugherty, *Man Induced Ecologic Change in El Salvador*, PhD. dissertation, University of California, Los Angeles, 1969.
2. *El Salvador Zonification Agricola* (Fase I), Organization of American States, Washington D.C., 1974, cited by Erik Eckholm, *Losing Ground*, Norton, for Worldwatch Institute, New York, 1976, p. 167.
3. George Borgstrom, 'Ecological Aspects of Protein Feeding – the case of Peru,' in eds. M. Taghi Farvar and John P. Milton, *The Careless Technology: Ecology and International Development*, The Natural History Press, Garden City, N.J., 1972, p. 901.
4. Food and Agriculture Organization, *Production Yearbook*, vol. 28-1, 1974.
5. Erik Eckholm, *Losing Ground*, Norton, for Worldwatch Institute, New York, 1976.
6. René Dumont, *False Start in Africa*, Deutsch, London, 1966, p. 69; originally, *L'Afrique est mal partie*, Seuil, Paris, 1962.
7. Jeremy Swift, 'Disaster and a Sahelian Nomad Economy,' in *Drought in Africa* eds. David Dalby and R. J. Harrison (London: Centre for African Studies, 1973), pp. 71-79; Douglas L. Johnson, 'The Response of Pastoral Nomads to Drought in the Absence of Outside Intervention,' paper commissioned by the United Nations Special Sahelian Office, 19 December, 1973; F. Fraser Darling and M. T. Farvar, 'Ecological Consequences of Sedentarization of Nomads,' in *The Careless Technology*; D. J. Stenning, *Savannah Nomads*, Oxford University Press, London, 1959.
8. Ibid., especially Stenning.
9. Helen Ware, 'The Sahelian Drought: Some Thoughts on the Future,' Special Sahelian Office, Food and Agriculture Organization, 26 March 1975, especially 3ff.
10. Claire Sterling, 'The Making of the Sub-Saharan Wasteland,' *Atlantic Monthly*, May 1974 98-105.

11. Ibid.
12. Eduardo Cruz de Carvalho, ' "Traditional" and "Modern" Patterns of Cattle Raising: A Critical Evaluation of Change from Pastoralism to Ranching,' *The Journal of Developing Areas* 8 January 1974.
13. Frank L. Lambrecht, 'The Tsetse Fly: A Blessing or a Curse?' in *The Careless Technology*, 72ff. and 775ff.
14. Frances M. Foland, 'A profile of Amazonia,' *Journal of Inter-American Studies and World Affairs*, January 1971: 72ff.
15. Cited in Vic Cox, 'Brazil: The Amazon Gamble,' *The Nation*, 11 October 1975: 328.
16. Dr Nelson Chaves, Head of the Nutrition Institute at the University of Pernambuco.
17. *World Environment Report*, Center for Environmental Information, New York, 1, no. 8, 12 May 1975.
18. José S. Da Veiga, 'Quand les multinationales font du ranching,' *Le Monde Diplomatique*, September 1975: 12.
19. Ibid., p. 13.

Chapter 5
The Price Scare

1. US Department of Agriculture, *Agricultural Statistics* – 1972 Government Printing Office, Washington, D.C., Tables 650, 755, and 759.
2. Lester Brown with Erik Eckholm, *By Bread Alone*, New York: Praeger, 1974, p. 60.
3. Helen Bryant, *Fertilizer: Part of the Solution, or Part of the Problem?* War on Want, London, 1975. Quoting Edwin Weheler, President of the Fertilizer Institute, at its annual meeting, 3 February 1975.
4. Joe Belden with Gregg Forte, *Toward a National Food Policy*, Exploratory Project for Economic Alternatives, 1519 Conneticut Ave, N.W., Washington, D.C. 20036, p. 132, citing USDA *Agricultural Statistics* 1974, p. 210.

Chapter 6
The Food Vs. Poison Trade-off

1. J. P. Hrabovszky, Senior Policy and Planning Coordinator, Agriculture Department, FAO, Rome, letter dated 18 March

1976, quoting Dr W. R. Furtick, Chief, Plant Protection Service.

2. Teodoro Boza Barducci, 'Ecological Consequences of Pesticides Used for the Control of Cotton Insects in Cañete Valley, Peru,' in *Careless Technology, Ecology and International Development*, eds. M. Taghi Farvar and John P. Milton, Natural History Press, Garden City N.J., 1972, 423ff.

3. M. Taghi Farvar, 'Relationship Between Ecological and Social Systems,' speech delivered to EARTHCARE conference, New York, 6 June 1975, p. 4.

4. M. Taghi Farvar, 'Ecological Implications of Insect Control,' Centre for the Study of Biological Systems, Research Report, 6 February 1970, pp. 6-8.

5. Farvar, 'Ecological Implications of Insect Control,' p. 11.

6. Robert F. Luck et. al, 'Chemical Insect Control, A Troubled Pest Management Strategy,' BioScience, 1977.

7. Farvar, 'Ecological Implications of Insect Control,' 1970, p.15.

8. Erik Eckholm and S. Jacob Scherr, 'Double Standards and the Pesticide Trade,' *New Scientist*, 16 February 1978, p. 440ff.

9. *New York Times*, 5 December 1976, p.39.

10. Eckholm, p. 443.

11. Farvar, 'Relationship Between Ecological and Social Systems,' 1975, p. 4.

12. Farvar, 'Ecological Implications of Insect Control,' 1970, p. 10.

13. *Environment* 17 (April/May 1975): 22.

14. *New York Times*, 6 February 1976, p. 12.

15. Richard Franke, 'The Green Revolution in a Javanese village' Ph.D. dissertation, Department of Anthropology, Harvard University, 1972, 39ff.

16. See James S. Turner, *A Chemical Feast: Report on the Food and Drug Administration* (Ralph Nader Study Group Reports), Grossman, New York, 1970, for a study of the influence in government of the chemical and drug companies; David Pimentel, 'Realities of a Pesticide Ban,' *Environment* 15, March 1973, gives extensive reference notes.

17. Fred Willman, 'Biogradable Pesticides,' *R. F. Illustrated*, Rockefeller Foundation, 2, 1, March 1975: 5.

18. Environmental Protection Agency, 'Strategy of the Environmental Protection Agency for Controlling the Adverse Effects of Pesticides,' EPA Office of Pesticide Programs, Office of

Water and Hazardous Materials, Washington D.C. 36pp cited by Pimentel, 1977.

19. Ibid.

20. David Burnham, 'Pesticide Work Suggested for Those Seeking Sterility,' *New York Times*, 27 September 1977.

21. *The New York Times*, 14 February 1975, citing Dr G. M. Woodwell, Marine Biology Laboratory, Woods Hole, Mass.

22. 'Man's Impact on the Global Environment,' Report of the Study of Critical Environment Problems, Massachusetts Institute of Technology, Cambridge, Mass, 1970, cited by Erik Eckholm, *Losing Ground*, Norton, New York, 1976, p. 162.

23. Martin Brown, 'An Orange Is an Orange,' *Environment* 17, July/August 1975: 6ff.

24. Van den Bosch, et. al., 'Investigation of the Effects of Food Standards on Pesticide Use,' Draft Report, Environmental Protection Agency, Washington D.C., cited by Pimentel, 1977, p. 180.

25. Pimentel, 1977, p. 178ff.

26. Michael Jacobson, 'Agriculture's New Hero: IPM,' *Nutrition Action*, January 1978, p. 4.

27. *New York Times*, 6 February 1976, p. 12.

28. Ibid., citing National Academy of Sciences 1976 study.

29. Smith and Reynolds, 'Effects of Manipulation of Cotton Agro-Systems on Insect Pest Populations,' p. 389.

30. A. Ayanaba and B. N. Okigbo, 'Mulching for Improved Soil Fertility and Crop Production,' *Organic Materials as Fertilizers*, Soils Bulletin 27, Swedish International Development Authority and FAO, Rome, 1975, p. 101.

31. *Pesticides*, The Journal of the Indian Pesticides Industry, February 1968, see entire issue.

32. Personal communication of L. More and T. F. Watson with Dr Robert van den Bosch, Division of Biological Control, University of California, Berkeley, cited in Dr van den Bosch's 'The Politics of Pesticides,' speech.

33. Richard Norgaard, 'Evaluation of Pest Management Programs for Cotton in California and Arizona,' Appendix C in *Evaluation of Pest Management Programs for Cotton, Peanuts and Tobacco*, Rosemarie von Rumker, consultant, RVR Project 66, Contact ‡EQ4Ac036, Environmental Protection Agency and the Council on Environmental Quality,

October, 1975; see also D. C. Hall, R. B. Norgaard, and P. K. True, 'The Performance of Independent Pest Management Consultants in San Joaquin Cotton and Citrus,' in *California Agriculture*, Division of Agricultural Sciences, University of California, 29, October 1975.

34. John S. Steinhart and Carol E. Steinhart, 'Energy Use in the U.S. Food System,' *Science*, April 1974; 3-4.

35. Erich H. Jacoby, *The Green Revolution in China* (Geneva: UNRISD, 18 December, 1973, pp. 11-12.

36. Robert F. Luck et al., 'Chemical Insect Control, A Troubled Pest Management Strategy,' *BioScience* 27, no. 9, Sept. 1977: 606-611.

37. Robert van den Bosch, *The Pesticide Conspiracy*, Doubleday and Company, New York, 1978.

38. Peter Feldman and David Lawrence, 'Social and Economic Implementations of the Large-Scale Introduction of New Varieties of Foodgrains,' Africa Report, Preliminary draft Geneva: UNRISD, 1975, pp. 198ff.

Chapter 7
Famines and History

1. M. Ganzin, 'Pour entrer dans une ère de justice alimentaire,' UNESCO *Courrier* May 1975, cited by Susan George, *How the Other Half Dies*, Penguin, Harmondsworth, 1976, p. 139.

2. 'Famine-Risk and Famine Prevention in the Modern World: Studies of food systems under conditions of recurrent scarcity' UNRISD, Geneva: June 976, p. 36.

3. Famine Inquiry Commission, *Report on Bengal*, Government of India Publication, Delhi, 1945, p. 28.

4. Famine Inquiry Commission, *Report*, pp. 106, 198.

5. George Blyn, *Agricultural Trends in India, 1891-1947*, University of Pennsylvania Press, Philadelphia, 1966, p. 102, cited by Gail Omvedt in 'The Political Economy of Starvation,' unpublished manuscript, 1974.

6. George Blyn, *The Agricultural Crops of India*, 1893-94 *to* 1945-46 University of Pennsylvania Press, Philadelphia, 1951.

7. Lester Brown and Gail Finsterbusch, *Man and His Environment: Food*, Harper and Row, New York, 1972, p. 7, cited by Omvedt, 'Political Economy of Starvation.'

8. Special Publication of the American Geographical Society, No. 6. p. 1.

9. *The Report of the American Red Cross Commission to China*, ARC 270, October 1929.

10. Joseph Needham, 'The Nature of Chinese Society: A Technical Interpretation.' a public lecture published in University of Hong Kong *Gazette*, 15 May 1974, cited by Harry Magdoff, 'China: Contrasts with the U.S.S.R.,' in 'China's Economic Strategy,' *Monthly Review* 27, July-August 1975: 15-16.

11. *China Reconstructs*, 23, no. 2, 2ff.

12. Richard Greenhill, 'Coping,' *New Internationalist*, June 1973: 14-15.

13. *China Reconstructs*, 23, no. 2, 2ff.

14. A. de Vajda, Senior Advisor, FAO, Rome.

15. Greenhill, 'Coping.'

Chapter 8
Drought in the Sahel

1. US Agency for International Development, Office of Science and Technology, *Desert Encroachment on Arable Lands: Significance, Causes and Control* (TA/OST 72-10) Government Printing Office, (Washington, D.C.: August 1972).

1. Douglas L. Johnson, 'The Response of Pastoral Nomads to Drought in the Absence of Outside Intervention,' paper commissioned by the United Nations Special Sahelian Office, 19 December 1973, p. 3.

2. Helen Ware, 'The Sahelian Drought: Some Thoughts on the Future,' paper commissioned by the United Nations Special Sahelian Office, 26 March 1975, especially pp. 2ff.

3. A. T. Grove, 'Desertification in the African Environment,' in David Dalby and R. J. Harrison, *Drought in Africa* Centre for African Studies, London: 1973, pp. 33-45.

4. *Christian Science Monitor*, quoted in *Environment* 1 December 1974.

5. D. Stamp, 'Some Conclusions,' in *A History of Land Use in Arid Regions* (Paris: UNESCO, 1961).

6. Thurston Clarke, *The Last Caravan*: Putnam, New York, 1978, pp. 7, 84-90.

7. 'Les ravages de la culture du coton,' *Le Monde Diplomatique* May 1976: 11.

8. Claude Raynaut, 'Le Cas de la region de Maradi (Niger), in *Sécheresses et Famines du Sahel* François Maspero, Paris: 1975, especially pp. 8-18.

9. Calculations based on Food and Agriculture Organization, *Yearbook of International Trade Statistics*, 1974.

10. Food and Agriculture Organization, *Production Yearbook* 1975.

11. Food and Agriculture Organization, *Trade Yearbook*, 1975.

12. Ibid., and *Production Yearbook*, 1975.

13. Personal communication from Dr Thierry Brun, Institut National de la Santé, Hospital Bichat, Paris, 17 November, 1975.

14. Lofchie, 'Political and Economic Origins of African Hunger,' pp. 554 and 561ff.

15. Food and Agriculture Organization, *Trade Yearbook*, 1975.

16. 'Social Institutions,' a study by the UN Special Sahelian Office, March 28, 1974, p. 80.

17. Calculations based on the Food and Agriculture Organization, *Yearbook of International Trade Statistics*, 1974.

18. Interview with Dr Marcel Ganzin, Director, Food Policy and Nutrition Division, FAO, 20 April, 1976.

19. Letter from Dr Marcel Ganzin, Director, Food Policy and Nutrition Division, FAO, dated 18 December 1975, (emphasis added.)

Chapter 9
Why Nations Can't Feed Themselves

1. Radha Sinha, *Food and Poverty*, Holmes and Merier, New York: 1976, p. 26.

2. John Stuart Mill, *Political Economy*, Book 3, Chapter 25 (emphasis added).

3. Peter Feldman and David Lawrence, 'Social and Economic Implications of the Large-Scale Introduction of New Varieties of Foodgrains,' Africa Report, preliminary draft UNRISD, Geneva: 1975, pp. 107-108.

4. Edgar Owens, *The Right Side of History*, unpublished manuscript, 1976.

5. Walter Rodney, *How Europe Underdeveloped Africa* Bogle-L'Ouverture Publications, 1972, pp. 171-172.

6. Ferdinand Ossendowski, *Slaves of the Sun*, Dutton, New York: 1928, p. 276.

7. Rodney, *How Europe Underdeveloped Africa*, pp. 171-172.

8. Ibid., p. 181.

9. Ibid, p. 185.

10. Ibid., p. 184.

11. Ibid., p. 186.

12. George L. Beckford, *Persistent Poverty: Underdevelopment in Plantation Economies of the Third World*: Oxford University Press, New York, 1972, p. 99.

13. Ibid., p. 99, quoting from Erich Jacoby, *Agrarian Unrest in Southeast Asia*, New York: Asia Publishing House, 1961, p. 66.

14. Feldman and Lawrence, 'Social and Economic Implications,' p. 103.

15. Special Sahelian Office Report, Food and Agriculture Organization, 28 March, 1974, pp. 88-89.

16. Alan Adamson, *Sugar Without Slaves: The Political Economy of British Guiana, 1838-1904* Yale University Press, New Haven and London: 1972, p. 41.

17. Eric Williams, *Capitalism and Slavery* Putnam, New York: 1966, p. 110.

18. Ibid., p. 121.

19. Gunnar Myrdal, *Asian Drama*, vol. 1 Pantheon, New York: 1966, pp. 448-449.

20. Feldman and Lawrence, 'Social and Economic Implications,' p. 189.

Chapter 10
The Legacy of Colonialism

1. Eduardo Galeno, *Open Veins in Latin America: Five Centuries of the Pillage of a Continent* Monthly Review, New York: 1973, p. 282.

2. George Beckford, *Persistent Poverty: Underdevelopment in Plantation Economies of the Third World* Oxford University Press, New York, 1972, p. 82.

3. Robert E. Gamer, *The Developing Nations, A Comparative Perspective* Allyn and Bacon, Boston: 1976, Chapter 2.

4. Edgar Owens and Robert Shaw, *Development Reconsidered* Heath, Lexington, Mass.: 1972, p. 150; also see Gunnar

Myrdal, *Asian Drama,* vol. 1 Pantheon, New York, 1966, part III, Chapter 10.

5. Francine R. Frankel, 'The Politics of the Green Revolution: Shifting Patterns of Peasant Participation in India and Pakistan,' in *Food, Population and Employment,* eds., Thomas T. Poleman and Donald K. Freebairn, Praeger, New York, 1973, p. 124.

6. Thomas P. Melady and R. B. Suhartono, *Development: Lessons for the Future* Orbis, Maryknoll, New York, 1973, p. 209.

Chapter 11
The Narrow Focus on Greater Food Production

1. Radha Sinha, *Food and Poverty* Holmes and Meier, New York, 1976, p. 7.

2. Cynthia Hewitt de Alcántara, 'A Commentary on the Satisfaction of Basic Needs in Mexico, 1917-1975,' Prepared by the Dag Hammerskjold Foundation, May 7, 1975, pp. 1 and 9.

3. Cynthia Hewitt de Alcántara, 'The Green Revolution as History,' *Development and Change,* 5, 2 1973-1974: 25-26.

4. Hewitt de Alcántara, 'Commentary on the Satisfaction of Basic Needs,' p. 10.

5. Hewitt de Alcántara, 'The Social and Economic Implications of the Large-Scale Introduction of New Varieties of Foodgrains,' *Country Report – Mexico* UNDP/UNRISD, Geneva: 1974, p. 30.

6. Ibid., p. 19.

7. Ibid., p. 156.

8. 'Mexico: Roosting Chickens,' *Latin America* 28 Nov., 1975: 375.

9. Andrew Pearse, 'Social and Economic Implications of the Large-Scale Introduction of New Varieties of Foodgrains,' Part 4, UNDP/UNRISD, pp. XI-19, XI-20.

10. Cited in Keith Griffin, *The Political Economy of Agrarian Change* Harvard University Press, Cambridge, Mass.: 1974, p. 55.

11. Ingrid Palmer, *Science and Agricultural Production* UNRISD Geneva: 1972, pp. 6-7.

12. World Bank, *The Assault on World Poverty – Problems of Rural Development, Education, and Health:* Johns Hopkins University Press, Baltimore, 1975, pp. 132-133.

13. Andrew Pearse, 'Social and Economic Implications of the Large-Scale Introduction of the New Varieties of Foodgrains, Part 2 UNDP/UNRISD, Geneva: 1975, p. II-7.
14. S. Ahmed and S. Abu Khalid, 'Why did Mexican Dwarf Wheat Decline in Pakistan?' *World Crops* 23: 211-215.
15. Charles Elliott, *Patterns of Poverty in the Third World – A Study of Social and Economic Stratification*, New York: Praeger, 1975, pp. 47-48.
16. North London Haslemere, *The Death of the Green Revolution*, Haslemere Declaration Group; London: Third World First, Oxford: p. 4.
17. Victor McElheny, 'Nations Demand Agricultural Aid,' *New York Times*, 3 Aug. 1975, p. 20.
18. Keith Griffin, *The Political Economy of Agrarian Change* Harvard University Press, Cambridge, Mass.: 1974, p. 205.
19. Pearse, 'Social and Economic Implications,' Part I, pp. 111-118.
20. Nicholas Wade, 'Green Revolution I: A Just Technology Often Unjust in Use,' *Science* Dec. 1974: 1093-1096.
21. Pearse, 'Social and Economic Implications,' Part 4, pp. XI-52, XI-53.
22. Pearse, 'Social and Economic Implications,' Part 3, pp. IX-23, IX-24.
23. Palmer, *Science and Agricultural Production*, p. 47.
24. Erich M. Jacoby, *The 'Green Revolution' in China*, UNRISD, Geneva: 1974, p. 6.
25. Food and Agricultural Organization, *Report on China's Agriculture*, prepared by H. V. Henle, 1974, pp. 144-145.

Chapter 12
The Results of the Green Revolution

1. Erna Bennett, Department of Plant Genetics, FAO, Rome, personal communication, April 1976.
2. Francine R. Frankel, 'The Politics of the Green Revolution: Shifting Patterns of Peasant Participation in India and Pakistan,' in *Food, Population, and Employment – The Impact of the Green Revolution*, eds., Thomas T. Poleman and Donald K. Freebairn Praeger, New York, 1973, p. 133.
3. Joan Mencher, 'Conflicts and Contradictions in the "Green Revolution": The Case of Tamil Nadu,' *Economic and Poli-*

tical Weekly 9, nos. 6, 7, 8, February 1974: especially 315.

4. 'Tamil Nadu – Starvation Deaths in a Surplus State, '*Economic and Political Weekly* 10, 22 February 1975: 348.

5. H. P. Singh, 'Plight of Agricultural Labourers. II, A Review,' *Economic Affairs* 16 June 1971: 283.

6. Wolf Ladejinsky, 'Ironies of India's Green Revolution,' *Foreign Affairs* July 1970: 762.

7. Robert d'A. Shaw, 'The Employment Implications of the Green Revolution,' Overseas Development Council Washington, D.C.: 1970, pp. 3-20.

8. A. Eugene Havens and William Flinn, *Green Revolution Technology – Structural Aspects of its Adoption and Consequences* UNRISD, Geneva, 1975, p. 25.

9. Ibid., p. 35.

10. Keith Griffin, *Land Concentration and Rural Poverty*, Macmillan, New York, 1976, p. 74.

11. Cynthia Hewitt de Alcántara, 'Social and Economic Implications of the Large-Scale Introduction of New Varieties of Foodgrains,' *Country Report – Mexico* UNDP/UNRISD, Geneva 1974, p. 148.

12. Gordon Gemmill and Carl K. Eicher, 'A Framework for Research on the Economics of Farm Mechanization in Developing Countries,' African Rural Employment Paper no. 6, African Rural Employment Research Network, Department of Agricultural Economics, Michigan State University, East Lansing, Michigan, 1973, pp. 32-33.

13. Susan George, *How the Other Half Dies*: Penguin, Harmondsworth 1976.

14. Edgar Owens and Robert Shaw, *Development Reconsidered: Bridging the Gap Between Government and People*: Heath, Lexington, Massachusetts, 1972, p. 74.

15. Food and Agriculture Organization, *Agricultural Development and Employment Performance and Planning: A Comparative Analysis*, Agricultural Planning Studies, no. 18, 1974, pp. 100, 102.

16. A. R. Khan, 'Poverty and Inequality in Bangladesh,' pp. 7-36.

17. For further discussion of women's issues, see Mary Roodkowsky and Lisa Leghorn, *Who Really Starves? Women and World Hunger*, Friendship Press, New York, NY, 1977.

18. A. R. Khan, 'Growth and Inequality in the Rural Philippines,' in *Poverty and Landlessness in Rural Asia*, pp. 11-13, 11-24.

19. A. R. Khan, 'Poverty and Inequality in Bangladesh,' in *Poverty and landlessness in Rural Asia,* pp. 7-21, 7-22.

20. E. Lee, 'Rural Poverty in Sri Lanka, 1963-1973,' in *Poverty and Landlessness in Rural Asia,* pp. 8-13.

21. Robert J. Ledogar, *Hungry for Profits: U.S. Food and Drug Multinationals in Latin America,* IDOC/North America Inc., New York, 1975, p. 96.

22. *Ceres,* May-June 1976: 8.

23. Ray Goldberg, *Agribusiness Management for the Developing Countries – Latin America,* Ballinger, Cambridge, Mass, 1974, p. 87.

24. *New York Times,* 3 March 1976, p. 2.

Chapter 13
Undermining the World's Food Security

1. Jon Tinker, 'How the Boran Wereng Did a Red Khmer on the Green Revolution,' *New Scientist* 7 August, 1975: 316.

2. Nicholas Wade, 'Green Revolution (II): Problems of Adapting a Western Technology,' *Science,* 186, 27 December, 1974: 1186-1187.

3. John Prester, 'The Green Revolution Turns Sour,' *Reports,* 7 December, 1974.

4. Andrew Pearse, 'Social and Economic Implications of the Large-Scale Introduction of the New Varieties of Foodgrains,' Part I: UNDP/UNRISD, Geneva, 1975, pp. II-8, II-9.

5. *Des Moines Register,* 17 April, 1974.

6. Ibid.

7. D. H. Timothy and M. M. Goodman, 'Plant Germ Plasm Resources – Future Feast or Famine?' paper, Journal Series of the North Carolina State University Agricultural Experiment Station, cites P. C. Mangelsdorf, *Proceedings of the National Academy of Science* (1966): 56, 370; and H. Garrison Wilkes, 'Too Little Gene Exchange,' letter to the editor of *Science,* 171, 12 March 1971: 955.

8. H. Garrison Wilkes and Susan Wilkes, 'The Green Revolution,' *Environment,* 14 October 1972: 33.

9. Robert A. Ginskey, 'Sowing the Seeds of Disaster?' *The Plain Truth* 61, June 1976: 35, quoting Wilkes.

10. Ibid.

11. Wade, 'Green Revolution' p. 1191.

12. Bettina Conner, 'Seed Monopoly,' *Elements*: Transnational Institute for Policy Studies, Washington, D.C., February 1975.
13. Ibid.
14. Frank B. Viets, Jr., and Samuel R. Aldrich, 'The Sources of Nitrogen for Food and Meat Production,' in *Sources of Nitrogenous Compounds and Methods of Control*, Environmental Protection Agency Monograph, p. 67, 73ff.
15. William Brune, State Conservationist, Soil Conservation Service, 823 Federal Building, Des Moines, Iowa, 50309, testimony before the Senate Committee on Agriculture and Forestry, July 1976.
16. Ramon Garcia, 'Some Aspects on World Fertilizer Production, Consumption and Usage,' paper, University of Iowa, 1975.
17. Swedish International Development Agency and Food and Agriculture Organization, 'Organic Materials as Fertilizers,' Soils Bulletin 27, 1975.

Chapter 14
The Mechanization of Farming

1. Robert d'A. Shaw, *Jobs and Agricultural Development* Washington, D.C.: Overseas Development Council, monograph no. 3, 1970, pp. 34-35.
2. Andrew Pearse, 'Social and Economic Implications of the Large-Scale Introduction of New Varieties of Foodgrains,' Part 3: UNDP/UNRISD, Geneva, 1975, p. IX-12.
3. T. J. Byres, 'The Dialectic of India's Green Revolution,' *South Asian Review* 5, January 1972: 109.
4. Donald K. Freebairn, 'Income Disparities in the Agricultural Sector: Regional and Institutional Stresses,' in *Food, Population, and Employment – The Impact of the Green Revolution*, Thomas Poleman and Donald Freebairn, eds. Praeger, New York: 1973, p. 108.
5. International Labour Office, *Mechanization and Employment in Agriculture*, Geneva, 1974, p. 8.
6. S. R. Bose and E. H. Clark, 'Some Basic Considerations on Agricultural Mechanization in West Pakistan,' *Pakistan Development Review* 9, 3 (Autumn 1969), cited by Owens and Shaw, *Development Reconsidered: Bridging the Gap Between Government and People*: Heath, Lexington, Massachusetts, 1972, p. 62.

7. Randolph Barker et al., 'Employment and Technological Change in Philippine Agriculture,' *International Labour Review* 106, 2-3 August-September 1972: 130.

8. Frank C. Child, and Hiromitsu Kaneda, 'Links to the Green Revolution: A Study of Small-Scale, Agriculturally-Related Industry in the Punjab,' *Economic Development and Cultural Change* 23, 1974: 5.

9. Amir U. Khan and Bart Duff, 'Development of Agricultural Mechanization Technologies at the IRRI (Manila),' paper no. 72-02, mimeographed (International Rice Research Institute), cited in *Mechanization and Employment in Agriculture*, p. 11.

10. Lester Brown, *Seeds of Change*: Praeger, New York, 1970, p. 59.

11. 'Companies – Massey-Ferguson's Success Story,' *Business Week*, 2 February, 1976, pp. 44.

12. *Mechanization and Employment in Agriculture*, p. 11.

13. Keith Griffin, *The Political Economy of Agrarian Change*, Harvard University Press, Cambridge, Mass.: 1974, p. 54.

14. Francine R. Frankel, 'The Politics of the Green Revolution: Shifting Patterns of Peasant Participation in India and Pakistan,' in *Food, Population, and Employment – The Impact of the Green Revolution*, eds., Thomas T. Poleman and Donald K. Freebairn: Praeger, New York, 1973, pp. 132-133.

15. M. Taghi Farvar, 'The Relationship Between Ecological and Social Systems,' Speech delivered to EARTHCARE conference, New York, 6 June, 1975, p. 9.

16. Ma Chu, 'Something on the Side,' *Far Eastern-Economic Review*, 14 April 1978, p. 30.

17. Joseph Hanlon, 'India Back to the Village: Does AT Walk on Plastic Sandals?' *New Scientist*, 26 May, 1977, p. 467ff.

18. *Christian Science Monitor*, 3 August, 1977.

19. Hanlon, 'India Back to the Village,' p. 469.

PART V THE INEFFICIENCY OF INEQUALITY
Chapter 15
The Productivity of Large and Small Farms

1. Edgar Owens and Robert Shaw, *Development Reconsidered: Bridging the Gap Between Government and People*: Heath, Lexington, Mass, 1972, p. 60.

2. World Bank, *The Assault on World Poverty – Problems of*

Rural Development, Education, and Health: Johns Hopkins University Press, Baltimore, 1975, p. 215.

3. Owens and Shaw, *Development Reconsidered*, p. 60.

4. World Bank, *Assault on World Poverty*, pp. 215-216.

5. Food and Agriculture Organization, *Report on the 1960 World Census of Agriculture*, Rome, 1971, cited in *The Assault on World Poverty*, World Bank, The Johns Hopkins University Press, 1975, p. 244.

6. Keith Griffin, *The Political Economy of Agrarian Change*, Harvard University Press, Cambridge, Mass.: 1974, p. 27.

7. World Bank, *Assault on World Poverty*, p. 105.

8. Sudhir Sen, *Reaping the Green Revolution*: Orbis, Maryknoll, New York, p. 11.

9. Griffin, *Political Economy*, p. 28.

10. Keith Griffin, *Land Concentration and Rural Poverty*: Macmillan, New York, 1976, p. 122.

11. International Labour Office, *Poverty and Landlessness in Rural Asia*, A Study by the World Employment Programme, edited by Keith Griffin and Azizur Rahman Khan, 1976, pp. 1-31.

12. Erich Jacoby and Charlotte Jacoby, *Man and Land* Knopf, New York, 1971, p. 79.

13. Hugh Brammer, FAO, Bangladesh, interviewed by Joseph Collins, January, 1978.

14. World Bank, *Assault on World Poverty*, p. 142.

15. Don Paarlberg of USDA, speech before the 55th Annual Convention of Milk Producers, 30 November, 1971.

16. Food and Agriculture Organization, *Agricultural Development and Employment Performance: A Comparative Analysis* Agricultural Planning Studies no. 18, 1974, p. 124.

17. Keith Griffin, *Land Concentration and Rural Poverty* Macmillan, New York, 1976, p. 190.

18. Milton J. Esman, *Landlessness and Near-Landlessness in Developing Countries*, Cornell University, Centre for International Studies, Ithaca, 1978.

Chapter 16
Land Reform Versus Production?

1. Theodore Bergman, *Farm Policies in Socialist Countries*, Lexington Mass.: 1975, pp. 203-204, 206.

2. Food and Agriculture Organization, *Progress in Land Reform – Sixth Report*, Rural Institutions Division, Rome, 1975, pp. III-8; and *Agricultural Problems: Agronomical Data*, Vietnamese Studies, Hanoi, pp. 19-20.

3. Food and Agriculture Organization, *op. cit.*

4. Food and Agriculture Organization, *Production Yearbook*, 1975.

5. Arthur MacEwan, *Agriculture and Development in Cuba*, a manuscript prepared for the International Labour Office, 1978.

6. Bergman, *Farm Policies in Socialist Countries*, p. 225.

7. McEwan, *Agriculture and Development in Cuba*, especially Chapter 16.

8. Bergman, *Farm Policies*, p. 219 and McEwan, *Agriculture and Development*, pp. 16-3.

9. McEwan, *Agriculture and Development*, Parts VI and VII.

10. Wilfred Burchett, 'Portuguese Defend Land Reform,' *Guardian*, 26 April, 1978, p. 24.

11. Leo Orleans, 'The Role of Science and Technology in China's Population – Food Balance,' prepared for the Subcommittee on Domestic and International Scientific Planning, Analysis and Cooperation of the Committee of Science and Technology of the US House of Representatives, September 1977, p. 55.

12. *Agricultural Problems*, pp. 19ff.

PART VI THE TRADE TRAP
Chapter 17
Doing What Comes Naturally

1. Frederick Clairmonte, 'Bananas,' in Payer, *Commodity Trade*, p. 131.

2. Payer, 'Coffee,' in *Commodity Trade*, 156ff.

3. UNDP, 'Changing Factors in World Development,' prepared by Don Casey, (Development Issue Paper 5, Global I,) UNDP, August 1975, p. 2.

4. Payer, 'Coffee,' in *Commodity Trade*, p. 158.

5. UNCTAD, 'Marketing and Distribution System for Cocoa,' (Report by the Secretariat), January 1975, p. 9.

6. Ibid., p. 6.

7. Payer, *Commodity Trade*, p. 185.

8. David Andelman, 'Malaysian Land Plan Thriving, but Snags Arise,' *New York Times*, 4 September 1976.

Chapter 18
The Losers

1. Susanne Jones and David Tobias, eds., *Guatemala*, North American Congress on Latin America, New York and Berkeley, 1974, pp. 9, 16.
2. Gamini Navaratne, 'Tea,' *New Internationalist*, April 1976: 11.
3. Thierry Brun, 'Démystifier la famine,' *Cahiers de Nutrition et de Dietique* 9 (2): 115, no date.
4. UNCTAD, 'Report of Intergovernmental Group on Least Developed Countries,' Geneva, 1975, p. 43.
5. Donal B. Cruise O'Brien, 'Cooperators and Bureaucrats: Class Formation in a Senegalese Society,'*Africa*, Journal of the International African Institute, 61, October 1972, 273.
6. UNCTAD, 'Marketing and Distribution System for Cocoa,' Report of the Secretariat, January 1975, p. 34.
7. Derek Byerlee and Carl K. Eicher, 'Rural Employment, Migration and Economic Development: Theoretical Issues and Empirical Evidence from Africa,' African Rural Employment Study, paper no. 1, Department of Agricultural Economics, State University, East Lansing, Mich., September 1972, pp. 13-14.
8. Ingrid Palmer, *Food and the New Agricultural Technology*, UNRISD, Geneva, 1972, p. 53.
9. Uma Lele, 'A Conceptual Framework for Rural Development,' presented to the Development from Below Workshop, the Association for the Advancement of Agricultural Sciences in Africa (AAASA), October 1973, pp. 8-9.
10. *Latin America* 10, 22 October 1976: 326.

Chapter 19
The Winners

1. Walter Hink, 'Mobutu on Tightrope as Crisis Hits Zaire,' *African Development* (September 1975): 48
2. United Nations Economic and Social Council Preparatory Committee for the Special Session of the General Assembly

Devoted to Development and International Cooperation, Second Session, 16-27 June 1975 (E/AC. 621/8) 5 May, 1975, p. 7.

3. Cheryl Payer, ed., *Commodity Trade in the Third World*, Wiley, New York, 1975, pp. 180, 184.

4. Gamini Navaratne, 'Tea,' *New Internationalist* (April 1976): 11.

5. Robert Shaplen, Letter from Manila, *The New Yorker*, 3 May, 1976, p. 92.

6. David Feldman and Peter Lawrence, 'Global II Project on the Economic and Social Implications of Large Scale Introduction of New Varieties of Food grains,' Africa Report, UNDP/UNRISD, Geneva, 1975, p. 52.

7. Peter Dorner, 'Export Agriculture and Economic Development,' Land Tenure Center. University of Wisconsin, Madison, statement before the Interfaith Center on Corporate Responsibility, New York, 14 September 1976, p. 6.

8. Keith Griffin, *The Political Concentration and Rural Poverty*, Macmillan, New York, p. 162.

9. Keith Griffin, *The Political Economy of Agrarian Change*, Harvard University Press, Cambridge, Mass., 1974, p. 105.

10. P. L. Raikes, 'Ujamaa and Rural Socialism,' *Review of African Political Economy*, May-October 1974: 36.

11. Cheryl Payer, *The Debt Trap – The IMF and the Third World* Penguin, 1974.

Chapter 20

Changing the Game

1. Interview conducted by Joseph Collins with US AID Mission, Santo Domingo, Dominican Republic, 26 November, 1976.

2. Arthur MacEwan, *Agriculture and Development in Cuba*, manuscript prepared for the International Labour Organization, 1978, Chapter 27, p. 2.

3. Pedro Alvarez Tabio, ed., *The Overall Situation of the Cuban Economy*, Instituto Cubano de Deportes, Havana, September 1975, 39ff.

4. Ibid., 2ff.

PART VIII THE MYTH OF FOOD POWER
Chapter 21
Bountiful Uncle Sam

1. The following comparisons regarding MSA countries are calculated from US Department of Agriculture, *Foreign Agriculture Trade Statistical Report*, Calendar Year 1974, May 1975.
2. Calculated from Food and Agriculture Organization, *Production Yearbook*, 1974, and *Yearbook of International Trade statistics*, 1974.
3. Calculated from US Department of Agriculture, *Foreign Agricultural Trade Statistical Report*, Calendar Year 1974.
4. Calculated from *Yearbook of International Trade Statistics*, 1974.

Chapter 22
The American Drive for Food Power

1. Richard Bell, Assistant Secretary for International Affairs and Commodity Programs, USDA, cited by Norman Faramelli, 'A Primer for Church Groups on Agribusiness and the World Food Crises,' Boston Industrial Mission, Boston, Mass., 1975.
2. *New York Times*, 19 August 1975, p. 16.
3. *Feedstuffs* 47, 8 September 1975: 4.
4. Richard Barnet and Ronald Mueller, *Global Reach: The Power of the Multinational Corporation*, Simon and Schuster, New York, 1973, p. 266.
5. United States Commerce Department, *Guide to Foreign Trade Statistics*, Government Printing Office, Washington DC: June, 1978.
6. North American Congress on Latin America (NACLA), 'U.S. Grain Arsenal,' *NACLA Report* 9, 7 October 1975, p. 4.
7. Commission on International Trade and Investment Policy, *United States International Economic Policy in an Interdependent World*, report to the President, Washington DC, July, 1971.
8. U.S. Department of Agriculture, *Foreign Agricultural Trade Statistical Report*, Fiscal Year 1971 and Fiscal Year 1974, Table 10.
9. Jimmy Minyard, 'Market Development Looks Ahead to New Markets and Programs,' also Darwin Stolte, 'Team Effort

Boosts U.S. Farm Exports,' *Foreign Agriculture* 13, 26 May 1975: 6, 9.

10. C. W. McMillan, 'Meat Export Federation to be Newest Cooperator,' *Foreign Agriculture* 13, 26 May 1975: 14. 14.

11. Philip B. Dwoskin and Nick Havas, 'Fast Foods in Japan – A Billion Dollar Industry?' *Foreign Agriculture* 13, 26 May 1975: 33.

12. William K. Chung, 'Sales by Majority-Owned Foreign Affiliates of U.S. Companies, 1976,' *Survey of Current Business*, March 1978, vol. 58 no. 3.

13. William Robbins, *The American Food Scandal – Why You Can't Eat Well on What you Earn*, Morrow, New York, 1974, p. 185.

14. Jim Hightower, *Eat Your Heart Out: How Food Profiteers Victimize the Consumer*, Crown, New York, 1975, p. 194.

15. Dan Morgan, *Washington Post*, January 2, 3, 1976, p. A5.

16. U.S. General Accounting Office, *Exporters' Profits on Sales of U.S. Wheat to Russia*, B-176943, 12 February 1974, 15ff.

17. Hightower, *Eat Your Heart Out*, p. 194.

18. Steven Bennett, 'U.S. Food Policy for Whom?' *Center Survey* 4 (1): 6, Center of Concern, Washington, D.C.

19. Cliff Connor, 'U.S. Agribusiness and World Famine,' *International Socialist Review*, September 1974, quoting James McHale, Secretary of Agriculture for the State of Pennsylvania.

20. Lawrence A. Mayer, 'We Can't Take Food for Granted Anymore,' *Fortune*, February 1974, p. 86.

21. Morgan, *Washington Post*, 2 January, 1976.

22. *The NFO Reporter*, Corning, Iowa, January 1978, p. 9.

23. James Flanigan, 'Question for Congress,' *Forbes*, 1 May 1978, p. 36.

24. Calculated from US Department of Agriculture, *Farm Income Statistics*, Annual Statistical Bulletin 557, Table 3D, July 1976, p. 60.

25. Ibid., Table 4D, 61.

26. Ibid., Tables 1D-4D.

27. *Time*, 24 October, 1977, p. 28.

28. Ibid.

29. *Forbes*, pp. 35, 40.

30. *Business Week*, 27 March, 1978, p. 79.

31. US Department of Agriculture, *Farmland Tenure Patterns in the United States*, USDA/ERS, February 1974, p. 3.
32. *Ag World*, 4, 3, March 1978: 13.
33. Don Paarlberg quoted in *Feedstuffs*, 16 August 1976, p. 10.
34. US Department of Agriculture, *The One-Man Farm*, prepared by Warren Bailey, USDA/ERS-519, August, 1973.
35. Calculated from *Farm Income Statistics*, Statistical Bulletin no. 547, Table 3D, USDA/ERS, July 1975, p. 60, and 'The Balance Sheet of the Farming Sector, By Value of Sales Class, 1960-1973,' supplement no. 1, *Agricultural Information Bulletin* no. 376, Table 2, USDA/ERS, Washington, D.C.: Government Printing Office, April 1975, p. 3.
36. Walter Goldschmidt, 'A Tale of Two Towns,' in *The People's Land*, Peter Barnes, ed., Emmaus, Pa: Rodale Press, 1975, 171 ff.

Chapter 23
Multinational Food Companies and Feeding the Hungry

1. George L. Baker, 'Good Climate for Agribusiness,' *The Nation*, 5 November, 1973, p. 460; NACLA, *Bitter Fruits*, September 1976, *Latin America and Empire Report*, 12ff.
2. Baker, 'Good Climate for Agribusiness,' p. 460.
3. 'Poverty in American Democracy: A study of Social Power,' US Catholic Conference, November 1974, cited in CNI *Weekly Report*, Community Nutrition Institute, Washington, D.C., 2 September 1976, p. 8.
4. Baker, *'Good Climate for Agribusiness.'*
5. Ernest Feder, 'The Penetration of the Agricultures of the Underdeveloped Countries by the Industrial Nations and Their Multinational Corporations,' Institute of Social Studies, The Hague, 1975, p. 8.
6. For commodity breakdowns see Ray Goldberg, *Agribusiness Management for Developing Countries – Latin America* (Cambridge, Mass.: Ballinger, 1974), 69ff. Calculations based on Goldberg, *Agribusiness Management*, Chapter 2; and US Department of Agriculture, *Foreign Agricultural Trade Statistical Report Fiscal Year 1975* (Washington, D.C.: Governmental Printing Office, 1975, 1976).
7. Cited by Goldberg, *Agribusiness Management*, p. 70.
8. Ibid., p. 70.

9. Ibid., 150ff. gives some figures. See also Food and Agricultural Organization, *Production Yearbooks*.

10. Ernest Feder, *Strawberry Imperialism: An Enquiry into the Mechanisms of Dependency in Mexican Agriculture*, Institute of Social Studies, The Hague: 1978.

11. Goldberg, *Agribusiness Management*, p. 147.

12. Ibid., p. 150.

13. Ibid., p. 87.

14. Ernest Feder, *Strawberry Imperialism*; unless otherwise noted, the facts on the strawberry industry in Mexico are drawn from Dr Feder's comprehensive documentation.

15. Unless otherwise noted, the sources for the analysis of Bud Senegal are: Kees Pels, 'Stijgende invoer van Afrikaanse groenten,' 1975; Jan Bunnik, 'Bud maakt Senegal groen,' *Vakblad voor groothandel in aardappelen, groeten en fruit*, February 6 and 13, 1975, pp. 11-15 and pp. 13-16; transcript of KRO (Netherlands) televised documentary 3 March 1975; 'Une remarquable reussite,' *Senegal 1960-1973: 14 ans de développement;* 'De situatie in Senegal,' *Landbouw Wereldnieuws*, 15 October 1974, 'Liefermoeglichkeiten Senegals,' *Mitteilungen der Bundesstelle feur Aussenhandelsinformation*, July 1974, 1ff.; and personal communication from Maureen M. Mackintosh, The Institute of Development Studies, completing a study of Bud Senegal, dated 5 October 1976.

16. International Finance Corporation, IFC T162, Appraised Report for Bud Senegal, 24 February 1976.

17. Lars Bondestam, 'Notes on Foreign Investments in Ethiopia,' in *Multinational Firms in Africa*, Carl Widstrand and Samir Amin, eds. Scandinavian Institute for African Studies, Uppsala: 1975), 139ff. The interview referred to is in SIDA-*rapport*, no. 8, Stockholm, 1972.

18. Bondestam, 'Notes on Foreign Investments.'

19. Alan Berg, *The Nutrition Factor: Its Role in National Development*, The Brookings Institution Washington, D.C.: 1973, p. 65.

20. *Wall Street Journal*, 27 July, 1972 and 7 January, 1970.

21. José da Veiga, 'Quand les multinationales font du Ranching,' *Le Monde Diplomatique*, September 1975, p. 13.

22. *New York Times*, 4 July 1972.

23. We are greatly indebted to the excellent study of Ralston Purina in Columbia researched by Rick Edwards and largely

forming Chapter 6 in Robert J. Ledogar, *Hungry for Profits: U.S. Food and Drug Multinationals in Latin America* (New York: IDOC, 1976). Unless otherwise noted, data on Ralston Purina in Columbia comes from this study.

24. Giovanni Acciarri, et al. 'Production Agropecuaria y Desnutricion en Colombia,' Universidad del Valle, Division de Ingenieria, Cali: 1973.

25. Ibid.

26. Calculations are based on figures in the US, Department of Agriculture, *U.S. Foreign Agricultural Trade Statistical Report, Fiscal Year, 1975*.

27. Interview with Gabriel Misas, DANE (National Department of Statistics) Bogotá, Columbia, 30 April 1973, confirmed as 'more or less correct' by the Embassy of Columbia in Washington, D.C., 14 January 1974.

28. A helpful source of data, largely compiled from US government statistics, can be found in Appendix J in Ray A. Goldberg, *Agribusiness Management*, pp. 359-374.

29. Overseas Private Investment Corporation, Annual Report, 1973.

30. Calculation taken from Henry Frundt, *American Agribusiness and U.S. Foreign Agricultural Policy PhD dissertation*, Rutgers University, May 1975.

31. Jane's *Major Companies of Europe* 1977

32. Susan George in *Economic and Political Weekly* (Bombay),

33. Ibid., Vol. XIII No. 37, pp. 159ff.

34. Ibid.

35. Nestlé Bulletin No. 20, International Union of Food and Allied Workers, Geneva.

36. UK Prices Commission Report No. 24 'Coffee' 1977. HMSO.

37. Nestlé Bulletin no. 20 op. cit.

38. Ibid.

39. Unless otherwise noted, the data in this section is from Susanne Jonas and David Tobias, *Guatemala*, NACLA, P.O. Box 226, Berkeley, Calif. pp. 127-131.

40. 'Bitter Fruits,' *Latin American and Empire Report*, NACLA, 10, September 1976: 30.

41. UNCTAD, *The Marketing and Distribution System for Bananas*, 24 December 1974, p. 24.

42. *Business Week*, 18 January 1969, p. 54.

43. Consultation with agroindustrial leaders in preparation for the

UN World Food Conference, September 10-11, 1974, Toronto, Canada.

44. *The Times,* 4 May 1973.

45. *Source for People* No. 34, 1976.

46. Hightower, *Eat Your Heart Out,* p. 165.

47. US Department of Agriculture, *Packers and Stockyards Administration,* prepared by Marvin L. McLain, 14 May 1974, p. 28.

48. Cited by Susan De Marco and Susan Sechler, *The Fields Have Turned Brown – Four Essays on World Hunger,* The Agribusiness Accountability Project, Washington, D.C., 1975, 73ff.

49. Harrison Welford, *Sowing the Wind* (New York: Grossman, 1972), 101ff.

50. Hightower, *Eat Your Heart Out,* p. 168. See also US Department of Agriculture, 'The Broiler Industry,' *Packers and Stockyards Administration* August 1967.

51. ABC-Television News, 'Food: Green Grow the Profits,' documentary, 21 December 1973, transcript, 46ff.

52. Vincent G. Cullen, 'Sour Pineapples,' *America* (6 November 1976): 300ff.

53. Liberation News Service, 22 June 1974.

54. Ismail A. Jami, 'Land Reform and Modernization of Farming Structure in Iran,' *Institute of Agricultural Economy* (no. 2, December 1973: 118-121. See also Julian Bharier, *Economic Development of Iran, 1900 – 1970,* Oxford University Press, London: 1971, especially p. 138.

55. *Agriculture and Agribusiness in Iran: Investment Opportunities* Paul R. Walter & Associates, Inc, New York: March 1975, p. 39. Also, much information was obtained through correspondence with two Iranian economists who, for reasons of their personal safety, have asked to remain anonymous. Also helpful was an interview with John Tobey, a senior investment officer to the Chase Manhattan Bank, 16 July 1975.

56. Frances Fitzgerald, 'Giving the Shah Everything He Wants,' *Harper's* November 1974, p. 55.

57. *International Agribusiness,* published by Hawaiian Agronomics (a subsidiary of C. Brewer and Company), Winter 1975, p. 3.

58. 'How Iran Spends Its New Found Riches,' *Business Week,* 22 June 1974.

59. Presentation by CPC International at the World Food System

Symposium, University of California, Berkeley, September 17-19, 1975. All quotes in this section are from this case presentation by CPC International.

Chapter 24
Changing Traditional Diets

1. See Frances Moore Lappé, *Diet for a Small Planet*, Ballantine Books, New York, revised edition, 1975.
2. *Business Week*, 1 December 1973, p. 89.
3. Joseph M. Winski, 'Back-to-Basics Trend,' *Wall Street Journal*, 29 May 1975, pp. 1, 25. See also Peter T. Kilborn, 'Food Industry Finds Shoppers' Tastes Are Changing,' *New York Times*, 28 April 1975, pp. 45, 49.
4. International Union of Food and Allied Workers Association Conference of Workers in the Dairy Industry, Geneva 1974.
5. Report of a survey in UK, Hairy and Schaller, Institut National de la Recherche Agronomique, Paris, December 1975.
6. Ibid.
7. Ibid.
8. 'Our Daily Bread,' Agricultural Group BSSRS 1978.
9. Media Expenditure Analysis Ltd. (Meal) 1977.
10. 'Our Daily Bread,' op. cit.
11. Peter Drucker, *The Age of Discontinuity*, Harper and Row, New York, 1969, p. 107.
12. *Food Processing and Packing Machinery and Equipment:* Mexico Office of International Trade Promotion, April 1971.
13. Andre van Dam, 'El Futuro de la Industria Alimenticia en America Latina,' speech delivered in Porto Alegre, 14 May, 1975.
14. *Financial Times*, 9 March 1973 quoted in CIS Anti-Report 11 'Unilever's World.'
15. Thomas Horst, *At Home Abroad*: Ballinger, Cambridge, Mass. 1974.
16. W. R. Grace and Co., *Annual Report*, 1969.
17. Quotations are from David F. Hawkins and Derek A. Newton, *Case Study on General Foods Corporation* Harvard Business School course materials, 1964.
18. Horst, *At Home Abroad*, p. 127.
19. Federal Trade Commission, 'Structure of Food Manufacturing,'

Technical Study, no. 8 Washington, D.C.: Government Printing Office, June 1966, p. 80.

20. Chris Wardle, *Changing Food Habits in the UK*. Resources Research Publication 1977.

21. *Guardian*, 31 December 1975.

22. Cited Hightower, *Eat Your Heart Out*, p. 52.

23. Federal Trade Commission, 'Structure of Food Manufacturing,' p. 81, n. 33.

24. Media Expenditure Analysis Ltd (MEAL) Monthly Digests, 1973, quoted in *Changing Food Habits in the UK*.

25. Robert J. Ledogar, *Hungry for Profits: U.S. Food and Drug Multinationals in Latin America*: IDOC, New York, 1976, 111ff.

26. We gratefully acknowledge the research on General Foods as coming from Henry Frundt, *American Agribusiness and U.S. Foreign Policy*, PhD dissertation, Rutgers University, 1975, especially pp. 194-198.

27. 'Insult or Injury?' Charles Medawar, Social Audit 1979.

28. We gratefully acknowledge much of the research for this section as that of Bernardo Kucinski, carried out for Robert Ledogar, *Hungry for Profits*, pp. 111-127. While the analysis may differ, the facts, unless otherwise noted, are from this source.

29. Cited by Richard Barnet and Ronald Mueller, *Global Reach* Simon and Schuster, New York, 1974, 183ff.

30. Letter to Robert Ledogar from Rev Crisoforo Florencio, parish priest of Olinala, Guerrero, Mexico, June 1974, cited by Robert Ledogar, *Hungry for Profits*, p. 113.

31. *Economic and Political Weekly* 4, 24 May 1969, 890ff.

32. Ibid.

33. Quoted in *Forbes*, 15 November, 1968.

34. Alan Berg, 'Industry's Struggle with World Malnutrition,' *Harvard Business Review* 50 January-February 1972, 135.

Chapter 25
The Baby Food Scandal

1. Roy J. Harris, Jr, 'The Baby Bust,' *Wall Street Journal*, 4 January, 1972; 'The Bad News in Babyland,' *Dun's Review* 100, December 1972: 104.

2. Mike Muller, *The Baby Killer*, pamphlet, War on Want,

London, 1975; 467 Caledonian Rd. Contains extensive references and bibliography.

3. Ruth Rice Puffer and Carlos V. Serrano, *Patterns of Mortality in Childhood*, Scientific Publication, no. 262: Pan American Health Organization, 1973, Washington, D.C., p. 161.

4. William A. M. Cutting, *The Lancet* 7870, 29 June, 1974: 1340, citing J. B. Wyon and J. E. Gordon, *The Khanna Study* Harvard University Press, Cambridge, Mass. 1971, p. 187.

5. Alan Berg, *The Nutrition Factor*, Washington, D.C.: The Brookings Institution, 1973, p. 95, citing D. S. McLaren, in *The Lancet* 7461, 27 August, 1966: 485.

6. Derrick B. Jelliffe and E. F. Patrice Jelliffe, 'An Overview,' in *The Uniqueness of Human Milk*, symposium reprinted from *The American Journal of Clinical Nutrition* 24 August, 1971.

7. *Times* London, 29, June, 1974.

8. Paul Gyorgy, 'Biochemical Aspects of Human Milk,' *The American Journal of Clinical Nutrition* 24 August, 1971: 970.

9. Hugh Jolly, 'Why Breast Feeding Is Food for Mother and Baby,' *Times*, London, 26 March, 1975.

10. Michael C. Latham, 'Introduction,' in *The Promotion of Bottle Feeding by Multinational Corporations: How Advertising and the Health Professions Have Contributed*, Ted Greiner, ed. Ithaca, N.Y.: Cornell University Monograph Series, no. 2, 1975, iiff.

11. Data from affidavit submitted for *Sisters of the Precious Blood, Inc.* vs. *Bristol Myers Co*, US District Court, Southern District of New York, 1976. See also V. G. James, 'Household Expenditure on Food and Drink by Income Groups,' paper delivered at Seminar on National Food and Nutrition Policy of Jamaica, Kingston, May 27-31, 1974 and Latham, 'Introduction,' p. ii.

12. The National Food and Nutrition Survey of Barbados, Scientific Publication, no. 237: Pan American Health Organization, Washington, D.C., 1972, cited Robert J. Ledogar, *Hungry for Profits: US Food and Drug Multinationals in Latin America*, IDOC, New York, 1976, 130ff.

13. This and the next example are from Muller, *The Baby Killer*, p. 7.

14. Ibid, p. 6.

15. Ibid.

16. Ibid.

17. *Report of an Ad-Hoc Committee on Young Child Feeding*, United Nations Protein Advisory Group, New York, 1971.

18. Ledogar, *Hungry for Profits*, p. 132, cites M. D. Samsudin, et al, 'Rational Use of Skim Milk in a Complete Infant Formula,' *The American Journal of Clinical Nutrition* 20, 1967: 1304; and John McKigney, 'Economic Aspects,' in *The Uniqueness of Human Milk*, p. 1009.

19. David O. Cox, 'Economics of Feeding Infants and Young Children in Developing Countries,' paper presented at the UN Protein Advisory Group Ad-Hoc Working Group meeting, Geneva, December 11-13, 1972.

20. Muller, *The Baby Killer*, 11ff.

21. *New York Times*, 14 September, 1975.

22. This and more extensive information on milk banks can be found in Ledogar, *Hungry for Profits*, 138ff.

23. *New Internationalist*, no. 7, September 1973, p. 2.

24. From various company promotion, all books cited and noted in Ledogar, *Hungry for Profits*, 133ff.

25. Ibid, p. 135.

26. *The Womanly Art of Breast Feeding*, Souvenir Press, 1975, p. 54.

27. Information obtained from Leah Margulies, Interfaith Centre on Corporate Responsibility, New York.

28. Alan Berg, 'The Economics of Breast-Feeding,' *The Saturday Review of the Sciences* 1, May 1973: 30.

29. *New Internationalist*, March 1975.

30. Ibid.

31. *Development Forum*, July-August 1976, Geneva: United Nations, Council for Economic and Social Information.

PART IX THE HELPING HANDOUT; AID FOR WHOM?
Chapter 26
Triage

1. Radha Sinha, *Food and Poverty*: Holmes and Meier, New York, 1976, p. 8.

Chapter 27
The Debt Trap

1. Howard M. Wachtel, *The New Gnomes: Multinational Banks*

in the Third World: Transnational Institute, Washington, D.C.: 1977, p. 11.

2. UNCTAD, *Money and Finance and Transfer of Real Resources for Development*, International Financial Co-operation for Development (Report by the UNCTAD Secretariat, TD/188/Supplement), February 1976, p. 32.

3. 'What one hand giveth . . .', *International Bulletin*, 22 May, 1978, p. 7.

4. UNCTAD, *Debt Problems in the Context of Development* Report by the Secretariat, 1974, pp. 1, 16.

5. Marcel Barang, 'Latest Theories Tested Here,' *Far Eastern Economic Review*, 19 May, 1978: 30.

Chapter 28
The World Bank's 'Assault On Poverty'?

1. Communication from Allison B. Herrick, State Department, Office of Planning and Budget, dated 24 February, 1978.

2. We are greatly appreciative of the paper 'Development vs the World System: A Model Policy Planning Country Study of Peru,' prepared by development consultant Guy Gran, Washington: AID, March 1978. It catalysed for us the discussion here of World Bank appraisal reports.

3. World Bank, *Rural Development: Sector Policy Paper*, Washington, D.C., February 1975, p. 18.

4. Committee on Government Affairs, 'U.S. Participation in the Multilateral Development Banks,' United States Senate, April, 1979, p. 9.

5. Betsy Hartmann and James Boyce, *Bangladesh: Aid to the Needy?* Center for International Policy, Washington D.C., June 1978.

6. Hartmann and Boyce, ibid., p. 7.

7. Per-Arne Stroberg, 'Water and Development: Organizational Aspects of a Tubewell Irrigation Project in Bangladesh,' Dacca, March 1977, pp. 80-81.

8. Hartmann and Boyce, *Aid to the Needy?* p. 7.

9. IDA News Release, no. 76/22, May 24, 1976.

10. Stroberg, 'Water and Development,' p. 82.

11. Interview with Hugh Brammer, FAO, Dacca, 25 January, 1978, conducted by Joseph Collins.

12. Interview with Errik Jansen, Dacca, 26 January, 1978, conducted by Joseph Collins.

13. World Bank, *Rural Development: Sector Policy Paper*, p. 40.

14. Speech by President Robert McNamara to the World Bank Board of Governors, Nairobi, Kenya, 1973.

15. World Bank, *Assault on World Poverty*, Johns Hopkins University Press, Baltimore, 1975, pp. 106, 118.

16. Ibid., p. 194.

17. Ibid., pp. 154-155.

18. Ibid., pp. 159-160.

19. Hartmann and Boyce, *Aid to the Needy?* p. 75.

20. 'Letter from London,' *Far Eastern Economic Review*, 7, February, 1975.

21. World Bank, *Assault on World Poverty*, p. 143.

22. Ibid., p. 143.

23. World Bank *Annual Report*, 1978, pp. 72-79.

24. World Bank, *Assault on World Poverty*, p. 125.

25. World Bank Annual Report, 1978, p. 28.

26. Uma Lele, *The Design of Rural Development*, A World Bank Research Publication, Johns Hopkins University Press, Baltimore, pp. 204ff.

27. Barry Newman, 'In Indonesia, Attempts by World Bank to Aid Poor Often Go Astray,' *Wall Street Journal*, 19 November, 1977, p. 1.

28. We have received various communications (some anonymous) from Indonesia on the peasants' resistance to the imposition of this World Bank project. One is an internal World Bank document (C18700/J23823/D2168 Annex 1).

29. World Bank internal document (C18700/J23823/D2168), especially pp. 51ff.

30. World Bank, *Assault on World Poverty*, pp. 139-140.

31. Newman, 'In Indonesia.'

32. Cyrus Vance, 'Foreign Assistance and U.S. Foreign Policy,' US Department of State, Office of Public Information, 1 May, 1978, p. 2.

33. World Bank, *Thailand: Appraisal of the National Agricultural Extension Project*, Report no. 1256a-TH, 10 March, 1977.

34. World Bank, *Policy and Operations: The World Bank Group*, September 1974, pp. 12ff.

35. World Bank, *Zaire – Appraisal of the Oil Palm Project*. Report no. 1407-ZR and P-2296-ZR, March 29 and April 3,

unpublished. See also Guy Gran, 'Zaire 1978: The Ethical and Intellectual Bankruptcy of the World System,' *Africa Today*, Vol. 25, No. 4, Oct.-Dec., 1978.

36. Ibid.
37. Ibid.
38. World Bank, document cited by Susan George, *How the Other Half Dies*, Penguin, Harmondsworth, 1976, p. 260.
39. Paul Boucher, in the *Guardian*, 12 June, 1975, cited in Susan George, op. cit.
40. 'World Bank Sets $2.9 Billion in Loans to Human Rights Violators for Fiscal Year 1979,' a research study published by Center for International Policy. Washington, D.C., 1978, p. 2.
41. Hon Tom Harkin, 'Human Rights and International Financial Institutions,' *Congressional Record*, 7 September, 1978, p. E4847.
42. World Bank, *Annual Report*, 1978, pp. 26f.
43. Hon Tom Harkin, 'Human Rights and International Financial Institutions,' p. E4848.
44. Geoffrey Barraclough, 'The Struggle for the Third World,' *New York Review of Books*, 9 November, 1978, pp. 47-49.
45. Howard M. Wachtel, *The New Gnomes: Multinational Banks in the Third World* (Washington, D.C.: Transnational Institute, 1977), p. 39.
46. *Manchester Guardian Weekly*, 11 June, 1978.
47. *The Washington Post*, 19, May 1978.
48. Guy Gran, 'Zaire 1978,' a paper presented at 21st Annual Meeting, African Studies Association, 4 November, 1978, unpublished.
49. World Bank, *Annual Report*, 1978, Appendix F, p. 147.

Chapter 29
The Value of Food Aid
1. EEC Background Report 'Food Aid' 11 March, 1978.
2. European Commission COM (76) 452 Final 1976.
3. European Parliament working document 492/77. 19 January, 1978.
4. *Financial Times* 21 February, 1978.
5. *Senegal en Chiffres* Dakar 1976.
6. *Financial Times* 7 January, 1976; 2 March, 1976.

7. European Commission COM (77) 161 final.
8. Study of EEC Food Aid – Institute of Social and Economic Research of Underdeveloped areas – Amsterdam.
9. UN Food Conference document E/conf. 65/3.
10. *Food Aid – a Curate's Egg.* Chris Stevens, Overseas Development Institute, 1979.
11. Report of bottle feeding. Ted Greiner, Cornell University.
12. *The Observer* 27 June, 1976, reporting Dr David Morley (Tropical Pediologist).
13. *Operation Flood – A Study.* National Dairy Development Board, India, 1976.
14. Letter from Chief of News Unit 5 March, 1974.
15. *Sunday Times* 4 January, 1976.
16. Annual Report of National Dairy Development Board 1977/78.
17. Dairy Industries International August 1976.
18. Dairy Industries International November 1974.
19. *Ibid.*
20. *The Times* 6 May, 1977.
21. John McClung, 'Dr Spitzer Views Food Resources as Tool in Defending Nation's System,' *Feedstuffs* 8 December, 1975: 7.
22. Betsy Hartmann and James Boyce, *Bangladesh: Aid to the Needy?* Center for International Policy, Washington, D.C., June, 1978.
23. Donald F. McHenry and Kai Bird, 'Food Bungle in Bangladesh,' *Foreign Policy*, Summer 1977, p. 74.
24. *Bangladesh: Food Policy Review,* World Bank, 12 December, 1977, p. 39.
25. McHenry and Bird, *Food Bungle in Bangladesh.*
26. *Bangladesh: Food Policy Review,* op. cit.
27. Cited by McHenry and Bird, *Food Bungle in Bangladesh,* p. 75.
28. Communication on file Dec. 1977.
29. Cited by McHenry and Bird, *Food Bungle in Bangladesh,* p. 78.
30. Cited in *Far Eastern Economic Review,* 19 May, 1978, p. 35.
31. F. Thomasson Jannuzi and James T. Peach, *Report on the Hierarchy of Interests In Land in Bangladesh* UNSAID, September 1977, p. 88.
32. W. L. Clayton, Assistant Secretary of State, US Congress, House of Representatives, *Hearings on House of Representa-*

tives 2211, Bretton Woods Agreement Act, Committee on Banking and Currency, 79th Congress, 1st Session, 9 March, 1945, pp. 275, 282, cited by Michael Hudson in *Super-Imperialism – The Economic Strategy of American Empire* Holt, Reinhart and Winston, New York, 1972, pp. 92-93.

33. 'U.S. Grain Arsenal,' Latin America and Empire Report, North American Congress on Latin America (NACLA) 9, 7 October 1975, p. 9.

34. Dan Morgan, 'Opening Markets: Program Pushes U.S. Food,' *Washington Post*, 10 March, 1975.

35. Dan Morgan, 'Impact on U.S. Food Heavy on South Korea,' *Washington Post*, 12 March, 1975.

36. North American Congress on Latin America, (NACLA) interview with George Shanklin, Assistant Administrator, Commercial Export Programs, 'U.S. Grain Arsenal,' *NACLA Reports*, October 1975, p. 23.

37. Arthur Mead, 'PL 480 – Humanitarian Effort Helps Develop Markets,' *Foreign Agriculture* (USDA) 13, 26 May, 1975: 29.

38. Dan Morgan 'Self-Interest, Markets Bedevil World Food Aid,' *Washington Post* 5 July, 1975.

39. Kim Changsoo, 'Korean Farmers Betrayed,' *New Asia News* 25 Nov, 1977, Tokyo.

40. Loren Fessler, 'Population and Food Production in South Korea,' *Fieldstaff Reports* XXII, 2, East Asia Series, American University.

41. Morgan, 'Impact on U.S. Food Heavy on South Korea.'

42. Leonard Dudley and Roger Sandilands, 'The Side Effects of Foreign Aid: The Case of P.L. 480 Wheat in Colombia,' *Economic Development and Cultural Change* January 1975: 321.

43. Ibid., pp. 331, 332.

44. Melvin Burke, 'Does "Food for Peace" Assistance Damage the Bolivian Economy?' *Inter-American Economic Affairs* 25 1971: 9, 17.

45. J. S. Mann, 'The Impact of Public Law 480 on Prices and Domestic Supply of Cereals in India,' *Journal of Farm Economics* 49, February 1969: 143.

46. US General Accounting Office, *Disincentives to Agricultural Production in Developing Countries*, Report to the Congress, 26 November, 1975, p. 25.

47. We are grateful to William Ruddell and Roland Bunch for interviews, August 1977, Antigua, Guatemala.
48. Pierre Spitz, 'L'Arme de l'Aide Alimentaire: Les Années d'Apprentissage 1917-1947,' *Critiques de l'Economie Politique* January-March 1974.
49. Pierre Spitz, 'Les aides alimentaires, techniques et culturelles dans la politique agricole des Etats-unis en Inde depuis la défaite du Koumintang.' *'Monde et Developpement'*, no. 4, Paris 1973.
50. Hubert Humphrey, testimony before the Senate Committee on Foreign Relations, 1959.
51. US Aid, *U.S. Overseas Loans and Grants and Obligations from International Organizations: Obligation and Loan Authorizations*, 1 July, 1945 – 30 June, 1973, Office of Financial Management.
52. *Washington Post*, October 26, 1974, p.7.
53. North American Congress on Latin America, p. 13.
54. Ibid., p. 14.
55. Morgan, 'Impact of U.S. Food on South Korea.'
56. North American Congress on Latin America, p. 14.
57. Editorial, *The New Republic*, 7 December, 1974.

Chapter 30
Working Toward Food Self-Reliance

1. 'The Struggle for Self-Reliance in Asia Today,' Pan Asian Assembly, May 1976, published by the World Student Christian Federation and the International Movement of Catholic Students Asia Region, PO Box 11 – 1473, Bangkok, Thailand, p. 8.
2. Joseph B. W. Kuitenbrouwer, 'Self-Reliance Without Poverty (An Analysis of Pakistan's Fifth Five-Year Plan, 1976-1981),' UN Economic and Social Commission for Asia and for the Pacific, Bangkok, Thailand, 1976, p. 94.
3. Lasse Berg and Lisa Berg, *Face to Face*, Ramparts, Berkeley, 1971, p. 125.
4. Ibid.
5. International Labor Office, *Land Reform in Asia*, Zubeda Ahmad, ed., World Employment Programme Research, Working Papers, 1976.
6. Takedazu Ogura, ed., *Agricultural Development in Mod-*

ern Japan, Japan FAO Association, Tokyo, 1976, p. 25.

7. Edgar Owens and Robert Shaw, *Development Reconsidered*, Heath, Lexington, Mass. 1972, p. 73.

8. *Captives on the Land*, Report of a Consultation on Land, Colombo, Sri Lanka, February, 1976, Christian Conference on Asia – Urban Rural Mission Office, 2–3–18 Nishi-Waseda, Shinjuku-ku Tokyo 160, Japan, p. 11.

9. Theodore Bergman, *Farm Policies in Socialist Countries*, Heath, Lexington, Mass. 1975, pp. 129ff.

10. Food and Agriculture Organization, Mission to China, confidential report, 1977.

11. Bergman, *Farm Policies*, pp. 197ff.

12. Yu-Hsi Chen, 'Rural Transformation in Mainland China and Taiwan: A Comparative Study,' May, 1976, manuscript, p. 7.

13. Ibid., p. 17.

14. P. L. Raikes, 'Ujamaa and Rural Socialism,' *Review of African Political Economy*,' no. 3, May-June 1975.

15. UN Asian Development Institute, 'Toward a Theory of Rural Development,' prepared by Wahidul Haque, et al., December 1975, 66ff.

16. Azizur Rahman Khan, 'China: The Great Exception,' in *Poverty and Landlessness in Rural Asia*, a study by the World Employment Programme, International Labor Office, 1977.

17. Roy Preiswerk, 'Sources of Resistance to Self-Reliance,' manuscript, Institut d'études du Developpement, Institut Universitaire de Hautes Études Internationales, Geneva, quoting an interview with Samir Amin in *Politique Hebdo*, no. 225, June 3, 1976.

18. Johan Galtung, 'Self-Reliance: Concepts, Practice, and Rationale,' Ecumenical Institute, Château de Bossey, CH-1298, Celigny, Switzerland, April 1976.

19. Dudley Jackson, 'Third World Food Crisis,' *New Society* 16, May 1974: 380.

20. David Feldman and Peter Lawrence, 'The Social and Economic Implications of the Large Scale Introduction of New Varieties of Food grains,' *Africa Report* UNRISD, Geneva, 1975, p. 215.

21. Chen, 'Rural Transformation,' p. 21.

22. Sortaj Aziz, 'The Chinese Approach to Rural Development,' *International Development Review* 15, 1973: 4.

23. Food and Agricultural Organization, 'First FAO Professional

Study Mission to China: Some Preliminary Observations,' October 1975, p. 7.

24. Preiswerk, 'Sources of Resistance,' p. 10.

25. Kuitenbrouwer, 'Self-Reliance Without Poverty,' p. 93.

26. Latin America Working Group Letter, vol. 2, no. 7 February–March 1975: 18-19.

27. Kuitenbrouwer, 'Self-Reliance Without Poverty,' p. 45.

Chapter 31
But Where Would Funds for Development Come From?

1. See Dudley Seers, 'The Meaning of Development,' in *The Political Economy of Development*, Norman T. Uphoff and Warren F. Ilchman, eds. University of California Press Berkeley: 1972.

2. Richard J. Barnet and Ronald Mueller, *Global Reach: The Power of the Multinational Corporation*, Simon and Schuster, New York, 1974.

3. Banco Central, cited in *Latin America Economic Report*, 9 January, 1976 Vol. 4, no. 2, p. 6.

4. J. Gurley, 'Rural Development in China,' in *Employment in Developing Nationals*, E. D. Edwards, ed. Columbia University Press, New York, 1974, p. 385.

5. Food and Agriculture Organization, *Progress in Land Reform – Sixth Report*, Rural Institutions Division, Rome, April 1975, pp. III-69, III-70.

6. Kathleen Gough, 'The "Green Revolution" in South India and North Vietnam,' *Social Scientist*, Kerala, India, August 1977, no. 61, and the *Bulletin of Concerned Asian Scholars* (forthcoming). See also, Gough, *Ten Times More Beautiful*, Monthly Review, New York, 1978.

7. Swedish International Development Authority and Food and Agriculture Organization, 'Use of Organic Materials and Green Manures as Fertilizers in Developing Countries' prepared by Ambika Singh, in *Organic Materials as Fertilizers*, Rome, 1975, p. 29.

8. Amulya Kumar and N. Reddy, 'The Trojan Horse,' *Ceres* March – April 1976: 43; for greater detail see Arjun Makhijani with Alan Poole, *Energy and Agriculture in the Third World* Ballinger, Cambridge, Mass. 1976, Chapter 4.

Chapter 32
The Passive Peasantry – Too Oppressed to Change

1. Wahidul Haque, et al., 'An Approach to Micro-Level Development: Designing and Evaluation of Rural Development Projects,' United Nations Asian Development Institute, February 1977, p. 15.
2. Lasse Berg and Lisa Berg, *Face to Face*, Ramparts, Berkeley, Calif. 1970, p. 154.

What We Can Do

1. Advertising Journal 1973 quoted in 'Changing Food Habits in the UK' by Chris Wardle, Earth Resources Research Publication 1977.
2. Ibid.
3. 'Unequal Shares' by Tony Atkinson, Allan Lane 1973
4. Baby Milk Action Coalition, c/o War on Want, 467 Caledonian Road, London N.1.
5. 'Seven Questions to Ask an Aid Project', quoted in full from the American edition of *Food First*, Ballantine Books 1979.
6. Ibid.
7. Ibid.

Index